# The Economics
# of Taxation

## Studies of Government Finance: Second Series

TITLES PUBLISHED

# The Economics
# of Taxation

HENRY J. AARON
MICHAEL J. BOSKIN
*Editors*

*Studies of Government Finance*

THE BROOKINGS INSTITUTION

*Washington, D.C.*

*Library of Congress Cataloging in Publication Data:*

Main entry under title:

The Economics of taxation.

(Studies of government finance : Second series)
Includes index.

1. Taxation—Addresses, essays, lectures.   2. Taxation—United States—Addresses, essays, lectures.
3. Fiscal policy—Addresses, essays, lectures.
4. Fiscal policy—United States—Addresses, essays,
lectures.   I. Aaron, Henry J.   II. Boskin, Michael J.
III. Series.

HJ2305.E27      336.2'00973      79-3774

ISBN 0-8157-0014-8
ISBN 0-8157-0013-X pbk.

9 8 7 6 5 4 3 2 1

THE BROOKINGS INSTITUTION is an independent organization devoted to nonpartisan research, education, and publication in economics, government, foreign policy, and the social sciences generally. Its principal purposes are to aid in the development of sound public policies and to promote public understanding of issues of national importance.

The Institution was founded on December 8, 1927, to merge the activities of the Institute for Government Research, founded in 1916, the Institute of Economics, founded in 1922, and the Robert Brookings Graduate School of Economics and Government, founded in 1924.

The Board of Trustees is responsible for the general administration of the Institution, while the immediate direction of the policies, program, and staff is vested in the President, assisted by an advisory committee of the officers and staff. The by-laws of the Institution state: "It is the function of the Trustees to make possible the conduct of scientific research, and publication, under the most favorable conditions, and to safeguard the independence of the research staff in the pursuit of their studies and in the publication of the results of such studies. It is not a part of their function to determine, control, or influence the conduct of particular investigations or the conclusions reached."

The President bears final responsibility for the decision to publish a manuscript as a Brookings book. In reaching his judgment on the competence, accuracy, and objectivity of each study, the President is advised by the director of the appropriate research program and weighs the views of a panel of expert outside readers who report to him in confidence on the quality of the work. Publication of a work signifies that it is deemed a competent treatment worthy of public consideration but does not imply endorsement of conclusions or recommendations.

The Institution maintains its position of neutrality on issues of public policy in order to safeguard the intellectual freedom of the staff. Hence interpretations or conclusions in Brookings publications should be understood to be solely those of the authors and should not be attributed to the Institution, to its trustees, officers, or other staff members, or to the organizations that support its research.

# Foreword

THE ESSAYS in this volume commemorate the twentieth anniversary of the Studies of Government Finance, a series established at Brookings in 1960 with the substantial financial commitment of the Ford Foundation to promote responsible public consideration of issues in government finance. The series—nearly fifty volumes and hundreds of scholarly articles published by Brookings and others—presents comprehensive discussions of sophisticated economic concepts in nontechnical language, providing legislators and the voting public with informed analyses of the probable consequences of adopting particular fiscal policies. These essays also constitute a tribute to Joseph A. Pechman for his distinguished direction of the Brookings Economic Studies program and for his particular role in guiding the Studies of Government Finance.

The editors, Henry J. Aaron of the Brookings staff and Michael J. Boskin of Stanford University, planned this tribute and enlisted the twenty-three scholars who contributed essays on the economics, politics, and legal problems of taxation. Presenting various approaches to economic theory and conflicting points of view, the essays include histories of recent developments in taxation and budgeting, empirical investigations, explorations of abstruse theoretical questions, and applications of economic theory to policy. In short, they represent the research interests that Joseph Pechman has pursued himself, the skills and approaches he has cultivated and encouraged in the staff of the Economic Studies program, and the wide range of debates about economic theory and policy the Brookings staff has engaged in under his direction.

The essays in this volume were reviewed by virtually all staff members of the Brookings Economic Studies program. The manuscript was edited for publication by Diane Hammond and Tadd Fisher and was typed by Kathleen Elliott Yinug. The index was prepared by Florence Robinson.

This volume—the thirteenth in the second series of Studies of Government Finance—was financed by a grant from the Ford Foundation. The views expressed are those of the contributors and should not be ascribed to the Ford Foundation, to Joseph A. Pechman, or to the trustees, officers, or other staff members of the Brookings Institution.

BRUCE K. MACLAURY
*President*

*May 1980*
*Washington, D.C.*

# Editors' Preface

FEW PEOPLE have contributed as much in recent decades to the study of the economics of taxation as Joseph A. Pechman has. During a career that has spanned government service, university teaching, and research at Brookings, he has contributed many scholarly articles and books; developed and skillfully managed one of the leading centers of policy-oriented economic research; aided, encouraged, advised, and befriended other researchers, many of whom have had views quite different from his own; and participated zestfully and constructively in debates about economic policy.

In this volume, more than a score of economists and lawyers reflect the contributions Joseph Pechman has made. The diversity of viewpoints and analytical methods of the contributors testifies to the pervasiveness of his influence, the breadth of his interests, and the affection and esteem in which both allies and opponents in policy debates hold him.

H. J. A.

M. J. B.

# Contents

## Figures

PART ONE

# The Distribution of Tax Burdens

A. B. ATKINSON  *London School of Economics*

# Horizontal Equity and the Distribution of the Tax Burden

JOSEPH PECHMAN and Benjamin Okner's *Who Bears the Tax Burden?* already is a modern classic and follows a distinguished tradition of studies of the distributional impact of taxation.[1] The

This paper is part of work on a program of research on Taxation, Incentives, and the Distribution of Income, financed by the Social Science Research Council. I am grateful to Michael J. Boskin, Harvey Brazer, and Mervyn King for helpful comments on an earlier version.

1. Joseph A. Pechman and Benjamin A. Okner, *Who Bears the Tax Burden?* (Brookings Institution, 1974). For other major investigations carried out in the United States, see Helen Tarasov, *Who Pays the Taxes? (Allocation of Federal, State, and Local Taxes to Consumer Income Brackets)*, Monograph 3, Temporary National Economic Committee: *Investigation of Concentration of Economic Power*, 76 Cong. 2 sess. (Government Printing Office, 1940); R. A. Musgrave and others, "Distribution of Tax Payments by Income Groups: A Case Study for 1948," *National Tax Journal*, vol. 4 (March 1951), pp. 1–53; Alfred H. Conrad, "Redistribution through Government Budgets in the United States, 1950," in Alan T. Peacock, ed., *Income Redistribution and Social Policy* (London: Jonathan Cape, 1954), pp. 178–267; and others. In the United Kingdom, calculations of the incidence of taxation by income class had been made by Stanley Jevons in 1869 (see Henry Roseveare, *The Treasury, 1660–1870* [London: Allen and Unwin, 1973]), and later contributions include Lord Samuel, "The Taxation of the Various Classes of the People," *Journal of the Royal Statistical Society*, vol. 82 (March 1919), pp. 143–82; Tibor Barna, *Redistribution of Income through Public Finance in 1937* (Oxford University Press, 1945); Allan Murray Cartter, *The Redistribution of Income in Postwar Britain: A Study of the Effects of the Central Government Fiscal Program in 1948–49* (Yale University Press, 1955; Port Washington, N.Y., and London: Kennikat Press, 1973); and J. L. Nicholson, *Redistribution of Income in the United Kingdom in 1959, 1957 and 1953* (London: Bowes and Bowes, 1964).

Pechman-Okner study represented a departure from earlier work in two major respects. First, the authors carried out a more detailed analysis of the sensitivity of the results to the assumptions made about the incidence of different taxes. Second, their use of a micro data file allowed them to examine the variation in individual tax burdens. In contrast to studies in which taxes are allocated to broad income classes,[2] Pechman and Okner calculated individual tax burdens and did not rely on the assumption that these burdens are uniform within an income class. Somewhat surprisingly this latter aspect has received relatively little attention. The authors themselves devoted only one paragraph of their summary chapter to it, and reviewers have tended to concentrate on the treatment of different incidence assumptions.

The neglect of this feature of the Pechman-Okner monograph is unfortunate, since it bears on the concept of horizontal equity, which is widely held to be a major objective of the tax system. Individuals with identical incomes and family circumstances may face different tax burdens because their incomes come from different sources, because they consume different goods, because they live in rural rather than urban areas, and so on. As a result, taxation may change the ranking between the pre- and post-tax distributions of income. The extent of such re-ranking is a question of considerable interest. Pechman and Okner were able to investigate the degree of variation in tax rates by using the Brookings MERGE data file and calculating the individual tax burdens of the 72,000 families represented.

In this paper I pursue this issue further, focusing in particular on the conceptual problems that arise. The first section describes the analytical framework within which the "mobility" induced by taxation may be examined. The second section reviews the concept of horizontal equity, the various ways it may be interpreted, and possible measures of it.

## The Redistributive Impact of Taxation

The standard approach to measuring the redistributive impact of taxation is to compare the distribution after tax with that assumed to

2. See, for example, Richard A. Musgrave, Karl E. Case, and Herman Leonard, "The Distribution of Fiscal Burdens and Benefits," *Public Finance Quarterly*, vol. 2 (July 1974), pp. 259–311.

hold in the absence of taxation (on the basis of specified assumptions about incidence). Before the introduction of taxes, individual $i$ has income $Y_i$, and this is converted into a post-tax income $Y_i^N$. The standard procedure considers the distribution $Y_i$ (ranked in increasing order $i = 1, \ldots, n$) and compares it with the distribution $Y_i^N$ (ranked in the same way $i = 1, \ldots, n$). Commonly, in empirical applications the data are grouped. The standard procedure then is to consider the distribution ranked according to average income before tax in each group, constructing, for example, the Lorenz curve, and to compare this with the distribution obtained for the same groups ranked in the same way.

This approach, however, ignores the fact that taxation may change the ranking of individuals in the distribution. The person or group at the top of the pre-tax distribution may be lower down the post-tax distribution. The people who were in the same range of pre-tax income may be in different post-tax ranges. As a result, measures calculated according to the pre-tax ranking, as in the standard approach, typically understate the inequality of post-tax incomes. The Gini coefficient, for example, calculated from the pre-tax ranks, can be shown to be less than or equal to that calculated using the correct post-tax rankings. It is therefore an important distinguishing feature of the Pechman-Okner study that estimation of the tax burden for individual units permits the authors to draw the Lorenz curve corresponding to the re-ranked distribution and to calculate more accurately the various summary measures derived from it.[3]

The process of re-ranking is of interest in its own right as well as in obtaining an accurate measure of redistribution. We are concerned not only with the position of the Lorenz curves but also with how much "mobility" is induced by taxation. Where do the people at the lower quartile of the before-tax distribution end up in the distribution of the after-tax incomes? How much variation is there in the post-tax incomes of individuals who are identically situated before tax? These questions, discussed below, are related to the concept of horizontal equity.

Before turning to a more formal analysis, a simple example may

3. For an earlier discussion of the movements from one income range to another, see Nicholson, *Redistribution of Income in the United Kingdom.*

help illustrate the effects of changes in rankings. Assume the following distribution of incomes before and after tax:

| Taxpayer | Class | Income Before tax | Income After tax |
|---|---|---|---|
| 1 | } Top 40 percent | 1,000 | 800 |
| 2 | | 1,000 | 640 |
| 3 | } Next 40 percent | 800 | 800 |
| 4 | | 800 | 512 |
| 5 | Bottom quintile | 640 | 640 |

Analysis of the data on an individual basis and calculation of the Gini coefficient indicates a fall (from 0.087 to 0.053) on the basis of the pre-tax rankings, whereas it is clear that a correct calculation based on the re-ranked data would show no change (the Lorenz curves are identical). What happens if one groups the data? The three income classes shown in the second column indicate a progressive rate structure (average tax rates from the bottom are 0 percent, 18 percent, and 28 percent), and the grouped Lorenz curve moves toward the diagonal.[4] The individual data show, however, that the fact that the tax on the average is progressive is offset by the differential treatment of people with the same before-tax income—by the mobility induced by the tax system.

Differences between the taxes paid by people with the same pre-tax income may arise for a number of reasons.[5] First, on equity grounds the government may recognize certain characteristics as warranting differential treatment. The most obvious examples are allowances for different family sizes or special provisions for the elderly or disabled. Second, the government may deliberately treat differently certain

4. It should be noted that methods of putting bounds on the Lorenz curves of grouped data, as suggested by Joseph L. Gastwirth ("The Estimation of the Lorenz Curve and Gini Index," *Review of Economics and Statistics,* vol. 54 [August 1972], pp. 306–16), would not apply in this case, since the curve (ranked by pre-tax income) is nonconvex.

5. The term "taxes paid" should be taken to include all sources of differences between income in the absence of the fiscal system, and the after-tax position with the fiscal system in operation. Thus, for example, in the case of tax-exempt bonds adjustment should be made for the interest differential. Moreover, although the issue is discussed with reference to taxation, the same questions arise with government spending.

types of income or taxpayer for efficiency reasons; for example, it may want to encourage owner-occupation or discourage people from consuming certain products. Third, some horizontal inequities not desired by the government may be inherent in the tax system—an unavoidable by-product. For example, where there is less than 100 percent checking of income tax returns, one person may be caught but another, identically situated, may successfully evade. Another example is that some people may have a stronger preference for goods the government cannot tax (for example, leisure).

The discussion that follows concentrates on the second and third categories. In other words, it is concerned with differential treatment that has no equity justification. The income, $Y_i^N$, of individual $i$ should, for example, be interpreted as having been expressed in per adult equivalent terms, using an appropriate equivalence scale.

### Tax Mobility Matrices

Starting with the case of individual taxpayers, the effect of taxation on the Lorenz curve may be decomposed into two stages. The first gives the after-tax income $Y_i^N$ corresponding to pre-tax income $Y_i$ for a fixed ranking $i$. The second is the permutation to give the ranking according to $Y_i^N$. Denoting this latter ranking by $k$, one can write $k = iP$, where $P$ is a permutation matrix. A tax that causes no change in ranking is associated with the identity matrix; a tax that completely reverses rankings has the opposite diagonal permutation matrix.

In any actual application the individual data are likely to be treated in groups. For convenience I take equal size groups, each containing a proportion, $1/n$, of the population. The generalization of the permutation matrix is then the transition matrix $A$ where $a_{ij}$ denotes the proportion of those in pre-tax group $i$ entering post-tax group $j$. This matrix is bistochastic (each row and each column add to 1), and the extent of mobility depends on the off-diagonal elements ($j \neq i$). The standard assumption described earlier is that these are zero, $A$ being the identity matrix. The study of tax mobility means in effect supplementing the measures defined over the $n$ pre- and post-tax groups by the $n \times n$ matrix mapping the movement of individuals between these groups.

There is a clear parallel with the measurement of social mobility across generations. In the extensive literature on this subject many attempts have been made to reduce the transition matrix $A$ to a single

measure of the extent of mobility; for example, Bartholomew suggests
the following measure of social mobility:

(1) $$B = \frac{1}{n} \sum_i \sum_j a_{ij} |i - j|,$$

which is zero when $A$ is the identity matrix.[6]

It is possibly more natural in the present case to relate the measure
to conventional indices of inequality. These, of course, do not depend
intrinsically on the ranking, but in some cases the ranking is an intermediate step in the calculation. The Gini coefficient is a good illustration, since it is often related to the area between the diagonal and the
Lorenz curve (hence depending on the ranking).

The mobility matrix can readily be calculated from micro-unit
data. For present purposes an illustrative matrix has been constructed
using the data on the distribution of tax rates contained in chapter 5
of *Who Bears the Tax Burden?* A number of assumptions were made
in the calculations (see notes to table 1) and it is not claimed that
the results closely approximate those that would be obtained from
the original MERGE file. It should also be stressed that there are
several reasons why the degree of mobility may be inaccurately
measured, even if the original file is used. For example, because the
data are not adjusted for family size, differences in tax rates may
reflect the intended unequal treatment of families with the same income but different needs. The data are derived from surveys, and
part of the variation may be due to recording errors. Working in the
opposite direction is the fact that in the MERGE file consumption is
based on averages for income classes and demographic groups and
hence would not capture all the variability in consumption patterns
(for example, the different tax burdens of smokers and nonsmokers).
Moreover, because the population is divided into only ten groups,
each covering a wide range of income, a substantial amount of mobility is not reflected in the table. Finally, the results depend on the
assumptions about incidence.

For these reasons, the matrix shown in table 1 should not be regarded as more than illustrative; and no attempt has been made to
carry out accurate calculations. Inspection of the table suggests that
the diagonal entries are dominant; at the same time, some of the ele-

6. D. J. Bartholomew, *Stochastic Models for Social Processes,* 2d ed. (Wiley,
1973), p. 24. For a discussion of this index, see A. F. Shorrocks, "The Measurement
of Mobility," *Econometrica,* vol. 46 (September 1978), pp. 1013–24.

**Table 1. Illustrative Tax Mobility Matrix**

| Pre-tax decile in order of increasing income | Post-tax decile in order of increasing income (percent) | | | | | | | | | |
|---|---|---|---|---|---|---|---|---|---|---|
| | 1 | 2 | 3 | 4 | 5 | 6 | 7 | 8 | 9 | 10 |
| 1 | 94 | 6 | | | | | | | | |
| 2 | 6 | 85 | 9 | | | | | | | |
| 3 | | 9 | 75 | 14 | 2 | | | | | |
| 4 | | | 16 | 67 | 14 | 3 | | | | |
| 5 | | | | 19 | 67 | 13 | 1 | | | |
| 6 | | | | | 17 | 66 | 16 | 1 | | |
| 7 | | | | | | 18 | 62 | 19 | 1 | |
| 8 | | | | | | | 20 | 66 | 14 | |
| 9 | | | | | | | 1 | 14 | 72 | 13 |
| 10 | | | | | | | | | 13 | 87 |

Sources & notes: Calculated from the information on median-quartile tax rates by decile (Joseph A. Pechman and Benjamin Okner, *Who Bears the Tax Burden?* [Brookings Institution, 1974], table 5-1, p. 67) and on pre-tax ranges (interpolated from the same source, table 4-5, p. 53). The calculations were adjusted to impose the row and column sum conditions (items less than 1 percent being neglected). The figures all relate to the "most progressive" set of incidence assumptions (Variant 1c). The calculations are intended only to be illustrative and should be read in conjunction with the qualifications in the text.

ments adjacent to the diagonal are quite large. The matrix is approximately tridiagonal, with the elements bordering the diagonal of the order of 10–20 percent for deciles 2–10, and the other off-diagonal elements close to zero. In other words, it appears from the table that variability in the tax rate tends to shift people but not typically further than one decile.

### Mobility and Inequality

Changes in the ranking of observations as a result of taxation do not in themselves affect the degree of inequality in the post-tax distribution. They do, however, influence certain ways of representing the distribution and of calculating summary measures of inequality. In this section I consider the effect of rank changes on the Lorenz curve and the Gini coefficient, both widely used in the analysis of the incidence of taxation.

In order to see the effect of changes in ranking I define the concentration curve, which gives the cumulative percentage of a particular variable, $X_i$, where observations are ranked according to a variable $Z_i$; that is

$$(2) \qquad C(m, X, r(Z))$$

denotes the cumulative total (expressed as a proportion of the overall total) for $m$ observations of variable $X_i$, ranked in increasing order of $Z_i$. This gives as a special case the Lorenz curve $C(m, X, r(X))$.[7]

The first result that is readily proved is that if a ranking $j$ is obtained by a permutation of the ranking $r(X)$, then the resulting concentration curve lies inside the Lorenz curve (or is coincident with it); that is

(3)                           $$j = r(X)P,$$

where $P$ is a permutation matrix, implies

(4)                           $$C(m, X, j) \geq C(m, X, r(Y))$$

for all $m$.

The proof may be seen by considering a sequence of transpositions in which the ranks of $X_i$ and $X_k$ ($k > i$, $X_k > X_i$) are reversed (see figure 1).

This result shows that calculating the shares in post-tax total income according to the rankings by pre-tax income gives too high a figure if there is any substantive change in ranking (that is, for persons with different post-tax incomes). There is indeed no reason why the concentration curve need be below the diagonal, as may be seen from the example where the first person ($X_1 < \overline{X}$, where $\overline{X}$ denotes the mean) and the last person ($X_n > \overline{X}$) are interchanged. The Lorenz curve then starts off above the diagonal and ends above it.

The direction of the effect of re-ranking is readily apparent; of more interest is its possible magnitude. Figure 1 shows that the transposition of $i$ and $k$ raises the curve for $i < m < k$ by an amount $(X_k - X_i)/n\overline{X}$. Thus in a population of 100 people switching the person at the lower quartile, with an income of, say, three-quarters of the mean, with the person at the upper quartile, with an income of one and one-half times the mean, raises the cumulative shares in the range 25–49 percent by 0.75 percent. It is also possible to calculate the effect on the Gini coefficient, which is reduced as a result of the re-ranking by

(5)                           $$\frac{2(k - i)}{n^2} \left( \frac{X_k - X_i}{\overline{X}} \right).$$

With the example of the interquartile range used above, this turns out to be the same as the change in the cumulative shares, that is, 0.75 percent.

---

7. For a discussion of the relation between concentration and Lorenz curves, see, for example, N. C. Kakwani, "Applications of Lorenz Curves in Economic Analysis," *Econometrica*, vol. 45 (April 1977), pp. 719–27.

**Figure 1. Effect of Transposition of Individuals $i$ and $k$ on the Lorenz Curve**

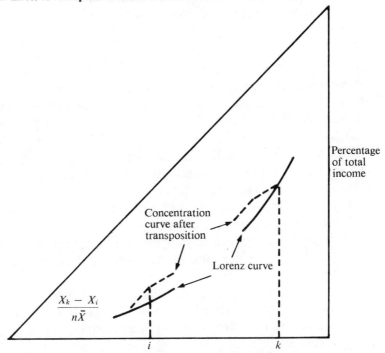

Percentage of total population

The effect of a general re-ranking may be built up from a sequence of such transpositions. In order to get some feeling for the overall effect, consider the case where the data are grouped into ranges with equal frequencies and the transition matrix is tridiagonal:

$$(6) \quad \begin{bmatrix} 1 - \alpha_1 & \alpha_1 & 0 & \cdots & 0 \\ \alpha_1 & (1 - \alpha_1 - \alpha_2) & \alpha_2 & \cdots & 0 \\ 0 & \alpha_2 & (1 - \alpha_2 - \alpha_3) & \cdots & 0 \\ 0 & 0 & \alpha_3 & \cdots & 0 \\ \cdot & \cdot & \cdot & \cdots & \cdot \\ \cdot & \cdot & \cdot & \cdots & \cdot \\ \cdot & \cdot & \cdot & \cdots & \cdot \\ 0 & 0 & 0 & \cdots & 0 \\ 0 & 0 & 0 & \cdots & \alpha_{n-1} \\ 0 & 0 & 0 & \cdots & 1 - \alpha_{n-1} \end{bmatrix}$$

The reduction in the Gini coefficient is then the sum of the individual transpositions and may be shown to equal

(7) $$\frac{2}{n^2} \sum_{i=1}^{n-1} \alpha_i^2 \left( \frac{X_{i+1} - X_i}{\bar{X}} \right)$$

(this may be seen geometrically from the Lorenz curve, where a fraction $\alpha_i$ is moved to the adjacent group). Suppose that the groups are deciles and that the value of $\alpha_i$ is taken as 0.15. The reduction in the Gini coefficient is then in percentage points $0.045 \times (X_n - X_1)/\bar{X}$. If, for example, the top income exceeds the bottom by six times the mean, then the Gini coefficient falls by 0.27 percent; if the relationship is 12:1, the fall is 0.54 percent. If the value of $\alpha_i$ is taken as 0.1, then the figures become 0.12 and 0.24, respectively; if $\alpha$ were 0.2, then the figures are four times larger.

This kind of difference may appear reassuringly small when compared with the absolute value of the coefficient (around 42 percent for the Pechman-Okner data); on the other hand, it is quite large when viewed in relation to the difference between before-tax and after-tax distributions. Thus Pechman and Okner report the following Gini coefficients for different assumptions about incidence, given here in percentages:[8]

| Variant | Before-tax income | After-tax income (families re-ranked) | Difference |
|---|---|---|---|
| 1a | 43.21 | 41.56 | −1.65 |
| 1b | 43.29 | 41.56 | −1.73 |
| 1c | 43.67 | 41.58 | −2.09 |
| 2a | 43.63 | 41.92 | −1.71 |
| 2b | 43.75 | 42.17 | −1.58 |
| 3a | 42.77 | 42.03 | −0.74 |
| 3b | 42.52 | 42.40 | −0.12 |
| 3c | 43.40 | 41.71 | −1.69 |

8. Pechman and Okner, *Who Bears the Tax Burden?* table 4-7, p. 56. The incidence assumptions of the variants are as follows: All variants distribute individual income tax payments among taxpayers and sales taxes among consumers in proportion to estimated consumption of taxed commodities. The corporation income tax is distributed among taxpayers according to estimated dividends received in Variants 2a and 2b, according to estimated property income in general in Variants 1a and 1b; under Variants 1c and 3c, half on the basis of dividends received and half on the basis of property income in general; under Variant 3a, half to dividends, one-fourth on the basis of consumption, and one-fourth on the basis of earnings; under Variant 3b, half on the basis of property income in general and half on the basis of con-

If the figures for the possible effect of re-ranking are at all realistic, they suggest that it might be quite significant in relation to the redistributive impact of taxation.

Finally, I make a comparison with the effects of interpolating grouped observations.[9] Unless the number of groups is very limited, the effect of re-ranking may warrant at least as much attention in empirical studies as that of grouping.

# Horizontal Equity and the Assessment of Tax Systems

In the previous section I set out a simple framework within which to examine the re-ranking induced by the tax system and suggested that it may be of some empirical significance. If one leaves to one side differences justified on equity grounds, such as those related to age and family size, the fact that people with identical pre-tax income pay different amounts of tax leads to horizontal inequity. Such inequity is frequently taken to be an undesirable feature of a tax system; however, relatively little consideration seems to have been given to the status of horizontal equity as a principle of tax design. The concept of horizontal equity is open to several different interpretations.

## Horizontal Equity and the Social Welfare Function

The first view is that horizontal equity is simply an implication of the more general principle of welfare maximization. Pigou stated this view explicitly: "Tax arrangements that conform to the principle of least sacrifice always and necessarily conform also to the principle of equal sacrifice among similar and similarly situated persons."[10] A more recent example is provided by Musgrave and Musgrave: "Both

---

sumption. The property tax is distributed on the basis of property income in general in Variants 1b and 1c and on the basis of land ownership in all other variants. The payroll tax on employees is distributed on the basis of employee compensation in all variants. The payroll tax on employers is distributed half on the basis of employee compensation and half on the basis of consumption under Variants 2b and 3b; under all other variants it is distributed on the basis of employee compensation. See ibid., pp. 35–39.

9. The results of Gastwirth based on census of population data give bounds, using his refined method, of 40.055 percent and 40.175 percent (the true value was 40.14 percent) for the case of twenty-eight groups. See "The Estimation of the Lorenz Curve and Gini Index," pp. 310–11.

10. A. C. Pigou, *A Study in Public Finance,* 3d rev. ed. (Macmillan, 1947), p. 45.

equity rules [horizontal and vertical] . . . follow from the same principle of equal treatment."[11]

The reasoning underlying this view has been set out clearly by Feldstein:

With the assumption that individuals all have the same utility function, the principle of horizontal equity requires nothing more than that individuals with the same consumption bundle (including leisure) should pay the same tax. . . . *Since violation of this condition would reduce aggregate social welfare,* the equal taxation of equals is implied directly by utilitarianism and does not require a separate principle of horizontal equity.[12]

Feldstein goes on to argue that this condition does not hold when there is diversity of tastes, but without introducing this complication the argument may be shown to be incorrect. Even if tastes are identical, the equal treatment of equals is not necessarily implied by welfare maximization—the italicized statement in the quotation above does not always hold. In particular, where the feasible set is nonconvex, treating otherwise identical individuals differently may increase social welfare.[13] If the feasible set has the (symmetric) shape drawn and the social welfare contour is as indicated (again symmetric), then differential treatment raises aggregate social welfare (see figure 2).

### Horizontal Equity as an Independent Principle

This brings me to the second view of horizontal equity—that it is an independent principle that has to be balanced with maximization of welfare. Although not usually made explicit, this interpretation appears to be what lies behind some treatments of the subject. The translation of the principle into an explicit measure has not, however, been widely attempted. The ideal of zero inequity is straightforward to define, but how can one compare the degrees of horizontal inequity in states that fall short of the ideal?

In a paper that has received relatively little attention, Johnson and Mayer discuss a number of ways in which an index of horizontal in-

11. Richard A. Musgrave and Peggy B. Musgrave, *Public Finance in Theory and Practice,* 2d ed. (McGraw-Hill, 1976), p. 216, note.

12. Martin Feldstein, "On the Theory of Tax Reform," *Journal of Public Economics,* vol. 6 (July-August 1976), p. 82 (emphasis added).

13. A. B. Atkinson and J. E. Stiglitz, "The Design of Tax Structure: Direct versus Indirect Taxation," *Journal of Public Economics,* vol. 6 (July-August 1976), p. 71; and Joseph E. Stiglitz, "Utilitarianism and Horizontal Equity: The Case for Random Taxation," ibid., forthcoming.

**Figure 2. Illustrative Nonconvex, Symmetric Feasible Set Showing that Social Welfare Is Maximized at Either *A* or *B* and that *C* Is a Minimum**

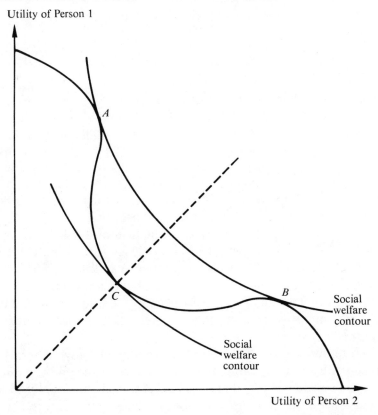

equity might be constructed.[14] They consider in effect persons with identical pre-tax incomes and suggest that the index might be a function of the number of inequities between people or of the differences in taxation. In the present context the former would lead to an index for pre-tax class $i$ (with a transition matrix $A$):

$$(8) \qquad J_i = 1 - \sum_j a_{ij}^2.$$

This reaches a maximum where $a_{ij} = 1/n$ and a minimum for $a_{ij} = 1$ for some $j$ (not necessarily $i$—a feature discussed later). Feldstein makes a number of interesting suggestions, among them that one

14. Shirley B. Johnson and Thomas Mayer, "An Extension of Sidgwick's Equity Principle," *Quarterly Journal of Economics,* vol. 76 (August 1962), pp. 454–63.

could take the after-tax variance of utilities of people with equal before-tax utility.[15] Thus, if the welfare of individuals in post-tax class $j$ is denoted by $U_j$, the measure of horizontal inequity for pre-tax class $i$ would be

(9) $$F_i = \sum_j a_{ij}(U_j - \bar{U}_i)^2,$$

where $\bar{U}_i$ is the mean for those in pre-tax class $i$.

One possible rationalization of these approaches follows a parallel with the Rawlsian "original position."[16] Rawls supposes that principles of justice are chosen as from behind a "veil of ignorance," with people unaware of their income. Suppose instead that individuals know their pre-tax income but are uncertain about the impact of taxation, knowing only the distribution of post-tax incomes conditional on gross income. The measure of horizontal equity may then be derived from the attitudes of individuals toward risk, given their ignorance about the impact of taxation. This characterization does not of course apply to certain factors that may lead to differential taxation and are known to the individual, but it is relevant to a number of aspects (including differences arising from successful and unsuccessful tax evasion,[17] and the "random" taxation considered by Stiglitz).[18]

The representation of the horizontal equity objective in terms of individual uncertainty captures some elements of the problem but is open to objections. First, it may be held to attach undue status to the pre-tax distribution. (The next section deals with this problem.) Second, even if one accepts the basic framework, there is the question as to how the "risk" associated with taxation should be measured. The related literature on portfolio theory indicates that one cannot expect to define a complete ranking without specification of the individual utility function, but it is possible to define the concept

15. Feldstein, "On The Theory of Tax Reform," p. 83. See also Melvin and Anne White, "Horizontal Inequality in the Federal Income Tax Treatment of Home Owners and Tenants," *National Tax Journal*, vol. 18 (September 1965), pp. 225–39.

16. John Rawls, *A Theory of Justice* (Harvard University Press, 1971).

17. To consider tax evasion in terms of expected income (as, for example, Nanak C. Kakwani does in "Income Tax Evasion and Income Distribution," in J. F. J. Toye, ed., *Taxation and Economic Development* [Frank Cass, 1978], pp. 161–73) obscures this issue and seems particularly unsatisfactory.

18. Stiglitz, "Utilitarianism and Horizontal Equity."

analogous to a mean-preserving spread.[19] Thus if the third row in the transition matrix is changed from (0, 0.2, 0.6, 0.2, 0) to (0, 0.1, 0.8, 0.1, 0), this matrix can be said to exhibit less horizontal inequity. This example also serves, however, to bring out a further shortcoming of this line of approach. Suppose that the third row had become (0, 0, 0.1, 0.8, 0.1). This is less dispersed, but the weight has shifted away from the pivotal $a_{33}$. In effect this treatment ignores the ranking of $i$ vis-à-vis other pre-tax groups, as noted by Feldstein: "[The variance] would be sensitive to unequal treatment of equals but would not reflect the utility reversals as such."[20] For the indices $J_i$ and $F_i$ to take the value zero it is necessary only that *some* $a_{ij} = 1$; it is not required that $a_{ii} = 1$.

This fact suggests that the measurement of horizontal equity should take explicit account of the distance moved from the pre-tax ranking.[21] Such a measure can be reduced to a single number, as with the example of the Bartholomew index $B$ given earlier, but any such summary statistic involves assumptions that may be little more than arbitrary. It may therefore be preferable to present the whole permutation or transition matrix; use of this matrix (or of the Lorenz curve) avoids the need to choose from the summary measures of inequality. In the same way, such a matrix can only provide a partial ordering of degrees of horizontal inequity; a comparison can be made where one ranking can be obtained from another by a sequence of rank-reversing transpositions.

### Status of Horizontal Equity

The ethical significance of horizontal equity may be seen as depending on the status of the pre-tax distribution (that is, the distribution in the absence of the state). On an entitlement view of justice, of the kind advanced by Nozick, the pre-tax position has a particular

19. See Michael Rothschild and Joseph E. Stiglitz, "Increasing Risk: I, A Definition," *Journal of Economic Theory,* vol. 2 (September 1970), pp. 225–43.

20. Feldstein, "On The Theory of Tax Reform," p. 83.

21. Note the affinity with Pyatt's "statistical game" interpretation of the Gini coefficient: "For each individual [*i*] we conduct an experiment. First, some income . . . is selected at random from the population of incomes. . . . If the income selected is greater than the actual income of the individual then he can retain the value selected: otherwise he retains his actual income. . . . if we now average these expected gains over all individuals, *i*, we obtain [the numerator of the Gini coefficient]." See G. Pyatt, "On the Interpretation and Disaggregation of Gini Coefficients," *Economic Journal,* vol. 86 (June 1976), p. 244.

claim on our attention,[22] and horizontal inequity is of central concern. In contrast, moral arguments based on end-result principles, such as utilitarian or Rawlsian theories, see the distribution of post-tax income as the sole matter for concern; no equity significance is attached to the degree of mobility induced by taxation.[23] A similar line has been taken in radical critiques of traditional normative tax theory that argue that the pre-tax income has no equity significance and that it is wrong to place "normative emphasis on the preservation of the ordinal ranking of individual labor incomes as one moves from the market to the post-tax-and-transfer distribution."[24]

There is, however, a third position: that horizontal equity is concerned, not with outcomes or with changes in position, but with the means by which they are achieved. In this view, horizontal equity is "a safeguard against capricious discrimination."[25] It may require, for instance, that the tax rate should not vary, ceteris paribus, with a person's race or religion. It is a restriction on the class of tax instruments the government may use. Thus in the case of indirect taxes the government may be constrained from varying the tax rate on commodities between which differences in consumption are mainly matters of taste (for example, taxing different brands of beer at different rates).[26]

The status of horizontal equity and the relationship of tax-induced mobility to social justice depend therefore on the position adopted. Even if one attaches no significance to mobility from an ethical point of view, however, this does not mean that the study of such mobility is redundant. The magnitude of changes in ranking induced by taxation is an interesting feature in its own right. Most important, it helps explain why the tax system is less progressive in effect than it nominally appears—the theme that runs through so much of Joseph Pechman's work.

22. See Robert Nozick, *Anarchy, State and Utopia* (Basic Books, 1974).

23. This may need to be modified where individuals are concerned about their *relative* position. It is possible, for example, that the "reference group" is defined with respect to pre-tax income.

24. David M. Gordon, "Taxation of the Poor and the Normative Theory of Tax Incidence," *American Economic Review*, vol. 62 (May 1972, *Papers and Proceedings, 1971*), p. 321.

25. Richard A. Musgrave, *The Theory of Public Finance: A Study in Public Economy* (McGraw-Hill, 1959), p. 160.

26. See Atkinson and Stiglitz, "The Design of Tax Structure."

BORIS I. BITTKER  *Yale University Law School*

# Equity, Efficiency, and Income Tax Theory: Do Misallocations Drive Out Inequities?

TRADITIONALLY, equity has been the standard applied by tax theorists to the structural details of the federal income tax. Equity theorists ask whether existing law treats equals equally (horizontal equity) and whether it differentiates appropriately among unequals (vertical equity). To determine whether taxpayers or groups of taxpayers are equals or unequals, equity theorists compare their pre-tax economic incomes. When equity theorists subject the U.S. Internal Revenue Code to this mode of analysis, most if not all of them find it woefully defective.

Equity is now being supplemented, even supplanted, by efficiency as the goal of economic policy. This mode of analysis asks whether the tax allowances of existing law promote or inhibit the efficient allocation of resources. Viewing existing tax law from this vantage point, efficiency theorists are as critical of its numerous exclusions, deductions, credits, and other allowances as are equity theorists.

Although the verdicts of these two schools of income tax analysis converge, I hope to show, first, that the behavioral assumptions on which their conclusions rest are so contradictory that their inde-

The author is indebted to Marvin Chirelstein for commenting on a draft of this paper.

19

pendent verdicts challenge—rather than reinforce—each other; second, that efficiency theory, if valid, calls into question the methodology employed by equity analysis in testing for horizontal and vertical equity; and third, that a fundamental task of income tax theory is to integrate these normative standards into a general theory.

In calling equity the traditional normative standard for judging the propriety of exclusions, deductions, credits, and other tax allowances, I have in mind such honored names as Edwin R. A. Seligman, Robert M. Haig, and, above all, Henry Simons—the only one of the three who wrote long enough after the vaguely defined income tax had been converted into a statutory reality to have a detailed charter before him for systematic analysis.

The influence of equity analysis has been pervasive. Examples of its application include the tax plan of Senator George McGovern to provide every American a $1,000 refundable credit and to drastically simplify the tax base and rate structure; U.S. Treasury Department studies of the tax liabilities of taxpayers with economic income over $200,000; the minimum tax on tax preferences; and countless other tax reform proposals. While equity theory is primarily concerned with the individual income tax, it has also inspired recent studies of the divergent tax rates to which corporations in different industries are subject.

While equity theorists condemn most tax allowances for imposing divergent tax burdens on taxpayers with equal economic incomes, efficiency theorists blame many of the same allowances for causing the misallocation of resources. An important difference so far as public attention is concerned, however, is that efficiency theorists have not succeeded in coining any passionate slogans to rival those contributed by equity theorists ("upside-down subsidies" and "tax relief for the rich," for example). The dominant tone of efficiency analysis is prudence, stemming from worries about the misallocation of resources, and this attitude is not easily converted into a fighting creed.

Efficiency analysis is associated primarily with a new generation of tax theorists, whose elders tend to be faithful instead to equity analysis. This situation is reminiscent of my colleague Leon S. Lipson's characterization, a decade ago, of the Yale Law School faculty as a combination of Old Turks and young fogies—a generation of idealists in their sunset years, still inspired by the ethics of compassion adopted in their youth, and a rising generation of skeptics insisting on the prudent calculation of costs before embarking on new ventures or endorsing old ones. There are, of course, some tax theorists who resist this bipolar classification; every taxonomy is a procrustean bed. By and large, however, equity and efficiency as modes of tax analysis are separated by a generational line as well as an intellectual one.[1] In saying this, I have our own day in mind. Taking a longer view, one might find that today's efficiency theorists differ from their parents but resemble their grandparents.[2]

## The Competing Behavioral Assumptions

As suggested, equity and efficiency as normative standards rest on divergent assumptions about the effect of tax allowances on the behavior of taxpayers and the citizenry as a whole.

The behavioral effect usually posited by equity-oriented theorists (more often implicitly than explicitly) is either that taxpayers continue to do just what they would have done without the allowances or that any changes in their economic conduct to take advantage of the allowances do not significantly alter the pre-tax yield or other economic benefits produced by the tax-favored behavior. It is assumed, in other words, that the soup does not have to be watered down, no matter how many taxpayers line up for the free lunch. Indeed, unless the after-tax benefit of a tax-sheltered activity is greater than the after-tax benefits of its unsheltered counterparts, it cannot produce horizontal inequity. The behavioral premise of equity theory is therefore

1. For what it is worth, I count myself as a troubled Old Turk whose chagrin, if my doubts about conventional equity analysis can be refuted, would be outweighed by the pleasure of having my faith resuscitated.

I am indebted to Henry J. Aaron for helping to clarify my thinking in this area with an exchange of letters in 1972 and 1973. For a more systematic analysis, see Martin J. Bailey, "Progressivity and Investment Yields under U.S. Income Taxation," *Journal of Political Economy*, vol. 82 (November-December 1974), pp. 1157–75. Bailey concludes (p. 1174) that "apparent horizontal inequities [in income tax burdens] as a rule shake out in competitive resource allocation and translate into misuse of resources." See also Martin Feldstein, "On the Theory of Tax Reform," *Journal of Public Economics*, vol. 6 (July-August 1976), pp. 77–104, in which the author argues that optimal tax reforms lead to a different tax structure than do optimal de novo designs when the effects of current rules on efficiency, horizontal equity, and property rights are taken into account.

2. See, for example, the views regarding the shifting of "special taxes on income" in Edwin R. A. Seligman, *Studies in Public Finance* (Macmillan, 1925), pp. 65–68.

reminiscent of the classical theory that the burden of an income tax cannot be shifted and hence remains on the nominal taxpayer.

The basic behavioral assumption of efficiency theory differs from that of equity theory in two respects: it is more likely to be explicit, and it presupposes an increase of tax-favored behavior at the expense of its unfavored alternative until the after-tax benefits of the two are equalized. This equalization assumption is as central to efficiency theory as it is damaging to equity theory.

As a standard for judging the income tax, efficiency does not, of course, *require* the behavioral assumption just described. One can envision an efficiency theorist who, on inspecting the exclusions, deductions, and other tax allowances of existing law, announces that they do not induce an inefficient misallocation of resources, because taxpayers either do not change their behavior under the impetus of the allowances or, if they do, there is no difference in economic yield. An efficiency theorist, in short, might hold that the allowances are harmless from a resource allocation perspective and that if they are objectionable at all, it is only on equity grounds. Conversely one can envision the mirror image of this efficiency theorist: an equity theorist who concludes that the allowances are nullified by declines in the pre-tax yield of the tax-favored activities and are therefore acceptable from an equity point of view, however much they might distort the allocation of resources.

But in real life both schools seem irresistibly drawn to behavioral assumptions that warrant gloomy conclusions: equity theorists seem drawn to a no-shifting premise that leads them to the conclusion that existing tax law is horizontally and vertically inequitable; efficiency theorists virtually always perceive equalized after-tax yields that are the hallmark of misallocated resources.

## Illustration of Conflicting Behavioral Assumptions

An illustration will disclose the conflicting implications of the divergent behavioral assumptions on which the equity and efficiency standards rest. The standard classroom example of a violation of horizontal equity is the comparison of A and B, both subject to a marginal tax rate of 70 percent and both realizing an additional $1,000 of interest income. Because A invested in taxable industrial bonds, he pays a tax of $700 and is left with $300; B, being more tax-conscious, invested in tax-exempt bonds of equal risk, so his $1,000 of interest is unscathed by any tax liability.

Students sometimes ask why they should be disturbed by this comparison, which implies that A suffers from a self-inflicted wound. He is a fool, they suggest, not a victim; let him follow B's example, and the alleged inequity will vanish. Whatever may be the reason for the persistent failure of some taxpayers to take advantage of the tax allowances open to them,[3] the instructor usually answers student objections by asserting that A should not be forced into unwanted investments in order to be equal to B.

An efficiency theorist, of course, can use this example to demonstrate that the exclusion generates a misallocation of resources rather than horizontal inequity. If A gets $1,000 interest from a taxable bond paying 10 percent a year, he must have invested $10,000. If B invested the same amount in tax-exempt bonds, the efficiency theorist points out, B gets only $300 interest because the after-tax yields of taxable and tax-exempt bonds are the same in a competitive market; and 3 percent on a taxable bond is the tax-free equivalent of 10 percent on a taxable bond if the investor is subject to a 70 percent marginal tax rate. Because of the resulting equalization of the after-tax receipts of A and B, there is no horizontal inequity between them; both are in the same boat, as they should be.[4] But the ability of cities and states to borrow at 3 percent when taxable projects of equal risk must pay 10 percent for capital results in a misallocation of resources because funds flow toward exempt projects of lower economic productivity.

3. See note 6.

4. The conventional equity criticism can be rehabilitated in a purely formal sense by the fact that B pays no taxes, even if his pre-tax income drops by the full amount of the unpaid taxes. But this quibble in turn is rebutted if the tax allowance is viewed as a device for (a) taxing the ostensibly exempt income and (b) transferring the hypothetical tax revenue to the tax-favored borrower. This view of the tax allowance should be congenial to advocates of tax expenditure analysis, which treats forgone taxes as tantamount to appropriations to the tax-favored function. See Stanley Surrey and Paul McDaniel, "The Tax Expenditure Concept and the Budget Reform Act of 1974," *Boston College Industrial and Commercial Law Review*, vol. 17 (June 1976), pp. 679–737, for the argument that imputing a tax equal to forgone income (that is, the tax-induced reduction in pre-tax yields on tax-favored investments) is "not a useful analytic technique for the policymaker as part of the determination of effective tax rates" (p. 703), though the authors seemingly accept (pp. 704–05) the concept of forgone income to the extent that it buttresses their theory that tax expenditures are inefficient.

At this point, the efficiency theorist's students may note that the horizontal equity to which their instructor points is produced by comparing persons who do not have equal amounts of economic income: A receives $1,000 in interest; B, only $300. If we return to the original hypothesis of two taxpayers with $1,000 of income each, the equity theorist's complaint that they do not pay the same amount of tax seems to regain its full original force.

In rebuttal, however, the efficiency theorist lays profane hands on the sacred ark by asserting that equal economic income, meaning pre-tax income, is not the proper base for measuring horizontal equity. A and B are equals, he argues, only if they have the same amount invested at the same risk. Their pre-tax economic receipts cannot be properly compared, because B's pre-tax income reflects its tax exemption.

The efficiency theorist therefore compares A, not with B, but with C, who, like A, has $10,000 to invest but who, unlike A, buys tax-exempt bonds and gets $300 of tax-exempt interest. As for B, his $1,000 of tax-exempt interest implies an investment of $33,333, if the interest rate is 3 percent. Hence B should be compared, not with A who has only $10,000 invested, but with D who (like B) has $33,000 invested. If D invests $33,333 in taxable bonds with a 10 percent yield, his after-tax yield is $1,000 (that is, $3,333 less 70 percent of $3,333), which is the same amount that B gets from his tax-exempt bonds. If these are the proper comparisons in testing for horizontal equity, the tax allowance gets a clean bill of health, since A and C, with equal amounts invested, enjoy the same after-tax yield, and so do B and D.

These comparisons are restricted to investment income. How are they affected when income from personal services is introduced into the examples?

As further evidence that horizontal equity is violated by the tax exemption accorded to state and municipal bond interest, traditional equity analysis offers the case of X, a taxpayer who (like A, B, C, and D) is subjected to a 70 percent marginal rate of tax and who earns an additional $1,000 of income from personal services, an action leaving him with $300 after taxes. When compared with B ($1,000 of tax-exempt interest), therefore, X is a victim of horizontal inequity. But the efficiency theorist argues, I presume, that X's skill, experience, and reputation are comparable to the $10,000 of capital invested by

**Table 1. Tax Liabilities and After-Tax Incomes of Taxpayers Subject to a 70 Percent Marginal Tax Rate, Assuming Equalized After-Tax Yields of Comparable Alternative Activities**

Dollars

| Taxpayer | Source of income | Amount invested | Pre-tax yield | Tax | After-tax yield |
|---|---|---|---|---|---|
| A | Taxable interest | 10,000 | 1,000 | 700 | 300 |
| B | Tax-exempt interest | 33,333 | 1,000 | ... | 1,000 |
| C | Tax-exempt interest | 10,000 | 300 | ... | 300 |
| D | Taxable interest | 33,333 | 3,333 | 2,333 | 1,000 |
| X | Taxable wages | a | 1,000 | 700 | 300 |
| Y | Taxable wages | b | 3,333 | 2,333 | 1,000 |

a. X's human capital is equivalent to $10,000 of financial capital.
b. Y's human capital is equivalent to $33,333 of financial capital.

A and C in taxable and tax-exempt bonds; that X, like them, takes $300 home; and that A, C, and X are therefore on a plane of horizontal equity.

For an analogue to B ($1,000 of tax-exempt interest), the efficiency theorist can conjure up Y, whose skill, experience, and reputation not only are comparable to the $33,333 of financial capital invested by B and D but enable him to earn $3,333 with the same time and effort that X must expend to earn $1,000. Being left with $1,000 after tax, Y occupies the same status as B and D, with whom (the efficiency theorist argues) he is properly comparable.

The conclusions reached by the foregoing efficiency analysis are shown in table 1.

Employing the same methods and standards of comparison, an efficiency theorist finds that the results set out in table 1 are consistent with vertical as well as horizontal equity. For this purpose assume that there are four taxpayers, A', D', X', and Y', who are subject to a 50 percent marginal tax rate and who realize additional income in the same amounts and from the same sources as do their counterparts, A, D, X, and Y, who are in the 70 percent bracket. The tax liabilities and after-tax incomes of the former are set out in table 2.

When A' and X' (both having $500 of after-tax yield from their pre-tax income of $1,000) are compared with A and X, the two pairs are separated by the "proper" distance, since the first pair is subject to a 50 percent tax rate and the second to a 70 percent rate. Since it is foolish for a taxpayer subject to a 50 percent marginal rate to invest in

**Table 2. Tax Liabilities and After-Tax Incomes of Taxpayers Subject to a 50 Percent Marginal Tax Rate**
Dollars

| Taxpayer | Source of income | Amount invested | Pre-tax yield | Tax | After-tax yield |
|---|---|---|---|---|---|
| A′ | Taxable interest | 10,000 | 1,000 | 500 | 500 |
| D′ | Taxable interest | 33,333 | 3,333 | 1,667 | 1,666 |
| X′ | Taxable wages | a | 1,000 | 500 | 500 |
| Y′ | Taxable wages | b | 3,333 | 1,667 | 1,666 |

a. X's human capital is equivalent to $10,000 of financial capital.
b. Y's human capital is equivalent to $33,333 of financial capital.

tax-exempt bonds paying only 3 percent, there are no realistic 50 percent analogues to C. But if A, C, and X are on a plane of horizontal equity, all three of them must also occupy a plane of vertical equity when compared with A′ and X′. By a parity of reasoning, since D′ and Y′ are properly separated from D and Y, they are also properly distinguished from B.

Although efficiency analysis thus results in favorable judgments on both vertical and horizontal equity, conventional equity analysis results in entirely different verdicts:

1. Horizontal equity is violated because B has the same pre-tax income as A and X ($1,000) and is subject in theory to the same marginal tax rate (70 percent) but pays no tax.

2. Vertical equity is violated because A′, D′, X′, and Y′ pay taxes at the marginal rate of 50 percent, while B and C, who are subject in theory to a higher rate (70 percent), pay no taxes.

## The Trickle-up Phenomenon

A recent analysis of tax-exempt interest offers a trickle-up theory of the exclusion's impact.[5] A brief examination of the relationship of this theory to equity and efficiency as normative standards is in order. Acknowledging that the benefit of the exclusion is competed away (and inures wholly to the borrowers) if all exempt bonds are purchased by investors subject to the highest marginal rate (currently 70 percent), trickle-up analysis points out that if bonds must be sold to

5. Susan Ackerman and David Ott, "An Analysis of the Revenue Effects of Proposed Substitutes for Tax Exemption of State and Local Bonds," *National Tax Journal*, vol. 23 (December 1970), pp. 397–406.

taxpayers subject to a lower marginal rate (for example, 50 percent) in order to clear the market, the tax benefit will be competed away only for this group of investors.[6] Thus to compete with 10 percent industrial bonds and attract these 50 percent taxpayers, the exempt securities will have to pay 5 percent. For these taxpayers, therefore, exempt bonds generate no lasting tax benefit; the net yield is 5 percent whether they buy taxable or exempt bonds. But for investors in the 70 percent bracket, exempt bonds offer a windfall profit of 2 percentage points above the after-tax yield of taxable bonds (that is, 5 percent tax-free versus 3 percent after-tax). Thus the excess of the interest rate on exempt bonds (5 percent) over the after-tax yield on taxable bonds (3 percent) trickles up to these 70 percent taxpayers.

This phenomenon should arouse the wrath of both efficiency and equity theorists because the tax allowance causes both a misallocation of resources (by diverting funds from investments with a 10 percent economic yield to investments yielding only 5 percent) and vertical inequity (that is, the same yield of 5 percent tax-free to taxpayers whether their marginal tax rate is 50 percent or 70 percent). But efficiency theorists should find the resulting misallocation less objectionable than the misallocation that arises when the tax allowance is monopolized by taxpayers subject to a marginal tax rate of 70 per-

6. The assumption that the tax-favored, tax-exempt bonds must be sold to middle-income taxpayers points up a deficiency in equity analysis that I wish to record here without attempting to pursue it further. Horizontal inequity can arise only if some members of the equal-income class under examination fail to take advantage of the allowance; if *everyone* in a given income class gravitated toward the allowance, they would all fit into the same boat, leaving no one for us to pity. But there is no adequate theory explaining the stubborn reluctance of numerous taxpayers in every income class to engage in tax-sheltered activities that according to equity analysis, confer benefits at no cost. In particular, why is the appetite of top-bracket taxpayers for tax-exempt bonds satiated so quickly? Conversely why do they buy *any* taxable bonds if their aggregate income from all sources brings the top marginal rate into force?

My economist friends tell me that the purchase of both taxable and tax-free bonds by top-bracket investors reflects a desire to avoid risks by diversifying their portfolios. Since tax-free bonds offer a wide spectrum of risks, with a higher yield *at every risk level* than the after-tax yields on taxable bonds of equal quality, the diversification theory does not persuade me. I am also skeptical about another explanation, that is, differing judgments about risks. Since the yield on the *safest* tax-free bonds is greater than the after-tax yield on the *riskiest* investment-grade taxable bonds (in 1978 conservative, middle-term, tax-free bonds yielded almost 6 percent, while extremely risky taxable "junk bonds" yielded less than 15 percent, or 4.5 percent after a 70 percent tax), only an extremely idiosyncratic judgment about risks could account for a preference for the latter over the former.

cent, since that stimulates borrowing for projects producing an economic yield of only 3 percent.[7]

The relationship of the trickle-up phenomenon to equity analysis is more complicated. Taxpayers at the 70 percent marginal rate who buy taxable bonds have only themselves to blame for the resulting disparity between their tax liabilities and those of their compatriots who invest in tax-exempt bonds. By contrast, taxpayers at the 50 percent level enjoy the same yield (5 percent) in the hypothetical case just described whether they buy taxable or tax-exempt bonds; hence there is no horizontal disparity among them.

Vertical inequity, however, is produced by the trickle-up phenomenon; taxpayers subject to a 70 percent marginal tax rate who invest in tax-exempt bonds get the same net yield (5 percent) as taxpayers subject to a 50 percent marginal tax rate who buy either taxable or exempt bonds.

A paradoxical aspect of the trickle-up phenomenon—disregarded by equity theorists so far as I can recall—is that vertical inequity *increases* in proportion to the tax allowance's popularity with low-income taxpayers. If tax-exempt bonds are offered in such volume that they must be sold to taxpayers subject to a marginal tax rate of, for example, 30 percent, the resulting interest rate (7 percent) will result in a windfall of 4 percentage points to top-bracket taxpayers, in contrast to their 2-point advantage when the market in tax-exempt bonds can be cleared by sales to taxpayers subject to a 50 percent marginal tax rate. For the rich, therefore, the best tax shelters are those that are patronized by the poor; on the other hand, the more exclusive the club, the less reason to join.

This conclusion, of course, is wholly contrary to the conventional equity assumption that the most inequitable tax allowances are those that are confined to top-bracket taxpayers.[8] If the trickle-up theory is valid, an upside-down subsidy (that is, one that goes *exclusively* to

7. The "efficiency" objection offered by equity theorists to tax allowances that trickle up is, of course, totally different from the efficiency theorist's misallocation-of-resources criticism discussed in the text. Equity theorists complain that the trickle-up phenomenon diverts to lenders some of the tax benefit intended by Congress for borrowers. From an allocation-of-resources point of view, however, this is a virtue, not a vice; the less the allowance is passed through to borrowers, the less they will be encouraged to indulge in uneconomic ventures.

8. See, for example, Harvey Galper and Dennis Zimmerman, "Preferential Taxation and Portfolio Choice: Some Empirical Evidence," *National Tax Journal,* vol. 30 (December 1977), pp. 387–97.

taxpayers subject to the highest marginal tax rate) causes a misallocation of resources but no vertical inequity. From an equity point of view, therefore, converting an upside-down allowance into one that is right-side-up would create—rather than eliminate—vertical inequity.

## Does the Conflict Matter?

If I am right that there is a fundamental conflict between old-style equity analysis and new-fashioned efficiency analysis, does the conflict matter? If both groups damn what they see and agree on the remedy (for example, a tax law based on the Haig-Simons definition of income), why be concerned if they prefer to reach their common destination by different roads?

In response I argue that each group's zeal for tax reform would (and should) diminish, if not evaporate, if it concluded that the other group's reason for wanting reform is valid. If the inequity perceived by equity theorists in a given tax allowance is in fact converted wholly into a misallocation of resources, a single-minded equity theorist has no reason to favor its repeal, unless he also objects to governmental interference with marketplace outcomes. Moreover, some equity theorists might well favor retention of a tax allowance if persuaded that it alters a particular marketplace outcome while producing little or no horizontal inequity. Conversely, a single-minded efficiency theorist has no reason to object on efficiency grounds to a tax allowance changing the distribution of horizontal tax burdens if it does not alter economic behavior; and particular tax allowances might be favored by an efficiency theorist who welcomes the resulting change in the distribution of the burden and sees no adverse impact on resource allocations.

## Terra Incognita

In the foregoing discussion I use tax-exempt bond interest in my examples because its exclusion from gross income is one of the few tax allowances that has been examined extensively by both equity and efficiency theorists, and especially because economists now seem to agree that a significant part of the tax allowance is competed away rather than retained by the taxpayer-lender. It is obvious that wholly different equity and efficiency conclusions would be reached with respect to tax allowances that do not affect taxpayer behavior. The $1,000 annual tax exemption for blind taxpayers is an example; there may be economists who think that this allowance encourages some taxpayers to neglect their eyes and thereby induces a misallocation of resources (for example, increased dependence on seeing-eye dogs and other after-the-fact palliatives), but they would more likely agree that the blindness exemption does not alter the pre-tax income of its beneficiaries. If this view is correct, the blindness exemption raises solely equity issues, untinctured by any misallocation of resources.

But most tax allowances cannot be readily assigned to one end or the other of the behavioral spectrum. On reviewing the items listed in the tax expenditure budget, for example, I am surprised at the paucity of reliable data to be found anywhere about the extent to which the ostensible benefits of particular exclusions, deductions, credits, and other allowances remain with the taxpayer claiming the allowance or are transferred to others.[9]

I have focused here on only one aspect of the problem, the possibility that market forces transfer the economic benefit of a tax allowance from the taxpayer-claimant to others. But one must also consider the possibility that the benefit is impounded by the early birds and does not pass to later claimants; if a tax allowance is capitalized when first granted, any resulting inequity may be a transitional rather than permanent phenomenon. It should also be noted that tax allowances can acquire a self-destruct device from sources other than market forces. For example, if the exclusion of social security benefits, military allowances, and other governmental payments from gross income is taken into account by Congress in fixing the amount of these payments, their exemption creates horizontal and vertical inequities only by virtue of the trickle-up phenomenon described earlier.

We know so little that it is perhaps superfluous to mention another source of uncertainty, that is to say, the difficulty in separating tax allowances from the structural features of a "normal" income tax. For example, if income taxation alters the pre-tax trade-off between

9. Despite the vast body of commentary on the tax shelter epidemic of the last decade, for example, there are no measures by tax economists of the influence of market forces. Was a Texas friend of mine right in saying that any gas or oil shelter that has to be marketed to Scarsdale orthodontists is a sure loser? If so, what does that imply about the ostensible tax benefits promised by the investment?

work and leisure, are statutory provisions reducing the tax on income from personal services, such as the 50 percent tax ceiling and the earned income credit commendable features, mitigating a misallocation that is otherwise inherent in the tax itself, or are they sources of affirmative misallocations? The same questions can be asked from an equity point of view: if a "pure" income tax is biased against labor, do these allowances correct, or create, an inequity?

## Conclusion

It is hard to see how the normative standards favored by either equity or efficiency theorists can be applied with confidence to existing law while the behavioral consequences of most tax allowances remain terra incognita. Only when they are mapped will we be able to say with assurance whether particular tax allowances generate inequities, misallocations, or some of each. Until then, intuition and political preferences will have to be the bases for analysis, because scholars, alas, can legitimately claim little more authority than the average citizen.

JAMES BUCHANAN *Virginia Polytechnic Institute*

GEOFFREY BRENNAN *Virginia Polytechnic Institute*

# Tax Reform without Tears

THIS PAPER traces the distributional implications of departures from an idealized tax base. Orthodox public finance specialists operating within the conventions of tax orthodoxy have traditionally been preoccupied with this question. Seeking the twin objectives of efficiency and equity, the standard analyst tries to specify both an ideal tax base and a rate structure that should be applied to that base in order to distribute the cost of public expenditures equitably. In theory nondistorting taxes make it possible simultaneously to achieve "perfect" vertical and horizontal equity (however defined) with no efficiency loss induced by the tax system. In practice these various objectives conflict with one another because perfectly nondistorting taxes do not exist. For example, a more progressive rate structure will distort leisure-effort choices more severely; it will discriminate more between people according to the time pattern of their income streams; and a minimally distorting tax will vary between otherwise economic equals according to their elasticities of demand for leisure.[1]

By a kind of perverse luck the tax system contains so many distortions that some reforms advance all objectives. Closing some of the major loopholes in the personal income tax is one such reform. Such loopholes not only reduce efficiency and discriminate unfairly among economic equals but also violate common norms of vertical equity by offering chinks in the fiscal armor through which the incomes of many of the richest taxpayers all but disappear.

1. Given that averaging schemes are characteristically imperfect.

33

Empirical support for this latter contention is not hard to find. Even the most cursory glance at the relevant statistics indicates that the rich use these loopholes far more than do the poor. In fact, some commentators see the departure of actual income tax payments from those implied by the nominal rate structure as a prime reason why the U.S. tax system as a whole is roughly proportional rather than progressive.[2] If such loopholes do indeed undermine the major instrument of progression in the federal tax system, hope for any genuine overall progressivity is scant. It is conceivable, moreover, that the effect of loopholes on vertical equity is more significant than the effect on horizontal equity; if people within income classes make much the same use of loopholes, and the major differences are among income classes,[3] then loopholes undermine *vertical,* not horizontal, equity. On this basis it is tempting to make vertical equity considerations a major—perhaps *the* major—justification for tax reform; many commentators over the past decade have yielded to such a temptation.

At the same time, popular discussion of tax reform has tended to relegate efficiency considerations to a secondary place. "Excess burden" issues, it is claimed, involve allocative losses that are "small and difficult to measure."[4] And even where excess burden is discussed it is often treated as if efficiency losses fall only in general and not on anyone in particular.

In this paper we explore the distributional impact of excess burdens. We claim that a direct relationship exists between the extent to which taxpayers exploit loopholes and the size of the excess burden those loopholes induce. We hold that this excess burden falls precisely on the exploiters themselves. Several conclusions follow. First, the empirical measures of effective progression that are based on the ratio of actual tax payments to an idealized tax base (for example, total income) are themselves misleading; the nominal rate structure offers a measure of true progression that is not obviously inferior to these estimates of "effective" rates. To the extent that the nominal rate structure is progressive, so generally will be burden sharing. Second,

2. See Joseph A. Pechman and Benjamin A. Okner, *Who Bears the Tax Burden?* (Brookings Institution, 1974), for much of the relevant data; and George F. Break and Joseph A. Pechman, *Federal Tax Reform: The Impossible Dream?* (Brookings Institution, 1975), for related commentary.

3. An outcome consistent with the scenario envisaged by Martin Feldstein in "On the Theory of Tax Reform," *Journal of Public Economics,* vol. 6 (July-August 1976), pp. 77–104.

4. Pechman and Okner, *Who Bears the Tax Burden?* p. 3.

and for the same reason, empirical estimates of horizontal equity exhibited by different taxes or tax regimes may be rather misleading. Third, far from being "small and difficult to measure," allocative losses must be concomitantly large if the exploitation of tax loopholes is as significant as the standard discussions relate; and the measurement of such losses presents few problems not also present in estimating effective progression.

This analysis suggests that failure to include the excess burden attributable to loopholes leads to exaggerated estimates of their distributional effects. By contrast, arguments for tax reform resting on inefficiencies caused by loopholes receive too little attention.

In fact, *efficiency* considerations allow ample scope for legitimate tax reform, and arguably they are ethically superior and politically more practical than arguments based on equity considerations. Instead of emphasizing the injustice or unfairness of the existing system, as evidenced by the alleged failure of the "rich" to pay their "fair shares," tax reformers should place more stress on economic waste, the burden of which is borne largely, if not exclusively, by those who find it advantageous to make behavioral adjustments in response to tax loopholes. Moreover, emphasis on increased progression, as an end in itself, may possibly represent a strategic mistake on the part of the reform protagonists. Tax reform may become a "possible dream" when it is recognized that after taxpayers have adjusted to loopholes, those who avail themselves of special rules and regulations are not materially better off than they would have been in the absence of such rules and regulations. *All* taxpayers might agree on a reform that improves the post-tax position of all parties, by reducing excess burdens. Meaningful tax reform can be, and should be, examined and discussed as a "positive-sum game" and not as the "zero-sum game" that it is often made out to be. A corollary, obscured in the standard reformist emphasis on increased progression, is that a reduction in excess burden and an accompanying increase in revenue collections could make possible lower marginal rates of tax, quite apart from any shift toward comprehensiveness of the tax base.

Very little in this paper is new. Most of the points are implicit in orthodox discussion, and for the purposes of this paper we accept that logic completely.[5] We merely emphasize certain oversights in tradi-

5. We *have* attacked it in another place. See Geoffrey Brennan and James Buchanan, "Towards a Tax Constitution for Leviathan," *Journal of Public Economics*, vol. 8 (December 1977), pp. 255–73.

tional tax reform literature and urge a more thorough integration of equity and efficiency norms. When this integration is made, the importance of those efficiency norms emerges.

Our argument proceeds as follows. First, we illustrate the problem by appeal to two simple, rather stylized, numerical examples. Then, we present a more general algebraic/diagrammatic treatment and introduce our central results. Next, we demonstrate the possibility of tax reform via marginal rate reduction, and then we refer to the strictly horizontal equity problems posed by consensual changes. Finally, we offer a brief conclusion.

Perhaps, however, one clarifying comment should be offered here. Not *all* departures from an ideally neutral comprehensive tax base induce adjustments by *all* taxpayers to minimize tax payments. But we do believe that all such departures have that tendency. We do not argue that all taxpayers can adjust equally easily. Thus we do not— and need not—argue that the horizontal and vertical equity case for closing tax loopholes is entirely inappropriate, except in the limiting cases that our numerical examples illustrate. For this reason our discussion is cast in terms of the "exploitation" of tax loopholes by "rich" taxpayers—the object of much indignation on the part of many tax reform specialists—although it is in fact somewhat more general. Both the horizontal and vertical equity cases for closing tax loopholes are overstated *to the extent that there is any behavioral adjustment to tax loopholes at all.* On that basis the relative importance of efficiency arguments correspondingly grows; and the possibility of genuinely consensual tax reform increases, together with its political practicability and ethical desirability.

## Two Numerical Examples

We first present two numerical examples based on highly restrictive assumptions with sharply contrasting results. In each example we assume that people are indifferent to alternative sources of income, that they face linear rates of transformation among these alternative income sources over relevant ranges of choice, and that the tax rate structure is a simplified two-bracket schedule. As noted below, the examples differ from each other in one critically important assumption.

The pre-tax setting is identical in the two examples. Consider a two-person model (which may be extended to include many persons so long as each additional person is assumed to be identical to one of the two described here). Person 1 earns $10,000 per period from some standard income source, while Person 2 earns $20,000 per period from the same source. A progressive tax of 10 percent on the first $10,000 and 20 percent on the second $10,000 is imposed on personal income. The government expects to collect $4,000—$1,000 from Person 1 and $3,000 from Person 2.

After a period of behavioral adjustment the results are different. Person 2 locates a source of nontaxable income and shifts some of his efforts to earning income from this source.[6] Person 1, by assumption, continues to earn $10,000 in pre-tax income from the taxable source and to pay the anticipated tax. Actual tax payments made by the two persons, when measured, prove to be roughly proportional to measured gross incomes (from both sources) rather than progressive.

Under what conditions can we properly infer that Person 2 has escaped his "fair share" of the tax and that an increase in the effective rate of progression is indicated, something that might be accomplished by taxing the nontaxable source?

### The Equity Model

Consider the following post-tax equilibrium. Suppose that Person 2 secures $15,000 from the taxable source and pays a total tax of $2,000; in addition he can earn $5,000 from a nontaxable source. His labor input is unchanged and his gross pre-tax income remains at $20,000. But he has increased post-tax income from $17,000 to $18,000 by shifting some of his income receipts to the nontaxable source. The government finds itself with $1,000 less than anticipated. Note that the government's loss is equal to Person 2's gain. From this it follows that there is *no* excess burden of the tax; there is no net allocative inefficiency involved in the tax-induced shift between income sources, because Person 2's productivity is the same in both the taxable and nontaxable activities.

---

6. Preferential tax treatment of income sources or income uses is often based on the actual or alleged presence of such external benefits. Legislatures may deliberately create tax-reducing options for the purpose of modifying private behavior. The analysis of this paper can readily be extended to include this, but to attempt to discuss the implications here would distract from the main argument. In any case the conventional emphasis has been on the absence of such spillover benefits or, more correctly, on the inappropriateness of such considerations for the structure of income taxation.

### The Countermodel

Suppose now that the nontaxable source of income is only four-fifths as productive as the taxable source. Suppose further that after a period of adjustment, Person 2 earns $18,888—$14,444 from the taxable source and $4,444 from the nontaxable source. In this situation, note that the tax actually collected from each person is 10 percent of gross income ($1,000/10,000 = 1,888/18,888).

But what is the distribution of the tax *burden* in this case? It is now wholly misleading to infer from the proportionality of actual revenues collected to gross incomes that the distribution of burden is also proportional, as it was in the equity model. To look at the tax burden, one needs to look at post-tax positions. The position of Person 1 is defined by a post-tax income of $9,000, as before. The government anticipated that Person 2 would have a post-tax income of $17,000 owing to his expected payment of $3,000 to the government. After adjustment, Person 2 still ends up with $17,000. Person 2 is no better off than he would have been without the nontaxable option, yet the government collects $1,112 less in revenue. This loss in economic value arises exclusively from the shift in Person 2's earnings from the more productive taxable source to the less productive nontaxable source. The revenue loss measures the difference between the total value of output produced in the no-tax and the post-tax situations, a difference that is generated solely by the imposition of the tax. It measures the excess burden of the tax, if excess burden is defined as the loss in social value as distinct from the actual payment to the government.

This counterexample has, of course, been deliberately contrived to demonstrate our central point while yielding the proportionality results. At a minimum this counterexample should give pause to those who try to assess relative tax burdens on the basis of statistics measuring actual tax payments.[7]

7. In the example, given the simplifying assumptions, Person 2 will remain in the same post-tax position with income at $17,000 at *any* level of taxable income between the $10,000 and $20,000 limits. The break between taxable and nontaxable income chosen in the illustration is the only one within these limits, however, that will precisely mirror the proportionality results where tax payments made by the two persons are proportional to gross incomes, despite the progressive rate structure. If Person 2 had remained wholly unresponsive to the tax, his post-tax income would have been the same, but actual payments to government would have been higher, and a conventional "effective progression" measure would have yielded progressive

# General Analysis

Both numerical examples contain extreme discontinuities. In this section we offer a more general model that reaches the same conclusion—reduction in excess burden is a more appropriate justification for tax reform than is increased progressivity, and it is equally feasible.

We continue to assume that potential taxpayers have no preference for one kind of work over another; it follows that normal utility-maximizing behavior will dictate an equalization of net-of-tax marginal rates of return in alternative employments. If the wage rate in a taxed activity, $W_T$, exceeds the wage in an untaxed activity, $W_U$, people will shift effort from taxed to untaxed labor as long as $W_U > W_T$ $(1 - t)$, where $t$ is the marginal tax rate. Only when $W_U = W_T (1 - t)$ will a person be indifferent between additional work in the two activities. If the wage rates measure marginal productivity, it is clear that *at the margin* the difference in productivity between the two income sources (the "excess burden") must be negligibly different from the tax saving, as determined by the marginal tax rate. Equally, in the pre-tax situation (that is, when the tax rate is zero), the difference in the productivity of the two sources is also negligibly different from zero: in the tax-free situation the individual is also indifferent between the sources at the margin. Over the entire range of substitution, therefore, the excess burden would be roughly half the tax avoided, given that there are no discontinuities or nonlinearities.

Precisely the same reasoning applies if particular expenditures are tax-favored. Rational behavior dictates that a person be indifferent between a dollar's worth of nondeductible and deductible outlays both before and after the tax is introduced. Hence he will make expenditures on tax-favored commodities that would not be worth making if expenditures on that commodity were treated equally with other expenditures. Once again a reasonable approximation to the excess burden under normal circumstances seems to be half the tax avoided.

The point can be made by appeal to the geometry of figure 1. To focus on the substitution of tax-exempt activities for taxable ones, we

---

results. On the other hand, if Person 2 had reduced taxable income to $10,000, the conventional measure would have suggested a *regressive* structure of revenue payments to government, despite the *progressivity* of the underlying tax burden.

**Figure 1. Labor Supply with and without Taxation**

Wage rate (dollars)

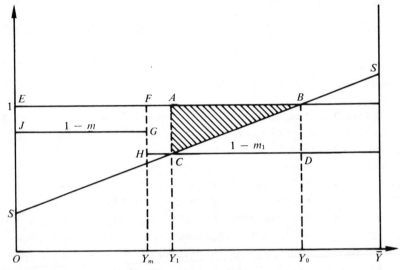

Income-generating activity

assume in figure 1 that the total amount of income-generating activity (this could be thought of as labor input) is fixed at $\overline{Y}$ units. The horizontal axis depicts how this total is divided between activities that are potentially taxable and activities that will not be subject to tax. Along the vertical axis we depict the return to the individual, per unit of labor effort, in the earning of taxable income. We define units of income-generating activity in such a way that the pre-tax return per unit of time spent in the taxable activity is $1.

The curve $SS$ shows the allocation of income-generating activity to taxable sources as the marginal return from those taxable sources changes. Read from right to left, therefore, $SS$ depicts the marginal productivity of the individual in deriving income from nontaxable activity.[8] (The demand for the worker's services in potentially taxable activities is taken to be infinitely elastic at the initial dollar wage.)

In the absence of tax the individual would devote $Y_0$ units of

_____

8. We ignore the possibility that the supply curve is backward bending, due to income effects, as an unnecessary complication. Because our major focus is on loopholes and their exploitation, the shape indicated seems most plausible to us.

income-generating activity to those activities that are to be taxed, and $\bar{Y}-Y_0$ units to those activities that are to be tax free and will earn income from those sources accordingly. His total initial income therefore consists of $Y_0$ from taxable sources, plus the area below $SS$ beyond $Y_0$ (area $SBY_0\bar{Y}$) from nontaxable sources.

Suppose that the tax to be introduced is a progressive income tax consisting of two rates (in line with our earlier examples): the tax rate $m$ applies over the first $Y_m$ dollars of taxable income earned, and the rate $m_1$ over all subsequent taxable earnings. The line $(1-m, 1-m_1)$ depicts this tax regime: tax revenue is given by the area between that line and the horizontal dollar line over the relevant range. Because the return on taxed income sources has declined as a result of the tax, the individual will substitute activity in nontaxed areas for activity in taxed areas, until the marginal return in each pursuit is once more identical: this occurs when the level of activity in the taxed area is $Y_1$, where $SS$ cuts the line $(1 - m_1)$. The individual's gross taxable income falls in response to the imposition of the tax from $Y_0$ dollars to $Y_1$ dollars. His nontaxable income increases from the area under $SS$ from $Y_0$ to $\bar{Y}$, to the area under $SS$ from $Y_1$ to $\bar{Y}$—an increase measured by area $BCY_1Y_0$. The tax he avoids paying is therefore $m_1(Y_0 - Y_1)$ dollars, or equivalently the area $ABDC$. Note that this amount is not the same as the tax revenue forgone by the exemption of the tax-free income sources, because the individual was earning some income from the tax-exempt income source before the imposition of the tax. Rather, $ABDC$ measures the amount of revenue forgone as a result of the taxpayer's behavioral response to the imposition of the tax.

The crucial point of this construction is that on the basis of $SS$ as drawn, the value of the redirected income-earning activity to the taxpayer is *not* $(Y_0 - Y_1)$ dollars. The taxpayer is induced by the tax to move to less efficient income-earning activities—activities that return him an amount equal to the area under the $SS$ curve over the range of adjustment. This is less than $(Y_0 - Y_1)$ dollars by the amount $ABC$; the taxpayer thus bears a burden of $ABC$ in addition to the tax revenue received by government. This is the excess burden, and assuming $SS$ to be linear over the range of adjustment, this is exactly one-half of the tax revenue the taxpayer avoids paying, that is, $ABC = \frac{1}{2} [m_1(Y_0 - Y_1)]$.

Within a similar geometric construction, we can set forth the ex-

**Figure 2. Labor Supply: Equity Example**

Wage rate (dollars)

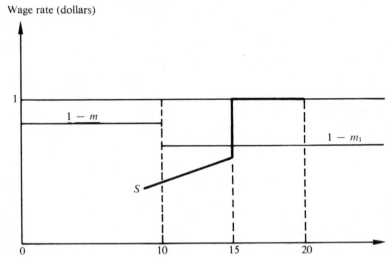

Income-generating activity (thousands of dollars)

treme assumptions that are implicit in both the equity-oriented and the counterequity arithmetical examples above. In both examples there is presumed to be *no* earning from tax-free sources before tax: that is, $Y_0$ and $\bar{Y}$ are identical. In the equity model the "rich" person is assumed to secure the full value of the tax avoided. Figure 2 depicts this situation. As in figure 1, $SS$ in figure 2 depicts the allocation of the taxpayer's activity between the taxed and untaxed forms of income as the marginal tax rate varies (or equally, read from right to left, the marginal productivity of untaxed income-earning activity). In the absence of tax the taxpayer earns $20,000 in the form of "taxable" income; in the presence of the tax with marginal rate $m_1$, he earns $15,000 in that form. Because $SS$ takes the shape it does, however, there is no excess burden induced by the adjustment: the tax-free earnings source generates virtually identical gross returns to those from the taxed source over the entire range to $15,000 and then drops to intersect the $(1 - m_1)$ line at that point. The line $SS$ must intersect $(1 - m_1)$ at $15,000, since otherwise the taxpayer would substitute untaxed for taxed activity over a different range. For example, if $SS$ were horizontal over the range from zero to $20,000, the taxpayer would never pay tax at all given this definition of taxable income; he would avoid tax entirely. In the case depicted in figure 2

**Figure 3. Labor Supply: Counterequity Example**

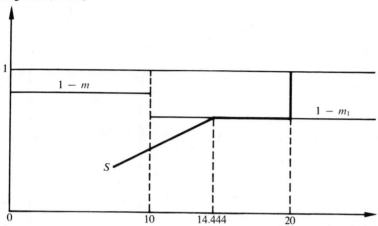

Income-generating activity (thousands of dollars)

(as in the numerical example) the activities substituted for taxed activities yield virtually a full $5,000 worth of value to the taxpayer.

The counterequity case is depicted in figure 3. In this case, productivity in the tax-exempt activity is no higher than $(1 - m_1)$ per unit of work effort. The taxpayer responds to the tax by substituting tax-free income-generating activity over the range from $20,000 to $14,444. Although he maintains his full input of income-generating activity, his gross income has fallen to $18,888 because income-generating activity in the tax-exempt area earns him negligibly more than he would receive net-of-tax from the taxed area. The individual is virtually indifferent between the two income sources over the range from $14,444 to $20,000. The key point of figure 3 is that each dollar of tax saved creates virtually one dollar of inefficiency and brings virtually no benefit whatsoever to the tax avoider. In this case, the excess burden and the tax saving are virtually identical.

Similar diagrammatics can be used to illustrate tax avoidance on the expenditure or "uses" side of income. In figure 4 expenditures are taxed at the rate $1/(1 - m_1)$ and the amount of commodity $X$ demanded is $X_1$. If the commodity $X$ becomes tax exempt, demand rises to $X_0$, where the price by assumption equals 1. Tax avoidance will be area $ABCG$, or $m_1(X_0 - X_1)$; and the excess burden associated with that outlay shift, given the assumption that $D$ is roughly linear over

**Figure 4. Excess Burden Resulting from Commodity Taxation**

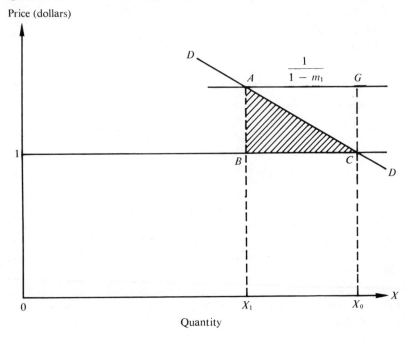

Price (dollars)

Quantity

the relevant range, will be area $ABCG$, or $m_1 (X_0 - X_1)$; and the excess burden associated with that outlay shift, given the assumption that $D$ is roughly linear over the relevant range, will be area $ABC$ or $\frac{1}{2} [m_1(X_0 - X_1)]$ as before.

It may be useful at this point to investigate some of the assumptions in the discussion so far. One assumption in both the numerical examples was that the lower-income individual did not adjust his behavior in response to the imposition of the tax on $Y$—an assumption that is inconsistent with the generalized continuity assumption adopted here. Denoting tax avoidance as $A$, where $A = m \cdot \Delta Y$, and using a definition of the elasticity of the supply curve, $SS$ in figure 1, as $\epsilon = (\Delta Y / Y_0)/(\Delta p/p)$, it follows that $A = m^2 \cdot \epsilon Y_0$ because the initial price is defined to be unity, and $m$ is the marginal tax rate.

If the elasticity, $\epsilon$, is taken to be the same at all income levels, then it follows that tax avoided will be *more than proportionately* larger for the rich than for the poor. For example, in the numerical illustration above, where Person 2's marginal tax rate (postadjustment) is twice Person 1's, then tax avoidance by Person 2 will be *four times as large a proportion* of his initial taxable income as tax avoidance by Person 1 is of 1's taxable income, even if there is no other difference. Given that 2's income is twice 1's, the absolute reduction in income earned in the taxed form will be four times as large for 2 as for 1, and the tax avoided eight times as large.

Thus the analysis explains why tax avoidance is particularly appealing to the rich and justifies in part the assumption made in the examples given above that tax avoidance by lower-income persons can be effectively ignored.

Until now we have assumed linear supply curves (on the sources side) and demand curves (on the uses side). We have also assumed that the marginal tax rate is unchanged over the relevant ranges. This assumption is much less reasonable. Generally the marginal tax structure consists of a considerable number of steps, or conceivably it could be smoothly progressive (as in figure 5). Although in such cases the excess burden remains as the area $ABC$ or $\frac{1}{2} [m_1 (Y_0 - Y_1)]$, the tax forgone is given by the area between the tax curve, labeled $(1 - m)$, and the horizontal unit price line and exceeds $m_1(Y_0 - Y_1)$ because the marginal rate at $Y_0$, $m_0$, is larger than that at $Y_1$. We can approximate tax forgone by the change in $Y$ times the *average* of $m_0$ and $m_1$.

Hence $A = \frac{1}{2} (m_0 + m_1) (Y_0 - Y_1)$ and the excess burden, $W$, equals $\frac{1}{2} [m_1(Y_0 - Y_1)]$.

Then, the ratio of excess burden $(W)$ to tax avoided $(A)$ will be

(1) $$W/A = m_1/(m_1 + m_0).$$

This expression depends on the rate of change of marginal tax rates as income rises rather than on the level of marginal rates, and this varies throughout the progressive rate scale. Because marginal rates are bounded at the upper end (at something below 100 percent), the ratio in equation 1 will tend to fall as one moves higher up the progressive rate scale. For the richest tax avoiders, those whose income after tax avoidance is subject to tax at rates near the maximum, $W/A$ is near the value of $\frac{1}{2}$ applying in the earlier discussion.

This theory generates two central conclusions. First, where tax avoidance is substantial, excess burdens in general will also be substantial. This conclusion implies that the scope for tax reform that makes virtually everyone better off is broader than the standard discussion seems to imply. The second conclusion is that the total tax

**Figure 5. Labor Supply and Excess Burden with Continuously Variable Wage Schedule**

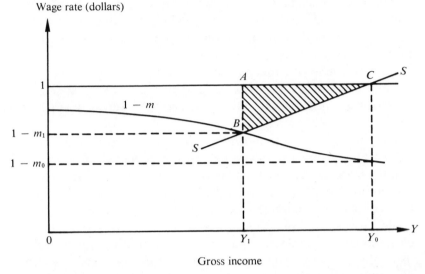

Gross income

burden, including excess burden, is distributed in a more progressive fashion than is normally indicated. Comparing, for example, any two persons whose post-tax taxable incomes are the same, the one who avoids the more tax (that is, whose pre-tax income was higher) endures a larger total burden.[9] If a tax structure that is progressive at pre-tax levels of $Y$ is transformed via tax avoidance into a structure in which actual tax payments are *proportional* in terms of initial levels of $Y$, then the true distribution of burdens (including excess burden) lies somewhere between the nominal and effective rate structures—and may not be too far removed from a simple average of the two. The tax burden, of course, would be precisely equal to that simple average if excess burden equaled *half* the tax avoided; the smaller the ratio of excess burden to tax avoidance (that is, as the elasticity of

9. We should note that it is not necessarily the case that for individuals whose *initial* levels of taxable income are identical, the one who avoids the most tax will have the largest excess burden. Whether or not this is so depends on the elasticity of the marginal tax rate structure because larger tax avoidance implies both a larger value of $(Y_0 - Y_1)$ and a *smaller* value of $m$. If the marginal rate reduction is proportionately greater than the increase in income diverted, excess burden will fall. Since $W = \frac{1}{2} [m(Y_1)] [Y_0 - Y_1]$, we can show this by differentiating $W$ with respect to $Y_1$, with $Y_0$ identical for both. Then $dW/d(Y_0 - Y_1) = \frac{1}{2} [m(Y_1)] + \frac{1}{2} (Y_0 - Y_1) dm/dY_1[dY_1/d(Y_0 - Y_1)]$. Because $dY_1/d(Y_0 - Y_1) = -1$, $dW/d(Y_0 - Y_1) > 0$ if and only if $1 > (dm(Y_1)/dY_1) (Y_0 - Y_1)/m(Y_1)$.

the marginal rate structure increases over the relevant ranges), the greater the weight that should be given to the effective rate structure.

## Tax Reform via Marginal Rate Reduction

Reformers who stress equity and seek to increase the effective progressiveness of tax payments try to ensure that the "rich" pay their "fair shares" of the total costs of government. In practice this approach leads to attempts to close loopholes, to eliminate the tax shelters, and to end the use of deductions or credits to shield income sources or income uses from taxation. This type of reform advocacy obscures an important avenue to genuine tax reform via *reduction* in the rate of tax progression.

In the counterexample shown in figure 3 the nontaxable income source is demonstrably less productive than the taxable source. In this setting a reduction in the top bracket rate can result in a complete elimination of excess burden as well as tax avoidance because the less productive tax-exempt source of income ceases to be worth pursuing. The tax becomes effectively comprehensive because no actual income source escapes tax. And most important, *all* parties may be made better off. The post-tax incomes of the "rich," who previously resorted to the nontaxable opportunity, increase, and the government collects *more* revenue from these same taxpayers. A conventional measure of tax payments would suggest progressivity, as desired by the reformists; furthermore, in this case payments would measure tax burdens.

The equity-oriented reformer might emphasize the possibility that in order to accomplish the same results, the effective marginal rate of progression might have to be cut so far that the tax structure would not yield the desired revenues. While this possibility exists, so do the opportunities for improved productivity that the efficiency-oriented reformer emphasizes.

The contrasting implications here may be illustrated readily in numerical terms. If the tax-exempt income source is only half as productive as the taxable source, any top bracket rate below 50 percent will eliminate the nontaxable source, without any explicit action toward making income from this source taxable. With appropriate adjustment to inframarginal rates of tax, the taxpayer could find his post-tax position improved by a shift to exclusive reliance on the taxable source; the government could collect more revenue than before the tax reduction, and almost as much as it had anticipated before it considered the existence of the nontaxable opportunity. There need be no loss in economic value produced by the tax under the appropriately revised rate schedule.

By contrast, if the tax-exempt income source yields 90 percent of that available from the taxable source at the pre-tax earnings position of the taxpayer, the top marginal tax rate would have to be less than 10 percent to ensure that there be no resort at all to the nontaxable opportunity. In this case rate adjustment alone, sufficient to eliminate both excess burden and tax avoidance, might make it impossible for the government to raise as much revenue as in the prereform situation. If the taxpayer is in equilibrium at the margin and is earning some nontaxable income, and if the rate structure is progressive, some reduction in marginal rates must exist along with appropriate inframarginal rate adjustment that will simultaneously improve the position of the taxpayer, increase governmental revenues, and reduce excess burden.[10]

Given that individuals with differing incomes must in practice face the *same* tax schedule, and given the assumption of continuity, the scope for tax reduction that increases public revenue, reduces excess burdens, and benefits all taxpayers is limited. Any inframarginal tax increases must in this scenario increase tax burdens imposed on people lower down the income scale who do not benefit from reduc-

10. The requirement that the taxpayer be in equilibrium at the margin rules out the possibilities of corner solutions analogous to those required for the numerical example of the equity-type model discussed earlier in the text. Consider a situation where two income opportunities are *equally* productive over a limited range but where beyond this the nontaxable source is not productive at all. In this case, regardless of the rate structure, the taxpayer will engage in the nontaxable activity up to the point where it ceases to be productive, regardless of the tax schedule. No change in tax rates can induce him to alter his effort in the nontaxable activity. On the other hand, if the tax schedule is everywhere progressive, the government can increase its revenue collections by increasing inframarginal rates of tax. But the taxpayer is necessarily made worse off in the process. No positive-sum game between government and the taxpayer can be constructed in this setting.

If the nontaxable source is nearly as productive as the taxable source over some range and significantly less productive beyond this range, there always exist tax adjustments that raise revenue, increase the taxpayer's welfare, and eliminate excess burden. In many cases, however, mutual gains may require a regressive rate schedule. If we rule out regressive rates, severe discontinuities in the productivity schedules for nontaxable options may preclude tax reform that reduces excess burden.

tions in high marginal rates. In some cases it is conceivable that revenue collected from an individual would increase due to a reduction in marginal tax rates without any increase in inframarginal rates. This situation arises if the reduction in marginal tax rates induces an increase in income from the taxable source ($Y$) sufficient to offset the loss in revenue caused by the marginal rate reduction; then revenue collected from that individual would go up, but the excess burden would go down sufficiently to leave him better off.

Suppose the marginal rate, $\bar{m}_1$, applies over the range from $Y_2$ to $Y_1$ and beyond. Then, the revenue ($R$) due to the excess of $m_1$ over some alternative marginal rate ($m$) that might have prevailed (say the rate applying on incomes over the previous range to $Y_2$) is $R_m = (Y_1 - Y_2)(m_1 - \bar{m})$. Then

$$dR/dm_1 = (Y_1 - Y_2) + m_1 \cdot dY_1/dm_1.$$

Now

$$Y_1 = Y_0(1 - \epsilon m_1),$$

where $Y_0$ is the income that would be earned from the taxable source in the absence of tax, $Y_1$ is income from the same source after imposition of tax, and $\epsilon$ is the elasticity of earning taxable income with respect to the wage net of tax; so

$$dR/dm_1 = Y_0(1 - \epsilon m_1) - Y_2 + m_1(-\epsilon Y_0)$$

$$= Y_0 - Y_2 - 2\epsilon m_1 Y_0.$$

This $dR/dm_1$ is less than zero if and only if

$$\epsilon > (Y_0 - Y_2)/(2m_1 Y_0).$$

Note that if $m_1 = 50$ percent, $\epsilon > 1$ is sufficient if $Y_2 > 0$; the implication is that for higher marginal rates the condition is not so very stringent.[11]

Beyond this possibility, however, the main policy thrust of the excess burden perspective accords with that of the equity view—a shift toward a comprehensive tax base reduces efficiency losses due to the tax system (although as we have pointed out, a move toward comprehensiveness need not be the only means of decreasing tax-caused

11. Note that this result is predicated on the assumption that the person in question is the highest-income taxpayer, since otherwise revenue lost exceeds $m_1(Y_1 - Y_2)$.

inefficiencies). Where the equity-oriented and the consensus philoso-
phies may diverge, however, is in the use each would make of the
revenue gained thereby. The equity-oriented reformer is likely to urge
cuts in tax rates on lower-income groups to increase the effective
progressivity of the tax system. In our alternative consensus perspective the distribution of the incremental revenue is constrained by the
requirement that no one is made worse off. Even within this constraint, however, there remains scope for alternative distributional
allocations of the gains from tax reform.[12]

12. A simple example will illustrate. Suppose that the tax rate schedule applicable
to income from source $Y$ is 10 percent on the first $10,000, 20 percent on the second
$10,000, and 30 percent on the third $10,000. In the absence of taxation, Individual 1
would earn $10,000 from income source $Y$ and $2,000 from other sources, pre-tax.
Individual 2 earns $20,000 from income source $Y$ and $4,000 from other sources,
pre-tax. The elasticity of supply of labor to earn income from source $Y$ is 1.64 for
both individuals. The post-tax equilibrium involves Individual 1 earning $8,333 from
income source $Y$ and $3,664 from other sources; and Individual 2 earning $13,333
from income source $Y$ and $10,664 from other sources. As a result, Individual 1 pays
$833 in tax, while 2 pays $1,666; the effective rate of tax is proportional (at a rate
of 8.3 percent if measured as a proportion of income earned from source $Y$ before
tax was imposed, or approximately 7 percent if measured against income of *all*
sources).
  The *actual* burdens (including excess burden) are $916.7 for Individual 1 and
$2,333 for Individual 2.
  Suppose we now move to a comprehensive tax system and that as a first step, we
leave the tax rates unchanged. Income sources will revert to their pre-tax proportions;
$1,400 will be raised from Individual 1 and $4,200 from 2. In order to maintain
revenue at the same aggregate level of $2,500, one possibility would be to opt for
maximum progression and to cut the rate on the first $10,000 to zero, leaving
Individual 2 to pay the full $2,500. Since this would necessarily leave 2 worse off, it
lies outside the limits imposed by consensus-type criteria.
  Within those consensus limits, however, very considerable variation remains
possible. Consider, for example, the following tax schedules:

  a.  1 percent over the first $10,000     Individual 1 pays $200; individual 2 pays
      10 percent over the next $10,000     $2,300
      30 percent over the next $10,000

  b.  5 percent over the first $20,000     Individual 1 pays $600;
      22.5 percent over the next $10,000   Individual 2 pays $1,900

  c.  Proportional at 7 percent           Individual 1 pays $840; individual 2 pays
                                           $1,680

*All* raise approximately the same revenue as the initial tax on $Y$ alone; *all* leave both
individuals better off (that is, enduring smaller total burdens) than the initial arrangement. Where the schemes differ is in the breakup of the total allocative gains,
which the shift toward comprehensiveness makes possible. These total allocative
gains are $750—$83 from Individual 1, and $667 from Individual 2—and this $750
can be divided between 1 and 2 in any manner desired.

## Rate Reduction and Horizontal Equity

If tax reform that increases revenue, reduces excess burden, and raises the welfare of all is possible, an explanation is required of the apparent dominance of reformist emphasis on increased progression. Why has the approach to reform that promises gains to all and that therefore holds a potential for agreement among all parties been so neglected? Presumably one response to this query would refer to the limited applicability of the analysis. Our analysis is restricted by the implicit assumption that everyone in a single income class or category responds identically to the imposition of tax. That is to say, we have taken no account of differences among the responses of taxpayers in the same income class to the advantages of nontaxable earning opportunities or income uses. In fact, only certain members of an income class respond to a tax through shifts to sources or uses of income that are fully or partially tax exempt. Those who exploit or exercise nontaxable options may seem to escape their "fair shares" relative to those within their own defined income class who fail to exercise such options.

But what does equality for tax purposes mean? Are taxpayers who respond differently to a tax, reflecting either differential tastes or differential capacities, to be arbitrarily defined as "similar" for tax purposes? Since Martin Feldstein has recently explored some of these questions in some detail, his argument will not be reviewed here.[13] General standards of "equal treatment" may nonetheless place severe limits on the adjustment in marginal and inframarginal rates of tax that may be worked out in the complex political bargaining process.

Within-class adjustment has received insufficient attention in the reformist discussion on the potential tax reduction that movement toward tax-base comprehensiveness would make possible. As noted, the emphasis has been placed almost exclusively on general rate reductions, over all classes, that would seem to become possible on the elimination of preferential treatment accorded to various income sources and uses. This emphasis is misplaced in the context of the alternative reform perspective that has been suggested in this paper. Marginal rate reductions, along with the appropriately designed inframarginal rate changes, are instrumental to the elimination of

13. Feldstein, "On the Theory of Tax Reform."

excess burden without necessary legal changes in the definition of income categories. Such reductions may, in the event, require that the spillover benefits of total tax cuts accrue to nonresponsive taxpayers who perchance are members of the classes most responsive to nontaxable options. To the extent that this is the case, the tax reduction prospect that is inherent in any tax reform may be largely if not wholly concentrated on members of those general income classes for which the nontaxable options are quantitatively important.[14] Tax reform viewed in this alternative perspective cannot readily be utilized as a handy means of implementing generalized rate reductions, and especially in such a manner as to further the liberal objectives of ever-increasing progressivity, as measured over income classes.

## Conclusion

The most important practical aspect of the alternative perspective suggested lies in its political rather than in its economic features. To the extent that those who suffer the excess burden of income tax by resort to preferentially treated sources or uses can be induced voluntarily to shift toward socially efficient behavior patterns, they will support rather than oppose reforms in the pull and haul of the legislative process. Agreement can emerge on genuine compromise solutions. Bargaining, of course, will continue to take place, but the object becomes the division of the net gains rather than the gains that are secured from the imposition of losses on members of losing political coalitions.

The alternative perspective outlined here also has ethical advantages that are too often neglected. Regardless of income level, those persons who have adjusted their behavior to the existing structure of taxation, and have done so legally, could be argued to have ethically legitimate expectations that the structure will not be arbitrarily modi-

14. This may be illustrated in the numerical example of note 12. Suppose that all or almost all of the behavioral adjustments to the prereform tax are made by persons in the same class as Individual 2 in the example. These persons can be made better off by the appropriate rate adjustments while moving to a more comprehensive income level. But these same rate adjustments must also be made available to those persons within the same income class who did not utilize nontaxable sources or uses of income before the reform. These persons will gratuitously benefit by a reduction in their tax payments. But this spillover effect dictated by principles of horizontal equity will constrain the set of distributional outcomes somewhat more than the arithmetical example of note 12 indicates.

fied. To impose damages on such persons through reform measures designed to attain some idealist version of comprehensiveness violates widely accepted equity norms. Ethical arguments against imposed reforms become stronger when it is recognized that essentially equivalent results can be attained by consensus. Agreement is surely preferred to conflict, whether within or without the arena of democratic politics.[15]

15. To a limited extent this approach is embodied in U.S. Department of the Treasury, *Blueprints for Basic Tax Reform* (Government Printing Office, 1977), largely through the emphasis on transitional problems involved in any major tax-law changes.

JOSEPH J. MINARIK  *Brookings Institution*

# Who Doesn't Bear the Tax Burden?

TAX EQUITY has received considerable public attention in recent years. Tax preferences were an important issue in the 1976 presidential election, and the winner promised fundamental reform of the income tax to broaden the personal income tax base. The public perception of the issue was influenced by analyses that showed graphically how much the various tax preferences reduced liability in different income classes.[1] This paper expands upon those analyses in three ways. First, it presents results showing the average effective tax rates paid at all income levels according to the tax schedule used and the number of exemptions claimed. Second, it shows which tax prefer-

Henry J. Aaron, Joseph A. Pechman, and Emil M. Sunley provided helpful discussion during the course of this project but should not be implicated in any errors. Richard A. Booth, James G. McClave, Jr., and Wing Thye Woo performed the computer programming under the supervision of Robin Mary Donaldson. The research was supported by a grant from the RANN program of the National Science Foundation. The views expressed herein are the author's and should not be attributed to the officers, trustees, or other staff members of the Brookings Institution, or to the National Science Foundation.

1. See Joseph A. Pechman, "Individual Income Tax Provisions of the Revenue Act of 1964," *Journal of Finance*, vol. 20 (May 1965), pp. 247–72; Joseph A. Pechman and Benjamin A. Okner, "Individual Income Tax Erosion by Income Classes," in U.S. Joint Economic Committee, *The Economics of Federal Subsidy Programs*, Compendium of Papers, Joint Economic Committee Print, 92 Cong. 2 sess. (Government Printing Office, 1972), vol. 2, pp. 13–40; Joseph A. Pechman and George F. Break, *Federal Tax Reform: The Impossible Dream?* (Brookings Institution, 1976); and Joseph A. Pechman, ed., *Comprehensive Income Taxation* (Brookings Institution, 1977).

ences are claimed by taxpayers with tax liabilities widely different from those characteristic of their income class and household status. Third, it also analyzes the effects of tax preferences used by groups of households according to the degree of difference between their taxes and the average. Comparisons can thus be made between groups of tax returns with similar use of tax preferences at different income levels and between others with different use of tax preferences at the same income levels. This analysis will be based on the Brookings 1970 MERGE file.[2]

## Determination of Average Effective Tax Rates

The public seems to be more interested in vertical equity—the fair differentiation of tax burdens borne by various income classes—than in horizontal equity—the equal treatment of families in the same income class. The latter question is the focus here, and evidence on variation in taxes at a given level of income will be presented. The public's fascination with vertical equity may arise because equal taxation of equals is a generally endorsed principle, while the standard for the appropriate treatment of unequals is a source of continuing and passionate disagreement. From a more pragmatic viewpoint any broadening or narrowing of tax preferences that did not change the distribution of average effective rates would not change total revenue, which is presumably set according to public sector needs rather than distributional preferences. This horizontal equity approach can provide insights to the need for and effects of tax reform independently of redistributional questions.[3]

A number of provisions of the tax law cause differences in tax liabilities at any given income level with no intervention by the taxpayer. Two taxpayers with the same incomes might pay taxes according to different tax rate schedules and claim different standard deductions and personal exemptions. These differences reflect the collective

2. The MERGE file is the result of linking responses to the March 1971 Current Population Survey with those from tax returns for 1970 on computer-readable magnetic tape. Working papers on the construction of the MERGE file are available from the author.

3. Two other issues in tax policy concern the relative treatment of incomes growing at different rates and of incomes that fluctuate around any trend. I do not deal with such distinctions between current and "permanent" income.

judgment that families of different sizes or marital status are not identically situated even if their incomes are identical. For that reason separate results are presented here for taxpayers filing each of the four different types of returns (married, filing jointly; married, filing separately; single; head of household). Furthermore, these results are based on a new income measure called standard taxable income that is used to compute average effective tax rates. Standard taxable income is defined as adjusted gross income plus excluded sick pay and moving expenses and the excluded half of long-term capital gains, less the appropriate standard deduction under the tax law in question, less the total amount of personal exemptions for the taxpayer(s) and dependents. These last two adjustments control for the varying family sizes and filing statuses of different taxpayers.

Deviations in effective tax rates around the average are measured relative to regression equations, one for each type of tax return. This approach avoids computational difficulties that would result from measuring deviations in effective tax rates relative to the average for an income bracket. With broad brackets and a progressive rate structure the average effective rate would be expected to increase from the bottom of each interval to the top. Thus the average for the entire interval would not be an appropriate standard for the extremes unless the interval were very small. With small income intervals, of course, the number of tax returns within that interval would be reduced, and therefore the sampling variation of the mean would increase.

The alternative chosen here, to estimate the average effective tax rate through a set of four regression equations, circumvented the problems of progressivity within income intervals and the sampling variation described above.

A simple single natural logarithmic transformation provided the best fit of effective tax rates (that is, liabilities, $T$, as a percentage of $STI$) to $STI$.

$$T/STI = a + b \, ln(STI),$$

where $T$ is tax liability and $STI$ is standard taxable income. In order to obtain a satisfactory fit, it was necessary to eliminate returns with negative standard taxable income and to truncate to zero the negative taxes of those low-income tax returns eligible for negative taxes under the refundable earned income credit. The regression results are shown

*The Economics of Taxation*

**Table 1. Estimates of Average Effective Tax Rates**

Dependent variable: tax/standard taxable income

| | | Coefficient[a] | | | |
|---|---|---|---|---|---|
| Type of return | Con-stant | Natural log of standard taxable income (thousands of dollars) | $\bar{R}^2$ | $F$[b] | Standard error of estimate |
| Single | 0.3614 (0.0014) | 0.0397 (0.0002) | 0.6546 | 25,785.60 (1; 13,604) | 0.036 |
| Joint | 0.3972 (0.0024) | 0.0543 (0.0005) | 0.2010 | 11,945.62 (1; 47,491) | 0.105 |
| Separate | 0.5467 (0.0158) | 0.0831 (0.0035) | 0.6377 | 569.54 (1; 322) | 0.069 |
| Head of household | 0.3632 (0.0035) | 0.0457 (0.0006) | 0.6129 | 5,304.64 (1; 3,349) | 0.042 |

Source: Brookings 1970 MERGE file, projected to 1977.
a. Figures in parentheses are standard errors.
b. Figures in parentheses are degrees of freedom.

**Table 2. Distribution of Tax Returns by the Relationship of Tax Liabilities to the Average, 1977**

| Tax rate as a percent of average tax rate for various income levels | Number of returns (millions) | Percent of all returns |
|---|---|---|
| 0 | 3.1 | 4.2 |
| 0–24[a] | 0.7 | 1.0 |
| 25–49 | 1.4 | 1.9 |
| 50–74 | 2.5 | 3.4 |
| 75–99 | 8.8 | 12.0 |
| 100 and over | 56.8 | 77.5[b] |
| Total | 73.2 | 100.0 |

Source: Brookings 1970 MERGE file, projected to 1977. Data are rounded.
a. Tax is 25 percent or less of the average effective rate for the income level but greater than zero.
b. The reason that over 50 percent of returns show taxes greater than average is that (1) the distribution of taxes as a percentage of the average is skewed toward zero, as explained in note 4 in the text, and (2) the regression equation used to estimate the average effective rate at each income level underestimates the actual mean because it is fit on the basis of the square of the deviation of each observation from the mean, rather than on the deviation itself.

**Figure 1. Influence of Various Provisions on Effective Rates of the Federal Individual Income Tax, 1976: All Taxpayers**

Effective rate (percent)

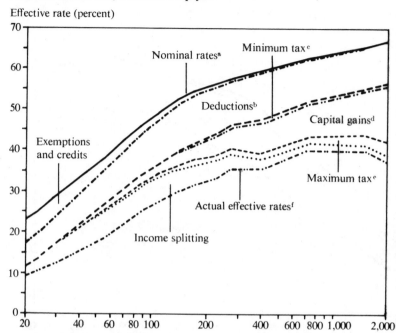

Comprehensive income (thousands of dollars, log scale)[g]

Source: Brookings 1970 MERGE file, projected to 1977. Curves are smoothed.

a. Rate schedule for married couples filing separate returns applied to comprehensive income.

b. Standard and itemized deductions plus dividend, sick pay, and moving expense exclusions.

c. Special calculation for tax preference items, except excluded net long-term capital gains. The net effect of this category was calculated by eliminating the minimum tax on preference items and including these items in comprehensive income to be taxed at the regular rates.

d. Combined effect of the alternative tax calculation for taxpayers with capital gains and excluded net long-term capital gains.

e. Effect of maximum marginal tax rate of 50 percent on earned taxable income.

f. Includes reductions for retirement and foreign tax credits, which are not shown separately.

g. Comprehensive income is the sum of adjusted gross income, excludable sick pay, excludable dividends, excludable moving expenses, and tax preference items as defined in the Tax Reform Act of 1969, including excluded net long-term capital gains.

in table 1,[4] and the distribution of tax returns by the relationship of tax liability to the average is shown in table 2.

4. The distribution of effective tax rates is such that there is a maximum value (that which results from taking the standard deduction with no exclusions) but no minimum other than zero. Thus the distribution tends to be truncated at the highest possible tax rate, and the regression curve underestimates the average rate somewhat. The result here is that the group selected as paying approximately the average effective rate includes returns paying somewhat less, and the group selected as paying less than average in fact pay even somewhat less than stated.

**Figure 2. Influence of Various Provisions on Effective Rates of the Federal Individual Income Tax, 1976: Taxes within 5 Percent of Average**[a]

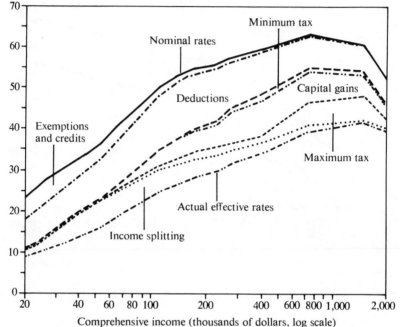

Effective rate (percent)

Comprehensive income (thousands of dollars, log scale)

Source: Brookings 1970 MERGE file, projected to 1977. Curves are smoothed.
a. See notes for figure 1.

## Tax Reduction Devices

Figures 1 through 6 show the distribution of effective tax rates by income class that would prevail if no deductions or exemptions whatever were permitted; they also show the change due to reinstating each preferential feature one by one until the final result is tax liability under 1976 law.

Figure 1 shows the effects of the individual tax features for all tax filers. The personal exemptions and personal credits in the law reduce taxes significantly at the lower income levels but become relatively less important as income rises. Personal deductions have a large impact at all levels, including lower incomes where the standard deduction is prevalent. Tax preference items excluded from the ordinary tax but subject to the minimum tax have a perceptible effect only at upper

**Figure 3. Influence of Various Provisions on Effective Rates of the Federal Individual Income Tax, 1976: Taxes between 75 and 100 Percent of Average**[a]

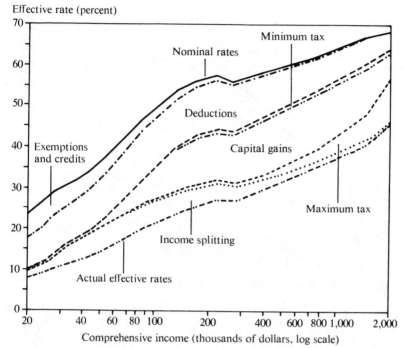

Source: Brookings 1970 MERGE file, projected to 1977. Curves are smoothed.
a. See notes for figure 1.

income levels;[5] the maximum tax on earned income has a similar impact. Income splitting reduces taxes by the largest relative amounts at moderately high income levels and less at the highest and lowest incomes.

The effect of the capital gains preference is striking.[6] While it has no perceptible effect on effective tax rates for households with comprehensive income below about $25,000, the exclusion of one-half of realized long-term gains (and the lower alternative tax rate) reduces taxes by sharply increasing amounts as income rises until it is the second most important revenue-reducing feature for the highest in-

5. Not including excluded long-term capital gains.
6. This paper does not deal with the issue of the inflationary component of capital gains. See Joseph J. Minarik, "The Size Distribution of Income During Inflation," *Review of Income and Wealth,* series 25 (December 1979), for estimates of the effect of inflation on after-tax incomes by income class.

62 The Economics of Taxation

**Figure 4. Influence of Various Provisions on Effective Rates of the Federal Individual Income Tax, 1976: Taxes between 50 and 75 Percent of Average**[a]

Effective rate (percent)

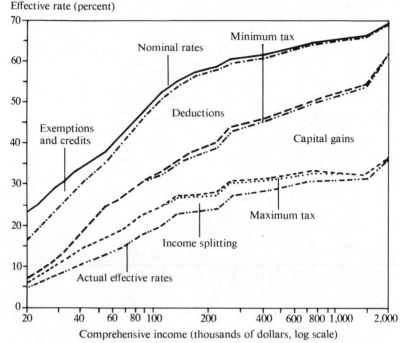

Comprehensive income (thousands of dollars, log scale)

Source: Brookings 1970 MERGE file, projected to 1977. Curves are smoothed.
a. See notes for figure 1.

come returns. This pattern suggests the possibility that capital gains play a leading role in cases of highly successful minimization of tax liability by upper-income taxpayers.

Figure 2 reinforces this conclusion. It shows that the upper-income taxpayer with liabilities near the average for his income class uses the capital gains preference less than do all of those with high incomes. By contrast, he uses the maximum tax on earnings more than do all those with high incomes, indicating that the high-income taxpayer with average liability receives a relatively large fraction of his income from labor. Below about $70,000 of income it is clear that the average taxpayer uses virtually no tax reduction devices beyond deductions and exemptions.

Figures 3 and 4 show effective rates for two other subgroups of the population: those whose taxes are between 75 and 100 percent, and 50 and 75 percent of the average for their income class, respectively. For upper-income returns in these groups it is clear that the capital

**Figure 5. Influence of Various Provisions on Effective Rates of the Federal Individual Income Tax, 1976: Taxes between Zero and 25 Percent of Average[a]**

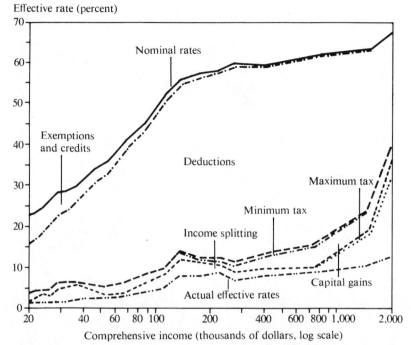

Source: Brookings 1970 MERGE file, projected to 1977. Curves are smoothed.
a. See notes for figure 1.

gains exclusion and the alternative tax are of primary importance. These preferences reduce the effective rates on taxpayers in the highest income classes by 20 percentage points for households with liabilities 25 to 50 percent of the average for their income class—more than all itemized deductions. The maximum tax has less effect for this group, a fact that reveals that these households have little earned income.[7] Income splitting also becomes relatively less important for lower tax rate groups, while tax preference items other than capital gains become more important. The tax reduction devices used at income levels below about $70,000 are again restricted largely to the various itemized deductions.

Figures 5 and 6 show the tax-reducing features used on returns

7. Alternatively they may have earned income that is ineligible for the maximum tax because they also have large amounts of excluded long-term capital gains. This "poisoning" feature has been repealed in the Revenue Act of 1978, effective in tax year 1979.

**Figure 6. Influence of Various Provisions on Effective Rates of the Federal Individual Income Tax, 1976: Nontaxable Returns**[a]

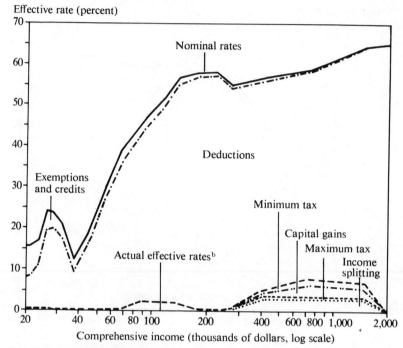

Source: Brookings 1970 MERGE file, projected to 1977. Curves are smoothed.
a. See notes for figure 1.
b. Bottom curve lies precisely on horizontal axis.

facing positive tax rates below 25 percent of the average for the income bracket and on nontaxable returns. The superficially surprising result is that the role of capital gains preferences is drastically reduced. The overwhelming effect is that of personal deductions, which by themselves reduce effective tax rates by 50 percentage points or more at the highest income levels. The only other appreciable effect is that of capital gains, which is less than 10 percentage points for both groups. The dominance of personal deductions below $100,000 of income is virtually unchanged. These results make it clear that different taxpayer groups with varying effective rates of tax make dramatically different use of different tax reduction devices.

A remaining question is the composition of the personal deductions taken at different income and effective tax rate levels. Figures 7–9 classify itemized deductions among five categories: medical,

**Figure 7. Selected Itemized Deductions as a Percentage of Total Itemized Deductions: Taxes Greater than Average**

Effective rate (percent)

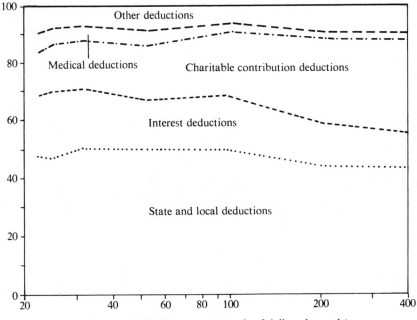

Standard taxable income (thousands of dollars, log scale)

Source: Brookings 1970 MERGE file, projected to 1977.

charitable, interest, state and local taxes, and all other. The results indicate that the relative use of different itemized deductions also varies significantly among households depending on whether their liabilities are close to or much below the average for their income bracket.[8]

Comparisons among the effective tax rate classes can best be made by broad income groupings. Between about $20,000 and $200,000 the low effective tax rate group shows a greater relative use of medical, charitable, and (with less consistency) miscellaneous deductions

8. It is important to remember two factors in considering figures 7–9: (1) The figures show the percentage breakdown of different types of deductions in total deductions; in the lower effective tax rate groups, however, the absolute amount of deductions is higher in any given income class than in the higher tax groups; and (2) they show the total amount of each deduction claimed in each income class; certain types of deductions might be claimed in very large amounts but on few returns, leading to a small total.

**Figure 8.** Selected Itemized Deductions as a Percentage of Total Itemized Deductions: Taxes between 50 and 75 Percent of Average

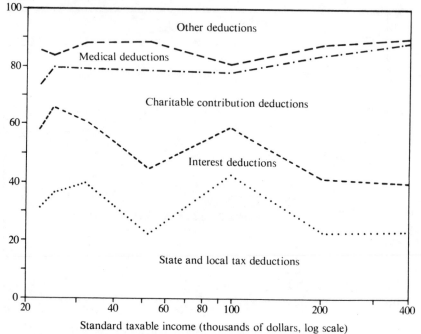

Effective rate (percent)

Standard taxable income (thousands of dollars, log scale)

Source: Brookings 1970 MERGE file, projected to 1977.

than tax returns with higher effective rates. The reliance on interest and state and local tax deductions is lower. Above $200,000, however, the low tax rate returns show distinctly greater relative use of interest and charitable deductions and less of medical and state and local tax deductions; miscellaneous deductions are largely unchanged. Interest and charitable deductions are, of course, easily manipulable by the taxpayer to minimize tax liability.

## Conclusions

These computations indicate that some qualification of earlier notions of the role of tax reduction devices may be in order. A view of the entire population indicates that preferences for realized long-term capital gains have an impact second only to personal deductions on

**Figure 9. Selected Itemized Deductions as a Percentage of Total Itemized Deductions: Taxes Less than 25 Percent of Average but Greater than Zero**

Effective rate (percent)

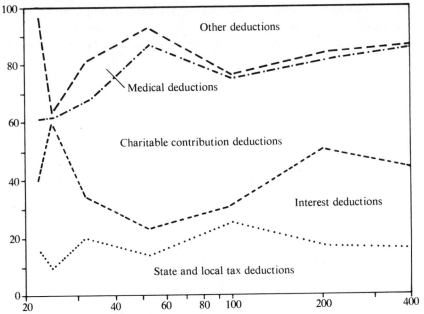

Standard taxable income (thousands of dollars, log scale)

Source: Brookings 1970 MERGE file, projected to 1977.

tax liabilities at the highest income levels. On tax returns showing high incomes and very low tax liabilities, however, personal deductions—principally for interest paid and charitable contributions—play a far more important role. Capital gains preferences show up more strongly on returns with liabilities between one-half of the average and the average. For returns showing taxes around the average, the maximum tax on earned income reduces liabilities most. At lower income levels, personal deductions are the major tax reduction feature.

An examination of the itemized personal deductions used to reduce taxes shows again that the use of various devices changes with the degree of tax reduction. Returns showing low tax liability between about $20,000 and $200,000 of income make heavier relative use of deductions for medical expenses and charitable contributions than do returns with the same income and higher taxes.

The major implication of these findings is for tax policy with regard to leakages from the income tax base. If a major concern for policy is the total reduction of tax liabilities at upper income levels, then the capital gains preferences are virtually as important as personal deductions. If, on the other hand, the major concern is extreme cases of tax minimization, then most effort should be concentrated on personal deductions.

BENJAMIN A. OKNER  *U.S. Department of the Treasury*

# Total U.S. Taxes and Their Effect on the Distribution of Family Income in 1966 and 1970

IN 1974 Joseph A. Pechman and I completed a study of total tax burdens in the United States for the year 1966.[1] At that time we stated that despite the many statutory changes that had been made since 1966, the general pattern of tax burdens in a more recent year would not be very different from that shown for 1966. A major reason for undertaking this paper is to confirm that statement. In addition, except for the 1966 work the distribution of total taxes among families by different income classes or with various demographic characteristics is not generally known. Thus another important purpose of this study is to reestimate for 1970 the effect of all U.S. taxes on the distribution of income and to compare the more recent results with those for 1966.

Validation of the 1966 results and examination of income distributions for specific population groupings required construction of a

The research reported here was completed before the author joined the Treasury Department, and the views expressed are solely his own and should not be attributed to any other staff members of the department. In addition to those persons whose assistance is acknowledged in *Who Bears the Tax Burden?* the author is grateful to Barry J. Eichengreen and Larry J. Tenison for their programming assistance in preparing the 1970 tax burden estimates.

1. *Who Bears the Tax Burden?* (Brookings Institution, 1974).

new data base containing linked demographic and tax return data. When the project began, the most up-to-date information available was for 1970; for that reason the comparisons in this paper are all between 1966 and 1970.[2]

## Major Concepts

All the estimates presented here are based on micro-unit files of information for representative samples of U.S. families (referred to as the 1966 MERGE data file and the MERGE-70 data file).[3] When properly weighted each sample accounts for the estimated total income received by all families in 1966 and 1970. In addition to income data the files contain demographic and other economic information about each sample unit (for example, homeownership, age, and house value). This information is available in machine-readable form and can be processed quickly and efficiently.

### Definitions of Income and Taxes

The income concept used in this chapter corresponds closely to the economist's comprehensive definition of income for household units. In addition to income earned in production (wages, interest, dividends, rents, and royalties) it includes transfer payments and total gains on capital assets accrued during the year (regardless of whether they are realized).[4]

2. The reader should remember that substantial changes in the age and family structure of the population have occurred during the last decade or so. While these may not be of major importance for the fairly short period between 1966 and 1970, they should not be totally ignored. For example, the number of unrelated individuals (that is, one-person families) increased by 25 percent between 1966 and 1970, while the number of families (two or more persons) rose by only 6 percent during the same time period. In addition the female labor force participation rate rose from 37.7 percent to 43.3 percent. These changes plus shifts in marriage and divorce rates and the changing age structure of the population all suggest that "family income" and its distribution may well connote quite different levels of well-being over time.

3. The techniques used to construct the MERGE-70 data file, prepared by Catherine Armington and Marjorie Odle, former staff members of the Brookings Institution, are discussed in a paper that is available on request from the Brookings Social Science Computation Center. The term "families" refers both to individuals living alone (one-person families) and to the conventional Census Bureau family consisting of two or more persons related by blood, marriage, or adoption.

4. This income definition excludes all imputed income to household production by persons but includes net imputed rent on owner-occupied dwellings. Because some estimates place the total value of nonmarket household imputed income at about one-third of GNP, the concept used here, while more comprehensive than most income measures, is still less than "true" economic income.

Transfer payment income includes cash payments under social security and railroad retirement, unemployment insurance, workmen's compensation, public assistance (welfare), veterans' benefits, and military retirement pay. In 1970 the value of medicare and medicaid benefits plus the bonus value of food stamps are also counted as transfer income. To convert income to a before-tax basis, indirect business taxes as well as direct taxes are included in income.[5]

The definition of taxes is also the same in both years. The starting point in deriving total taxes is "government receipts," as defined in the national income accounts.[6] From this amount all nontax receipts and estimated corporate income taxes paid by fiduciaries and other groups not in the family household population are subtracted. Finally, in keeping with the 1966 procedure, customs duties and estate and gift taxes are subtracted.[7] In total, 1970 taxes included in the study amounted to about $40 billion less than the $302 billion of federal and state-local government receipts in the national income accounts.[8]

## Tax Incidence

The incidence of a tax—or the tax burden—is measured by the reduction in real income that results from its imposition. Thus taxes may reduce the incomes of individuals in their roles as producers or they may increase the prices of consumer goods and thus reduce the purchasing power of a given amount of money income. The former effect is the burden of taxes on the sources of income; the latter, the burden of taxes on the uses of income. While both effects are included in this analysis, no attempt is made to measure any tax burden that results from the reallocation of economic resources in consumption or production.

Although much progress in the methods used to study tax incidence

5. Direct taxes, of course, are included in factor incomes; indirect taxes are allocated to individual families in proportion to their share of factor incomes.

6. For some purposes it might be desirable also to include "implicit taxes," which arise in some tax avoidance situations. For example, if Mr. A received $10,000 of interest on municipal bonds that yield 6 percent, and at the same time taxable bonds yield 9 percent, it can be argued that Mr. A's income should be grossed up by $5,000 and that the $5,000 in forgone interest should be considered a tax burden. This adjustment was omitted from the study on practical grounds.

7. See Pechman and Okner, *Who Bears the Tax Burden?* p. 17, and app. B, pp. 93–104.

8. Computation of the 1966 and 1970 figures derived from the U.S. national income accounts was completed before the revisions published by the Bureau of Economic Analysis in January 1976. Therefore small differences may exist between the data cited here and the most up-to-date statistics.

**Table 1. Tax Incidence Assumptions Used in This Study**

| Tax and basis of allocation | Most progressive variant | Least progressive variant |
|---|:---:|:---:|
| *Individual income tax* | | |
| To taxpayers | X | X |
| *Sales and excise tax* | | |
| To consumption of taxed commodities | X | X |
| *Corporation income* | | |
| Half to dividends; half to property income in general | X | ... |
| Half to property income in general; half to consumption | ... | X |
| *Property tax on land* | | |
| To landowners | ... | X |
| To property income in general | X | ... |
| *Property tax on improvements* | | |
| To shelter and consumption | ... | X |
| To property income in general | X | ... |
| *Payroll tax on employees* | | |
| To employee compensation | X | X |
| *Payroll tax on employers* | | |
| To employee compensation | X | ... |
| Half to employee compensation; half to consumption | ... | X |

has been made in recent years, economists still disagree about the incidence of several of the most important taxes. In the 1966 study eight different sets of incidence assumptions were used; however, the 1970 results presented here include only those under the most progressive set of assumptions—Variant 1c—and the least progressive set—Variant 3b.[9] These are summarized in table 1 and are described briefly below.

The most progressive assumptions are distinguished from the least progressive mainly by the way the corporation income and property taxes are treated. Under the most progressive assumptions these taxes

9. For a discussion of all eight incidence variants and the economic assumptions underlying them, see Pechman and Okner, *Who Bears the Tax Burden?* chap. 3, pp. 25–43. The incidence assumptions are also presented briefly in note 8, p. 12, in the present volume.

are assumed to be taxes on income from capital, while under the least progressive assumptions half the corporation income tax and the property tax on improvements are assumed to be paid by consumers through increases in the relative prices of housing and other goods and services. The assumption under the most progressive variant is that half the corporation income tax is borne by corporate stockholders and the other half is borne by owners of capital in general.

Other differences between the variants are that the property tax on land is assumed to be paid by owners of capital in general under the most progressive variant and by landowners under the least progressive, and that the employer payroll tax is borne by employees under the most progressive variant and shifted to consumers under the least. Under both sets of incidence variants the individual income tax is assumed to be borne by the income recipients, sales taxes and excises are assumed to be paid by consumers, and employee payroll taxes are assumed to be paid by workers.

## Overall Results

Data from the MERGE files indicate that no significant changes in the pattern of relative tax burdens occurred between 1966 and 1970. Both the 1966 and 1970 tax burdens were high at the very bottom of the income scale and then dropped sharply until the $3,000 to $4,000 income level was reached. Between $4,000 and $10,000 the 1970 effective rates were lower than the 1966 ones. Effective rates in 1970 then rose slightly above the 1966 rates and remained in the 20 to 30 percent range between $10,000 and $50,000, with no discernible differences between 1966 and 1970 tax burdens. In 1966 effective tax rates rose to almost 50 percent for families with incomes of $1 million or more. In 1970 the average tax rate rose somewhat more rapidly and reached 53 percent for families with incomes of $1 million or more.[10]

In both 1966 and 1970 tax burdens under the least progressive incidence assumptions also displayed a quite similar pattern. For those at the very bottom of the income scale effective tax rates were somewhat higher in 1970 than they were in 1966. Then there was

10. For 1966, tables containing these data are given in Pechman and Okner, *Who Bears the Tax Burden?* chap. 4, pp. 44–65. The 1970 data are given in tables 2 and 3 in the present chapter.

**Table 2. Comparison of Effective Rates of Federal, State, and Local Taxes by Adjusted Family Income Bracket under the Most and Least Progressive Incidence Variants, 1966 and 1970**

Percent

| Adjusted family income (thousands of dollars) | Most progressive incidence variant | | Least progressive incidence variant | |
|---|---|---|---|---|
| | 1970 | 1966 | 1970 | 1966 |
| 0–3 | 22.2 | 18.7 | 31.4 | 28.1 |
| 3–5 | 19.4 | 20.4 | 24.4 | 25.3 |
| 5–10 | 22.4 | 22.6 | 25.2 | 25.9 |
| 10–15 | 24.1 | 22.8 | 26.3 | 25.5 |
| 15–20 | 24.5 | 23.2 | 26.3 | 25.3 |
| 20–25 | 25.0 | 24.0 | 26.1 | 25.1 |
| 25–30 | 25.7 | 25.1 | 26.2 | 24.3 |
| 30–50 | 27.3 | 26.4 | 26.5 | 24.4 |
| 50–100 | 32.7 | 31.5 | 29.3 | 26.4 |
| 100–500 | 39.1 | 41.8 | 30.6 | 30.3 |
| 500–1,000 | 51.9 | 48.0 | 36.7 | 30.3 |
| 1,000 and over | 52.7 | 49.3 | 32.9 | 29.0 |
| All incomes | 26.1 | 25.2 | 26.7 | 25.9 |

Sources: For 1966 data: Joseph A. Pechman and Benjamin A. Okner, *Who Bears the Tax Burden?* (Brookings Institution, 1974), table 4-3, p. 49. Data for 1970 were computed from the MERGE-70 file.

very little difference in effective rates—they ranged from 25 percent to 30 percent—for those with incomes of up to $500,000 (see table 2). In 1970 average tax rates under 3b rose only slightly and reached 33 percent for those with incomes of $1 million and over. While this is a sizable increase over the top rate of 29 percent in 1966, it is far below the 53 percent effective tax rate for those at the top of the income scale under Variant 1c.[11]

Thus for both years the differences between tax burdens under the two sets of incidence variants were very small over virtually the entire income scale. Under the least progressive variant the tax system remained essentially proportional for the vast majority of all family units, with average effective rates of 24 to 25 percent. Under the most progressive variant effective rates rose slightly with income for taxpayers in the bottom half of the income distribution. In both years

11. It should be noted that data regarding average effective tax rates at different income levels conceal a great deal of variation of rates among family units with similar levels of income. For a more extensive discussion of this, see ibid., pp. 67–70.

**Table 3. Comparison of Effective Rates of Federal, State, and Local Taxes by Income Deciles and Selected Percentiles under the Most and Least Progressive Incidence Variants, 1966 and 1970**

Percent

| Population ranking by income level | Most progressive incidence variant | | Least progressive incidence variant | |
|---|---|---|---|---|
| | *1970* | *1966* | *1970* | *1966* |
| *Decile* | | | | |
| Lowest[a] | 18.8 | 16.8 | 25.8 | 27.5 |
| Second | 19.5 | 18.9 | 24.2 | 24.8 |
| Third | 20.8 | 21.7 | 24.2 | 26.0 |
| Fourth | 23.2 | 22.6 | 25.9 | 25.9 |
| Fifth | 24.0 | 22.8 | 26.4 | 25.8 |
| Sixth | 24.1 | 22.7 | 26.2 | 25.6 |
| Seventh | 24.3 | 22.7 | 26.2 | 25.5 |
| Eighth | 24.6 | 23.1 | 26.4 | 25.5 |
| Ninth | 25.0 | 23.3 | 26.1 | 25.1 |
| Highest | 30.7 | 30.1 | 27.8 | 25.9 |
| *Percentile* | | | | |
| 95th | 26.3 | 24.5 | 26.1 | 24.1 |
| 96th | 26.4 | 25.7 | 26.1 | 24.6 |
| 97th | 27.0 | 25.2 | 26.1 | 24.0 |
| 98th | 29.0 | 26.7 | 27.7 | 24.4 |
| 99th | 30.2 | 28.3 | 27.4 | 25.2 |
| Top | 39.0 | 39.2 | 31.0 | 28.6 |

Sources: Data for 1966 are from Pechman and Okner, *Who Bears the Tax Burden?* table 4-9, p. 61, and table 4-4, p. 51. Data for 1970 were computed from the MERGE-70 file.

a. Includes only units in the sixth to tenth percentiles.

effective rates rose sharply only at the very top of the income scale (see tables 2 and 3). Under Variant 1c effective rates remained below 30 percent through the ninety-eighth population percentile. Under 3b the average effective tax rate exceeded 30 percent only for those in the topmost percentile.

Although the data suggest that the overall tax structure became slightly more progressive between 1966 and 1970, the changes are too small to affect the overall measures of progressivity.[12] The major exception is that effective rates near the bottom of the income scale are somewhat lower in 1970 than in 1966.

12. This issue is treated in the "Distributional Effects" section.

## Other Results

The remainder of this chapter presents detailed information on tax burdens, the role of state and local taxes versus the role of federal taxes, and the impact of taxes on particular groups of people.

### State-Local versus Federal Tax Burdens

Between 1966 and 1970 total effective tax rates rose by just under 1.0 percentage point. The average effective federal tax rate fell slightly; at the same time, the average effective state-local rate increased by about 1.1 percentage points. The overall hike is the net result of these two changes.

Effective state-local tax rates rose at virtually all income levels and under both incidence variants between 1966 and 1970. But again there is no change from the pattern of rates found for 1966. Under the most progressive assumptions effective tax rates still exhibit a U-shaped pattern; they fall from 15 percent for those at the bottom of the income scale to about 7.5 percent in the middle-income range, and then rise to 19 percent at the highest income levels. Under the least progressive assumptions state-local taxes fall continuously as income rises; the rate falls from about 20 percent for those in the lowest income class to 6 percent for those at the top of the income scale.

The crucial nature of the assumptions regarding the incidence of the corporation income and property taxes is obvious when effective rates are examined separately for federal taxes and for state-local taxes (see table 4). Because the federal government relies heavily on individual and corporation income taxes, average effective federal tax rates in both years were mildly progressive throughout most of the income scale. This pattern held whether the corporation income tax was assumed to be borne by owners of capital or partly shifted to consumers.

When federal rates in 1966 are compared with those in 1970, however, a distinct change is seen in the pattern of tax burdens under the two incidence variants. For families with incomes below the $10,000–$15,000 range, effective tax rates in 1970 are lower than or equal to the 1966 rates under the most progressive variant. Then, at income levels between $15,000 and $50,000 the 1970 rates ex-

**Table 4. Comparison of Effective Rates of Federal Taxes and of State-Local Taxes, by Adjusted Family Income Bracket, under the Most and Least Progressive Incidence Variants, 1966 and 1970**

| Adjusted family income (thousands of dollars) | *Most progressive incidence variant (percent)* | | | | *Least progressive incidence variant (percent)* | | | |
|---|---|---|---|---|---|---|---|---|
| | *Federal* | | *State-local* | | *Federal* | | *State-local* | |
| | *1970* | *1966* | *1970* | *1966* | *1970* | *1966* | *1970* | *1966* |
| 0–3 | 7.0 | 8.8 | 15.3 | 9.8 | 11.0 | 14.1 | 20.4 | 14.0 |
| 3–5 | 8.6 | 11.9 | 10.8 | 8.5 | 10.7 | 14.6 | 13.7 | 10.6 |
| 5–10 | 13.7 | 15.4 | 8.7 | 7.2 | 14.6 | 17.0 | 10.6 | 8.9 |
| 10–15 | 16.4 | 16.3 | 7.7 | 6.5 | 16.9 | 17.5 | 9.3 | 8.0 |
| 15–20 | 17.0 | 16.7 | 7.6 | 6.5 | 17.4 | 17.7 | 8.9 | 7.6 |
| 20–25 | 17.6 | 17.1 | 7.4 | 6.9 | 17.9 | 17.8 | 8.2 | 7.4 |
| 25–30 | 18.2 | 17.4 | 7.5 | 7.7 | 18.4 | 17.2 | 7.9 | 7.1 |
| 30–50 | 18.7 | 18.2 | 8.6 | 8.2 | 18.6 | 17.7 | 7.9 | 6.7 |
| 50–100 | 21.7 | 21.8 | 11.0 | 9.7 | 20.9 | 20.1 | 8.4 | 6.3 |
| 100–500 | 25.2 | 30.0 | 13.9 | 11.9 | 22.4 | 24.4 | 8.2 | 6.0 |
| 500–1,000 | 33.6 | 34.6 | 18.3 | 13.3 | 29.5 | 25.2 | 7.1 | 5.1 |
| 1,000 and over | 33.3 | 35.5 | 19.4 | 13.8 | 27.0 | 24.8 | 5.9 | 4.2 |
| All incomes | 17.4 | 17.6 | 8.7 | 7.6 | 17.6 | 17.9 | 9.1 | 8.0 |

Sources: Data for 1966 are from Pechman and Okner, *Who Bears the Tax Burden?* table 4-10, p. 62. Data for 1970 were computed from the MERGE-70 file.

ceed the 1966 ones. And finally, for those with incomes of $50,000 and over, 1966 rates again exceed the 1970 ones. Under the least progressive variant federal effective tax rates in 1970 are lower than the 1966 rates for families with incomes below $20,000. Then, except for a small number of units in the $100,000–$500,000 income range, 1970 effective tax rates exceed those for all families with incomes of $20,000 and above.

These results are not surprising in light of the federal tax changes enacted between 1966 and 1970. In 1970 federal individual and corporation income tax rates were up somewhat due to the Vietnam surcharge; individual liabilities for families at the low end of the income scale were down substantially because of the increase in the low-income allowance; and the social security payroll tax rate and the taxable earnings base were both up from their 1966 levels, a change that particularly affected those in the low-income and lower-middle income classes.

Changes in state and local tax burdens between 1966 and 1970

Table 5. Effective Federal, State, and Local Tax Rates for Families Headed by Persons under and over Sixty-five under the Most and Least Progressive Incidence Variants, 1966 and 1970
Percent

|  | 1966 | | | | 1970 | | | |
|---|---|---|---|---|---|---|---|---|
|  | Most progressive | | Least progressive | | Most progressive | | Least progressive | |
| Type of tax | Under 65 | Over 65 | Under 65 | Over 65 | Under 65 | Over 65 | Under 65 | Over 65 |
| Individual | 8.7 | 6.9 | 8.6 | 7.2 | 10.1 | 7.2 | 9.9 | 7.6 |
| Corporation | 3.2 | 8.2 | 4.1 | 6.6 | 2.0 | 6.8 | 2.7 | 4.6 |
| Property | 2.5 | 5.9 | 3.2 | 4.4 | 2.7 | 6.8 | 3.6 | 4.3 |
| Sales and excise | 5.2 | 4.5 | 5.1 | 4.7 | 5.1 | 4.1 | 5.0 | 4.3 |
| Payroll | 4.9 | 1.9 | 4.6 | 2.8 | 5.3 | 1.8 | 5.1 | 2.7 |
| Personal property | 0.3 | 0.2 | 0.3 | 0.2 | 0.6 | 0.6 | 0.6 | 0.7 |
| Total | 24.8 | 27.6 | 25.9 | 25.9 | 25.9 | 27.3 | 27.0 | 24.3 |

Sources: Data for 1966 are from Pechman and Okner, *Who Bears the Tax Burden?* table 5-3, p. 72. Data for 1970 were computed from the MERGE-70 data file. Figures are rounded.

are more marked, with significant increases in tax rates particularly at the bottom and the top of the income distribution. Several states had adopted income taxes for the first time; and real and personal property tax rates had increased generally during the 1966–70 period. In addition, of course, under progressive rate structures increases in income automatically push taxpayers into higher marginal tax brackets and thereby raise average individual income tax liabilities.

### Tax Burdens for Selected Population Groups

The MERGE files used in this study contain a large number of demographic and economic characteristics for each family and may be used to study taxes paid by different subgroups of the population.

AGED AND NONAGED. In both 1966 and 1970 family units headed by a person aged sixty-five or over paid a smaller fraction of their income in individual income, sales and excise, and payroll taxes than did families headed by persons under age sixty-five; but the aged paid a higher fraction in corporation income and property taxes (see table 5).

Individual income taxes for the aged are low partly because older persons generally have low current incomes and partly because they receive preferential treatment under federal and most state income taxes. They pay low payroll taxes because most of them are retired and pay lower consumption taxes because they generally spend relatively less for the consumption of highly taxed commodities than do the nonaged.

The aged pay high corporation income and property taxes because they own more property and consume more shelter per dollar of income than do the nonaged. Thus the relative tax burdens of families headed by aged and nonaged persons depends crucially on the assumptions made about the incidence of the corporation income and property taxes. If it is assumed that these taxes are borne by owners of capital (most progressive variant), the aged paid 2.5 times and 2.9 times as much corporation income and property taxes relative to their income as did the nonaged in 1966 and 1970, respectively.

If part of the corporation income and property taxes is assumed to be passed on to consumers, as under the least progressive variant, the aged paid about 1.5 times as much of these taxes as did the nonaged in 1966 and 1.4 times as much in 1970.

TAXES ON FAMILIES BY MAJOR INCOME SOURCE. Tax burdens depend heavily on the sources from which families derive their income. Table 6 shows effective tax rates for families classified by their largest source of income in 1970. Results for 1966 are not shown but are virtually identical.

The largest source of income for families is as follows:

| Source of income | Percent of families |
|---|---|
| Wages | 70 |
| Business income | 6 |
| Property | 10 |
| Transfer payments | 14 |

Under the most progressive variant, tax rates are highest for families that derive the major portion of their income from property or business. Those whose major income source is transfer payments have the lowest rates. The tax burdens of families who rely on wages are lower than the tax burdens of families relying on property income or business income and higher than those of families relying on transfer payments. Under the least progressive variant taxpayers whose principal income source is wages pay taxes at about the same rate as those whose principal source is property income.

The relative burdens imposed by the major taxes on each group

**Table 6. Effective Federal, State, and Local Tax Rates under the Most Progressive and Least Progressive Incidence Variants, by Type of Tax, and Major Source of Income, 1970**

Percent

| Family's major source of income[a] | Individual income tax | Corporation income tax | Property tax | Sales and excise taxes | Payroll taxes | Personal property and motor vehicle taxes | Total tax |
|---|---|---|---|---|---|---|---|
| | | | Most progressive variant | | | | |
| Wages[b] | 10.1 | 1.1 | 1.7 | 5.4 | 6.2 | 0.6 | 25.1 |
| Business[c] | 12.0 | 2.7 | 5.3 | 4.2 | 2.2 | 0.5 | 26.9 |
| Property[d] | 9.0 | 12.2 | 11.0 | 2.8 | 0.7 | 0.6 | 36.3 |
| Transfers[e] | 1.4 | 1.5 | 2.9 | 6.0 | 0.6 | 0.8 | 13.2 |
| | | | Least progressive variant | | | | |
| Wages[b] | 9.8 | 2.4 | 3.0 | 5.2 | 5.7 | 0.6 | 26.7 |
| Business[c] | 11.5 | 3.6 | 7.6 | 4.0 | 3.2 | 0.5 | 30.3 |
| Property[d] | 10.4 | 6.6 | 4.2 | 3.2 | 1.6 | 0.7 | 26.8 |
| Transfers[e] | 1.3 | 3.1 | 5.3 | 5.9 | 2.0 | 0.8 | 18.5 |

Source: Computed from the MERGE-70 data file.

a. Families are classified on the basis of the largest absolute amount of income. Thus a family with a larger business loss than it had positive income from wages, property, or transfer payments is classified as receiving its major source of income from businesses. Families with no major income source are excluded.

b. The sum of wages, salaries, and wage supplements.

c. The sum of farm and nonfarm business income.

d. The sum of interest, corporation profits before tax, rents, royalties, and other gains on capital assets.

e. The sum of social security benefits, unemployment insurance, workmen's compensation, public assistance, medicare and medicaid, veterans' benefits, and the bonus value of food stamps.

depend heavily on which incidence assumption is used. Under both variants the corporation tax is the heaviest tax for property income recipients, while the individual income tax is the heaviest for those with business income. Recipients of transfer payments pay very little individual income tax under either variant, but under 3b they are heavily burdened by the property and consumption taxes. They also pay high consumption taxes. Under both sets of assumptions the payroll taxes are the second largest tax paid by wage-earning families. On the average, under both variants the burden of the payroll tax on wage-earning families is exceeded only by that of the income tax.

### Distributional Effects

Because tax burdens in both 1966 and 1970 differ so little for the mass of the population and are higher for both the poor and the rich than for those in between, the U.S. tax system is found to have very little effect on the overall distribution of income.[13] Under both sets of incidence assumptions the Gini coefficients for the distributions of after-tax income are less than for the before-tax distributions (that is, the after-tax Lorenz curves lie closer to the line of equal distribution than the before-tax curves). The movement toward equality is relatively small, however—just under 5 percent under the most progressive variant in both 1966 and 1970 (table 7). Although the movement toward equality under the least progressive variant was somewhat larger in 1970 than in 1966, the reduction in the area of inequality was still only about one-fourth that found under the most progressive assumptions.[14]

Table 8 illustrates another way of viewing the small amount of redistribution effected by the U.S. tax system. It classifies families by their relative income positions before taxes and transfers. As can be seen, taxes have a very small effect on the distribution of income, both for the total population and (when viewed separately) for those under and over age sixty-five (compare columns 1 and 3). The largest change in the distribution of income results from transfer income (compare column 5 with either column 1 or column 3). The shift in the distribution of income after taxes and transfers is greatest among the aged. For these units after-tax and after-transfer income shares are increased by the receipt of transfer payments at all income levels up to the eightieth percentile.

## Conclusion

The overall effective tax rate increased by about 1 percentage point between 1966 and 1970. Within each of the two polar incidence variants, however, little change was found between the pattern of 1966 and 1970 tax burdens.

For both years relative tax burdens still depend mainly on the

13. Since the pre-tax income distribution is not independent of the tax system, however, it is not completely accurate to infer that the difference in the before- and after-tax income distribution is the net result of only the tax system.

14. It is interesting to note that the 1970 before-tax distributions of income, as measured by the Gini coefficient, appear considerably less unequal than the 1966 before-tax distributions. This shift may be due in large measure to the more comprehensive definition of transfer income used in 1970.

Table 7. Comparison of Gini Coefficients for the Distribution of Income before and after Taxes, 1966 and 1970

| Incidence variant | 1966 Gini coefficient[a] | | | 1970 Gini coefficient[a] | | |
|---|---|---|---|---|---|---|
| | Before-tax income distribution | After-tax income distribution | Percentage decrease in area of inequality[b] | Before-tax income distribution | After-tax income distribution | Percentage decrease in area of inequality[b] |
| Most progressive | 0.4367 | 0.4158 | −4.79 | 0.4192 | 0.3991 | −4.79 |
| Least progressive | 0.4252 | 0.4240 | −0.28 | 0.4121 | 0.4067 | −1.31 |

Sources: Data for 1966 are from Pechman and Okner, *Who Bears the Tax Burden?* table 4-7, p. 56. Data for 1970 were computed from the MERGE-70 file.

a. The Gini coefficient is the ratio of the area of the area between a Lorenz curve and the 45-degree line (the line of equal distribution) to the entire area below the 45-degree line. The coefficients are based on the distribution of families ranked by their before-tax incomes and then reranked by their after-tax incomes.

b. Reductions in the Gini coefficient indicate decreasing inequality.

**Table 8. Combined Effect of Federal, State, and Local Taxes and Transfer Payments on the Distribution of Income, 1970**
Percent

| Population category and income quintile (dollars) | Income before taxes and transfers[a] (1) | Total taxes paid[b] (2) | Total income after taxes (3) | Transfers[c] (4) | Income after taxes and transfers (5) |
|---|---|---|---|---|---|
| *Total population* | | | | | |
| 0–20 | 4.9 | 4.4 | 5.0 | 42.8 | 8.2 |
| 20–40 | 11.1 | 9.9 | 11.5 | 38.9 | 13.9 |
| 40–60 | 16.1 | 14.4 | 16.6 | 11.0 | 16.1 |
| 60–80 | 22.2 | 20.5 | 22.8 | 5.3 | 21.3 |
| 80–100 | 45.8 | 50.8 | 44.0 | 2.1 | 40.4 |
| Total | 100.0 | 100.0 | 100.0 | 100.0 | 100.0 |
| *Under age 65* | | | | | |
| 0–20 | 4.3 | 4.1 | 4.4 | 16.8 | 5.5 |
| 20–40 | 10.1 | 9.3 | 10.4 | 16.4 | 10.9 |
| 40–60 | 14.6 | 13.6 | 15.0 | 4.7 | 14.1 |
| 60–80 | 19.8 | 18.6 | 20.3 | 2.4 | 18.8 |
| 80–100 | 37.8 | 40.5 | 36.8 | 0.6 | 33.7 |
| Total | 86.7 | 86.0 | 86.9 | 40.8 | 83.0 |
| *Age 65 and over* | | | | | |
| 0–20 | 0.5 | 0.4 | 0.6 | 26.4 | 2.8 |
| 20–40 | 1.0 | 0.6 | 1.1 | 22.5 | 3.0 |
| 40–60 | 1.4 | 0.9 | 1.7 | 6.3 | 2.1 |
| 60–80 | 2.4 | 1.9 | 2.6 | 2.9 | 2.6 |
| 80–100 | 7.9 | 10.2 | 7.2 | 1.5 | 6.7 |
| Total | 13.3 | 13.9 | 13.1 | 59.2 | 17.1 |

Source: Derived from the MERGE-70 data file. Figures are rounded.
a. Adjusted family income less transfers as defined in the text.
b. Total taxes distributed among families under the most progressive incidence assumptions (Variant 1c). For details, see Pechman and Okner, *Who Bears the Tax Burden?* chap. 3.
c. Transfer income includes social security and railroad retirement receipts, veterans' benefits, military retirement payments, workmen's compensation, unemployment insurance, public assistance (welfare), medicaid and medicare benefits, and food stamp bonus value.

assumptions made with respect to who pays the corporation income tax and the property tax. Because property income is heavily concentrated among higher-income families, effective tax rates under the most progressive assumptions continue to rise sharply at the very top of the income scale. On the other hand, because the ratio of consumption to income falls as income rises, the average effective rate of tax rises more moderately under the least progressive assumptions.

Thus the speculation in *Who Bears the Tax Burden?* that there would be few differences between the 1966 results and those for a later year appears to have been accurate. Most families experienced only a slight increase in effective tax rates (resulting primarily from state-local taxes) during this period. By and large total 1970 tax burdens were still proportional among families at virtually all income levels.

# PART TWO

# The Concept of Tax Expenditures

GERARD M. BRANNON *Georgetown University*

# Tax Expenditures and Income Distribution: A Theoretical Analysis of the Upside-Down Subsidy Argument

ADVOCATES of broadening the income tax base often stress that providing incentives through deductions, exclusions, and nonrefundable credits generally helps rich people a lot, ordinary-income people only a little, and poor people not at all.[1] The apparent absurdity of these upside-down subsidies has been graphically described by Stanley Surrey.

Indeed, it is doubtful that most of our existing tax incentives would ever have been introduced, let alone accepted, if so structured [as expenditures] and many would be laughed out of Congress. . . . What HEW Secretary would introduce a program under which social security benefits would be unaffected if the recipient's total income including the benefit were under $2,050, would be automatically increased by 14 percent if the recipient's income were between $2,050 and $2,550, by 15 percent if between $2,550 and $3,050, and so on up to 70 percent if over $100,000?[2]

The upside-down-subsidy argument has been important politically in the United States because it provides a populist appeal to the

---

1. Joseph A. Pechman, *Federal Tax Policy,* 3d ed. (Brookings Institution, 1977), pp. 83–92; and Henry C. Simons, *Personal Income Taxation: The Definition of Income as a Problem of Fiscal Policy* (University of Chicago Press, 1938), pp. 114–15.

2. Stanley S. Surrey, *Pathways to Tax Reform: The Concept of Tax Expenditures* (Harvard University Press, 1973), p. 136.

relatively technical argument for tax reform. (Or is it a technical appeal to the populist argument for progressivity?)

The argument for base-broadening tax reform also claims that a lower rate of income tax on a broader base would reduce market distortions.[3] Such an antiseptic argument for tax reform has far less political appeal than does former Treasury Secretary Joseph W. Barr's reference to 155 high-income taxpayers who paid no tax in 1967.[4] The message that tax expenditures are "welfare for the rich" makes a banner to which troops will rally.[5]

The upside-down-subsidy argument deserves some intensive analysis. Surrey is right that it is passing strange to adopt subsidies that encourage, say, contributions of rich people more than those of poor or average-income people. The deduction for charitable contributions does not seem so strange, however, if one justifies it as follows: instead of taxing all rich people at an average rate of, say, 40 percent and all middle-income people at, say, 20 percent, we tax generous rich people at, say, 35 percent and stingy rich people at, say, 45 percent; the spread for corresponding degrees of generosity and stinginess for average incomes is 17.5 percent and 22.5 percent, with the average at 20 percent. This line of argument can be extended to other allowances as well.

This description of the contributions deduction makes clear that the structure of the contributions subsidy and the progressivity of the tax system are in principle different things. A tax system could be enacted in which the average tax on rich people was 40 percent or 60 percent. With either average, one could introduce a variety of tax rate differentials between generous and stingy taxpayers: 0 percent, $\pm$ 2.5 percent, $\pm$ 10 percent, and so forth. The differential can be centered on any average. There are logically two separate questions here: how progressive the tax system should be and how tax subsidies to charity should be structured.

Despite this logical separability, issues of income-tax structure and

3. See Simons, *Personal Income Taxation;* and Joseph A. Pechman and Benjamin A. Okner, "Individual Income Tax Erosion by Income Classes," in Joint Economic Committee, *The Economics of Federal Subsidy Programs,* 92 Cong. 2 sess. (Government Printing Office, 1972), pp. 13–40.

4. For a brief history of events leading to the Tax Reform Act of 1969, see Roger A. Freeman, *Tax Loopholes: The Legend and the Reality* (American Enterprise Institute for Public Policy Research, 1973), pp. 6–18.

5. For the use of this banner, see Philip M. Stern, *The Rape of the Taxpayer* (Random House, 1973).

progressivity continue to be confused. Much discussion centers on the high-income bias of tax expenditures, and not uncommonly the argument against a provision is that it helps the rich.

This paper is not a restudy of the whole case for or against base-broadening tax reform. It is concerned with the narrower issue of the high-income bias of tax incentives.

To put this in context consider a deduction that is not related to economic income. Such a deduction tends to distort individual choice. Whether such a tax deduction is good social policy involves such questions as the following: (1) Is there some external benefit in the activity involved in the deduction that justifies a subsidy? (2) Should the subsidy be treated as a tax provision and administered by the Internal Revenue Service or treated as an expenditure and administered by an agency with subject matter expertise? (3) Is it efficient to structure the subsidy to encourage rich people—an income-level bias—which is usually the case with tax subsidies?

This paper examines only question 3. Frequently the answers to questions 1 and 2 provide a strong case against the deduction, but here it is assumed that the deduction passes these tests. Because of the political importance of question 3, it deserves particular scrutiny.

The first section explores the issues of income-level bias in theoretical terms. The second section examines income-level bias in connection with a number of specific tax allowances for contributions, taxes, investments, and so forth. The third section offers some conclusions.

# The Tax Base and the Distribution of the Tax Burden

## Income-Level Bias

A high-income bias in a tax expenditure is the property of providing more dollar tax relief, in relation to the amount subject to *special* treatment, for high-income taxpayers than for low-income taxpayers.

The word "special" carries a lot of freight. A deduction for cost of goods sold produces more tax relief for a high-bracket taxpayer than for a low-bracket taxpayer. This is not called a high-income bias because a deduction for cost of goods sold removes from taxation a part of gross receipts that is not net income. The deduction prevents those receipts from being taxed at whatever rates they would have been taxed without the deduction. The value of such a deduction quite properly depends on the payer's tax bracket. Income-level *bias,* however, is associated only with features of the tax law not directly related to the measurement of economic income. While not all tax provisions are clearly necessary or unnecessary for the definition of economic income, this fuzziness is not critical.[6]

I define income-level bias in terms of the ratio of tax relief to the amount subject to special treatment.[7] A refundable tax credit is free of income-level bias because tax relief is the same percentage of contributions at each income level. That the rich contribute more than the poor is not necessarily evidence of bias. In another sense there may be high-income bias even in a refundable tax credit for some expenditure common in rich families and rare in poor families, such as hiring household servants.

### Base-Broadening Tax Reform and Tax Rate Progressivity

To highlight the distinction between issues of tax structure (in other words, the tax base) and those of progressivity (in other words, tax rates), I define as "progressivity constant, revenue constant" (PC-RC) any tax reform that broadens the tax base and adjusts tax rates so that tax revenue from each income bracket is unchanged after taxpayers adjust their behavior to take account of the change in rates and bases.

Such a change reforms the tax system in two ways: it removes a tax distortion, which increases or decreases the attractiveness of the previously untaxed or undertaxed activity relative to all other taxable activities; it also permits a reduction in tax rates, which may reduce the distortions that any tax system imposes.[8] If the latter occurs, it is

6. For a debate about the possibility of making such distinctions, see Boris I. Bittker and others, *A Comprehensive Income Tax Base? A Debate* (Federal Tax Press, 1968). One may argue whether or not a tax allowance for child care expense of working parents is a tax expenditure or a business cost. Is it an expense of getting income or an expense of having children? That this question is raised justifies examining the question of how the dollar tax relief should vary in relation to the expenses at each income level. If one concludes that there is good ground for relieving 50 percent of expenses for the 50 percent taxpayer and 20 percent for the 20 percent taxpayer, this is an operational answer to the question, namely, child care expenses are costs of income.

7. I reject the argument that high-income bias is necessarily evidenced by larger dollar relief per tax return on high-bracket returns than on low-bracket ones.

8. Thus one reformer states in reference to exclusions and deductions that "eliminating them and reducing marginal tax rates would yield substantial gains. Horizontal equity—the equal treatment of equals—would be improved, and the incentives to work, to save, and to take risks would be increased." (Emil M. Sunley, Jr., "Employee Benefits and Transfer Payments," in Joseph A. Pechman, ed., *Com-*

necessary to moderate the claim made earlier that it does not matter whether we tax all rich people at 40 percent or adopt a higher rate schedule with a contribution that results in generous rich people paying 35 percent and stingy rich people 45 percent.

These two ways of taxing rich people differ in the incentive effects of deductions and exemptions. "Incentive effect" means encouraging some action that the taxpayer would not take without the tax provision. From the taxpayer's standpoint a simultaneous expansion of the tax base and reduction of the tax rates reduces excess burden. Presumably the point of these deductions and exemptions is that they induce actions that are not worth the before-tax cost to the taxpayer.

When one considers incentive effects, however, one sees that broadening the tax base, with PC-RC rate changes, does reduce the marginal *burden* of the tax, even if it does not reduce effective tax *rates*. Repealing the tax advantages of homeownership and correspondingly reducing statutory rates would reduce the excess burden of incentives in two ways: taxpayers would be less likely to buy housing than they would have been with the subsidy, and because of the lower marginal rates they would be less likely to alter labor supply, to give to charity, and to invest in oil wells.

The subtle connection between base-broadening and tax rates is that removing some tax expenditures weakens all the others (which suggests that tax reform a little at a time is quite satisfactory). The use of tax incentives does not increase average tax rates but does increase marginal tax rates, thereby adding a burden to the tax. When these incentives involve income-level bias, they add particularly to the burden of the progressive part of the income tax.

### *Tax Allowance Techniques*

Exclusion from gross income of a type of income is equivalent to the combination of taxing it fully and providing the taxpayer a subsidy of $tI/(1-t)$, where $I$ is the excluded income and $t$ is the marginal tax rate. The subsidy is zero when $t$ is zero, 25 percent when $t$ is 0.20, and 233 percent when $t$ is 0.70, a clear high-income bias.

The failure to "gross up" a tax credit—in other words the failure

---

*prehensive Income Taxation* [Brookings Institution, 1977], p. 75.) The Treasury Department notes that "a low-rate, broad-based tax promises a general improvement in incentives." (U.S. Department of the Treasury, *Blueprints for Basic Tax Reform* [GPO, 1977], p. 53.)

to add the credit to income—is a kind of exclusion and therefore contains some high-income bias, but it is less than a full exclusion of the item on which the credit is allowed. The difference is related to the size of the credit. For example, replacing the municipal bond exclusion with a 50 percent tax credit, not grossed up, would cut the income-level bias of exempt interest in half.

A tax credit that is grossed-up currently and is refunded when the net tax after credits is negative is in all respects like a taxable payment to the recipient and thus involves no income-level bias. The income-level bias of deductions and exclusions normally is the same because both remove a certain amount of income from taxation. The income-level bias of personal deductions is actually greater than that of ordinary deductions and exclusions because of the standard deduction. The 1978 standard deduction is equivalent to an extra personal deduction of $2,200 for the taxpayer or $3,200 for taxpayer and spouse, coupled with a disallowance of $2,200 or $3,200 of itemized personal deductions. A disallowance of a fixed amount constitutes a relatively larger disallowance for low-income taxpayers than for high-income taxpayers.[9]

## The Income-Level Bias of Some Specific Tax Expenditures

How significant is the high-income bias in specific tax expenditures, and does such bias make sense as subsidy policy? I assume that Congress has achieved the degree of income tax progressivity that it wants and that if a tax expenditure were repealed it would be in a PC-RC fashion. I deal here with only two questions: Does being upside-down make the tax expenditure less efficient or otherwise less desirable as a subsidy? Does it make the tax system less or more progressive in ways other than by the rates?

### Contributions

Criticisms of the high-income bias of the charitable-contributions deduction have been frequent and vociferous, usually concluding in

9. Contrast this provision with the disallowance floor of 5 percent of adjusted gross income proposed by President Kennedy in 1963 (see "Special Message to the Congress on Tax Reduction and Reform," *Public Papers of the Presidents: John F. Kennedy, 1963* [GPO, 1964], p. 85) or with the 3 percent floor on medical deductions.

favor of a tax credit or a system of fractionally matching the contributions of taxpayers and nontaxpayers alike.[10]

Hard analysis provokes puzzlement over why liberal tax reformers should wish to eliminate the high-income bias in the contributions deduction. The total burden of the tax system is the sum of the tax paid plus the excess burden associated with the induced contributions. If the contributions deduction were converted into a refundable tax credit and at the same time tax rates were changed so that the reform was PC-RC, it would follow that while maintaining the progressivity of the formal tax system, some of the excess burden connected with induced contributions would be shifted from the rich to the poor, making the total system more regressive. This fact suggests that ignoring excess burden and focusing only on the distribution of taxes lead analysts to understate the true progressivity of the tax system.

Figure 1 shows the excess burden. $D$ is the demand curve for contributions. With no deduction, the cost to the taxpayer for every dollar contributed is a dollar; the contribution is $AB$. For a taxpayer in the 50 percent tax bracket, deductibility reduces the cost to 50 cents for every dollar contributed and increases contributions to $AC$: the area $EFG$ represents the excess burden for donors in the 50 percent tax bracket. Under the PC-RC assumption tax rates must be increased for taxpayers whose marginal tax rates are less than the credit percentage and decreased for taxpayers whose marginal tax rates are greater than the credit percentage. These changes are required because high-bracket taxpayers, for example, will reduce their contributions (the "price" of contributing has increased), lowering their deductions; the decline in contributions together with the reduced tax-offset percentage will increase tax liabilities. To keep the change PC-RC, rates must be reduced. The argument is the reverse for low-income taxpayers. Accordingly conversion of the contributions deduction to a credit, in a PC-RC change, shifts more of this excess burden to lower-income groups. The nub of this argument is that in the analysis of PC-RC changes, the rich are going to pay a given amount of net tax whether there is a contributions deduction or not. With the contributions de-

---

10. See, for example, Paul R. McDaniel, "A Study of Federal Matching Grants for Charitable Contributions," in Commission on Private Philanthropy and Public Needs, *Research Papers,* vol. 4: *Taxes* (U.S. Department of the Treasury, 1977), pp. 2417–2532; and David A. Good and Aaron Wildavsky, "A Tax by Any Other Name: The Donor Directed Automatic Percentage Contribution Bonus, A Budget Alternative for Financing Governmental Support of Charity," ibid., pp. 2389–2416.

**Figure 1. Effect of Deductibility for Charitable Contributions on the Amount of Contributions**

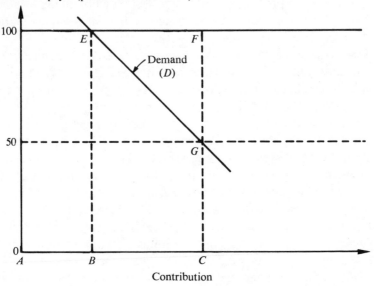

Cost to taxpayer (percent of contribution)

Contribution

duction, the rich can get to this tax only by contributing more to charity than they "really" want to contribute.

Having high-income bias in the contributions deduction (an upside-down subsidy) is consistent with the usual purpose of a progressive tax, which is to reduce the inequalities of living standards. The argument for this thesis is seen by pushing it further, converting the contributions deduction to a credit without changing tax rates—a change that appears to favor the poor because their taxes are cut and the taxes of the rich are raised. But if the price elasticity of contributions at every income level is greater than one, as recent research suggests,[11] then converting the contributions deduction to a credit that yields the same total revenues while making no changes in tax rates increases the income available for personal consumption and savings of the rich while decreasing that of the poor. The taxes of the rich would increase, but their contributions would fall even more. The reverse is true of the poor. By the criterion of relative total burden

11. Martin S. Feldstein and Charles Clotfelter, "Tax Incentives and Charitable Contributions in the United States: A Microeconometric Analysis," in Commission on Private Philanthropy and Public Needs, *Research Papers*, vol. 3: *Special Behavioral Studies, Foundations, and Corporations*, pp. 1393–1417.

of the tax system, converting the contributions deduction to a credit without changing tax rates is favorable to low-income groups; by the criterion of disposable income for personal purposes, such a change is unfavorable to low-income groups.

I think that the disposable-income-for-personal-purposes criterion is the more useful one in this case. If the goal of a tax system is to reduce inequality, it can be achieved by permitting the rich to exchange some of the tax redistribution for a larger amount of redistribution through charity. Apparently the rich are willing to make such an exchange because of the personal satisfaction, name memorialization, or other reward that comes from giving. This sort of "consumption" is harmless as long as the public regulation of charity precludes private benefits to donors.

The upside-down subsidy also efficiently uses forgone revenues to increase contributions and to reduce differences in personal spending. Assume that expenditures by charity serve the public good as well as welfare expenditures by government.[12] Removing the contributions deduction would reduce contributions by *BC* (figure 1), and if there were no change in rates, the tax increase would be *EFGH*. Recent research suggests that contributions decline more than taxes increase.[13] Consequently the charitable contribution reduces private spending inequalities more than would a PC-RC repeal of the deduction, and the net burden on low-income donors of induced contributions is only *EFG* before donor satisfaction is subtracted. It should please equalitarians to achieve this goal in a less burdensome way.

I conclude that the income-level bias of the charitable contribution deductions is a desirable tax policy.

### State Income and Sales Taxes

Another apparent peculiarity of the federal tax law is that it allows high-income people to offset more of their state income taxes and sales taxes than it allows low-income people. The influence of federal tax deductibility on state tax policy complicates matters. Suppose that deductibility of state income taxes were repealed, effective four years hence. Each state would have reason to reexamine the allocation of

12. For such an argument, see *Giving in America: Toward a Stronger Voluntary Sector,* Report of the Commission on Private Philanthropy and Public Needs (Washington, D.C.: The Commission, 1975), chap. 1.

13. Feldstein and Clotfelter, "Tax Incentives and Charitable Contributions."

state tax burdens because the net costs that state tax laws impose on their citizens would be altered significantly.

The income-level bias in the federal treatment of state income taxes makes a progressive tax less costly to high-income taxpayers. With deduction, a state can impose a net cost of $3,000 on a taxpayer in the 50 percent bracket and collect $6,000 in revenue. If state income tax deductibility were repealed in a PC-RC way, states would tend to make their income taxes less progressive or would repeal them altogether, and the total progressivity of the tax system would decline.

The income-level bias makes state and local sales taxes more regressive by reducing their net cost for upper-bracket taxpayers. It is difficult to see how this deduction serves the purposes of a progressive federal income tax. A more neutral way of reducing the cost to taxpayers of state sales taxes is to give those states revenue grants measured by their sales tax collections. To balance the burden that progressive taxes place on the rich, especially if the political cost of progressivity increases, states are likely to strike a balance at less progressivity.

### Other Deductions and Exclusions

The high-income bias of the standard deduction and personal exemptions amounts to excluding from income tax, at the taxpayer's marginal rate, the increase in the official poverty-level income associated with the addition of one dependent. Above-poverty-level income seems to me to be the appropriate tax base.[14]

Exclusion of transfer payments is a singularly inappropriate instance of high-income bias. The basic idea behind transfer payments is a perceived need of the recipient, but most transfers are made as a matter of right without means tests. If the amount of transfers varied systematically with taxable income, it would be possible in principle for Congress to vary them with perceived need. But the amount of, say, social security or unemployment insurance payments may be the same for families with widely different amounts of taxable income from other sources. Exclusion of transfers from income tax provides the greatest tax advantage for those least in need, which contradicts progressivity.

14. Gerard M. Brannon and Elliott R. Morss, "The Tax Allowance for Dependents: Deductions versus Credits," *National Tax Journal*, vol. 26 (December 1973), pp. 599–609.

## Investment Incentives

Many investment incentives are provided through extra deductions or exclusions, accelerated depreciation, or lower tax rates (oil and gas well development costs, building depreciation, capital gains rates, and so forth). Each technique involves high-income bias. The investment tax credit has less high-income bias than accelerated depreciation, but it still has some because it is neither refundable nor grossed-up. One argument for the investment credit in 1961–62 was that it had less high-income bias than the obvious alternative, more accelerated depreciation.[15]

It is inefficient to provide investment incentives with high-income bias. The effect is to expand the supply of a particular investment and reduce the before-tax rate of return on it. The favored investment is attractive for high-income taxpayers even when the rate of return declines sufficiently to make it relatively unattractive to low-income taxpayers. The increase of investment in the favored activities by high-bracket taxpayers in part replaces investment by low-bracket taxpayers and in part causes a net expansion of the investment.

Such a pattern is clear in the market for tax-exempt municipal bonds. Because top-income taxpayers are reluctant to concentrate investment in a specialized security, they typically hold only a portion of their portfolios in municipal bonds. As a result, the interest rate on municipal bonds must be sufficiently high to induce taxpayers below the top brackets to invest in them. The net return on these bonds to top-bracket taxpayers is higher than net returns on similarly risky bonds that are taxable. It is precisely for this reason that many tax reformers advocate a tax credit payable by the federal government to states and municipalities that agree to issue taxable bonds. An incentive with less high-income bias will not only provide greater federal revenues but, because it appeals to a broader market, promises to enable states and municipalities to borrow as much as they now do at less cost to themselves.

This costly and inefficient aspect of high-income-biased investment incentives will become aggravated as more types of investment are selected for tax-expenditure subsidy, all to be financed by a narrow section of the investment market.

15. E. Cary Brown, "Tax Incentives for Investment," *American Economic Review*, vol. 52 (May 1962, *Papers and Proceedings, 1961*), pp. 335–45.

## Conclusion

Hard-bitten veterans of tax reform wars will find it strange to read in this essay about reforms that leave the revenue and progressivity constant. Many tax reformers seek more progressivity by linking repeal of some high-income-biased tax expenditures with an across-the-board rate reduction. There is one good argument for considering the repeal of these tax expenditures and an increase of tax progressivity: statutory tax rates are straightforward and can be taken as the popular will. Tax expenditures, however, are complex and those biased toward high incomes lend themselves to being lobbied in Congress by well-paid pressure groups. If they are parts of the same project, the public would understand how they undercut progressivity.[16]

If this near-conspiracy theory of why high-income-biased tax expenditures are in the law is true, then it follows that tax expenditures especially favorable to high incomes ought to be repealed for just that reason—because they are upside-down subsidies, because they are welfare for the rich.

I find the conspiracy theory of tax expenditures plausible but not compelling. After a quarter of a century of broaden-the-tax-base debates, it is fairly well known that the tax system is much less progressive than the statutory rate schedule. If this much is understood, then it follows that tax reform and greater progressivity are different things and we could buy either one without the other.

Given the separability of tax reform and greater progressivity, the upside-down-subsidy or welfare-for-the-rich arguments per se are not convincing. There may be good reasons for structuring particular subsidies to provide greater incentives to the rich than to the poor. Because the basic tax rates can offset the average value of the tax incentive, it is inappropriate to describe the subsidy merely as more generous for the rich. The tax system in this case is more burdensome for rich taxpayers who do not qualify for the subsidy.

Whether tax expenditures should be structured to produce greater differentials for the rich than for the poor turns out to be something that should be looked at for each tax expenditure. My examination suggests that in some cases, but not always, high-income bias is a defect of tax expenditures.

16. For an exposition of this argument, see Randall Bartlett, *Economic Foundations of Political Power* (Free Press, 1973), pp. 117–18.

MARTIN FELDSTEIN *Harvard University and the National Bureau of Economic Research*

# A Contribution to the Theory of Tax Expenditures: The Case of Charitable Giving

ALTHOUGH tax incentives play a central role in the practice of public finance, theoretical studies continue to ignore them. This chapter begins a theoretical examination of this important subject. In sharp contrast to the common assertion that tax reform should eliminate all tax expenditures, this chapter shows that tax incentives should be used to encourage charitable gifts that will promote the achievement of desired social goals.

It is easy to understand how the intellectual tradition in public finance has caused tax incentives to be overlooked. Early contributors to the normative theory of public finance focused on the problem of raising required revenue with least distortion or minimum sacrifice. The appropriate pattern of government spending received little or no attention. Of course, economists have long prescribed that government expenditure should be expanded until its marginal benefit equals its marginal cost, including the excess burden of the associated tax revenues.[1] But a common feature of all these studies is that they focus

1. This principle was recognized by A. C. Pigou in *A Study in Public Finance* (London: Macmillan, 1928) and remains a central idea in the modern theory of optimal taxation and government spending, beginning with F. P. Ramsey's seminal article, "A Contribution to The Theory of Taxation," *Economic Journal,* vol. 37 (March 1927), pp. 47–61, and continuing with the following recent reformulations

on the optimal level of public spending and ignore the possibility that collective purposes can be satisfied by private action. In particular, the analyses ignore the use of government incentives for private action.

This focus of public finance theory contrasts sharply with actual practice throughout the world. Governments use not only public expenditures but also a variety of other techniques, including tax incentives, to achieve desired public purposes.

Special features of the U.S. Internal Revenue Code encourage American taxpayers to make charitable contributions; to buy homes; to purchase insurance; to invest in such things as common stock, municipal bonds, and natural resource exploration; and to engage in a whole host of other activities. Although the list of tax subsidies is somewhat arbitrary and therefore elastic, the U.S. Treasury recently estimated that the fiscal year 1979 forgone revenue cost of its list of individual and corporate "tax expenditures" will be more than $130 billion.[2]

The two basic forms of tax expenditures are (1) the deduction of certain expenses or exemptions in the calculation of taxable income and (2) the complete or partial exclusion of certain receipts from taxable income. The tax expenditures are thus defined relative to the Haig-Simons concept of a broad-based income tax.[3] For example, people can deduct the full value of their charitable gifts and mortgage interest payments and take a tax credit of up to $400 for the costs of caring for one child ($800 for two or more children). Similarly the capital gain that is implicit in gifts of appreciated property is excluded from taxable income along with employer contributions to private pension plans and 60 percent of realized long-term capital gains.

---

and extensions: William J. Baumol and David F. Bradford, "Optimal Departures from Marginal Cost Pricing," *American Economic Review,* vol. 60 (June 1970), pp. 265–83; Peter A. Diamond and James A. Mirrlees, "Optimal Taxation and Public Production I: Production Efficiency," ibid., vol. 61 (March 1971), pp. 8–27; and others. Agnar Sandmo, "Optimal Taxation: An Introduction to the Literature," *Journal of Public Economics,* vol. 6 (July-August 1976), pp. 37–54; and A. B. Atkinson and J. E. Stiglitz, "The Design of Tax Structure: Direct versus Indirect Taxation," ibid., pp. 55–75, provide excellent surveys of recent contributions to this literature.

2. See *Special Analyses: Budget of the United States Government, Fiscal Year 1979,* table G-1, pp. 158–60. These estimates are based on the overly simple assumption that all behavior is unaffected by the tax rules. Eliminating a particular feature may cause behavioral changes to reduce tax liabilities.

3. An alternative set of tax expenditures would be defined relative to a consumption tax.

More generally, tax expenditures are officially defined as the revenues forgone because of

tax provisions that either have been enacted as incentives for the private sector of the economy or have that effect even though initially having a different objective. The tax incentives usually are designed to encourage certain kinds of economic behavior instead of employing direct expenditures or loan programs to achieve the same or similar objectives.[4]

The use of tax expenditures has been the subject of substantial controversy and the focus of debate among those who are concerned with tax policy. Some analysts seem to hold that all tax expenditures are bad and should either be eliminated or be replaced by direct public spending.[5] This view is well summarized in Surrey's authoritative book:

What, then, is the balance sheet regarding these two methods of Government assistance, direct expenditures and tax incentives? I conclude from

4. *Estimates of Federal Tax Expenditures,* prepared for the House Committee on Ways and Means and the Committee on Finance by the Department of the Treasury and the Joint Committee on Internal Revenue Taxation, 94 Cong. 1 sess. (Government Printing Office, 1975), p. 1. The term "tax expenditure" was coined by Stanley Surrey when he was assistant secretary of the treasury for tax policy. Surrey, now a professor at Harvard Law School, discusses the origin of the tax expenditure budget in his *Pathways to Tax Reform: The Concept of Tax Expenditures* (Harvard University Press, 1973). Not all tax expenditures are really incentives; for example, the additional exemption for the blind. Therefore Henry Aaron ("Inventory of Existing Tax Incentives—Federal," in Tax Institute of America, *Tax Incentives* [Heath Lexington Books, 1971], pp. 39–49) uses the term "tax incentives" for those tax expenditures that are intended to influence behavior. The terms "tax expenditures," "tax subsidies," and "tax incentives" will be used interchangeably in my paper.

5. See, for example, George F. Break and Joseph A. Pechman, *Federal Tax Reform: The Impossible Dream?* (Brookings Institution, 1975); R. A. Musgrave, "In Defense of an Income Concept," *Harvard Law Review,* vol. 81 (November 1967), pp. 44–62; Richard A. Musgrave and Peggy B. Musgrave, *Public Finance in Theory and Practice,* 2d ed. (McGraw-Hill, 1976), pp. 264–66; Joseph A. Pechman and Benjamin A. Okner, "Individual Income Tax Erosion by Income Classes," in Joint Economic Committee, *The Economics of Federal Subsidy Programs,* pt. 1, *General Study Papers,* 92 Cong. 2 sess. (GPO, 1972), pp. 13–40. For a contrary view see Boris I. Bittker, "A 'Comprehensive Tax Base' as a Goal of Income Tax Reform," *Harvard Law Review,* vol. 80 (March 1967), pp. 925–85; "Accounting for Federal 'Tax Subsidies' in the National Budget," *National Tax Journal,* vol. 22 (June 1969), pp. 244–61; "Income Tax 'Loopholes' and Political Rhetoric," *Michigan Law Review,* vol. 71 (May 1973), pp. 1099–1128; and Roger A. Freeman, *Tax Loopholes: The Legend and the Reality* (American Enterprise Institute for Public Policy Research and Hoover Institution on War, Revolution and Peace, Stanford University, 1973). The current extra tax on "preference income" represents partial elimination of all of the tax expenditures that are currently regarded as favoring primarily high-income individuals or corporations; see Surrey, *Pathways to Tax Reform,* chap. 8; and Break and Pechman, *Federal Tax Reform,* pp. 78–82.

the above observations that, as a generalization, the burden of proof should rest heavily on those proposing the use of the tax incentive method. In any particular situation—certainly any new situation—the first approach should be to explore the various direct expenditure alternatives. Once the most desirable of these alternatives is determined, if one still wishes to consider the tax incentive method for the same program, the question must be what clear advantages can be obtained by using the tax method. Again, as a generalization, I think it is unlikely that clear advantages in the tax incentive method will be found.[6]

Surrey concludes that

most of the tax expenditure programs should either be scrapped because the federal financial assistance they provide is not warranted . . . or be replaced by direct assistance measures that can readily be devised.[7]

The common presumption that direct government spending is better than tax expenditures is false. This paper will show in particular that a tax subsidy for private charitable giving is generally a more efficient method of achieving a desired purpose than a direct government expenditure.[8] Although the magnitude of the optimal tax subsidy must be considered explicitly in each case, my analysis shows that when public and private actions are close substitutes a wide range of circumstances exists in which there should be a tax subsidy but no direct government spending.

Several issues should be clarified before proceeding to the formal discussion.

First, my analysis does not show that every tax expenditure is appropriate. Some current tax subsidies should no doubt be eliminated completely, while others should be changed to incorporate different rates of tax subsidy. Each case requires an explicit analysis of the kind that is presented here for charitable giving.

Second, my rejection of the presumption that all tax expenditures are bad implies no criticism of the valuable idea of the "tax expenditure budget"; calculating the revenue implications of different features of the tax law is clearly a necessary first step in the process of

6. Surrey, *Pathways to Tax Reform,* p. 148.
7. Ibid., p. 209. Surrey's single exception to this general rule is the investment tax credit.
8. For a quite different analysis of charitable giving as private income redistribution see A. B. Atkinson, "The Income Tax Treatment of Charitable Contributions," in Ronald Grieson, ed., *Public and Urban Economics: Essays in Honor of William S. Vickrey* (Heath, 1976), pp. 13–27.

evaluating alternative tax policies. The fact that experts disagree about which provisions should be considered tax expenditures does not reduce the usefulness of any estimates of particular tax subsidies.[9] There are serious conceptual and technical problems with the method of estimating the revenue loss and its distribution among income classes. In particular it is assumed in making these estimates that the law has no effect on the behavior of taxpayers even though most tax expenditures were actually introduced in order to influence that behavior. One implication of this false behavioral assumption is that the incidence of all tax expenditures is assumed to be on the taxpayers who receive the favored treatment. Additional research on each type of tax expenditure is needed to assess its real impact on tax revenue and on the distribution of net income.

Third, the method employed here to assess the desirability of using tax subsidies is an extension of the theory of optimal commodity taxation pioneered by Ramsey.[10] The criterion is thus an explicit utilitarian social welfare function.[11] Moreover, the analysis is limited to the problem of de novo design of optimal tax subsidies and does not include the issues involved in changing an existing system of tax subsidies.[12]

Finally, I make a number of simplifications by assuming an econ-

9. In *Pathways to Tax Reform,* Surrey provides a detailed rationale for the list of provisions adopted by the U.S. Treasury and the House Ways and Means Committee. Aaron ("Inventory of Existing Tax Incentives") and Pechman and Okner ("Individual Income Tax Erosion") suggest alternative lists, while Bittker, in the articles cited in note 5, argues that the concept is too vague to be useful.

10. "A Contribution to the Theory of Taxation."

11. This is in sharp contrast to the practice of Break and Pechman in *Federal Tax Reform;* of Musgrave in "In Defense of an Income Concept," of Surrey in *Pathways to Tax Reform,* and of others who adopt the ad hoc Haig-Simons proposition that the income tax should be levied on the most comprehensive measure of income with no personal deductions. It is better to regard such comprehensive Haig-Simons taxation as a conceivable (but unlikely) outcome of this welfare optimization. The Haig-Simons approach was developed by Henry C. Simons in *Personal Income Taxation: The Definition of Income as a Problem of Fiscal Policy* (University of Chicago Press, 1938). Unfortunately Surrey and other lawyers have concluded that this is the "economists' criterion" that lawyers should adopt. See Martin Feldstein, "On the Theory of Tax Reform," *Journal of Public Economics,* vol. 6 (July-August 1976), pp. 77–104, for an explicit critique of the Haig-Simons approach. Also see Sandmo, "Optimal Taxation," and Atkinson and Stiglitz, "The Design of Tax Structure."

12. For a general discussion of the difference between de novo tax system design and the problem of reforming an existing system see Feldstein, "On the Theory of Tax Reform."

omy of identical individuals and by focusing on the choice of efficient subsidies and ignoring the issues of vertical and horizontal equity. The concluding section deals with these problems as well as with other issues.

In the next section a simple case is examined in which it is easily shown that a tax subsidy is preferable to direct government spending. The succeeding section then explores a more general model and presents calculations of the welfare costs of using either a tax subsidy or direct government spending to increase the consumption of a good that is favored by public policy. This is followed by an examination of the conditions under which some tax subsidy is desirable, that is, the conditions under which the welfare cost of a *new* subsidy is less than the welfare cost of achieving the same increment in consumption of the favored good by direct government spending; it establishes the conclusion that under a variety of plausible conditions at least some tax subsidy should be used in lieu of direct government spending. Then the size of the optimal tax subsidy is considered. In a wide range of cases, particularly when private and government spending are equally efficient, it is optimal to rely exclusively on the tax subsidy to achieve the desired consumption of the favored good. A brief conclusion points the direction for future work.

## The Basic Case for Subsidizing Charitable Gifts

Charitable organizations play major roles in education, health care, the visual and performing arts, social welfare services, and other important public activities. The government can encourage these organizations by subsidizing private gifts. Alternatively the government can produce the desired services or provide direct government grants to private organizations. If both private and public support are equally effective, the efficient method is the one with least cost in government revenue per dollar spent on the favored activity. Minimizing the revenue cost is appropriate because raising government revenue creates an excess burden by distorting labor supply, saving, and investment.

The basic question is therefore whether a tax subsidy for private giving uses more or less government revenue than does a direct government expenditure that provides equal additional funds to the favored activity. If one dollar of government spending adds one dollar to the total expenditure on the favored activity, the required comparison depends on the sensitivity of private giving to the tax subsidy. The charitable deduction lowers the net price to the donor of a dollar received by a donee organization. I and a number of colleagues recently completed several econometric studies with different bodies of data, all of which indicate that the absolute price elasticity of charitable giving is slightly greater than one.[13] This fact means that charities receive more in additional contributions because of the tax subsidy than the Treasury forgoes in revenue and therefore that the tax subsidy is more efficient than direct government spending if each dollar of government expenditure adds one dollar to the total spending on the favored activity.[14]

It is unlikely, however, that government spending adds an equal amount to total spending on the activity. Individual donors make charitable gifts until the point at which they believe that the benefit of another dollar spent on the charity's activity is equal to the value of retaining the net cost of such a contribution for their own consumption. When the government increases spending on a charity's activity

13. See Martin Feldstein, "The Income Tax and Charitable Contributions: Part I —Aggregate and Distributional Effects," *National Tax Journal,* vol. 28 (March 1975), pp. 81–99; Feldstein, "The Income Tax and Charitable Contributions: Part II —The Impact on Religious, Educational and Other Organizations, ibid., vol. 28 (June 1975), pp. 209–26; Martin Feldstein and Charles Clotfelter, "Tax Incentives and Charitable Contributions in the United States: A Microeconomic Analysis," *Journal of Public Economics,* vol. 5 (January-February 1976), pp. 1–26; Martin Feldstein and Amy Taylor, "The Income Tax and Charitable Contributions," *Econometrica,* vol. 44 (November 1976), pp. 1201–22; and Michael J. Boskin and Martin Feldstein, "Effects of the Charitable Deduction on Contributions by Low and Middle Income Households: Evidence from the National Survey of Philanthropy," *Review of Economics and Statistics,* vol. 59 (August 1977), pp. 351–54.

14. More specifically, let $G_0$ be charitable giving if there were no tax subsidy and $G_1$ be giving when gifts can be deducted from taxable income with marginal tax rate $t$; that is, when the price of giving is $p = 1 - t$. The cost to the Treasury Department $(tG_1)$ is less than the additional gifts received by the donee $(G_1 - G_0)$ if $G_1 - G_0 > tG_1$ or $-(\partial G/\partial p)t > tG_1$. This is equivalent to $(1/G_1)\partial G/\partial p < -1$. Since the price is one when there is no deduction, this implies that the price elasticity of giving must be less than minus one. (Note that with a constant elasticity function, $G_1 = G_0 (1 - t)^\eta$ and $G_1 - G_0 > tG_1$ if $(1 - t)^\eta - 1 > t (1 - t)^\eta$ or $(1 - t)^{\eta+1} > 1$, implying $\eta < -1$.) The price elasticity estimated in the references cited in note 13 satisfies this condition and thus implies that each dollar of revenue forgone because of the charitable deduction adds more than one dollar to the receipts of the donee. Thus the evidence that $\eta < -1$ implies that the tax subsidy is more efficient than direct government spending if each dollar of expenditure adds one dollar to the total spending on the favored activity.

the perceived marginal value of funds for the charitable organization tends to decline and thus induces people to reduce their giving until a new equilibrium is established.

If donors are fully rational, they will regard the government's spending as equivalent to an equal increase in their total private budget constraint. They will reduce their private giving and increase their personal consumption until the total spending on the favored activity has increased only by the product of the donors' marginal propensity to give to the charity and the amount of the government's expenditure.

Each dollar of direct government spending (other than matching grants perhaps) would therefore increase the charity's budget by only this marginal propensity to give ($m$). A tax subsidy is therefore more efficient than government spending if each dollar of revenue loss adds more than $m$ dollars to the donee's receipts. This result is assured because the introduction of a tax incentive that reduces revenues by one dollar not only increases the income of the donor by one dollar, causing his contributions to rise by $m$, but also reduces the price of giving, which will further increase giving.[15]

In the remainder of this paper the strong assumptions that have been used to obtain this result are relaxed.

## The Welfare Costs of a Tax Subsidy and of Direct Spending

The economy analyzed in this paper contains $n$ identical individuals. Each individual faces a wage rate, $w$, and chooses to supply labor, $L$. The labor income is taxed at a constant rate, $t$. The individual uses his net income to purchase quantity $c$ of the general consumption good and quantity $x$ of the special "favored" good. The price of the favored good is $p$ while the general consumption good is the numeraire. The favored good enjoys a tax subsidy at rate $s$; that

15. More formally, a tax subsidy is thus more efficient if $G_1 - G_o > mtG_1$ or $-(\partial G/\partial p)t > mtG_1$. Since $(1/G)$ $(\partial G/\partial p) = \eta$, the subsidy is more efficient than direct spending if $\eta < -m$. The usual Slutsky decomposition of the price elasticity implies that $\eta = E - m$, where $E$ is the compensated own-price elasticity of demand. The required condition $\eta < -m$ can therefore be written $E - m < -m$ or $E < 0$. Since the compensated own-price elasticity of demand is always negative, the subsidy is always more efficient than direct government spending.

is, the individual subtracts $spx$ from his tax liability. If each individual has exogenous nonlabor income $a$, the individual budget constraint is

(1) $$(1 - t)wL + a = c + (1 - s)px.$$

Each individual's utility depends on his leisure, his general consumption, and his consumption of the favored good, $f$:

(2) $$u = u(c, 1 - L, f).$$

The government provides quantity $g$ of the favored good. If the favored good is a purely private one, each individual consumes one $n$-th of the government's total provision:

(3) $$f = x + g/n.$$

More generally the favored good may involve externalities, that is, the purchase of $x$ by one person may give satisfaction to the others, and each individual may "consume" more than one $n$-th of total government provision. Equation 4 allows for different possible degrees of externality. Each individual $i$'s consumption of the favored good, $f_i$, will be written

(4) $$f_i = x_i + \xi \sum_{j \neq i} x_j + (g/n)[1 + \xi(n - 1)].$$

If $\xi = 0$, the favored good is a purely private one and equation 4 is equivalent to equation 3. The purchase of pensions for old age or of medical care are examples of such favored goods. Alternatively, if $\xi = 1$, the favored good is a pure public good; a unit of $x$ purchased by anyone or by the government gives equal satisfaction to all. Charitable contributions—for example, gifts to support public television —may exemplify such a pure public good in an economy of identical individuals. Other types of charitable gifts, for example, support of a local museum, are neither purely private nor purely public, so that $0 < \xi < 1$.

If the government wishes to increase everyone's consumption of the favored good by one unit, $df = 1$, this can be done either by increasing the rate of subsidy ($ds > 0$) or by direct government spending ($dg > 0$). In either case, the tax rate, $t$, must be increased if the government wishes to keep the budget balanced. To allow for the possibility that the government is either more or less efficient in the purchase of the favored good, the government budget constraint may be written

(5)                          $n(twL - spx) - epg = r$,

where $r$ is the government revenue required for other purposes, $e < 1$ if the government is more efficient in the provision of the favored good, and $e > 1$ if it is less efficient. The problem of the government is to maximize the sum of individual utilities subject to the government budget constraint (equation 5) and to the constraint that consumption of the favored good rises by one unit ($df = 1$). To achieve a small increase in $f$, it is optimal for the government either to cause private purchases to rise by increasing the tax subsidy, $s$, or to provide the favored good directly itself, but not to do both. It is sufficient, therefore, to calculate the effects on social welfare of achieving the increase by each method separately and then to compare the two welfare changes. Equivalently, since the same level of $f$ is fixed for both methods, it is sufficient to compare the welfare costs in terms of the reduced value of leisure and other consumption that is required by the two methods.

In general a subsidy will affect not only the consumption of the favored good but also the supply of labor. The subsidy can therefore increase or decrease the welfare loss that results from tax-caused distortions between leisure and all other goods. To focus on the use of the subsidy in increasing consumption of the favored good, I will avoid this issue by assuming that the individual's utility is separable between leisure and other goods.[16]

As a background for this calculation, it is necessary to examine the

16. If the utility function (equation 2) is *not* separable between leisure and the other goods, that is, unless $u = u (1 - L, \phi (c,f))$, it is optimal to have a positive or negative subsidy on good $f$ if there is a tax on labor income. This is equivalent to different rates of excise taxes on $c$ and $f$ with no tax on labor income. See A. B. Atkinson, "Housing Allowances, Income Maintenance, and Income Taxation," in Martin S. Feldstein and Robert P. Inman, eds., *The Economics of Public Services* (MacMillan, 1977), pp. 3–16. Thus a subsidy on $f$ might be optimal even if there were no desire to increase expenditure on this good. In order to eliminate this effect from the results to be obtained below and thus to study whether a subsidy is optimal for the purpose of encouraging expenditure on $x$, I will assume the necessary separability condition. This in turn implies that the compensated demand for leisure is independent of the price of the favored good: $\partial(1 - L)/\partial ps = 0$. From the symmetry of the Slutsky matrix, this also implies that the quantity demanded of the favored good is independent of compensated changes in the net wage rate: $\partial x/\partial(1 - t)w = 0$.

first-order conditions for utility maximization by the typical individual. Equations 1 and 2 imply the Lagrangian maximand:

(6)  $W = u(c, 1 - L, f) + \lambda[(1 - t)wL + a - c - (1 - s)px]$,

where $f$ is given by equation 4. The first-order conditions for the optimum with respect to consumption and leisure are

(7)  $$u_c = \lambda$$

and

(8)  $$u_{(1-L)} = \lambda(1 - t)w.$$

The first-order condition with respect to $x$ is more complex because when there are externalities ($\xi > 0$), a change in $x_i$ will alter all $x_j$'s, which in turn affects the utility of individual $i$. Since an explicit expression for this first-order condition is not required in what follows,[17] it will not be presented.

## The Tax Subsidy

Consider now the welfare effect of increasing the consumption of the favored good by an increase in the rate of tax subsidy with no change in government provision ($dg = 0$). Since social welfare ($W$) is the sum of the individual utilities and all individuals are alike, then from equation 2

(9)  $$dW = n[u_c dc + u_{(1-L)}d(1 - L) + u_f df].$$

Since $df = 1$ and is the same for the tax subsidy and the direct government provision, it is unnecessary to evaluate $u_f$ and the criterion can be rewritten using equations 7 and 8, as

(10)  $$dW' = n\lambda(dc - (1 - t)wdL).$$

Dividing $dW'$ by $-n\lambda$ yields the welfare cost per individual of increasing each $f$ by one unit through an increased tax subsidy:

(11)  $$C_s = -\left(\frac{\partial c}{\partial s} - (1 - t)w \frac{\partial L}{\partial s}\right) ds - \left(\frac{\partial c}{\partial t} - (1 - t)w \frac{\partial L}{\partial t}\right) dt.$$

Differentiating the individual's budget constraint, equation 1 with respect to $s$ implies

(12)  $$\frac{\partial c}{\partial s} - (1 - t)w \frac{\partial L}{\partial s} = px - (1 - s)p \frac{\partial x}{\partial s}.$$

17. It is obtained implicitly from the budget constraint.

Similarly, differentiating with respect to $t$ yields

(13) $\quad \dfrac{\partial c}{\partial t} - (1 - t)w \dfrac{\partial L}{\partial t} = -\left(wL + (1 - s)p \dfrac{\partial x}{\partial t}\right).$

Substituting these into equation 11 gives an alternative expression for the cost of increasing $f$:

(14) $\quad C_s = -\left(px - (1 - s)p \dfrac{\partial x}{\partial s}\right) ds + \left(wL + (1 - s)p \dfrac{\partial x}{\partial t}\right) dt.$

The values of $ds$ and $dt$ must satisfy two constraints. First, the requirement $df = 1$ implies

(15) $\quad \left(\dfrac{\partial f}{\partial s}\right) ds + \left(\dfrac{\partial f}{\partial t}\right) dt = 1.$

Second, the requirement that the tax increase is sufficient to keep the budget balanced implies (from equation 5) that

(16) $\quad \left(\dfrac{\partial r}{\partial s}\right) ds + \left(\dfrac{\partial r}{\partial t}\right) dt = 0.$

Thus

(17) $\quad ds = \dfrac{\partial r/\partial t}{\Delta_1} \quad$ and $\quad dt = \dfrac{\partial r/\partial s}{\Delta_1},$

where

(18) $\quad \Delta_1 = \dfrac{\partial f}{\partial s} \dfrac{\partial r}{\partial t} - \dfrac{\partial f}{\partial t} \dfrac{\partial r}{\partial s}.$

Since both $ds$ and $\partial r/\partial t$ are positive, equation 17 implies $\Delta_1 > 0$. The values of $\partial r/\partial s$ can be derived from equation 5 as

(19) $\quad \dfrac{\partial r}{\partial t} = n\left(wL - tw \dfrac{\partial L}{\partial(1 - t)} + sp \dfrac{\partial x}{\partial(1 - t)}\right)$

and

(20) $\quad \dfrac{\partial r}{\partial s} = n\left(-px - tw \dfrac{\partial L}{\partial(1 - s)} + sp \dfrac{\partial x}{\partial(1 - s)}\right).$

Finally, the evaluation of $C_s$ requires the values of $\partial f/\partial (1 - s)$ and $\partial f/\partial (1 - t)$. Since all individuals are alike,

(21) $\quad \dfrac{\partial f}{\partial(1 - s)} = (1 + (n - 1)\xi) \dfrac{\partial x}{\partial(1 - s)}$

and

$$(22) \qquad \frac{\partial f}{\partial(1-t)} = [1 + (n-1)\xi]\frac{\partial x}{\partial(1-t)}.$$

Note that the derivatives of the subsidized good $(x)$ and the supply of labor $(L)$ with respect to the tax subsidy $(s)$ and the tax rate $(t)$ reflect not only the direct effect of the associated price change but also the indirect impact of each person's consumption of $x$ on the well-being of others where there are externalities (that is, through $\xi\Sigma_{j\neq i}\, x_j$). It is important to be clear that the derivatives correspond to the observable consequences of changes in tax rates rather than to the unobservable effects that would be relevant if individuals assumed that no one else would respond to the tax change.[18]

It is convenient to rewrite these expressions in terms of elasticities and budget shares. Let the net price of the subsidized consumption good be $p_n = (1-s)p$ and the net wage be $w_n = (1-t)w$, and the fraction of net labor income spent on the favored good will be $\pi = p_n x / w_n L$. Also let $\theta = t/(1-t)$ and $\sigma = s/(1-s)$. Then, for example, from equation 19

$$(23) \qquad \frac{\partial r}{\partial t} = nwL\left(1 - \frac{t}{L}\frac{\partial L}{\partial(1-t)} + \frac{sp}{wL}\frac{\partial x}{\partial(1-t)}\right)$$

$$= nwL(1 - \theta\eta_{Lw} + \sigma\pi\eta_{xw}),$$

where

$$\eta_{Lw} = (w_n/L)\partial L/\partial w_n = [(1-t)/L][\partial L/\partial(1-t)].$$

Substituting these expressions into equation 11 yields

$$(24) \quad C_s = \frac{(1-s)p[\pi(1+\eta_{xp})(1-\theta\eta_{Lw}+\sigma\pi\eta_{xw})}{\pi[1+\xi(\eta-1)][\eta_{xp}(1-\theta\eta_{Lw}+\sigma\pi\eta_{xw})} \cdots$$

$$\cdots \frac{-(1-\pi\eta_{xw})(\theta\eta_{Lp}+\pi-\sigma\pi\eta_{xp})]}{+\eta_{xw}(\theta\eta_{Lp}+\pi-\sigma\pi\eta_{xp})]}.$$

$C_s$ is the cost per person of increasing everyone's consumption of the favored good by one unit as the result of an increase in the rate of subsidy.

### Direct Government Spending

The welfare cost of a unit increase in everyone's consumption of the favored good brought about by direct government spending will

18. Thus the partial derivative $\partial x_i/\partial(1-s)$ implies holding $t$, $a$, and $g$ constant but allowing $\Sigma_{j\neq i}x_j$ to change.

now be evaluated. Now the government keeps the tax subsidy constant and increases $g$ directly by enough to increase each person's consumption by one unit ($df = 1$). Of course, the increase in $g$ will require an increase in tax. Moreover, each individual will respond to the provision of $g$ and to the tax increase by altering, and probably reducing, his own spending on $x$. The government's direct provision must be large enough to offset these individual reactions.

By calculations similar to equations 9 through 11, one obtains the welfare cost per individual of increasing each $f$ by one unit through increased government provision with $s$ unchanged:

$$(25) \quad C_d = - \left( \frac{\partial c}{\partial g} - (1 - t)w \, \frac{\partial L}{\partial g} \right) dg - \left( \frac{\partial c}{\partial t} - (1 - t)w \, \frac{\partial L}{\partial t} \right) dt.$$

Differentiating the individual budget constraint (equation 1) with respect to $g$ yields

$$(26) \qquad \frac{\partial c}{\partial g} - (1 - t)w \, \frac{\partial L}{\partial g} = - (1 - s)p \, \frac{\partial x}{\partial g}.$$

The corresponding expression for the coefficient of $dt$ was already found in equation 13. Thus

$$(27) \qquad C_d = \left[ (1 - s)p \, \frac{\partial x}{\partial g} \right] dg + \left[ wL + (1 - s)p \, \frac{\partial x}{\partial t} \right] dt.$$

The values of $dg$ and $dt$ must satisfy two constraints. First, the requirement that $df = 1$ implies

$$(28) \qquad\qquad (\partial f/\partial g) \, dg + (\partial f/\partial t) \, dt = 1.$$

Second, the balanced budget expenditure implies

$$(29) \qquad\qquad (\partial r/\partial g) \, dg + (\partial r/\partial t) \, dt = 0.$$

Together these equations imply

$$(30) \qquad\qquad dg = \frac{\partial r/\partial t}{\Delta_2} \quad \text{and} \quad dt = - \frac{\partial r/\partial g}{\Delta_2},$$

where

$$(31) \qquad\qquad \Delta_2 = \left( \frac{\partial f}{\partial g} \right) \left( \frac{\partial r}{\partial t} \right) - \left( \frac{\partial f}{\partial t} \right) \left( \frac{\partial r}{\partial g} \right).$$

Since both $\partial r/\partial t$ and $dg$ are positive, equation 30 implies that $\Delta_2 > 0$.[19]

The values of $\partial r/\partial t$ and $\partial f/\partial t$ were calculated in equations 19 and 22. From equation 5,

$$(32) \qquad \frac{\partial r}{\partial g} = n\left[tw\,\frac{\partial L}{\partial g} - sp\,\frac{\partial x}{\partial g}\right] - ep.$$

Equation 4 implies that

$$(33) \qquad \frac{\partial f}{\partial g} = [1 + \xi(n - 1)]\frac{1}{n} + \frac{\partial x}{\partial g}.$$

Finally, it is necessary to evaluate $\partial x/\partial g$ and $\partial L/\partial g$. An increase in direct government provision has two effects on each individual's own purchase of $x$. An increase in $g$ is equivalent to a grant of income. If the favored good is a normal one, this induces some increase in the individual's demand for $f$. The more important effect of the increase in government provision is to increase the supply of $f$ and therefore to permit each individual to reduce his own spending on $x$. Thus an increase in $g$ will reduce $x$ to the extent that the marginal propensity to consume $x$ is less than one.[20] When there are externalities in consumption the actual effect is somewhat more complex. More formally, the effect of $dg$ can be written:

$$(34) \qquad \frac{\partial x_i}{\partial g} = \frac{\partial x_i}{\partial \hat{a}_i}\frac{\partial \hat{a}_i}{\partial g} - \frac{\partial f_i'}{\partial g},$$

where $f_i' = f_i - x_i$ and $\hat{a}_i$ is exogenous income expanded to include the value of government provision and of externalities. Equation 34 states that the individual adjusts $x$ to eliminate the difference between the increased demand and the increased supply. If the individual's marginal propensity to spend on $x$ is denoted by $m_x = \partial(p_n x)/\partial\hat{a}$, the result is $\partial x/\partial\hat{a} = m_x/p_n$. The value to the individual of the increased government provision is

$$(35) \qquad \partial\hat{a}_i/\partial g = p_n\partial f_i'/\partial g,$$

19. Under certain conditions it may actually be impossible for a small increase in government spending to increase the consumption of the favored good if the budget constraint must be satisfied. I ignore these cases because the subsidy is then the only possible method of increasing provision of $f$, and efficiency comparisons are meaningless.

20. This assumes that the individual would purchase some $x$ if the government provided no $g$; that is, $x > 0$ if $g = 0$.

while from equation 4

(36)         $\partial f_i'/\partial g = (n - 1)\xi \partial x/\partial g + [1 + \xi(n - 1)]/n.$

Therefore,

(37)         $$\frac{\partial x}{\partial g} = - \frac{(1 - m_x)}{n} \frac{1 + \xi(n - 1)}{1 + \xi(n - 1)(1 - m_x)}.$$

Note that for a purely private good ($\xi = 0$), equation 37 implies that $\partial(nx)/\partial g = -(1 - m_x)$; that is, total private purchases are reduced to the extent that the marginal propensity to consume is less than one.

The effect of $g$ on individual labor supply can be derived in a similar way. Thus

(38)         $$\frac{\partial L}{\partial g} = \frac{\partial L}{\partial \hat{a}} \frac{\partial \hat{a}}{\partial g}.$$

Writing $-m_L$ for the marginal propensity to purchase leisure, that is, $-m_L = \partial w_n(1 - L)/\partial \hat{a}$ or $m_L = w_n(\partial L/\partial \hat{a})$ implies $\partial L/\partial \hat{a} = m_L/w_n$. Therefore, using equations 33 and 36,

(39)         $$\frac{\partial L}{\partial g} = m_L \frac{p_n}{w_n} \left[ \frac{1 + \xi(n - 1)}{n} + \xi(n - 1) \frac{\partial x}{\partial g} \right].$$

Substituting from equation 37 yields

(40)         $$\frac{\partial L}{\partial g} = \frac{m_L}{n} \frac{p_n}{w_n} \frac{1 + \xi(n - 1)}{1 + \xi(n - 1)(1 - m_x)}.$$

All the terms required to evaluate $C_d$ have now been derived. After making the necessary substitutions to obtain elasticities, equation 27 yields

(41)   $$C_d = - \frac{(1 - s)p}{1 + \xi(n - 1)} \cdot$$

$$\frac{J(1 - m_x)(1 - \Theta\eta_{Lw} + \sigma\pi\eta_{xw}) + (1 - \pi\eta_{xw})[J(\Theta m_L + \sigma(1 - m_x)) - e(1 - \sigma)]}{[1 - J(1 - m_x)](1 - \Theta\eta_{Lw} + \sigma\pi\eta_{xw}) + \pi\eta_{xw}[J(\Theta m_L + \sigma(1 - m_x)) - e(1 - \sigma)]},$$

where $J = [1 + \xi(n - 1)]/[1 + \xi(n - 1)(1 - m_x)]$. Note that $J = 1$ if the favored good has no externalities.

# When Should Some Subsidy Be Used?

Whenever $C_d > C_s$ an increase in the consumption of the favored good should be achieved by increasing the rate of subsidy with direct government provision unchanged. If there is currently direct government spending but no subsidy, the condition $C_d > C_s$ implies that government spending should be reduced and a subsidy introduced.

The values of $C_d$ and $C_s$ are themselves functions of the subsidy rate, $s$.[21] It may be optimal to use a subsidy instead of direct spending when the subsidy rate is below some level but to use direct spending when the subsidy rate has reached that level. Before evaluating this critical level of the maximum optimal subsidy, I will examine the conditions under which at least some subsidy should be used to increase consumption of the favored good.

More formally if $C_d > C_s$ when $s = \sigma = 0$, the optimal way to increase consumption of the favored good should include at least some subsidy. A special case will help to focus attention on the fundamental aspects before considering the general condition. Consider therefore the case in which the favored good has no externalities ($\xi = 0$ and $J = 1$) and in which government and private provision are equally efficient ($e = 1$). Equations 22 and 41 then imply, after some simple but tedious algebra, that $C_s < C_d$ if and only if[22]

(42)

$$(1 - \Theta\eta_{Lw})\Theta[\eta_{Lw}(\eta_{xp} + m_x) + \eta_{Lp}(m_x - \pi\eta_{xw})/\pi - m_L(\eta_{xp} + \pi\eta_{xw})] < 0.$$

Equation 42 can be further simplified by substituting terms involving compensated price elasticities ($E_{ij}$) for the uncompensated elasticities ($\eta_{ij}$). Recall that to avoid confusing the subsidy desired to increase spending on the favored good with the subsidy desired to mitigate the effect of the labor income tax, I assumed above that $E_{Lp} = E_{xw} = 0$. It then follows from the traditional Slutsky equations that[23]

(43) $$\eta_{xp} = E_{xp} - m_x,$$

(44) $$\eta_{Lw} = E_{Lw} + m_L,$$

(45) $$\eta_{Lp} = -\pi m_L,$$

and

(46) $$\eta_{xw} = \pi^{-1}m_x.$$

21. See equations 22 and 41 and note that $\sigma = s/(1 - s)$.

22. This uses the facts that the denominator of equation 22 is negative and the denominator of equation 41 is positive.

23. Note that $\partial L/\partial w = -\partial(1 - L)/\partial w$, so that $\eta_{Lw}$ and $E_{Lw}$ are labor supply elasticities but can be derived from the demand for leisure.

After substitution equation 42 is equivalent to $C_s < C_d$ if and only if

(47) $$(1 - \Theta\eta_{Lw})\Theta E_{Lw}E_{xp} < 0.$$

Since $\sigma = 0$,

(48) $$1 - \Theta\eta_{Lw} > 0,$$

and the condition in 48 implies that[24]

(49) $$E_{Lw}E_{xp} < 0.$$

Note that $E_{xp}$ is an own-price compensated elasticity of demand and that therefore $E_{xp} < 0$; similarly, $E_{Lw}$ is an own-price compensated supply elasticity and therefore $E_{Lw} > 0$. Thus $C_s < C_d$, that is, a subsidy should be used.

When there are positive externalities associated with consumption of the favored good, $\xi > 0$ and

(50) $$J = \frac{1 + \xi(n - 1)}{1 + \xi(n - 1)(1 - m_x)} > 1.$$

Equations 26 and 42 now imply that $C_s < C_d$ if and only if[25]

(51) $$\eta_{Lw}(\eta_{xp} + m_x) + \frac{\eta_{Lp}}{\pi}(m_x - \pi\eta_{xw}) - m_L(\eta_{xp} + \pi\eta_{xw})$$

$$< (J - 1)\left[\left(\eta_{Lw} + \frac{\eta_{Lp}}{\pi}\right)(1 - m_x) + (\eta_{xp} + \pi\eta_{xw})m_L\right].$$

After substituting compensated elasticities (using 43 through 46) equation 51 is equivalent to

(52) $$E_{Lw}E_{xp} < (J - 1)[(1 - m_x)E_{Lw} + m_L E_{xp}].$$

The left-hand side is the same as equation 49. Since positive externalities imply $J - 1 > 0$, the existence of externalities increase the attractiveness of the subsidy relative to direct government spending (that is, increases $C_d - C_s$) because the bracketed expression on the right-hand side of equation 52 is positive.

Finally, the necessary and sufficient condition for the use of some subsidy to be optimal can be extended to allow for differences in

24. Equation 25 shows $dr/dt > 0$ if and only if $(1 - \Theta\eta_{Lw} + \sigma\pi\eta_{xw}) > 0$.
25. The reader will note that a factor of $(1 - \Theta\eta_{Lw})\Theta$ has been eliminated from both sides of the inequality.

efficiency between government and private purchases of the favored good. When $e \neq 1$, one obtains $C_s < C_d$ if and only if

$$(53) \quad E_{Lw}E_{xp} < (J - 1)[(1 - m_x)E_{Lw} + m_L E_{xp}] + (1 - e)E_{xp}\theta^{-1}.$$

If the government is more efficient than private purchasers, $1 - e > 0$. Since $E_{xp}$ is negative, this reduces the value of the right-hand side and makes the inequality more difficult to satisfy. Of course, if private purchasers are more efficient than the government, $1 - e < 0$ and the condition for $C_s < C_d$ is more easily satisfied.

Note in particular that a subsidy of individual purchasers may be optimal even if the government is a more efficient purchaser; that is, even if $e < 1$. Consider, for example, the simple case in which there is no externality ($J = 1$). Then equation 53 implies that $C_s < C_d$ if $(1 - e) < \theta E_{Lw}$; if the relative efficiency of direct purchase, $1 - e$, is less than the product of the tax ratio ($\theta$) and the compensated labor supply elasticity ($E_{Lw}$), it is optimal to subsidize inefficient private purchases. An increase in $E_{Lw}$ militates against direct finance because it increases the welfare loss per dollar of additional tax revenue. Similarly the higher the initial tax rate (and therefore $\theta$), the greater the welfare cost of additional taxation.

## The Maximum Optimal Tax Subsidy

The previous section established that under a wide range of likely conditions *some* subsidy should be used as part of a government policy to increase the consumption of a favored good, but it did not indicate how much reliance should be placed on subsidies. In the current section, therefore, I turn to the proper mix of tax subsidy and direct spending. The question to be answered here is: if the conditions are satisfied for at least *some* subsidy to be used, what is the maximum optimal rate of subsidy? That is, if $C_s < C_d$ at some value of $\sigma \geq 0$, at what value of $\sigma$ (if any) does $C_s = C_d$?

A very striking result is obtained when government spending and private purchases are equally efficient ($e = 1$). In this case the elasticity condition that is necessary and sufficient for $C_s < C_d$ at $\sigma = 0$ is also necessary and sufficient for all values of $\sigma \geq 0$. *It is optimal to rely as much as possible on the subsidy to achieve any desired expenditure on the favored good.*

This conclusion is reinforced whenever the government is less efficient than the private purchasers of the favored good—when $e > 1$. When the government is a more efficient purchaser of the favored good ($e < 1$) the optimality condition is more complex.

The condition for the maximum optimal $\sigma$ will now be derived. It follows from equations 26 and 42 that $C_s < C_d$ if and only if[26]

(54) $E_{Lw}E_{xp} - (J - 1)[(1 - m_x)E_{Lw} + m_L E_{xp}] - (1 - e)E_{xp}\theta^{-1}$
$$< \sigma(1 - e)E_{xp}\theta^{-1}.$$

With $e = 1$, the right-hand side equals zero and the left-hand side is identical with inequality (equation 53); that is, with the condition for $C_s < C_d$ at $\sigma = 0$ when $e = 1$. Thus when $e = 1$ the value of $\sigma$ plays no *direct* role in the condition that determines the relative size of $C_s$ and $C_d$. Because equations 53 and 54 are identical in this case, $C_s < C_d$ at $\sigma = 0$ implies $C_s < C_d$ for all values of $\sigma$; that is, that if any subsidy is to be used, the maximum possible subsidy should be used before any direct spending.

Consider finally the condition in which the government is a more efficient purchaser of the favored good, $e < 1$. Condition 54 can be written conveniently as

(55) $$Q < \sigma(1 - e)E_{xp}\theta^{-1},$$

where $Q$ equals the left-hand side of equation 54. Note that $Q < 0$ is the condition required in equation 53 for $C_s < C_d$ at $\sigma = 0$. Since the right-hand side of equation 55 is negative, the condition for $C_s < C_d$ at $\sigma = 0$ is not sufficient at $\sigma > 0$. The greater the relative efficiency of the government as a provider (that is, the greater is $1 - e$), the lower will be the maximum optimal rate of subsidy.

The special case of $J = 1$ (no externalities) can again provide useful insights. With these restrictions, equation 54 is equivalent to

(56) $$1 + \sigma < \frac{\theta E_{Lw}}{1 - e}.$$

Note first that a greater efficiency of government purchasing ($e < 1$) limits but does not preclude reliance on the subsidy. For example, if $E_{Lw} = 0.3$, $e = 0.8$, and $\theta = 1$ (a 50 percent tax rate), the maximum optimal $\sigma$ is 0.5. This implies a maximum optimal subsidy rate of $s = \frac{1}{3}$. Direct government spending is appropriate only if the desired

---

26. This factors out $1 - \theta\eta_{Lw} + \sigma\pi\eta_{xw} > 0$ from both sides of the inequality. Equation 25 shows that $\partial r/\partial t > 0$ implies $1 - \theta\eta_{Lw} + \sigma\pi\eta_{xw} > 0$.

level of consumption of the favored good cannot be achieved with a subsidy rate of up to $s = \frac{1}{3}$.

Equation 56 also implies that the optimal subsidy is increased by higher values of both $\Theta$ and $E_{Lw}$. This finding is easily understood. Because the subsidy entails a smaller tax increase than does direct governmental provision, and because higher values of both $E_{Lw}$ and $\Theta$ increase the welfare cost of any tax rate, they clearly favor the subsidy. Finally, equation 56 shows the obvious property that an increase in the relative efficiency of government purchasing (that is, in $1 - e$) lowers the maximum optimal rate of subsidy.

It is important to note in concluding this section that all the results have been derived on the assumption that $x > 0$ at all levels of $s \geq 0$ —that there is some private consumption of the favored good even in the absence of the subsidy. When private consumption would be zero if there were no subsidy, the sufficient conditions for the use of a subsidy may be more stringent.[27] Although I have not investigated this fully, it is useful to consider the implication of $x = 0$ in the important special case in which there are no externalities ($\xi = 0$), in which public and private spending are equally efficient ($e = 1$). In this case, $x > 0$ implies that a subsidy is always the optimal way to increase consumption of the favored good (see equation 54).

This conclusion remains valid when $x = 0$ at some values of $s > 0$. Consider the situation in which $x = 0$ for $s = 0$. Only when the rate of subsidy has been increased sufficiently does $x$ become positive. If it is optimal to increase $s$ until $x > 0$, the previous analysis of this section becomes relevant for determining the maximum rate of subsidy that is optimal. For the current special case of $\xi = 0$ and $e = 1$, it therefore follows that the subsidy should be relied on exclusively if it is optimal to use any subsidy at all. The key question is therefore whether it is optimal to increase $s$ until $x = 1$ is achieved. To answer this question, it is necessary to repeat the derivation of $C_s$ and $C_d$ with the condition $x = 0$.

With $x = \pi = 0$, it can be shown that[28]

(57)
$$C_s = \frac{p_n(1 + \sigma - \Theta m_L)}{1 - \Theta \eta_{Lw}}$$

27. When $x = 0$, direct provision by the government cannot reduce private consumption of the favored good.

28. These derivations use the facts that $x = 0$ and $E_{Lp} = 0$ imply $\partial x / \partial t = -wLm_x/p_n$ and $\partial L / \partial s = 0$. Also, at $x = 0$, $\partial x / \partial g = 0$ and $\partial f / \partial g = 1$.

and

(58) $$C_d = \frac{p_n(1 - m_x)(1 + \sigma - \Theta m_L)}{1 - \Theta \eta_{Lw} - m_x(1 + \sigma - \Theta m_L)}.$$

Since both denominators are positive, it follows that $C_s < C_d$ if and only if $\sigma > -\Theta (\eta_{Lw} - m_L)$. Since $\eta_{Lw} - m_L = E_{Lw} > 0$, this condition is always satisfied. Thus the condition $x = 0$ leaves unchanged the previous conclusion that it is desirable to rely as much as possible on the subsidy in the important case when $J = e = 1$ and $E_{Lp} = 0$. Investigation of other cases would clearly be desirable.

## Conclusion

This paper has begun the examination of the optimal use of tax subsidies by studying in detail the question of subsidizing charitable giving. Some very strong results have been obtained by focusing on an economy of identical individuals. Within this context the analysis indicates that tax subsidies should generally be used as much as possible to achieve the desired increase in the expenditure on an activity favored by public policy.

The theoretical analysis should now be extended in two ways: to an economy of heterogeneous individuals and to a wider range of tax expenditures. In an economy in which individuals have different wage rates and different tastes, a subsidy may be optimal in some income classes and demographic groups but not in others. In the presence of externalities, for example, it may be best to concentrate subsidies on groups with high price elasticities. Although the actual price elasticity was irrelevant in the current analysis, it would become important if differential subsidies were possible.[29]

Such an extension of the current analysis to an economy of heterogeneous individuals would show why *tax* subsidies to consumers are preferable to *market* subsidies to producers. In the current paper, since all individuals are alike, the same rate of subsidy must be optimal for everyone. Such a subsidy could therefore be achieved either by an income tax subsidy to the individual or by a matching grant to

29. The deduction is, of course, a differential subsidy, the rate of subsidy being the individual's marginal tax rate. On the general issue of deductions versus credits, see Atkinson and Stiglitz, "The Design of Tax Structure"; and Joseph E. Stiglitz and Michael J. Boskin, "Some Lessons from the New Public Finance," *American Economic Review*, vol. 67 (February 1977, *Papers and Proceedings*), pp. 295–301.

the charity; more generally, a market subsidy could take the form of a negative excise tax on the favored good. But an economy with heterogeneous individuals is likely to require subsidies at different rates that therefore cannot be achieved by matching grants or product subsidies. Although varying the subsidy rate among individuals would not be possible for goods that are readily marketed, varying rates of subsidy are possible for charitable gifts and for such other expenditures that currently benefit from special tax treatment as home-ownership, pension saving, or insurance purchases.

Although a subsidy may be more efficient than direct government expenditures, it may undesirably alter the distribution of tax burdens. Choosing the optimal rate of subsidy requires balancing efficiency and distributional equity. The actual price elasticity of demand for the favored good would be important in such an analysis.

The current study should be extended to the other types of tax subsidy that are now used or contemplated: the mortgage interest deduction, accelerated depreciation, intangible drilling costs, a possible deduction for personal educational expenses, and so on. The analysis of tax expenditures to foster some desirable activity also has obvious implications for the problem of controlling undesirables. The government can engage in direct spending activities (cleaning up pollution), can subsidize corresponding private activities (a tax subsidy for private spending on pollution control), or can tax harmful activities (a tax on activities that create pollution). Although there has been significant recent interest in the use of Pigovian taxes to control externalities,[30] these studies have not examined the optimal mix of direct government activities and tax subsidies (positive and negative) along the lines suggested here.

In spite of the clear need to extend the current analysis in a number of ways, the results already suggest some conclusions of significance for tax policy. The common presumption that the aim of tax reform should be to eliminate all current tax subsidies is clearly unfounded.

---

30. See, for example, William J. Baumol, "On Taxation and the Control of Externalities," *American Economic Review*, vol. 62 (June 1972), pp. 307–22; Peter A. Diamond, "Consumption Externalities and Imperfect Corrective Pricing," *Bell Journal of Economics and Management Science*, vol. 4 (Autumn 1973), pp. 526–38; Jerry Green and Eytan Sheshinski, "Direct Versus Indirect Remedies for Externalities" (manuscript, 1974); Agnar Sandmo, "Direct versus Indirect Pigovian Taxation," in Sandmo, ed., *Essays in Public Economics* (Lexington Books, 1978), pp. 175–87.

In a number of important cases, the tax subsidy may be better than direct spending. Moreover, it may now be desirable to introduce new subsidies to replace some current forms of government activity. It would be useful to examine empirically whether tax subsidies would be better than current or proposed government spending in such areas as health insurance, retirement savings, the finance of higher education and the support of local public services through revenue sharing.

Much of the criticism of tax expenditures has focused on what is perceived to be inadequate legislative and administrative care in the voting of expensive tax subsidies. The official tax expenditure budget serves the important purpose of directing the attention of Congress and of the administrative agencies to these effects of tax law. The new Congressional Budget Office and special budget committees are now charged by law to consider both tax expenditures and the traditional direct expenditures. Nevertheless, if tax expenditures are to continue to play an increasing role in the achievement of social goals, it may well be appropriate to alter the process of legislative and administrative review. An analysis of such procedural reforms clearly lies beyond the scope of the current study. It would, however, be a perversion of logic to seek to eliminate tax expenditures instead of trying to improve the legislative and administrative process.

In conclusion, I must reiterate that this paper should not be construed as a defense of any particular tax expenditures. Each current or proposed subsidy requires specific empirical analysis. It is important, however, to begin that analysis without any prejudice against the use of tax expenditures to achieve desired social purposes. My analysis suggests that tax expenditures may be the appropriate instrument of public policy in a number of important instances.

STANLEY S. SURREY *Harvard Law School*

PAUL R. McDANIEL *Boston College Law School*

# The Tax Expenditure Concept
# and the Legislative Process

IN THE PERIOD since 1968, when the Treasury Department published its first tax expenditure budget, the concept of tax expenditure
has been widely applied and has been adopted for official use by
Congress, the Office of Management and Budget, at least one state,
and other nations.[1] The term "tax expenditure" refers to the fact that

1. *Annual Report of the Secretary of the Treasury on the State of the Finances
for Fiscal Year 1968*, pp. 326–40. The Congressional Budget Act of 1974 included
the tax expenditure concept in the new congressional budget process. Since January
1975 the U.S. budget has contained a special analysis entitled "Tax Expenditures."
(*Special Analyses, Budget of the United States Government, Fiscal Year 1976*,
Special Analysis F, pp. 101–17. See also Special Analysis F in subsequent annual
budget documents. For the fiscal year 1979 budget and thereafter this material is in
Special Analysis G.) In 1976 the House and Senate Budget committees set a target
for reducing tax expenditures through tax reform legislation, a step that affected the
Tax Reform Act of 1976. (Stanley S. Surrey, "Reflections on the Tax Reform Act of
1976," *Cleveland State Law Review*, vol. 25 [Fall 1976], pp. 303–30; also in *Tax
Notes*, vol. 6 [March 20, 1978], pp. 291–305.) In 1976 a California statute directed
that a report on tax expenditures be included in the governor's budget. (Chapter 575,
California Statutes of 1976. In 1971 in chapter 1762, California Statutes of 1971,
the state had directed the Department of Finance to prepare a biennial tax expenditure report.) In 1976 and 1977 the two major international tax organizations chose
the concept of tax expenditures as a principal subject for their annual meetings—
the International Fiscal Association at its 1976 Jerusalem Congress ("Tax Incentives
as an Instrument for Achievement of Government Goals," *Cahiers de droit fiscal*,
International Fiscal Association, vol. 51a [1976] and the International Institute of
Public Finance at its 1977 Varna Congress (*Subsidies, Tax Reliefs and Prices* [IIPF,

123

many of the provisions of the U.S. tax laws are intended, not as necessary structural parts of a normative tax, but rather as tax incentives or hardship relief provisions. These provisions are thus really spending measures. Direct outlays could be designed that are equivalent in their effects to the tax expenditure provisions that favor certain groups or that encourage certain forms of activity and favor certain sources of income; for example, it would be easy to design an investment subsidy identical to the investment tax credit in its effects on investors and on the federal budget deficit. It is being increasingly recognized that unless attention is paid to tax expenditures, a country does not have either its tax policy or its budget policy under full control.

This paper focuses on the impact of the tax expenditure concept on the legislative process.[2] Legislative actions in the 1976–78 period brought into sharper focus two related but distinct effects of the concept. The first concerned the effect of the Congressional Budget Act of 1974 on the procedures for dealing with tax legislation. The second concerned the question of committee jurisdiction over tax expenditures and procedures for identifying areas where tax and direct measures overlap.

---

forthcoming]). Germany has published a tax expenditure budget since 1966. In 1976 the Netherlands Finance Ministry appointed a commission to study the tax expenditures in the Netherlands tax system. In 1977 the president of the United States asked the Treasury Department for a detailed report on the desirability of each listed tax expenditure. In 1977 Congress again recognized the role played by tax expenditures in its considerations of "sunset" review for federal programs and of the jurisdiction of the Senate Appropriations Committee over "refundable" tax credits. A tax expenditure list for the United Kingdom was published in J. R. M. Willis and P. J. W. Hardwick, *Tax Expenditures in the United Kingdom* (London: Heinemann Educational Books, 1978), pp. 6–9. In 1978 Canada began work to identify tax expenditures in its income tax system.

   2. Primarily, legislative developments in the period 1976 to mid-1978 are covered here. For a more comprehensive analysis that carries the story through 1978, see Stanley S. Surrey and Paul R. McDaniel, "The Tax Expenditure Concept: Current Developments and Emerging Issues," *Boston College Law Review,* vol. 20 (March 1979), pp. 225–369. For a discussion of developments in 1974–75 and early 1976, see Surrey and McDaniel, "The Tax Expenditure Concept and the Budget Reform Act of 1976," *Boston College Industrial and Commercial Law Review,* vol. 17 (September 1976), pp. 679–737. For discussions of recent developments in the tax legislative process, see Stanley S. Surrey, "The Federal Tax Legislative Process," *Record Association of Bar of City of New York,* vol. 31 (November 1976), pp. 515–43; and Paul R. McDaniel, "Federal Income Tax Simplification: The Political Process," *Tax Law Review,* vol. 34 (Fall 1978), p. 27.

# Tax Expenditures and the Congressional Budget Process

This section is an analysis of the impact on the tax legislative process produced by the inclusion of tax expenditures in the congressional budget process.

## The Tax Reform Act of 1976

The Tax Reform Act of 1976 provided the first major test of the procedures established by the 1974 budget act to subject tax expenditures to the new congressional budget process.

THE FIRST CONCURRENT RESOLUTION. In early 1976, as the Budget committees began consideration of the First Concurrent Resolution on the Budget for Fiscal Year 1977, they sought ways to reduce tax expenditures. The committees could have placed a limit on the dollar total of tax expenditures permissible for the following year, although this approach suffers from a number of shortcomings, not the least of which is that a reduction could be accomplished by such actions as a simple rate reduction (or increase in the standard deduction) with no change in the tax base. In this way a stipulated reduction in tax expenditures could be achieved without repealing or modifying the actual provisions that give rise to tax expenditures.

Members of the Senate Finance Committee, especially the chairman, Senator Russell B. Long, were quite sensitive to what they considered a potential intrusion on the committee's jurisdiction. Pursuant to section 301(c) of the budget act, the Senate Finance Committee on March 15, 1976, submitted to the Senate Budget Committee its view that revenues for fiscal year 1977 should be cut $19.6 billion.[3] The Finance Committee did not specify how it intended to achieve such reductions.

In the meantime, as the Finance Committee commenced hearings on the Tax Reform Act of 1976, Senator Long made clear his displeasure with the interest in tax expenditures shown by the Senate

3. See *Fiscal Year 1977 Allocations under Section 302(b), Congressional Budget Act*, S.Rept. 94-916, 94 Cong. 2 sess. (Government Printing Office, 1976). For background material, see Staff of Senate Finance Committee, *Data and Materials for the Fiscal Year 1977: Finance Committee Report under the Congressional Budget Act*, Committee Print, 94 Cong. 2 sess. (GPO, 1976).

Budget Committee and the Congressional Budget Office.[4] He also argued before the Budget Committee, during its markup of the First Concurrent Resolution on the Budget for Fiscal Year 1977, that it was unrealistic to anticipate any significant revenue gains from tax reform in fiscal 1977 because it was too late to enact revenue-raising tax measures that would affect the current fiscal year.[5]

It was thus obvious that if the budget process was to exert any control over tax expenditures in fiscal 1977, the First Concurrent Budget Resolution had to refer specifically to tax expenditures. The Senate Budget Committee report therefore provided a net revenue increase of $2 billion from reductions in existing tax expenditures.[6]

The resolution itself, however, merely called for $15.3 billion in revenue reductions.[7] The Budget Committee report made it clear that the $15.3 billion figure was to be reached by netting the revenue loss of $17.3 billion from extension for a full year of the temporary tax cuts enacted in the previous year and the $2 billion revenue gain from cutting back on existing tax expenditures.[8] The House Budget Committee took a similar stand.[9] In the end, the Conference Committee report stated that the resolution was based on an assumed $2 billion revenue gain from "tax reform."[10]

THE TAX BILL. House bill 10612, as reported to the Senate floor in June 1976, reflected the influence of the budget resolution's revenue targets, but the Finance Committee did not comply with the Budget Committee method of reaching the target. Furthermore, the Budget

4. *Tax Reform Act of 1975*, Hearings before the Senate Finance Committee, 94 Cong. 2 sess. (GPO, 1976), pt. 1, p. 406.

5. "Chairman Long before the Budget Committee," *Tax Notes*, vol. 4 (April 12, 1976), pp. 5–10. Senator Edward M. Kennedy pointed out prior legislation that conflicted with Senator Long's position. See *Congressional Record*, daily edition (March 31, 1976), p. S4711; and *Tax Reform Act of 1975*, Hearings, pt. 4, pp. 1587, 1699–1705.

6. *First Concurrent Resolution on the Budget, Fiscal Year 1977*, S.Rept. 94-731, 94 Cong. 2 sess. (GPO, 1976), pp. 6, 8.

7. S. Con. Res. 109, 94 Cong. 2 sess. (GPO, 1976).

8. *First Concurrent Resolution on the Budget, Fiscal Year 1977*, S.Rept. 94-731, p. 6.

9. *First Concurrent Resolution on the Budget, Fiscal Year 1977*, H.Rept. 94-1030, 94 Cong. 2 sess. (GPO, 1976), pp. 23–24.

10. *Congressional Record*, daily edition (May 7, 1976), p. H4133. The use of the term "tax reform" rather than "tax expenditures" was not intended as a change in meaning and was never treated as such. The $2 billion figure was selected because it represented approximately a 2 percent reduction in tax expenditures, which corresponded to the 2 percent reduction in direct programs being recommended.

Committee felt that the tax bill had been produced in violation of the spirit of the budget act despite technical compliance with it.[11] The Finance Committee bill provided "reductions" of nearly $15 billion for fiscal 1977, slightly less than the $15.3 billion target of the resolution. The $15 billion figure, however, included only $980 million in revenue from "tax reforms." It achieved additional savings of $1.8 billion by terminating temporary tax cuts on June 30, 1977, rather than allowing them to run throughout fiscal 1977 as contemplated by the budget resolution.[12]

Thus the Finance Committee bill provided neither a $17.3 billion tax cut nor the $2 billion reduction in tax expenditures the budget resolution had called for. Indeed, even the $980 million cut in tax expenditures in 1977 was suspect. The Finance Committee made the revenue gainers in the bill retroactive and deferred the effective dates of the prospective revenue losers (in some instances skipping fiscal 1977 completely). As a result, revenue gains were artificially bunched in fiscal 1977, and in fact the Finance Committee's actions would have reduced revenues for all fiscal years after 1977.[13]

In its manipulation of effective dates, the Finance Committee simultaneously achieved technical compliance with the budget act and defeated the goal of the Budget Committee to reduce tax expenditures. Although the Finance Committee obviously felt pressured in 1976 to comply with the letter of the budget resolution, it also demonstrated a remarkable ability to avoid and to subvert the goals the resolution sought to achieve.

The Budget Committee fought back on the Senate floor. Senator Edmund S. Muskie, chairman of the Budget Committee, and Senator Henry Bellmon, the ranking Republican member, argued that the Finance Committee bill violated the First Concurrent Resolution on the Budget. They held that in adopting the resolution, Congress had also stipulated the method to be employed in reaching the target. That method, as reflected in the Budget Committee report, was designed to produce specified economic results—a certain form of fiscal stimulus from a full-year extension of the tax cuts and a degree of fiscal restraint from cuts in both direct and tax expenditures. The

11. *Congressional Record,* daily edition (June 16, 1976), pp. S9568–84; and ibid. (June 17, 1976), pp. S9711–26.

12. Ibid. (June 16, 1976), pp. S59570–71.

13. *Tax Reform Act of 1976,* S.Rept. 94-938, 94 Cong. 2 sess. (GPO, 1976), pt. 1, p. 22.

Finance Committee changed the mix of tax cuts and tax increases, and its bill would produce different economic results from those approved by Congress.[14]

Senator Long and members of the Finance Committee argued that only the budget resolution figures had to be met and that the $2 billion cut in tax expenditures appeared only in the Budget Committee report, not in the resolution. The report simply expressed the Budget Committee's views, not those of Congress, on how best to reach the $15.3 billion figure. The Finance Committee was free to disagree and the full Senate could then work its will. Senator Long also invoked fears that the Budget Committee might encroach on the jurisdictions of other committees if the Muskie-Bellmon views were upheld.[15] The debate ended inconclusively.

In the end the Senate rejected almost all the tax reform amendments and added a host of new tax expenditures. When House bill 10612 left the Senate floor, instead of a $2 billion reduction in tax expenditures for fiscal 1977, there was a $260 million increase (which would quickly accelerate to almost $850 million by fiscal 1981).

While no clear-cut votes had been taken, obviously the budget process had failed to constitute a significant force in achieving particular tax reforms on the Senate floor. A number of factors may have accounted for this failure. Some Senators opposed the necessary revenue-raising reforms on their merits; some may have feared a power grab by the Budget Committee. Others, as the defeats for tax reform and the victories for new tax preferences mounted, simply concluded that the bill would be cleaned up in conference; and still others apparently had not been persuaded that preferential tax provisions are equivalent to federal spending and had difficulty seeing how the policies of the budget act really applied to tax provisions. Whatever the reasons, the budget act had little impact in 1976 on Senate action on particular issues.[16] The Conference Committee faced

14. *Congressional Record,* daily edition (June 16, 1976), pp. S9568–84; and ibid. (June 17, 1976), pp. S9711–26.

15. Ibid. (June 16, 1976), p. S9573.

16. On the other hand, at the conclusion of the Senate floor debate Senator Long himself added an amendment that it was the sense of the Senate that the Senate members of the Conference Committee seek to reduce the net revenue reductions in the bill to the $15.3 billion figure targeted in the budget resolution. *Congressional Record,* daily edition (August 6, 1976), pp. S13784–85.

the formidable task of reconciling the Senate bill with House bill 10612, which provided a $1.7 billion revenue gain from cuts in tax expenditures for fiscal 1977 (increasing to a projected $2.5 billion in calendar year 1981).[17] The Conference Committee produced a compromise, with reductions in tax expenditures of $1.6 billion in 1977 (increasing to $2.47 billion in 1981),[18] an outcome much closer to the totals in the House bill and one that reflected a reassertion of the discipline sought by creators of the congressional budget process.

THE SECOND CONCURRENT RESOLUTION. When work on the Second Concurrent Resolution on the Budget for Fiscal Year 1977 began, the Senate assumed a fiscal 1977 revenue gain of $1.1 billion from tax reform; the House and the Conference Committee report assumed a $1.6 billion gain, the same as that provided by the Conference Committee on the Tax Reform Act of 1976.[19]

The effectiveness of the budget process in controlling tax expenditures in 1976 was uneven. On the one hand, the Budget committees' $2 billion target figure appears to have exerted a significant influence on the deliberations of the tax-writing committees and on the Conference Committee.[20] On the other hand, the budget process had little impact on the Senate floor.

17. See *Tax Reform Act of 1975*, H.Rept. 94-658, 94 Cong. 1 sess. (GPO, 1975), p. 19. The figures in the text vary somewhat from those shown in the committee report, reflecting subsequent revisions in the revenue estimates by the staff of the Joint Committee on Taxation.

18. Staff of Joint Committee on Taxation, *Summary of The Tax Reform Act of 1976* (GPO, 1976), p. 108.

19. S.Rept. 94-1204, 94 Cong. 2 sess. (GPO, 1976), p. 7; H.Rept. 94-1457, 94 Cong. 2 sess. (GPO, 1976); and H.Rept. 94-1502, 94 Cong. 2 sess. (GPO, 1976), p. 5 (all entitled *Second Concurrent Resolution on the Budget, Fiscal Year 1977*).

20. Another effect of the budget process subsequently was realized. The Senate version of H.R. 10612 contained a number of tax expenditures for energy conservation and production. The conferees agreed to drop all these provisions from the bill with the understanding that the Finance Committee would add them to H.R. 6860, the energy tax bill enacted by the House in 1975 and then still pending before the Finance Committee. The Finance Committee took this action but added to H.R. 6860 an increase of one-half cent per gallon in the federal gasoline tax. The tax increase was necessary because H.R. 6860 was scheduled for floor action after the passage of the Second Concurrent Resolution on the Budget. If only the tax expenditures had been included in H.R. 6860, the bill would have been subject to a point of order under section 311 of the budget act, since it would have reduced revenue levels below the mandatory figure established by the budget resolution. The Senate then lost its enthusiasm for energy-related tax expenditures if they had to be financed by higher taxes, and H.R. 6860 was allowed to die.

The approach to the process mandated by the Congressional Budget Act in the House differed strikingly from that in the Senate. Cooperation, rather than confrontation, marked the relationship between the House Budget Committee and the Ways and Means Committee.[21] Once the tax bill reached the House floor, the customary modified closed rule protected it from numerous amendments.

While the Finance Committee felt constrained by the budget resolution, much of its effort was devoted to circumvention, owing in part, no doubt, to the philosophical and personal differences between Senator Muskie and Senator Long. And once the tax bill reached the Senate floor, it was fair game for amendments under the customary Senate open rule. Nevertheless, the budget process apparently motivated an amendment that committed the Senate conferees to try to report a bill consistent with the budget resolution; and it enabled Senator Muskie to emphasize for the Congress and the press that the absence of significant tax reform contradicted assumptions underlying the budget resolution and really undercut a rational budget process.

### The 1977–78 Experience

The passage of the Tax Reduction and Simplification Act of 1977, the Energy Tax Act of 1978, and the Revenue Act of 1978 continued the interaction between the budget process and the tax legislation that had been experienced in 1976.

#### Budget Resolutions and the Tax Credit for Higher Education Costs

The issue of tax expenditures arose next when Congress considered the Second Concurrent Budget Resolution for Fiscal Year 1978. Proponents of tax expenditures added to that resolution the revenue necessary to fund a tax credit to offset partially the costs of higher education. Congressman Robert N. Giaimo, chairman of the House Budget Committee, opposed the addition until such time as the Ways and Means Committee had approved this type of credit. Nevertheless, the House adopted the amendment.[22]

21. In part this difference was due to Congressman Al Ullman, chairman of the House Ways and Means Committee, who was instrumental in securing enactment of the 1974 budget act and who served for a time as chairman of the House Budget Committee.

22. See *Congressional Record,* daily edition (September 8, 1977), pp. H9028–32.

Senator Muskie opposed a similar amendment offered by Senator William V. Roth, Jr., stating that the budget resolution was not the appropriate vehicle for approving individual tax provisions. Senator Long announced that he would vote for the Roth amendment; all the members of the Finance Committee followed his lead, and the amendment passed.[23] By adopting the Roth amendment the Senate created more "room" in the budget for his later amendment adding the tuition tax credit to the social security bill.[24]

The reaction of the administration to the Roth amendment dramatizes the interchangeability between tax and direct expenditures. In an effort to divert Congress from tuition tax credits, the president in early 1978 proposed to expand direct financial assistance to students from low- and middle-income families. The House Committee on Education and Labor adopted its own Middle-Income Student Assistance Act of 1978 increasing this assistance. Although the Ways and Means Committee initially neither recommended enactment of tuition tax credits nor urged provision in the budget resolution for such tax credits, it subsequently reported out a bill to provide tuition tax credits for the costs of higher education. The full House then approved this bill after adding credits for the costs of elementary and secondary education as well.

The House Budget Committee report on the First Concurrent Resolution on the 1979 budget provided $1.4 billion to finance the proposed direct financial assistance program but specifically recommended against enactment of tuition tax credits. The Budget Committee preferred the direct financial assistance approach because, unlike the tax credits, financial assistance was not provided to high-

23. Ibid. (September 9, 1977), pp. S14510–16. Senator Long's position may seem inconsistent with his earlier opposition to the inclusion of specific tax assumptions in the Budget Committee report. The distinction is that a floor vote on a particular item expresses the will of the Senate; the Senate never votes on a Budget Committee report as such.

Acceptance by Senator Long and the Finance Committee of the Roth amendment to the budget resolution can hardly be taken as general acquiescence in such a procedure. One could expect substantial opposition from the Finance Committee to an amendment to a budget resolution that proposed, for example, an increase in revenues to make room in the budget for repeal of a tax expenditure such as the deduction for intangible drilling and development costs.

24. See ibid. (November 4, 1977), pp. S18792–803. The Conference Committee, however, deleted the Senate-passed college tuition tax credit from the final version of H.R. 9346, the Social Security Financing Amendments of 1977. See *Social Security Amendments of 1977*, H.Rept. 95-837, 95 Cong. 1 sess. (GPO, 1977), pp. 78–79.

income families, and therefore direct assistance was less expensive than tuition tax credits.[25]

During consideration of the First Concurrent Resolution on the 1979 budget on the House floor, an amendment was offered to provide $635 million more in revenue to accommodate the tuition tax credits than the Budget Committee had recommended. Despite arguments that the revenue reductions provided in the budget resolution were sufficient to accommodate tuition tax credits if adopted, the House passed the floor amendment.[26]

The Senate Budget Committee report on the First Concurrent Resolution for fiscal 1979 took no position on tuition tax credits. Instead it recommended a revenue floor that "would allow for a number of legislative proposals including a college tuition tax credit."[27]

The Conference Committee report on the First Concurrent Resolution for fiscal 1979 provided a revenue floor that would accommodate both a tuition tax credit and funds for direct student assistance, although less than recommended by the House. Subsequent House debates revealed that both proponents and opponents understood

25. Recognizing the political force behind the tax credit approach, however, the report stated: "In line with views expressed by the Appropriations Committee, the Committee recommends that if Congress agrees to a revenue reduction to accommodate tuition tax credits, then the additional budget authority and outlays provided in this function (education) for the proposed Middle-Income Student Assistance Act should be eliminated." (*First Concurrent Resolution on the Budget, Fiscal Year 1979,* H.Rept. 95-1055, 95 Cong. 2 sess. [GPO, 1978], p. 7.) As to other tax expenditure matters: "The Committee strongly supports tax reform to reduce unnecessary tax expenditures. It assumes that any reduction in individual or corporate taxes beyond the level recommended by the Committee will be offset, dollar for dollar, by revenue gains achieved through tax reform." (Ibid., p. 13.) The report also showed total tax expenditures for each budget function.

26. *Congressional Record,* daily edition (May 4, 1978), pp. H3595–607.

27. *First Concurrent Resolution on the Budget, Fiscal Year 1979,* S.Rept. 95-739, 95 Cong. 2 sess. (GPO, 1978), p. 36. The Senate adopted the First Concurrent Budget Resolution without a discussion of the tuition tax credit issue. (*Congressional Record,* daily edition [May 15, 1978], p. S7458.) At the time of the floor consideration of the budget resolution, the Senate Finance Committee had approved a tax credit approach, and the Senate Education Committee had approved a direct assistance approach.

As to other tax expenditure matters, the Senate Budget Committee report made no assumptions about the elimination or reduction of tax expenditures, reiterating, however, the committee's view that "it is as important to control the growth of tax expenditures as it is to control the growth of direct spending programs." (S.Rept. 95-739, p. 36.) In addition, the Senate Budget Committee for the first time set forth in its report the tax expenditures related to each budget function. Indeed, the tax expenditure data provided by the Senate Budget Committee was more detailed than that in the corresponding House Budget Committee Report.

clearly that tax credits were to be considered an alternative to direct assistance and that the same standards—distribution of benefits by income classes, the balance of costs and benefits, constitutionality (under the House bill tax credits would benefit religious elementary and secondary schools), ease of administration—should be applied to each. Ultimately the House and the Senate passed the tax credit and the direct educational assistance measures. The tax credit, however, died in conference and the direct assistance bill was enacted.[28]

### Budget Resolutions and the Energy Bill

Senate debate on the energy bill occasioned a number of exchanges reminiscent of the debate between Senators Long and Muskie over the effect of the 1977 budget resolution. At the beginning of floor consideration in late 1977 the Budget Committee, and later Senator James Abourezk, challenged the energy bill on the ground that it provided $800 million more in tax reductions than the budget resolution permitted. Senator Abourezk lodged a number of points of order under various sections of the budget act, arguing first that the energy bill exceeded budget authority for 1978 and later that it contained tax provisions that would first become effective in fiscal year 1979, in apparent violation of the budget act's prohibition of such legislation until the First Concurrent Budget Resolution for that fiscal year had been enacted.[29] The chairman accepted none of Senator Abourezk's points of order and the energy bill moved ahead.[30]

### Other Aspects of the Budget Process

The House Budget Committee's Task Force on Tax Expenditures has held hearings on such proposed tax expenditures as the college tuition tax credit.[31] The Congressional Budget Office has cautiously

28. *Congressional Record,* daily edition (June 1, 1978), pp. H4727–4800, and (October 14, 1978), pp. S19141–44.

29. *Congressional Record,* daily edition (October 25, 1977), pp. S17679–84.

30. Many of the points of interaction between the budget process and the tax legislation process, which began in the 1976–77 period discussed in the text, were brought into sharper focus in the Revenue Act of 1978. Space does not permit discussion of that experience here. For a full discussion of the 1978 period, see Surrey and McDaniel, "The Tax Expenditure Concept: Current Developments."

31. *College Tuition Tax Credits,* Hearings before the Task Force on Tax Expenditures of the House Committee on the Budget, 95 Cong. 1 sess. (GPO, 1977). See also the task force hearings on the impact on cities of President Carter's proposed change in the investment tax credit (February 15, 1978). The Senate Budget Committee abandoned the use of its tax expenditure task force during 1976–78.

accelerated its activities with respect to tax expenditures. The Budget
Act of 1974 requires the CBO to provide information to the Budget
Committees on tax expenditures and upon request to any other committee or member of Congress "to the extent practicable."[32] The CBO
has prepared studies on real estate tax shelter subsidies and direct
subsidy alternatives, on the effects of various tax and nontax programs to provide financial assistance to middle-income families in-
curring costs of higher education, and on the refundable tax credit
for intercity bus companies contained in the energy tax bill in 1977.[33]

## Tax Expenditures and the Authorization-Appropriations Process

The impact of the tax expenditure concept on issues of committee
jurisdiction and the need to coordinate tax and direct programs were
brought into clearer focus during the 1976–78 legislative period.

### *Treatment of Refundable Tax Credits in the Budget Resolutions*

The proper treatment of refundable tax credits must be resolved
under the congressional budget process. Before the Third Concurrent
Budget Resolution for fiscal 1977, the House and Senate Budget
committees had reached a temporary accommodation on how to treat
the refundable portion of the earned income credit in the budget
resolutions. The House Budget Committee, following the policy of
the Office of Management and Budget on the president's budget, had
held that the refundable portion of a credit was an outlay. The Senate
Budget Committee, largely at the urging of Senator Long and the
Finance Committee, had held that the full cost of all credits should
be shown as a reduction in revenues. This debate continued, with
each side changing its position until agreement was reached by the
Conference Committee on the First Concurrent Budget Resolution

32. 88 Stat. 304, sec. 202(a)3 and sec. (c)1.

33. See Congressional Budget Office, *Real Estate Tax Shelter Subsidies and Direct
Subsidy Alternatives* (GPO, May 1977); CBO, *Federal Aid to Post-Secondary Students: Tax Allowances and Alternative Subsidies* (GPO, January 1978); *Congressional Record,* daily edition (October 26, 1977), p. S17826 (statement of Senator
Heinz); and CBO, *President Carter's Energy Proposals: A Perspective* (GPO, June
1977).

for 1979. The agreed upon position was that originally espoused by the House; the refundable part of tax credits would be treated as an outlay, not as a reduction in revenues.[34] This decision has some practical implications, although the budget deficit or surplus is unaffected by it.

First, the "scorekeeping" function established by the budget act requires the Budget committees to report periodically the effect on revenue and budget "outlays" of existing and proposed legislation. Treating the refundable portion of a tax credit as an outlay will make the item more visible than if it is submerged in total revenue figures.

Second, if the refundable portion of tax credits is classified as an outlay, the requirement of the budget act becomes operative that "outlays" and "new budget authority" must be allocated in the conference report on a concurrent budget resolution among each committee that has jurisdiction over bills and resolutions providing such new budget authority. The Finance Committee, for example, would then be limited by the "outlays" allocated to it. If the Finance Committee reported out a tax bill with refundable credits in excess of such outlays, the bill would have to be referred to the Appropriations Committee under section 401 of the budget act.

Third, if a refundable credit is an outlay, it would seem to follow that it also is spending authority under the act.[35] If so defined, a refundable tax credit effective in the next succeeding fiscal year would be subject to a point of order if it were considered before enactment of the first concurrent resolution for that fiscal year; no such point of order would lie if the tax credit were considered a reduction in revenue. Furthermore, the Appropriations committees would obtain jurisdiction to study the refundable tax expenditure "spending au-

34. For the full history of this exchange, see the following reports: (1) under the title *Third Concurrent Resolution on the Budget, Fiscal Year 1977*—H. Rept. 95-12, 95 Cong. 1 sess. (GPO, 1977), p. 6; S. Rept. 95-9, 95 Cong. 1 sess. (GPO, 1977), p. 13; and H. Rept. 95-30, 95 Cong. 1 sess. (GPO, 1977), p. 5; (2) *Second Concurrent Resolution on the Budget, Fiscal Year 1978,* H. Rept. 95-428, 95 Cong. 1 sess. (GPO, 1977), p. 5; (3) *First Concurrent Resolution on the Budget, Fiscal Year 1978,* S. Rept. 95-134, 95 Cong. 1 sess. (GPO, 1977), p. 5; (4) under the title *First Concurrent Resolution on the Budget, Fiscal Year 1979,* S. Rept. 95-739, p. 36; H. Rept. 95-1055, p. 150; and H. Rept. 95-1173; and (5) the daily edition of the *Congressional Record* for February 22, 1977 (pp. S2907–08); and September 15, 1977 (pp. S14971–72).

35. The terms "outlays" and "spending authority" are defined in 31 U.S.C., pars. 1302(a)(1) and 1351(c)(2), respectively.

thority" provisions and report from time to time their "recommendations for terminating or modifying such provisions."[36]

Finally, treating refundable credits as outlays would subject that portion of the resulting tax expenditure to the overall spending ceilings established by the budget resolution. As a result, tax expenditures would be required to compete with direct outlay programs in annual congressional appropriations. Furthermore, the freedom of the Finance Committee to use any mix it chooses of tax cuts and tax expenditures to achieve a given tax reduction would be circumscribed. Tax expenditures now escape such discipline.

### Energy Tax Legislation in 1977

The Finance Committee's real concern with the treatment of refundable tax credits may well stem from its realization that the exclusivity of its jurisdiction over tax expenditure aspects of tax legislation is at stake. The 1977 energy tax legislation illustrated this issue.[37]

ACTION IN THE HOUSE OF REPRESENTATIVES. When the president submitted his national energy plan, Speaker Thomas P. O'Neill, Jr., took a major step in implementing rational procedures for coordinating tax and direct expenditure programs by establishing an Ad Hoc Committee on Energy to receive and coordinate the reports of five standing committees, including the Ways and Means Committee, with jurisdiction over the National Energy Act.[38] The ad hoc committee had the unprecedented power to choose direct methods instead of tax approaches to energy problems, even if the Ways and Means Committee had already favorably reported tax measures. In fact, the various committee chairmen with responsibility for the energy legislation cooperated to a remarkable degree. Under this impressive procedure, the ad hoc committee considered over 113 separate legisla-

36. No point of order could be lodged, however, if the tax credit took effect two or more years after the fiscal year during which it is being considered. The relevant provisions of the budget act are sections 303(a), 303(b), 401, and 402(f), pp. 28, 36–38.

37. See Surrey and McDaniel, "The Tax Expenditure Concept: Current Developments," for a discussion of the 1978 aspects of the energy tax bill.

38. Executive Office of the President, Energy Policy and Planning, *National Energy Plan* (GPO, 1977). See H. Res. 508, 95 Cong. 1 sess. (GPO, 1977). For the House floor consideration of the resolution, see *Congressional Record,* daily edition (April 21, 1977), pp. H3349–55.

tive initiatives that had been proposed by some 200 House members of the standing committees.[39]

Chairman Ullman expressed the view that the procedure by the House on the energy legislation would have to be employed in the consideration of other complex issues.[40] The success of the technique, however, appeared to rest on two essential ingredients: strong leadership from the Speaker and the willingness of committee chairmen to work cooperatively. Neither of these factors was present as the Senate took up the energy tax legislation.

ACTION IN THE SENATE. The Senate abandoned the unified approach of the House. The tax portions of the House bill were referred to the Finance Committee and the nontax portions to the Energy Committee. The Finance Committee rejected the president's proposal, most of which had been approved by the House, to rely on excise taxes to curtail use of oil and gas. The Finance Committee recommended, instead, new tax expenditures (including five refundable tax credits) reducing federal revenues by a total of $40 billion through 1985.[41]

When the energy tax bill reached the Senate floor, Senator Ernest F. Hollings moved to refer the bill to the Appropriations Committee with instructions to report the bill back to the Senate with an amendment deleting the refundable portions of those tax credits that had not previously been approved by a full Senate vote. The Appropriations Committee position was that the refundable portion of each of

39. See *Report of the House Ad Hoc Committee on Energy,* H. Rept. 95-543, 95 Cong. 1 sess. (GPO, 1977); and *Congressional Record,* daily edition (August 1, 1977), p. H8173.

40. *Congressional Record,* daily edition (August 1, 1977), p. H8183. Congressman Ullman's view gains some support from the rather similar arrangements instituted for consideration of President Carter's welfare reform plan, The Program for Better Jobs and Income. This bill was referred to a special subcommittee consisting of selected members of the committees on Ways and Means, Agriculture, and Education and Labor. Whether chairmen of standing committees will be willing to surrender such powers in the future remains to be seen.

41. See *Energy Production and Conservation Tax Incentive Act,* S. Rept. 95-529, 95 Cong. 1 sess. (GPO, 1977), p. 122. The bill included refundable credits for (1) residential insulation costs; (2) residential solar, wind, and geothermal costs; (3) business investment in "alternative energy property"; (4) business investment in "specially defined energy property"; and (5) intercity bus transportation. The House bill did contain some new tax expenditures. For a critical analysis of those provisions, see Senator Kennedy's statement in *Congressional Record,* daily edition (September 7, 1977), p. S14272-78.

the credits constituted "spending authority" as defined in the budget act.[42]

Somewhat surprisingly Senator Long agreed to the referral to the Appropriations Committee.[43] However, he rejected the view that the budget act required such a referral. He argued that spending authority includes only payments "the budget authority for which is not provided for *in advance* by appropriations Acts."[44] The bill treated creditable amounts in excess of tax liability as overpayments of tax, thus triggering a refund. Because tax refunds are made under a permanent appropriation enacted in 1948,[45] Senator Long held that budget authority for refundable credits had been provided in advance and thus fell outside the purview of the budget act.

When Senator Hollings agreed to delete the reference to the budget act, Senator Long agreed to have the bill referred to the Appropriations Committee, which immediately reported it back to the floor with an amendment deleting the refundable portions of the credits.[46] The full Senate reversed the Appropriations Committee amendment and the refundable credits remained in the bill.[47]

Referral of the bill to the Appropriations Committee implied acceptance of the principle that the refundable portion of a tax credit is spending authority, because otherwise there was no reason to refer the energy bill to the Appropriations Committee. Senator Long's reliance on the 1948 permanent appropriation for tax refunds, however, seems misplaced. That act applies only to refunds of "moneys erroneously received," not to refundable credits correctly made under law.[48] Thus the language in the budget act should not be interpreted

42. Senator Hollings's motion was based on section 401(b)(2) of the budget act, which provides that in certain circumstances a bill reported by a committee containing new "spending authority" must be referred to the Appropriations Committee for up to fifteen days. Section 401(c)(2) defines spending authority. Section 401(b)(2) also requires that the legislation, if enacted, not exceed the budget authority allocated to the Finance Committee under the crosswalk provisions of section 302(b) of the budget act. The Finance Committee bill did not violate this provision if the refundable portions of the credits constituted spending authority. The floor debate on the Appropriations Committee motion appears in *Congressional Record,* daily edition (October 28, 1977), pp. S18037–52.

43. See *Congressional Record,* daily edition (October 28, 1977), pp. 18039–40.

44. 88 Stat. 317, par. 401(c)(2), p. 36 (emphasis added).

45. 31 U.S.C., sec. 711(3).

46. *Congressional Record,* daily edition (October 28, 1977), p. S18043.

47. Ibid., pp. S18044–52.

48. 31 U.S.C., sec. 711(3).

to exclude refundable credits from the definition of "spending authority."

The 1977 floor experience on the refundable energy tax credits revealed the need for carefully delineated procedures if the appropriations process is to be protected from circumvention by refundable tax expenditures. In fact, the same issue is presented by the nonrefundable portion of tax expenditures.

Recognition of this fact led Senator Kennedy to propose that whenever the Finance Committee reports a bill containing or extending a refundable or a nonrefundable tax expenditure (or a tax expenditure floor amendment is offered by, on behalf of, or with the approval of the committee), the measure must be referred to the Appropriations Committee and to each other committee with legislative jurisdiction over the subject matter encompassed by the tax expenditure provision.[49] Each committee would have fourteen days to consider the tax expenditure and report its recommendations to the Senate.

## Legislating Tax Expenditures

Full application of tax expenditure analysis requires nontax committees and staff to participate in the tax legislative process. Members and staffs of these committees have come to realize that tax expenditures have a significant effect on policies they are pursuing through direct programs. This section highlights the actual and potential involvement of nontax committees in the consideration of tax legislation.

### Senate Procedure

The standing rules of the Senate provide for joint referral of a bill to two or more committees on a motion of the majority and minority leaders. Technically this procedure permits referral of bills that include tax expenditures to both the Finance Committee and the legis-

---

49. *Amending Standing Rules . . .* , S. Res. 326, 95 Cong. 1 sess. (GPO, 1977). For a description of the extent of the overlap of the jurisdiction of the Senate Finance Committee and the House Ways and Means Committee (as a result of tax expenditures) with the jurisdictions of committees with legislative and appropriations responsibilities for direct programs in the areas covered by the tax expenditures, see Congressional Budget Office, *Five-Year Budget Projections: Fiscal Years 1979–1983, Supplement on Tax Expenditures, June 1978* (GPO, 1978), pp. 7–14; and the statement of Senator Kennedy, *Congressional Record,* daily edition (April 17, 1978), pp. S5703–04.

lative committee with jurisdiction over the subject matter covered by the tax expenditure. Senator Long in one instance at least defended the exclusive jurisdiction of the Finance Committee over tax expenditures by objecting to a proposed joint referral of a tax expenditure bill.[50]

### Senate Resolution 4

In 1977 the Senate reorganized the structure and jurisdiction of its committees through Senate Resolution 4. In the original version of Senate Resolution 4 each standing committee of the Senate would have been empowered to "study and review tax expenditures related to subject matters within its jurisdiction, and submit reports and its recommendations with respect thereto."[51] Senator Long, appearing before the Temporary Select Committee to Study the Senate Committee system, objected that the nontax committees already had the power to conduct such studies and that formalization in the Senate rules would lead to unnecessary duplication of committee work and staff personnel.[52] As a result, Senate Resolution 4, as reported by the Select Committee and adopted by the Senate, did not contain the language quoted above.[53]

### Hearings and Reports by Nontax Committees and Staff

Committees other than the Budget committees have involved themselves in tax legislation by holding hearings and issuing reports on tax expenditures within their legislative jurisdiction.[54] And as a result, the staffs of these committees have become more aggressive participants in the tax legislative process. In addition the Congressional Research Service of the Library of Congress has developed the staff

50. *Congressional Record,* daily edition (February 7, 1977), p. S2373.
51. Ibid. (January 4, 1977), p. S10.
52. Ibid. (January 18, 1977), p. S1629, S1640.
53. Ibid. (February 1, 1977), p. S1827; and ibid. (February 4, 1977), p. S2307.
54. See *Federal Tax Policy and Urban Development,* Hearings before the Subcommittee on the City of the House Committee on Banking, Finance and Urban Affairs, 95 Cong. 1 sess. (GPO, 1977); and *An Analysis of the Federal Tax Treatment of Oil and Gas and Some Policy Alternatives,* Senate Interior Committee, 93 Cong. 2 sess. (GPO, 1974). Some committees have involved themselves in tax provisions that are not tax expenditures. See, for example, *Foreign Tax Credits Claimed by United States Petroleum Companies,* Report of the Subcommittee on Commerce, Consumer and Monetary Affairs, House Government Operations Committee, H. Rept. 95-1240, 95 Cong. 2 sess. (GPO, 1978).

capacity to deal with tax expenditure issues and has prepared reports on various provisions that have proved influential in congressional deliberations.[55]

Increasing involvement by nontax committees and staffs appears inevitable and desirable as the tax expenditure concept becomes integrated into congressional thinking and procedures, although this involvement complicates the tax legislative process. At a minimum the substantive expertise of these committees and staffs should improve the equity and efficiency of those tax expenditure programs that are employed. More broadly, better coordination of tax and direct-spending programs could result, with questions being raised more frequently about the wisdom and propriety of using the tax route.

*Sunset Legislation*

In 1976 and again in 1977 legislation was proposed to terminate authorizations of federal programs every five years—on a staggered basis—unless reenacted. Moreover, all programs, including tax expenditures, would be required to undergo a review by the executive branch (and by the appropriate congressional committees if necessary) before reenactment to see whether they should be retained. The purpose of the legislation was to ensure regular review of the need, effectiveness, and efficiency of each authorization.[56]

The 1977 proposal called for the termination of all tax expenditures after five years unless reenacted by the tax-writing committees after a "sunset" review.[57] Predictably the inclusion of tax expenditures in the sunset process aroused controversy. Director of the Office of Management and Budget Bert Lance supported the inclusion of tax expenditures, noting that a review of outlay programs in a given area

55. See J. Gravelle, Kent Hughes, and Warren E. Farb, "The Domestic International Sales Corporation (DISC) Provision and its Effect on Exports and Unemployment" (April 30, 1976), in *Congressional Record,* daily edition (May 3, 1976), pp. S6323–27; R. Tannenwald and W. E. Farb, "Comparative Cost-Effectiveness of Alternative Investment Tax Incentives" (June 7, 1976), in *Congressional Record* (June 8, 1976), pp. S8684–89; J. Gravelle, "Provisions Reducing the Effective Tax Rate of Commercial Banking Organizations" (January 19, 1977); J. Gravelle and Donald W. Kiefer, "Deferral and DISC: Two Targets of Tax Reform" (February 3, 1978), in ibid. (February 6 and 7, 1978), pp. S1286–91, S1409–13; and J. Gravelle and D. W. Kiefer, "U.S. Taxation of Citizens Working in Other Countries: An Economic Analysis" (April 20, 1978), in ibid. (April 24, 1978), pp. S6193–202.

56. Michael J. McIntyre, "The Sunset Bill: A Periodic Review for Tax Expenditures," *Tax Notes,* vol. 4 (August 9, 1976), p. 6.

57. See *Congressional Record,* daily edition (January 10, 1977), p. S144.

"without also reviewing tax expenditures (in the same area) would surely be inappropriate."[58]

Secretary of the Treasury Michael Blumenthal did not oppose sunset legislation for tax expenditures, but he dwelled on technical problems in implementing such a procedure. He held that terminating a tax expenditure is more complicated than terminating a direct program, in part because termination of one code provision frequently requires changes in others. He warned that interrelationships among tax provisions would require extensive study to determine the full economic effects of a given tax expenditure. Furthermore, substantive legislation, not mere termination dates, would be required to terminate tax expenditures resulting from regulations and rulings such as the exclusion for social security benefits and deferral of taxation of income earned by foreign subsidiaries of U.S. corporations. He also asserted that the influence of taxes on business and economic decisions creates the risk that total termination without transition rules might prove unfair.[59] While the Treasury statement identified problems, it did not address itself to their solutions.

Actually all the problems raised by the Treasury were soluble. Senator Kennedy pointed out that many of the problems identified by the Treasury were also problems in terminating direct programs. And he suggested that the requisite budgetary and legislative expertise existed to solve the problems in each case.[60]

The "problems" raised by the Treasury, not surprisingly, provided part of the ground for Senator Long to recommend that tax expenditures be exempted from sunset legislation.[61] The full Government Operations Committee accepted the amendment of Senators William Roth and John C. Danforth to retain the requirement that tax expenditures be reviewed periodically but to delete the automatic termination date. Feeling that review was no improvement on existing procedures, Senator John Glenn, the sponsor of the proposal to in-

58. *The Sunset Act of 1977,* Hearings before the Subcommittee on Intergovernmental Relations of the Senate Committee on Intergovernmental Affairs, 95 Cong. 1 sess. (GPO, 1977), p. 93.
59. Ibid., pp. 109, 114.
60. Ibid., p. 329. For example, the Treasury and Joint Committee staffs could be directed to prepare draft legislation in advance of the scheduled termination date that would include suggested termination and transition language. The Treasury staff, on further reflection, recognized that definitional problems did not really exist and submitted a letter from Secretary Blumenthal to that effect (ibid., pp. 120–22).
61. Ibid., p. 484.

clude tax expenditures, moved to eliminate mention of tax expenditures from the committee's bill so that he could seek full inclusion of tax expenditures on the Senate floor.[62]

Many question the overall desirability of sunset legislation, but it is clear that if sunset legislation is enacted, it should apply to tax and direct expenditure programs alike. The technical problems envisioned by the Treasury are soluble. And a sunset process that excludes tax expenditure programs expending almost 25 percent of total federal funds would undoubtedly prove as unsatisfactory and ineffectual as a budget control process that failed to cover tax expenditures.[63]

*Development of Mechanisms to Coordinate Tax and Direct Expenditures*

At the end of 1977 implementation of a rational procedure to consider and coordinate direct expenditures and tax expenditures remained far from realization. Nonetheless, in particular instances effective coordination has taken place. In addition there were signs of movement toward a better system, although as expected, the path to reform has not proved an easy one.

The 1976–77 legislative experience did suggest some lessons to be learned and some possibilities for additional steps to move the legislative process toward integration of tax expenditures with direct spending programs.

First, achievement of the goal requires both forceful support by the leadership of each house and cooperation between the tax and nontax committees. That combination existed in the House of Representatives in its consideration of the 1977 energy legislation. It has not occurred in the Senate.

Second, the Budget committees can move to bring tax expenditures under control by using task forces on tax expenditures to hold hearings and to issue reports on tax expenditures; by requesting the Congressional Budget Office to prepare comprehensive reports on the tax

62. See Common Cause, "Sunset Process for Tax Loopholes," *In Common,* vol. 8 (Summer 1977), p. 14; Stanley S. Surrey, "Tax Expenditures Not in Sunset Bill," *Tax Notes,* vol. 5 (July 4, 1977), p. 7. Compare Senator Philip A. Hart's bill, S.921, to provide periodic review (but not termination) of tax expenditures; see *Congressional Record,* daily edition (March 4, 1977), p. S3489.

63. The text discussion of the sunset legislation is updated and elaborated in Surrey and McDaniel, "The Tax Expenditure Concept: Current Developments." Paul R. McDaniel, "Institutional Procedures for Congressional Review of Tax Expenditures," *Tax Notes,* vol. 7 (May 28, 1979), pp. 659–64.

expenditures selected for hearings; and by requesting program evaluations of tax expenditures conducted by the Office of Management and Budget, the Treasury, and other executive agencies.[64]

Third, the Budget committees should include in the body of the budget resolutions, and not just in the accompanying committee report, directions to reduce existing tax expenditures by a specified amount. The budget act provides authority for such an action in section 301(a)(6), which directs that the First Concurrent Budget Resolution shall include not only the recommended levels of revenues and the aggregate level of revenue increases or decreases, but also "such other matters relating to the Budget as may be appropriate to carry out the purposes of (the Budget) Act."

Fourth, the budget act should be amended to require closer coordination of tax and direct-spending programs between the tax committees and the authorizing and appropriations committees, perhaps along the lines of the resolution introduced by Senator Kennedy. The support of the chairmen of the nontax committees is, of course, essential to the success of such an effort.

Finally, without formal coordination, each authorizing committee can hold hearings and obtain from the CBO reports on particular tax expenditures. To date, neither tax-writing committee has shown any great interest in obtaining the objective studies necessary for intelligent evaluation of tax expenditures. The nontax committees could fill this vacuum by bringing their expertise to bear on proposed tax expenditures.

64. Section 801 of the budget act authorizes such requests. See also *Can Congress Control the Power of the Purse?* Hearings before the Senate Budget Committee, 95 Cong. 2 sess. (GPO, 1978).

# PART THREE

# The Tax Base

MICHAEL J. BOSKIN *Stanford University*

# Factor Supply and the Relationships among the Choice of Tax Base, Tax Rates, and the Unit of Account in the Design of an Optimal Tax System

THE EXTENSIVE DEVELOPMENT of the theory of optimal taxation has led to many important insights into the design of an optimal tax system.[1] While these insights are developed in the context of stylized models, they are considerably more rigorous than academic tax policy debates in past decades. The importance of the insights that these new analytical techniques provide is heightened by the enormous absolute and relative growth in the public sector in most economies in recent years, and by the concomitant increase in concern with tax, spending, and budget policy.

---

1. For some important discussions, see, for example, A. B. Atkinson and J. E. Stiglitz, "The Structure of Indirect Taxation and Economic Efficiency," *Journal of Public Economics,* vol. 1 (April 1972), pp. 97–119; Atkinson and Stiglitz, "The Design of Tax Structure: Direct vs. Indirect Taxation," ibid., vol. 6 (July-August 1976), pp. 55–75; Peter A. Diamond and James A. Mirrlees, "Optimal Taxation and Public Production, I: Production Efficiency," *American Economic Review,* vol. 61 (March 1971), pp. 8–27, and "Optimal Taxation and Public Production, II: Tax Rules," ibid. (June 1971), pp. 261–78; and J. A. Mirrlees, "An Exploration in the Theory of Optimum Income Taxation," *Review of Economic Studies,* vol. 38 (April 1971), pp. 175–208.

The most important general lesson from the theory of optimal taxation is the crucial dependence of optimal tax and spending policies on the induced behavior of the private sector of the economy. It simply does not make sense to analyze such questions as the appropriate rate of discount for use in cost-benefit analysis, the proper unit of account for personal taxation, and the most desirable tax base without paying considerable attention to whether, how much, and when alternative tax and spending programs would affect such private decisions as the supply of labor, saving, investment, and demands for different commodities.

Except under very special circumstances, the spending and taxing decisions of the government are not separable, for each change in tax base or rate, or in spending, will affect private demands for goods and supplies of factors of production and thus will affect tax revenues as well.[2]

Among the most important economic decisions of the public sector are:

*Spending*

—How much should the government spend on goods and services and how should such expenditures vary through time?

—How should the government divide its spending between investment and consumption and, within each category, among alternative projects?

—How large should transfer payments be and how should they vary through time?

*Financing expenditures*

—What is the appropriate mix among tax, debt, and inflationary finance?

—What types of taxes should be employed and how should tax burdens be divided among persons? (This issue involves the choice of tax base, rates, and the unit and time period of account.)

*The appropriate level at which activity is to be carried out*

—What level of government should make tax and spending decisions?

—To what extent should the government seek to achieve collec-

---

2. See Lawrence J. Lau, Eytan Sheshinski, and Joseph E. Stiglitz, "Efficiency in the Optimum Supply of Public Goods," *Econometrica*, vol. 46 (March 1978), pp. 269–84, for a discussion of separability conditions.

tive goals through regulation or mandated private activity rather than taxation or public expenditures?

In principle all these decisions are closely related and should be made jointly. For example, if the government invests in roads, it may increase the productivity of private resources and hence increase tax revenues in future periods. Going beyond such simple observations is difficult in practice because thinking about one problem at a time is much easier than weighing many simultaneously. Too often statements about a particular feature of the desirable tax or spending system are made *unconditionally*. Almost always such statements about particular features should be made *conditional* on the other features of the system.

This paper illustrates this basic point by focusing on some of the key interrelationships among the choice of tax base, tax rates, and the unit of account for tax purposes. It ignores spending, debt, and monetary policy, although in principle they should be considered simultaneously. It is concerned with why statements such as "the appropriate tax base is income" should not be made without simultaneously considering the rate structure and unit of account.

The first section presents the archetypical optimal tax problem by focusing on a special linear case. An important conclusion of this section (and the optimal tax literature in general) is that the optimal progressivity of the tax-transfer system depends crucially (and inversely) on the compensated elasticity of labor supply.

The second section addresses the issue of the appropriate unit of account for personal taxation. Again, the compensated labor supply elasticities of husbands and wives play a crucial role.

The third section presents a heuristic discussion of the choice of tax base in an intertemporal setting. In a stylized life cycle model the optimal base depends crucially on compensated own- and cross-elasticities of labor supply and working period and retirement consumption.

The final section addresses the interrelationship of these issues. Because each depends crucially on labor supply elasticities and other economic parameters, they must be closely interrelated. The optimal rates, base, and taxable unit each depend on these elasticities and other parameters, including other tax provisions. *Thus setting each tax policy places restrictions on the optimal design of other features of the tax system.* For this reason, the prescriptions emerging from analyses that ignore such interrelationships are likely to be inconsistent.

## The Optimal (Linear) Income Tax–Transfer System

Debate about taxation is no doubt as old as taxes themselves. Adam Smith propounded four canons of taxation: equality, certainty, convenience of payment, and economy in collection.[3] The modern counterparts of these principles are such widely used criteria as equity, ability to pay, and equal sacrifice. A host of ninteenth- and twentieth-century writers has advanced the precision and rigor of tax analysis.[4] The utilitarian approach of these writers has been applied to a wide variety of problems, both in and out of public finance. Its unifying theme is the study of how to achieve such goals as raising revenues in order to maximize, or at least improve, social welfare (which in turn depends on the welfare of individuals) under certain assumptions regarding the behavior of consumers, investors, and other economically relevant actors.

This approach to public finance problems has been applied to such diverse issues as the desirability of housing subsidies, public utility pricing, congestion tolls, optimal indirect taxation, the choice between credits and deductions, and tax expenditures.[5] A series of recent papers has relaxed some of the more restrictive assumptions

3. Adam Smith, *An Inquiry into the Nature and Causes of the Wealth of Nations*, vol. 2 (Oxford: Clarendon Press, 1976), pp. 825–27.
4. See Jules Dupuit, *Troite théorique et pratique de la conduite et de la distribution des eaux* (Paris, 1854); F. Y. Edgeworth, "The Pure Theory of Taxation," *Economic Journal*, vol. 7 (March 1897), pp. 46–70; F. P. Ramsey, "A Contribution to the Theory of Taxation," ibid., vol. 37 (March 1927), pp. 47–61; A. C. Pigou, *A Study in Public Finance*, 3d ed. (London: Macmillan, 1947); Harold Hotelling, "The General Welfare in Relation to Problems of Railroad and Utility Rates," *Econometrica*, vol. 6 (July 1938), pp. 242–69; M. Boiteux, "Sur la gestion des monopoles publics astreint à l'équilibre budgétaire," ibid., vol. 24 (January 1956), pp. 22–40; and Arnold C. Harberger, "The Measurement of Waste," *American Economic Review*, vol. 54 (May 1964, *Papers and Proceedings, 1963*), pp. 58–76.
5. See Atkinson and Stiglitz, "The Design of Tax Structure"; Herbert Mohring, "The Peak Load Problem with Increasing Returns and Pricing Constraints," *American Economic Review*, vol. 60 (September 1970), pp. 693–705; Diamond and Mirrlees, "Optimal Taxation and Public Production, I and II"; Joseph E. Stiglitz and Michael J. Boskin, "Some Lessons from the New Public Finance," *American Economic Review*, vol. 67 (February 1977, *Papers and Proceedings, 1976*), pp. 295–301; and Martin Feldstein, "The Theory of Tax Expenditures" (Harvard University, n.d.).

of the theory, although generally at the expense of considerably complicating the optimal tax rules.[6]

The earliest rigorous analysis of optimal direct taxation was that of Edgeworth.[7] He argued that if all people have identical declining marginal utility of income functions, the maximization of the sum of utilities (his measure of social welfare) required equalization of income! Of course, this analysis ignores the potential disincentives to supply labor and to save that are created by extremely high tax rates. Incredibly the optimal tax problem was not analyzed within the utilitarian approach incorporating disincentive effects until quite recently. Starting with a remarkable paper by Mirrlees, there has been a series of analyses of the income tax rate structure that shows what structure maximizes social welfare, subject to a government revenue requirement, to a skill distribution, to individual preferences for income and leisure (more generally, producing income versus not producing income—for example, supplying labor, saving, educational investment, and so on), and to production possibilities.[8] Mirrlees' surprising result is that for a utilitarian social welfare function (the sum of utilities), a Pareto or lognormal skill distribution, and elasticity of substitution between goods and leisure of unity (that is, a very elastic labor supply), the optimal tax rates are quite low and actually decline over some income ranges; rather little redistribution is optimal under Mirrlees' specification.

Other authors have extended Mirrlees' analysis to consider alternative social welfare functions, concern for relative income, the implications of endogenous wage rates, and alternative skill distributions and labor supply elasticities. In general the optimal marginal tax rates on different income classes depend on the concavity of the social welfare function, the distribution of ability or productivity, and the elasticity of labor supply.[9]

6. Useful surveys of the area may be found in Agnar Sandmo, "Optimal Taxation: An Introduction to the Literature," *Journal of Public Economics*, vol. 6 (July-August 1976), pp. 37–54; and Atkinson and Stiglitz, "The Structure of Indirect Taxation and Economic Efficiency." An interesting history of the development of this line of thought may be found in William Baumol and David Bradford, "Optimal Departures from Marginal Cost Pricing," *American Economic Review*, vol. 60 (June 1970), pp. 265–83.

7. Edgeworth, "The Pure Theory of Taxation."

8. See Mirrlees, "An Exploration in the Theory of Optimum Income Taxation."

9. See, for example, Anthony B. Atkinson, "How Progressive Should Income Tax Be?" in M. Parkin, ed., *Essays in Modern Economics* (London: Longmans, 1973); N. Stern, "On the Specification of Models of Optimum Income Taxation," *Journal of Public Economics*, vol. 6 (July-August 1976), pp. 123–62; Michael J. Boskin and

The generic optimal redistributive tax problem may be described as follows: people differ in "ability," which I index by $n$; $f(n)$ is the probability density of $n$, so that $\int f(n)\,dn = 1$. Individual utility depends on the consumption of goods and leisure:

(1) $$U = U(C_n, L_n),$$

where $C_n$ and $L_n$ are consumption and labor supply of persons with ability $n$. Income depends on ability and labor supply:

(2) $$Y = y(n, L_n) \quad \text{with} \quad \begin{aligned} y_n &> 0 \\ y_L &> 0. \end{aligned}$$

Because the government cannot measure ability, $n$, it cannot tax it; it can measure income, a compound of ability and labor supply. A linear negative income tax is imposed solely to attempt to redistribute income; the refundable credit to a person with no income is $g$, and the marginal tax rate is $t$. On the assumption that the budget must be balanced,

(3) $$g = t \int y(n, L_n) f(n)\,dn.$$

Hence the budget constraint for a person with ability level $n$ is

(4) $$C_n \leq y(n, L_n) + g - ty(n, L_n).$$

Individual maximization of equation 1 subject to condition 3 yields

(5) $$\begin{aligned} C_n^* &= C_n^*(g, t) \\ L_n^* &= L_n^*(g, t). \end{aligned}$$

In choosing $g$ and $t$, the government seeks to maximize social welfare subject to formula 3 and the behavior of individuals (defined by formula 5). This social welfare function may be represented as

(6) $$\int W(U_n(C_n^*, L_n^*))f(n)\,dn.$$

Eytan Sheshinski, "Optimal Redistributive Taxation When Individual Welfare Depends upon Relative Income," *Quarterly Journal of Economics*, vol. 92 (November 1978), pp. 589–601; Martin Feldstein, "On the Optimal Progressivity of the Income Tax," *Journal of Public Economics*, vol. 2 (November 1973), pp. 357–76; and J. A. Ordover and E. S. Phelps, "Linear Taxation of Wealth and Wages for Intragenerational Lifetime Justice: Some Steady-State Cases," *American Economic Review*, vol. 65 (September 1975), pp. 660–73.

Stiglitz has derived a simple formula for the calculation of the optimal $t$.[10] It simply equals the ratio of the normalized covariance between income and the marginal social utility of income to the average compensated labor supply elasticity:

$$(7) \qquad t = \frac{cov(Y, \, MSUY)/\bar{Y}}{\bar{n}_L},$$

where $MSUY$ is the marginal social utility of income (varying with $n$) and $\bar{Y}$ and $\bar{n}_L$ are average income and the average compensated labor supply elasticity, respectively.[11]

From the government's budget constraint—in this world where the tax system is used to finance transfer payments only—the optimal tax rate is also the relative income guarantee:

$$(8) \qquad t = \frac{g}{\bar{Y}}.$$

Hence the larger the covariance between income and the marginal social utility of income (reflecting greater dispersion of $n$ and greater concavity of $W$) is and the *smaller* the average compensated elasticity of labor supply, the more progressive the tax transfer system will be.

Put another way, the lower the elasticity of labor supply, the greater the degree of tax-transfer progression that appears to be justified. Low elasticities of labor supply also have important implications for the choice of tax base and the unit of account for personal taxation.

## The Unit of Account for Personal Taxation

The appropriate tax treatment of the family has been a basic issue in the design and implementation of taxation in every country employing direct taxation. Many countries use some combination of

10. Joseph Stiglitz, "Simple Formulae for Optimal Income Taxation and the Measurement of Inequality," IMSSS Technical Report 215 (Stanford University, August 1976).

11. Note that this covariance is itself dependent on $t$. The same may also be true of the labor supply elasticities; hence the optimal tax rate is not given by formula 7 explicitly as a function of the currently observed elasticities and covariance. The remaining discussion should therefore be considered heuristic. Stiglitz presents alternative explicit formulas for special cases of preferences and the skill distribution. See "Simple Formulae for Optimal Income Taxation and the Measurement of Inequality."

personal exemptions, deductions, and credits varying with family size. Several countries, including the United States, allow or require some type of income splitting among family members, while others rely on the individual as the unit of account for personal taxation. Income splitting, or pooling, creates a situation in which family members—for example, husbands and wives—face the same marginal tax rate however a given amount of earnings is divided between them. Because optimal tax theory implies heavier taxation of goods or factors in relatively inelastic demand, the question arises whether it is desirable to tax earnings of husbands and wives at the same rate.[12]

Consider the simplest case of a three-good economy where all persons are paired into households. Assume each household has a utility, $U$, of the form:

$$(9) \qquad\qquad U = U(C, L_1, L_2),$$

where $C$ denotes consumption of goods, $L_1$ is labor supplied by the husband, and $L_2$ is labor supplied by the wife.[13] The earnings of husbands and wives should be taxed equally, which is stipulated in U.S. tax law, if and only if their labor supplies have equal compensated cross-elasticities with respect to goods consumption. If the cross-substitution effect on labor supply is small relative to the own-substitution effects, the worker with the smaller own-compensated wage elasticity should be taxed more heavily.

If society is averse to inequality and relatively able husbands tend to marry relatively able wives, the results are more complex than otherwise, but the qualitative results are unaltered.[14] Wives account for a large and growing fraction of the market labor supply among married couples. Econometric studies suggest that the compensated labor supply elasticity for wives is about 1.0 and exceeds that of husbands.[15] Because labor supply elasticities of husbands run about one-

12. The inverse elasticity rule, cited in the text, is sometimes called the Ramsey rule after the British economist, Frank Ramsey, who first propounded it. It is approximately correct when cross-elasticities are small relative to own-elasticities. The general theorem is that the optimal tax system induces equi-proportionate reductions in compensated quantities demanded.

13. See Michael J. Boskin and Eytan Sheshinski, "Optimal Tax Treatment of the Family: Married Couples," *Journal of Public Economics*, 1980, forthcoming.

14. See ibid.

15. See, for example, Harvey S. Rosen, "Tax Illusion and the Labor Supply of Married Women," *Review of Economics and Statistics*, vol. 58 (May 1976), pp. 167–72; and James Heckman, "Shadow Prices, Market Wages, and Labor Supply," *Econometrica*, vol. 42 (July 1974), pp. 679–94.

sixth this size, it is clear that short-run efficiency requires much higher tax rates on husbands (more accurately, primary earners) than on wives (secondary earners). Over the long run, of course, husbands and wives could exchange roles as primary earners.

This principle, however, is related to the rule on progressivity presented above. Much progressivity is indicated if labor supply elasticities are low on the average. But labor supply elasticities can be low on the average only if the compensated labor supply of wives is not much more elastic than that of husbands. Thus the low average labor supply elasticities associated with a high degree of optimal progression are consistent with current income-splitting rules. Those implying taxation of individuals rather than families argue against extreme progression.[16]

## The Choice of Tax Base

Dropping the atemporal setting and considering the choice of tax base, again in a stylized model, let

$$(10) \qquad U = U(C_w, C_r, L_w),$$

where $C_w$ is the annual flow of consumption during working years, $C_r$ the annual flow of consumption during retirement, and $L_w$ the annual flow of leisure during working years. In such a model the optimal tax system requires heavier taxation in the period in which consumption is a weaker substitute for leisure.[17] If $C_w$ and $C_r$ are equally good substitutes for $L_w$, they should be taxed equally; that is, a consumption tax is optimal.[18] A heavier tax on $C_r$ than on $C_w$ implies taxation of interest income; the reverse implies its subsidization.

16. The analysis could be extended from the simple analysis in the section on the unit of account for taxation to the three-good case, based on a joint density of husbands' and wives' wages (assortive mating).

17. See Stiglitz and Boskin, "Some Lessons From the New Public Finance"; Atkinson and Stiglitz, "The Design of Tax Structure: Direct vs. Indirect Taxation"; Martin Feldstein, "The Welfare Cost of Capital Income Taxation," *Journal of Political Economy*, vol. 86 (April 1978), pp. S29–51; Michael J. Boskin and Lawrence J. Lau, "Taxation and Aggregate Factor Supply: Preliminary Estimates," in U.S. Department of the Treasury, *1978 Compendium of Tax Research* (GPO, 1978) pp. 3–19; and Michael J. Boskin, "Taxation, Saving and the Rate of Interest," *Journal of Political Economy*, vol. 86 (April 1978), pp. S3–27.

18. Adjusting for different lengths of the periods *C* and *R*. In a growing economy the argument is somewhat more complex. For a beginning on this problem, see Ordover and Phelps, "Linear Taxation of Wealth and Wages."

Hence the tax rates on capital income and earnings depend, as one expects, on the compensated own- and cross-price elasticities of current and future consumption and labor supply.

While many other features of the economy might affect such a decision, a major concern in the choice of tax base is the relative elasticities of labor supply and saving. If labor supply is completely inelastic and bequests are ignored, it is optimal to tax labor income only or, equivalently, consumption. If consumption is perfectly inelastic, it is optimal to tax only capital income (if sufficient revenue can be raised).

Heuristically speaking, given some nonzero elasticity of consumption,[19] the smaller the wage elasticity of labor supply, the less desirable is capital income taxation on efficiency grounds. An interesting conflict occurs, via the compensated wage elasticity of labor supply, between increasing progression and the taxation of capital income. As noted above, if the average compensated wage elasticity of labor supply is small, substantial progression may be optimal, but in a consumption tax, not an income tax. If the wage elasticity of labor supply is large, taxes on interest income will be desirable, but the amount of progression that is socially desirable is severely limited.

## Conclusion

I have briefly reviewed the application of the theory of optimal taxation to three crucial choices in tax policy: among tax rates, among tax bases, and among units of account. The optimal degree of progression, the choice between the individual and the family as the unit of account, and the appropriate tax base all depend crucially on private economic behavior, especially regarding labor supply and saving.

Empirical information on this behavior strongly affects the optimal tax system. Most important, policies concerning each of these issues should be set jointly. While these policies may be discussed separately, they ought to be analyzed simultaneously. For example, the analysis presented here suggests potential inconsistencies in support-

---

19. A nonzero forward price elasticity of consumption is *not* the same thing as a nonzero interest elasticity of saving. Indeed, the price elasticity of consumption is one plus the saving elasticity. Hence it would require an enormous negative saving elasticity to create a zero elasticity of current consumption. See Feldstein, "The Welfare Cost of Capital Income Taxation."

ing a highly progressive income tax on pooled family income. Consistency may require those arguing for substantial progression in a family-based personal tax to change their views about the desirable tax base, away from income toward consumption; or it may require those arguing for consumption as the appropriate base to change their views about the unit of account and the optimal degree of progression.

As the accuracy and reliability of information concerning labor supply and saving improve, perhaps the wide disparity of opinion concerning the desirable tax base, unit of account, and degree of progression will diminish.

RICHARD GOODE *International Monetary Fund*

# Long-Term Averaging of Income for Tax Purposes

THE POSSIBILITY that fluctuating incomes will be taxed more heavily than stable incomes under a progressive income tax has long been recognized. In the 1920s Australia and the state of Wisconsin attempted to reduce this inequality by permitting taxpayers to average taxable incomes over periods of five years and three years, respectively. In 1939 William Vickrey set out a plan for averaging income for tax purposes over many years, ideally the taxpayer's whole adult lifetime.[1] Lifetime averaging has been endorsed by other eminent scholars and in the final days of the Ford administration was endorsed by the Treasury Department.[2] Other writers and at least two official bodies have rejected it without much discussion.[3] Indeed, except for

I gratefully acknowledge detailed criticisms and suggestions generously made by William Vickrey, who is not responsible, however, for any remaining errors of interpretation or analysis.

1. "Averaging of Income for Income-Tax Purposes," *Journal of Political Economy,* vol. 47 (June 1939), pp. 379–97, reprinted in Richard A. Musgrave and Carl S. Shoup, eds., *Readings in the Economics of Taxation* (Irwin for the American Economic Association, 1959), pp. 77–92.

2. Richard A. Musgrave endorsed the idea in a qualified way in *The Theory of Public Finance: A Study in Public Economy* (McGraw-Hill, 1959), p. 170. Carl S. Shoup did so emphatically in *Public Finance* (Aldine, 1969), pp. 325–26. Also see U.S. Treasury Department, *Blueprints for Basic Tax Reform* (Government Printing Office, 1977), p. 25.

3. The Carter Commission of Canada rejected long-term averaging both because it would be administratively complex and because it is, in the commission's judgment,

Vickrey's publications and articles by Bravman and Steger, there have been few, if any, detailed examinations of long-term averaging.[4]

Long-term averaging as used here means all plans for averaging income for tax purposes over periods of more than five or six years. Such plans are intended not only to take account of erratic fluctuations and cyclical movements of income but also to adjust for rising or falling trends. In principle, averaging would extend over a person's adult lifetime, but an averaging period might have to be terminated when an important change in the taxpayer's status—such as marriage, divorce, death of spouse, or emigration—occurred.

Supporters of long-term averaging maintain that it is more equitable and simpler than annual taxation and that it facilitates using the income tax for economic stabilization.

This paper describes methods of long-term averaging, appraises the claims made for it, and comments on its probable operating characteristics and problems.

## Methods of Long-Term Averaging

The long-term averaging plans considered here are versions of cumulative or progressive averaging. Under these plans tax liability

---

not justifiable in principle; see *Report of the Royal Commission on Taxation,* vol. 3: *Taxation of Income* (Ottawa: Queen's Printer, 1966), p. 257. An Australian official committee was attracted to lifetime averaging on equity grounds and even remarked that "more than a single lifetime is relevant when the fairness of taxation upon an individual's capacity to do his duty to his heirs is considered" but added that "this lifetime perspective is not, of course, a practicable basis for taxation." See *Taxation Review Committee Preliminary Report, 1 June 1974* (Canberra: Australian Government Publishing Service, 1974), p. 16; the same passage appears also in *Taxation Review Committee Full Report, 31 January 1975* (Canberra: AGPS, 1975), p. 14.

4. See the following work by William Vickrey: "Averaging of Income for Income-Tax Purposes"; "The Effect of Averaging on the Cyclical Sensitivity of the Yield of the Income Tax," *Journal of Political Economy,* vol. 53 (September 1945), pp. 275–77; *Agenda for Progressive Taxation* (Ronald Press, 1947; Clifton, N.J.: Kelley, 1972), pp. 164–97, 285–87, 417–27; "Tax Simplification through Cumulative Averaging," *Law and Contemporary Problems,* vol. 34 (Autumn 1969), pp. 736–50; "Cumulative Averaging after Thirty Years," in Richard M. Bird and John G. Head, eds., *Modern Fiscal Issues: Essays in Honor of Carl S. Shoup* (University of Toronto Press, 1972), pp. 117–33. See also M. Francis Bravman, "Equalization of Tax on All Individuals with the Same Aggregate Income over Same Number of Years," *Columbia Law Review,* vol. 50 (January 1950), pp. 1–28; and Wilbur A. Steger, "Lifetime Income Averaging: What It Means for the Professional," *Tax Law Review,* vol. 12 (May 1957), pp. 427–33; and Steger, "Averaging of Income for Income Tax Purposes," in *Tax Revision: Compendium of Papers on Broadening the Tax Base,* submitted to the House Committee on Ways and Means (GPO, 1959), vol. 1, pp. 589–620.

in any year is related to a cumulative average that includes the income of the current year and all preceding years of the averaging period. Thus the income of the first year of the period enters into the cumulative average calculated in each subsequent year of the period. A cumulative average differs from a moving average, in which the earliest year is dropped when the latest year is added, and from a block average, which is computed at the end of the period with each year entering into the average only once.

## The Simple Method

The simplest method of long-term averaging would be to calculate tax liability each year by applying the current tax rates to cumulative average income. Clearly this method is unacceptable because it would create a severe liquidity problem or possible insolvency for persons experiencing a sharp decline in income. In a year of low or negative income following a period of high income, the taxpayer would face a liability based on a much higher cumulative average income. During the Great Depression this characteristic led to the repeal of the Wisconsin averaging plan, which used a three-year moving average.

## The Australian Method and an Alternative

Two methods, which have been used or suggested for short-term averaging but which could be adapted to long-term averaging, would reduce the problem inherent in the simple method. One was used in Australia in a general averaging system between 1921 and 1937 and is still used in a system confined mainly to primary producers (but covering their income from all sources). Under this method, the tax liability for each year is calculated by applying to the income of that year the effective rate in the current year's tax schedule on an income equal to the average income (a moving average in Australia but a cumulative average if desired).[5] In 1949 Holt suggested a modification of the Australian system to make tax liability respond more quickly to changes in income.[6] Under Holt's method the tax in any year would be the sum of two parts: (1) the stabilized tax, computed by applying the progressive rate schedule to average income; and (2) a fluctuation adjustment, equal to the product of the stabi-

5. When the average income exceeds the current income, the Australian tax is now determined by reference to the current income rather than the average income; this important change, effective July 1, 1978, is not reflected elsewhere in this paper.

6. Charles C. Holt, "Averaging of Income for Tax Purposes: Equity and Fiscal-Policy Considerations," *National Tax Journal,* vol. 2 (December 1949), pp. 349–61.

Table 1. Tax Liability under Two Income Assumptions, Using Annual Taxation and Three Averaging Methods[a]
Dollars

| | Income and tax | |
|---|---|---|
| Item | Taxpayer A | Taxpayer B |
| Income period | Taxable income | |
| Years 1–10 | 400,000 | 400,000 |
| Year 11 | 7,000 | 73,000 |
| Years 1–11, cumulative average | 37,000 | 43,000 |
| Method of taxation | Tax liability in year 11 | |
| Annual | 586 | 27,610 |
| Simple averaging | 9,416 | 12,050 |
| Australian-type averaging[b] | 1,781 | 20,455 |
| Holt-proposal averaging[c] | −3,184[d] | 25,550[e] |

a. U.S. 1977 tax rate schedule; taxpayers are married and filing joint returns; no allowance is made for the general tax credit and the maximum tax on earned income.

b. Effective rate is derived from average income over years 1 through 11.

c. Charles C. Holt, "Averaging of Income for Tax Purposes: Equity and Fiscal Policy Considerations," National Tax Journal, vol. 2 (December 1949), pp. 349–61.

d. A 42 percent stabilized marginal tax rate results in a fluctuation adjustment of −$12,600, which is summed with the tax derived by simple averaging ($9,416).

e. A 45 percent stabilized marginal tax rate results in a fluctuation adjustment of $13,500, which is summed with the tax derived by simple averaging ($12,050).

lized marginal tax rate (from the progressive rate schedule at the average income level) and the difference between the current income and the average income. (Holt's suggestion includes other features, which are not essential to this discussion.) The three averaging methods are illustrated in table 1 (which also shows the tax liability under annual taxation) for taxpayer A, whose income decreases in year eleven of an averaging period, and for taxpayer B, whose income increases in year eleven.

### Vickrey's Proposal

Vickrey's highly sophisticated proposal is intended to allow both for income variations and for the time at which tax is paid. The purpose is to make the income tax neutral, or as nearly so as feasible, with respect to the timing of a given amount of income over a period of years. Neutrality in this context means that the present value of tax payments during an averaging period would be the same regardless of when the income was reported and tax paid on it. Vickrey's plan, as he succinctly described it, would involve

considering all payments of income tax, with respect to income reported since some base starting date, as interest-bearing deposits in a tax-payer's account with the treasury. The accumulated balance in this account would then be available as a credit against whatever tax is found to be due for the entire period to date, on the basis of the total income thus far reported for the period, according to a tax schedule appropriate to the period covered.[7]

The interest credited on the tax account would be included in cumulative taxable income.

Under Vickrey's proposal separate tax rate schedules would be required for different numbers of years of cumulative averaging. These tables would be similar to the present one-year tables but would have wider income brackets: the distance between the boundaries for two years would be somewhat more than twice that for one year, for three years somewhat more than three times that for one year, and so on. The tax rates in the multiyear tables would be somewhat higher than in the one-year schedule to allow for interest. To illustrate, assume an interest rate of 8 percent a year and consider a married couple filing a joint tax return. In the 1977 (one-year) tax rate table income between $23,000 and $27,200 was subject to a rate of 32 percent. In a two-year table the corresponding bracket would be $46,750.40 through $54,852.80 and the bracket rate 32.859 percent. For three years, the bracket would be $70,679.23 through $82,994.62 and the rate 33.741 percent.[8] The tables apply to cumulative income rather than average income, but of course they could easily be converted to an average income basis if desired.

## Equity

Under a progressive rate schedule the tax liability on a given amount of income may be greater if income fluctuates than if it is received steadily. Because income averaging reduces such differences, most tax analysts agree that some form of short-period averaging is desirable and that the more progressive the tax rates, the stronger the case for averaging. But no consensus exists about the fairness of long averaging periods.

Those who favor lifetime averaging seem to regard it as intuitively obvious that taxpaying ability should be measured by lifetime income

7. "Cumulative Averaging after Thirty Years," pp. 117–18.
8. These numbers could be rounded without seriously affecting the system. For an explanation of the construction of the tables and illustrative tables, see Vickrey, *Agenda,* pp. 417–22.

(or consumption). Sometimes they appear to assume that people in fact plan their affairs on the basis of their expectations for their life-times. This assumption is compatible with the permanent-income hypothesis concerning the consumption function and with human capital theory. By saving and dissaving, individuals can obtain a smoother pattern of consumption than of income. Hence the case for long-term averaging would be weaker under an expenditure tax than under the income tax. Some advocates of the expenditure tax, how-ever, support long-term averaging for that tax to lessen discrimination against lumpy consumption outlays and gifts and bequests (if classi-fied as taxable consumption).[9]

Critics of long-term averaging reject the assumption of continuity underlying it, stressing changes in an individual's needs and capacities and in the economic environment over long periods of time. They argue that lack of foresight and imperfections in the capital market severely constrain the possibility of optimizing consumption rates over a person's life cycle and they imply that the marginal utility of income may be lower and ability to pay taxes greater during peak in-come years than at other times. They conclude that it is reasonable that people be exposed to the full rigors of tax progressivity during the part of their life cycles when income is highest without the possi-bility of obtaining tax rebates after retirement.[10]

Changes in statutory tax rates raise other issues. While long-term averaging would be simpler if statutory rates were constant, rate changes could be made under all averaging plans. Under simple aver-aging, the Australian method, and the Holt modification no adjust-ment for rate changes would be made; current rates would be used in all tax computations. Under Vickrey's proposal the multiyear tables would reflect the statutory rates in force in each of the years covered. Changes in personal exemptions, personal deductions, and tax credits presumably could be taken into account under all plans by averaging the income after exemptions and deductions and applying tax credits

9. See ibid., pp. 195–97; and Institute for Fiscal Studies, *The Structure and Reform of Direct Taxation: Report of a Committee Chaired by Professor J. E. Meade* (London: Allen and Unwin, 1978), pp. 38–39, 185.

10. These arguments are more prominent in the oral tradition of tax specialists than in the literature. See, however, Louis Shere, "Federal Corporate Income Tax—Revenue and Reform," *National Tax Journal*, vol. 2 (June 1949), pp. 117–18; John Willis, *The Mitigation of the Tax Penalty on Fluctuating or Irregular Incomes*, Canadian Tax Papers, no. 2 (Toronto: Canadian Tax Foundation, 1951), pp. 35–36; and Steger, "Averaging of Income for Income Tax Purposes," pp. 593–95.

to the tax computed under the averaging scheme, more or less as is now done in short-term averaging.

Endorsement of long-term averaging implies the judgment that persons having equal incomes, equal personal deductions, and equal personal exemptions in any year should pay different amounts of tax in that year if their previous taxable incomes, even in the distant past, differ. Under Vickrey's version of long-term averaging, moreover, persons who had earned equal incomes in each year from the beginning of their employment would face different marginal tax rates if their working careers, and hence their individual averaging periods, were unequal in length. These differences would be due to the interest factor and to changes in statutory (one-year) tax rates during the averaging period that would affect the multiyear tables for later years.[11]

Long-term averaging would reduce, or eliminate, the tax consequences of interaction between changes in statutory tax rates and fluctuations of income. Thus a person whose income happened to be unusually high in a year in which tax rates were temporarily increased would be less affected by the rate change than under the present system. Similarly a person whose income was unusually low in a year of reduced tax rates would benefit more under long-term averaging than under the present system. Advocates of long-term averaging regard these results as desirable on equity grounds. Critics argue that the interaction between variations of tax rates and variations of income is appropriate. Tax rate changes, they maintain, imply changes in social priorities that should not be blurred by averaging. Increased tax rates during a war or other defense emergency, for example, imply that people with unusually large incomes during that period should be subject to the full weight of the higher rates.

Important questions of equity—and of tax design and administration—arise from changes in the purchasing power of money. When lifetime averaging was originally proposed, these problems seemed unimportant. Now probably all would agree that adjustments for

---

11. See the illustrative rate schedules and computations in Vickrey, *Agenda*, pp. 417–19. Assume that in each of the years 1947 and 1948 taxpayer A received $6,000 of surtax net income (exclusive of interest credited on the tax paid in 1947) and that taxpayer B began his averaging period in 1948 with a net income of $6,000. In 1948 both A and B would owe $1,386 of tax. But A's marginal tax rate that would have applied if his income had risen somewhat above $6,000 (as the result of, say, overtime work) would be 36.5331 percent, and B's marginal rate would be 30 percent.

inflation would be an essential feature of long-term averaging. Further reference is made to this subject below.

Judgments on the equity issues are largely subjective, and readers will differ in their appraisals. My conclusion is that the arguments on equity grounds for long-term averaging are not persuasive.

## Stabilization

The significance of long-term averaging for economic stabilization is related to its influence on the built-in flexibility of tax liabilities and on the use of discretionary changes in the income tax for stabilization purposes.

### Built-in Flexibility

Long-term averaging would lessen variations in the marginal tax rates applicable to changes in income. This characteristic would tend to reduce built-in flexibility in periods of economic expansion, when incomes are rising; however, other features of the averaging plans have to be taken into account. In periods of recession, when incomes are falling, the plans would differ in their effects on built-in flexibility.

The simplest long-term averaging plan, under which current-year tax liabilities would depend solely on cumulative average income, would result in the longest lags between changes in income and changes in income tax. The hardships that taxpayers might suffer in years when their income drops sharply make this plan unacceptable. The Australian method, while avoiding extreme disparities between tax liability and current income, is characterized by slow changes in effective tax rates (and in implied marginal rates). It also would have considerably less built-in flexibility than the present system during both expansions and contractions of income. The reduction in built-in flexibility would be greater in a long-term averaging system using the Australian method than it is with the five-year moving mean used in Australia for primary producers.

Both Vickrey and Holt were mindful of the stabilization aspects of averaging. Their plans would increase built-in flexibility in periods of falling income. These authors concentrated on the possibility of countering a recession by automatic and discretionary tax reductions, but they gave far less attention to ways of modifying tax policy when income is rising too rapidly—an attitude widely shared and fully understandable when they wrote.

Basically, in Vickrey's scheme a person's marginal tax rate would depend on his whole income record during the averaging period. In tables covering many years the brackets would be very broad; hence the marginal tax rate would be stable for wide fluctuations in income. When income rose, the marginal tax rate would increase less than under annual assessment. This factor would tend to cause tax liability to increase less. On the other hand, because of the interest factor, effective marginal tax rates would be somewhat higher than under an annual system with stable statutory rates (see the illustrative brackets and rates above), and this would enhance the increase in tax liability. The net effect would depend on the steepness of tax progressivity, the interest rate applied, the length of the averaging period, and other factors. It seems likely that in periods of expansion the widening of the brackets would predominate and that built-in flexibility would be lessened. When income declined, the marginal rate would fall less than under a strict annual system, but the credit for the cumulative amount of tax paid in previous years of the averaging period, plus accrued interest on this sum, would reduce the additional amount to be paid and could result in tax refunds. Built-in flexibility would be enhanced during periods of contraction.[12]

Holt's averaging method would reduce built-in flexibility in periods of rising income because the effective marginal tax rate would be determined by reference to average incomes rather than to the higher current incomes. Under the method he suggests for calculating a fluctuation adjustment, taxpayers who suffered an abrupt fall of income would often receive greater tax reductions than under an annual system because the (negative) adjustment would be calculated at a fixed, rather than a declining, marginal rate. Built-in flexibility would

12. Built-in flexibility can be illustrated using the two-year and three-year tables based on the 1977 (one-year) rate table, from which excerpts are given in the text. Assume that the couple's taxable income was $25,200 in each of years 1 and 2. If in year 3 their taxable income should increase to $50,400, their tax would be $14,343 under Vickrey's system, compared with $15,660 under strict annual taxation. Their weighted marginal rates (the change in tax between years 2 and 3 divided by the change in income) under the two systems would be 36.996 percent and 42.222 percent, respectively. Alternatively, if their taxable income should fall to $12,600 in year 3, their tax would be $915 under Vickrey's system, compared with $1,688 under strict annual taxation. Their weighted marginal rates under the two systems would be 32.579 percent and 26.444 percent, respectively.

be increased. There appears to be no simple way of comparing the degree of built-in flexibility in Vickrey's scheme with that in a long-term averaging system incorporating Holt's method of determining the tax rate. It should be emphasized that Holt proposed short-term averaging, not long-term, with recent years weighted more heavily than earlier years. He was confident that his system would exhibit more built-in flexibility than Vickrey's cumulative long-term averaging system.

### Discretionary Changes

Vickrey and Holt argued that the adoption of averaging would lessen the reluctance to adopt discretionary changes in tax rates for stabilization purposes because averaging would reduce inequities suffered by persons who have unusually high incomes in years of temporarily high tax rates or unusually low incomes when tax rates are temporarily reduced. As asserted above, however, the opposite view of equity seems at least as attractive. Holt suggested that averaging would make it easier to separate political debate about the right degree of progressivity from decisions about discretionary tax changes for stabilization purposes. This hope may have been reasonable in 1949, but the subsequent record does not generate optimism about the possibility. With or without income averaging, the obstacles to successful use of discretionary tax changes for stabilization purposes in the United States are likely to remain formidable.

## Administration and Compliance

Paradoxically, critics of long-term averaging often dismiss it as complex and impracticable, whereas its advocates represent it as an important simplification of the income tax. For example, Due and Friedlaender, at the end of their brief discussion of Vickrey's cumulative averaging proposal, comment that "the major limitation is the apparent complexity of the proposal, which has prevented it from receiving serious attention."[13] Vickrey stresses simplification as a major advantage of his proposal. Shoup agrees and goes so far as to say that "if lifetime averaging were adjudged somewhat undesirable on equity

---

13. John F. Due and Ann F. Friedlaender, *Government Finance: Economics of the Public Sector*, 6th ed. (Irwin, 1977), p. 248.

grounds, there would remain a strong case for it on grounds of simplification of the tax law and consequent savings in administrative and compliance expense."[14] Evidently the critics and the supporters are looking at different aspects of long-term averaging. The critics concentrate on problems of record-keeping and computation and, more fundamentally, public understanding. The supporters emphasize the avoidance of the difficulties of allocating business and investment income to particular years and the quieting of controversy due to the tax consequences of variations of income.

### Record-Keeping and Computations

Although tax liability would depend on the income of an averaging period that could extend over many years, the individual taxpayer would not necessarily have to keep elaborate accounts or extensive records. The taxpayer could obtain the information for calculating cumulative average income from the previous year's tax return or from a statement provided by the tax administration agency. The prior return or the statement would also show the cumulated tax on past income required under the Vickrey plan. If the tax liability had been fully paid, the taxpayer would then multiply the cumulated tax by the established interest rate to ascertain the interest to be credited to his tax account. The interest would be added to the cumulated tax and to the cumulated income brought forward from the previous year. The current year's income would be added to the cumulated income, as increased by the accrued interest, and tax would be computed on this amount using the table for the number of years included in the taxpayer's individual averaging period. The amount to be paid —or the refund due—would be the difference between the tax so computed and the balance in the cumulated tax account. The Holt method would omit the interest computation but would require a more complicated tax computation.

It would not be prudent to rely on all taxpayers to keep copies of their previous returns and to make correctly the computations required for long-term averaging. However, the development of automatic data processing and taxpayer master files appears to have made the record-keeping and computations more feasible for the Internal Revenue Service than they were when long-term averaging was originally proposed. The IRS now checks most income tax returns for

14. *Public Finance,* pp. 325–26.

arithmetic accuracy and will compute the tax due on simple returns (not including returns using income averaging) if requested to do so.[15]

A requirement that income records from the distant past be used may seem inconsistent with the thinking on which the statute of limitations is based. In the absence of fraud this statute bars the IRS from going back more than three years to correct errors and omissions in tax returns. The rationale is that it would be unreasonably burdensome to require the taxpayer to maintain the files and records—or to obtain other evidence—to support returns for earlier years. Nevertheless, information about transactions that occurred in the distant past can affect tax liability at present, notably in establishing the basis for determining long-term capital gains and losses. And in the determination of social security benefits, employment and contribution records for the individual's whole working life may be taken into account. On balance, the objection based on analogy with the statute of limitations is not weighty.

### Existing Averaging Provisions

Long-term averaging would supplant the present five-year averaging system, which was introduced in 1964 and modified in 1969. Computations probably would be no more complicated for long-term averaging than for the present system, but many more taxpayers would be affected. From 1964 through 1974 income averaging was used on only 0.38 percent to 3.29 percent of all returns.[16] Averaging was voluntary, and it appears that only a minority of those eligible elected it despite the tax savings obtainable.[17] The compulsory nature of the long-term averaging plans under discussion would aggravate compliance problems.

Long-term averaging would also replace certain special provisions intended to smooth out irregularities of taxable income, including the carry-over of business net operating losses and proration for

15. In 1976, 79.3 million individual income tax returns were verified by computer; arithmetic errors were detected in 8.8 percent of them. (Commissioner of Internal Revenue, *Annual Report, 1976*, p. 18.)

16. Eugene Steuerle, Richard McHugh, and Emil Sunley, *Income Averaging: Evidence on Benefits and Utilization*, U.S. Treasury Department, Office of Tax Analysis, Paper 24 (Treasury Department, 1977), p. 6.

17. In 1971 only 31 percent of the eligible taxpayers included in a Treasury Department panel study elected averaging. (Ibid., p. 12.)

lump-sum distributions from qualified pension plans. A small simplification would result from dropping these provisions.

### Capital Gains and Losses

The institution of long-term averaging could be credited with a major tax simplification if it were a necessary and sufficient condition for the elimination of special treatment of capital gains and losses. The preferential rates for long-term capital gains and the limitations on the deductibility of capital losses against other income make it essential to distinguish between capital gains and losses and other income and losses, though the economic differences are often small or nonexistent. Perhaps the most common form of tax avoidance for individuals is the conversion of ordinary income into capital gains, and attempts to prevent this have added to the length and complexity of the U.S. Internal Revenue Code and the regulations. Classification of transactions is a source of dispute and administrative difficulty. Because of the limitations on the deductibility of capital losses, moreover, the timing of transactions resulting in capital gains and losses sometimes becomes highly significant and induces artificial transactions and causes disputes. Surrey concluded that the capital gains provisions are "the subject singly responsible for the largest amount of complexity" in "probably the most complex revenue law ever enacted in the fiscal history of any country"—the Internal Revenue Code.[18]

In my judgment, however, long-term averaging is neither a sufficient nor a necessary condition for reform of capital gains taxation. While the irregularity of capital gains and their accrual in some cases over long periods of time are cited as justifications for preferential tax rates on them, the alleged incentive effects and the need to allow for inflation figure more prominently in debates on the subject. The adoption of long-term averaging would not negate the latter arguments. To be sure, some form of averaging would be needed to make full taxation of capital gains and full deductibility of capital losses acceptable, but short-term averaging or a simple proration system would be adequate.[19] Long-term averaging—especially Vickrey's

18. Stanley S. Surrey, "Definitional Problems in Capital Gains Taxation," in *Tax Revision Compendium*, vol. 2, p. 1203; for an earlier version of this paper, see *Harvard Law Review*, vol. 69 (April 1956), pp. 985–1019.

19. Richard Goode, *The Individual Income Tax*, rev. ed. (Brookings Institution, 1976), pp. 191–95.

version—would reduce incentives to postpone realization of taxable gains and thus would alleviate the lock-in problem. But this problem can also be attacked by other means, including provisions treating gifts and bequests as constructive realizations of gains and an adjustment to reduce the advantages of deferring tax on accrued gains until they are realized.[20]

### Timing of Income and Tax Payments

Those who believe that long-term averaging would help simplify the income tax also believe it would de-emphasize or eliminate many questions about the time of accrual or realization of income. These questions include when to expense and when to capitalize outlays intended to produce income, what depreciation rates to use, what bad debt and other contingency reserves to maintain, how to handle bond premiums and discounts, when to declare a property or claim worthless, and how to recover the cost of annuities. Vickrey argues that long-term averaging, together with full taxation of capital gains, would allow elimination of the corporation income tax and would make inconsequential for taxation the extent of retention or distribution of profits.

It is true that long-term averaging would lessen the influence of timing of income on tax liabilities and could therefore be expected to diminish controversies about this subject. But the postponement of tax payment would remain advantageous for taxpayers. Provisions designed to prevent postponement by establishing the time of income accrual or realization would continue to be needed, though enforcement perhaps could be somewhat more relaxed than at present.

Vickrey's proposal to credit interest on tax payments is intended to counteract the attractions of postponement and to make the system neutral with respect to the distribution over the taxpayer's life of his income and tax payments. This is the unique and most intriguing feature of Vickrey's scheme. In his opinion, taxpayers could safely be given complete freedom about when to report income and to pay tax, with a final settlement made at death or at the termination of the averaging period for other reasons. Settlement would involve valuation of the taxpayer's assets to bring to account the balance of previously unreported gains and losses and the payment of any final tax or

20. Roger Brinner, "Inflation, Deferral and the Neutral Taxation of Capital Gains," *National Tax Journal*, vol. 26 (December 1973), pp. 570–71.

refund. Many of the rules about the timing of income, Vickrey asserted, would become redundant and could be dropped. He estimated that the Internal Revenue Code could be cut in half and the regulations cut even more.[21] Measures to prevent understatement of income receipts, overstatement of costs, and the transfer of income between persons would still be needed, he acknowledged.

In my opinion, these claims are unjustified. Hardly any accounting rules for income determination could safely be eliminated under Vickrey's plan, as I shall try to demonstrate.

The clearest reason why existing accounting provisions would have to be continued after the adoption of cumulative averaging is that it would not be feasible to apply the system to nonresident aliens. Tax on corporate profits would have to be assessed to reach non-resident shareholders. (Some may argue that the corporation tax, even if it had no independent role, would be needed also to reach U.S. tax-exempt organizations that hold shares.) Other forms of income received by nonresident aliens from U.S. sources would have to be reported currently, to determine the applicable regular tax or withholding tax. Vickrey almost completely neglects the international aspects of his proposal, an omission that may have been excusable in 1939, when he originally advanced the idea, and in 1947, when he first elaborated it, but one that is not justified today.

With regard to residents, the appropriateness of the interest rate would be crucial. If the interest rate credited on tax payments equaled "the" discount rate, the timing of tax payments would be unimportant, provided adequate guarantees of ultimate payment exist. But imperfections in capital markets assure that no one interest rate can be appropriate for the Treasury and all taxpayers. The literature on the social discount rate for cost-benefit studies reveals the difficulties. They are underscored by the wide range of interest rates prevailing at any time. In mid-1977, for example, rates were about 7 percent on U.S. Treasury bonds, 8 percent on high-grade corporate bonds, and 9 percent on new home mortgages. Average rates on short-term commercial and industrial loans of commercial banks ranged from about 7.25 percent on loans of $1 million and over to about 9.25 percent on loans of less than $25,000.[22] Consumers earned 5 percent to 5.25 per-

---

21. "Tax Simplification through Cumulative Averaging," p. 744; "Cumulative Averaging after Thirty Years," p. 120.

22. *Federal Reserve Bulletin,* vol. 63 (November 1977), pp. A-26–27, A-40.

cent on passbook savings accounts but were generally paying about 18 percent on department store credit and credit card debts.

While crediting interest on the tax account under the Vickrey proposal would reduce the attractions of tax postponement, taxpayers whose subjective discount rate exceeded the interest rate applied to tax accounts would still wish to defer their tax payments. Those whose discount rate was lower than the interest rate would wish to accelerate their payments. Rates prevailing on loans and investments would, of course, influence taxpayers' preferences. Frequent adjustments of the interest rate on tax accounts would be advisable.

An extreme version of cumulative averaging would set the taxpayer's adult lifetime as the averaging period and would allow complete freedom in the time at which income was reported and tax paid, with final settlement of any outstanding tax liability or refund at death, after valuation of assets and liabilities. This system, in practice, would allow taxpayers the option of borrowing or lending to the Treasury at the established interest rate. A taxpayer might justifiably regard the current payment of income tax as voluntary. One who was unconcerned about the size of his estate might disregard an accumulating tax liability.

Even if these attitudes were unusual and the interest rate on tax accounts were set high enough to encourage early payment by most taxpayers, a substantial risk of insolvency and default would exist. The Treasury would be lending for long periods of time without collateral. The persons most inclined to accumulate large tax debts would be the most improvident and most speculatively inclined. Insolvency resulting from losses on bad investments would be an acceptable reason for nonpayment to the extent that the losses wiped out previous income, but insolvency resulting from consumption or gifts would be another matter. As a safeguard, Vickrey suggested that a taxpayer not be allowed to write down the book value of his net worth, on a tax accounting basis, to a negative or nominal amount.[23] This would impose a weak check on deferral of income and tax payment but would require the continuation of existing accounting rules.

The risks of revenue losses from insolvency would be reduced if the averaging period were shorter than a lifetime, but then the allocation of income between averaging periods could be highly significant. Such allocation, of course, requires ordinary accounting procedures and rules that Vickrey hopes to eliminate.

23. "Tax Simplification through Cumulative Averaging," pp. 740, 742.

For these reasons and because of other problems touched on in the next section, the present provisions of the Internal Revenue Code and regulations and the accompanying accounting rules would have to be continued. Cumulative long-term averaging provisions would be added to them and would not replace them.

### Possibility of Limited Coverage

Vickrey suggested that in a transitional period, long-term averaging could be confined to a small number of high-income people.[24] This limitation would greatly simplify record-keeping and computations, but clearly it would not permit any of the simplifying changes in tax law and regulations that have been represented as advantages of cumulative averaging. The suggested restriction of coverage would be objectionable on equity grounds. Long-term averaging would often be advantageous to taxpayers and the restriction of its benefits to a few could not be justified. High-income people do not suffer the most from overtaxation of fluctuating incomes. The loss of the benefit of personal exemptions and sharp changes in marginal tax rates are experienced by low-income people who move in and out of the taxable area. Most employed people, regardless of their earnings, experience a decline in taxable income after retirement, and it would not be defensible to allow those with high earnings, but not others, to recover in later years income taxes paid during their middle years, as would be possible under Vickrey's proposal and some other long-term averaging systems.

## Operating Characteristics and Problems

This section touches on several operating characteristics and problems of long-term averaging, though most of them can equally well be regarded as relating to the design of an averaging system.

### Inflation Adjustments

In present and foreseeable conditions it is regrettably not realistic to expect the purchasing power of money to be stable or to change so slowly that money amounts of income received in different years will be sufficiently comparable to justify their aggregation over many years without adjustment and taxation under a common schedule of progressive rates. Even with an essentially annual income tax, ad-

24. *Agenda*, pp. 192–93.

justment for inflation is widely discussed.[25] Comprehensive measures
adjusting for the effects of inflation on personal exemptions and tax
bracket rates and on the items entering into the measurement of income, including capital gains and losses, would be highly complex
and might not be practicable. The adoption of long-term averaging,
however, would not increase the need for adjusting the income computation. Indexing the reported amounts of money income, however
the income is determined, would overcome the decisive objection to
the aggregation of these amounts over periods when the price level
rose significantly. This limited adjustment would not be administratively difficult, though differences of opinion about the choice of a
suitable price index no doubt would arise.

### Termination of Averaging Periods

Generally the longer the averaging period the more advantageous
averaging would be for taxpayers. The determination of the circumstances that would require the termination of an averaging period
therefore would be important and would be controversial. A possible
approach would be to start the first averaging period for a person at
the age when participation in the labor force customarily begins and
to continue it until marriage, or death if the person never marries.
A new period would begin when a taxpayer married or a marriage
was ended by divorce or death. Termination of an averaging period
when a change in marital status occurred could be supported on the
grounds that new consumer units are created on these occasions and
that their taxpaying abilities should be evaluated separately from
those of the units that existed before. Allocation of income and taxes
between spouses would thus be simplified. Continuation of an averaging period after a change in marital status would be possible,
though clumsy and perhaps not practicable.[26] But a seemingly minor
technical provision for the termination of an averaging period whenever a change in marital status occurred could have financial consequences that might be considered undesirable in many cases. For
example, a single person whose income had been rising rapidly might
find that marriage would cause the loss of a tax benefit from averaging current income with lower income of prior years, whereas for a

25. See Henry J. Aaron, ed., *Inflation and the Income Tax* (Brookings Institution,
1976).
26. Vickrey, *Agenda*, pp. 285–87.

married couple with rising income divorce might have similar tax consequences. Under systems such as those proposed by Vickrey and Holt that would allow part of prior-year taxes to be refunded when income declines, the death of a spouse or a divorce shortly before or after the normal retirement age could prevent the widowed or divorced person from benefiting from averaging low postretirement income with higher income earned in earlier years. In view of the controversy recently excited by rather small differences under present law in the taxation of married and single people, it can be predicted that no solution to the problems for long-term averaging posed by changes in marital status would command universal support.

### Special Problems under Vickrey's Proposal

The derivation of multiyear tax rate tables under Vickrey's proposal and their adjustment when statutory rates were changed would cause confusion. While there are few objective standards by which to judge a conventional tax schedule, the multiyear tables would at least have to relate to each other in a logical and equitable way. It would be essential to explain fully the derivation of the tables to Congress. Taxpayers would not have to know exactly how the tables were drawn up in order to use them, but citizens should understand the procedure well enough to be satisfied that persons using different tables were being fairly treated. A lack of such understanding could hinder acceptance of the system and damage voluntary compliance.

A permissive version of cumulative averaging, which allows taxpayers great flexibility in the timing of income reporting and tax payments, would handicap stabilization policy and even revenue estimation. If the authorities attempted to check an inflationary boom by tightening credit and increasing income tax rates, businessmen and investors could resist the squeeze by reporting less taxable income, thus "borrowing" from the Treasury. In slack times the interest on tax accounts might be more attractive, and some catching-up of payments could occur.

When a person emigrated his averaging period would have to close. This would mean that people who left the country in late middle age would lose the opportunity of averaging their low postretirement incomes with their peak incomes. Under a permissive version of long-term averaging, tax liabilities that would have to be settled at the time of emigration could be an obstacle to leaving. A settlement requirement would resemble the present requirement that aliens obtain a certificate that their income tax liabilities have been discharged before they leave the country, but it would be more onerous because it could cover a long period of time and would deny emigrants advantages enjoyed by others. It could, in practice, infringe on an important civil right.

## Conclusions

In my opinion long-term averaging of income for taxation would not be desirable on equity grounds. After a few years the merits of adaptation to changing circumstances outweigh the attractions of continuity in assessing the income tax. All the methods discussed in this paper (except possibly Vickrey's proposal) would diminish built-in flexibility of income tax liabilities during periods of rising income, but some of them would increase built-in flexibility when income is declining. It is doubtful that the adoption of long-term averaging would do much to remove obstacles to discretionary changes in tax rates for stabilization purposes. On examination the possibility of simplifying the income tax through long-term averaging is chimerical. While a highly permissive version of cumulative averaging, giving taxpayers freedom to decide when to report income and pay taxes, would allow many complexities to be eliminated or disregarded, it would be subject to abuse and defaults and would handicap stabilization policy. The present rules concerning income determination and the timely discharge of tax liabilities would have to be retained, and long-term averaging would merely add complexity. More serious than the record-keeping requirements and procedural complications might be the difficulty of gaining popular understanding and acceptance of the system and the consequent risk of discouraging voluntary compliance.

PETER MIESZKOWSKI *University of Houston and*
*Federal Reserve Bank of Boston*

# The Advisability and Feasibility
# of an Expenditure Tax System

FOLLOWING the publication of Kaldor's classic book advocating the adoption of an expenditure tax in place of the income tax, analysts paid little attention to the administrative feasibility and specific details of such a system.[1] Recently, however, a number of studies dealing with the practical aspects of the expenditure tax have appeared, along with arguments that this tax is superior to the income tax on grounds of equity, efficiency, and administrative simplicity.[2] Three governments—the United States, the United Kingdom, and Sweden —have produced major reports on the practical aspects and the advantages of adopting a progressive expenditure tax in place of an

1. Nicholas Kaldor, *An Expenditure Tax* (London: Allen and Unwin, 1955).
2. The most notable of these studies is an article by W. D. Andrews, "A Consumption-Type or Cash Flow Personal Income Tax," *Harvard Law Review,* vol. 87 (April 1974), pp. 1113–88, that is now well-known to lawyers and economists. See also Advisory Commission of Intergovernmental Relations, *The Expenditure Tax,* M-84 (Government Printing Office, March 1974); and Peter Mieszkowski, "The Cash Flow Version of an Expenditure Tax," Office of Tax Analysis Paper 26, *OTA Papers,* vol. 2, U.S. Treasury (GPO, August 1977). For earlier work on the subject, see Patrick L. Kelley, "Is An Expenditure Tax Feasible?" *National Tax Journal,* vol. 23 (September 1970), pp. 237–53; and Richard E. Slitor, "Administrative Aspects of Expenditures Taxation," in Richard A. Musgrave, ed., *Broad-Based Taxes—New Options and Sources* (Johns Hopkins University Press, 1973), pp. 227–63.

income-based system, and the tax was the subject of a Brookings Institution conference in October 1978.[3]

One of the main themes of this paper is that the widely held view that the expenditure tax is too difficult to administer is simply false;[4] there are, in fact, no fundamental problems associated with administering an ongoing expenditure tax. The transitional problems of moving from income to expenditure taxation, however, particularly in a world economy characterized by both personal and corporation income taxes, are serious.

I am inclined to downplay the administrative advantages of an expenditure tax and to emphasize its advantages in improving tax equity and promoting efficiency.

## Equity Arguments for and against an Expenditure Tax

The case for an expenditure tax is strongest in a world of complete certainty where a person enters the labor force at a prescribed age and where wages and a rate of interest are given.[5] In such a world, in the absence of inheritance and bequests the present value of a person's lifetime wage stream is equal to the present value of his lifetime consumption expenditure. This present value can be viewed as a person's endowment. Two people with the same endowment would be viewed as equal and would be assessed the same tax. Such a tax on endowment would be completely neutral with respect to the timing or composition of consumption. A person who saves a great deal and consumes in the latter stages of life would pay the same tax (measured in

3. U.S. Treasury Department, *Blueprints for Basic Tax Reform* (GPO, January 1977); J. E. Meade, *The Structure and Reform of Direct Taxation,* report of a committee chaired by J. E. Meade, Institute for Fiscal Studies (London: Allen and Unwin, 1978); and Sven-Olof Lodin, *Progressive Expenditure Tax—An Alternative?* Richard Cox, trans. (Stockholm: Liberförlag, 1978). See the Swedish Budget Department's final report, *Oversyn av skattesystemet: Slutbetankande av 1972 års skatteutredning* (Review of the tax system) (Stockholm: Statens Offentliga Utredningar, 1977). See also Joseph A. Pechman, ed., *What Should Be Taxed: Income or Expenditure?* (Brookings Institution, 1980).

4. See R. A. Musgrave and Peggy B. Musgrave, *Public Finance in Theory and Practice* (McGraw-Hill, 1973), p. 375; and Joseph A. Pechman, *Federal Tax Policy,* rev. ed. (Brookings Institution, 1971), pp. 164, 168.

5. Richard A. Musgrave, "ET, OT and SBT," *Journal of Public Economics,* vol. 6 (July-August 1976), pp. 3–16.

present value) as the person who borrows for consumption when young and spends most of his life getting out of debt.

A tax on interest or profit income, although called for under the income, or accretion, principle of taxation, is discriminatory since it imposes a higher rate of tax on those persons who are more inclined to save. In essence the argument that favors consumption on equity grounds reduces to the principle that taxation should not depend on how or when a person disposes of his wealth or endowment during his lifetime.

The introduction of uncertainty does not change this argument in any essential way. It does make the application of a single-payment endowment tax impractical. But in the absence of bequests, a proportional expenditure tax would be equivalent to a wage tax on endowment calculated ex post at the end of a lifetime. A person whose wage income went up unexpectedly would pay higher taxes when he consumed. A windfall capital gain would be reflected in higher taxes when consumption increased, and a loss would be reflected in lower taxes when consumption decreased.

How to treat bequests is a difficult question. Musgrave argues that bequests could be taxed as consumption at the death of the donor because the bequest is an option or part of the endowment of the donor.[6] I personally find this argument compelling since it is implied by the principle that individuals should be taxed on the basis of lifetime endowment. But some advocates of an expenditure tax will undoubtedly find this treatment of bequests unappealing because bequests would be taxed both as the consumption of the donor and as the consumption of the donee (when consumed). Such double taxation weakens the efficiency argument for an expenditure tax, as consumption of the donor is favored at the expense of bequests.

According to another line of reasoning, bequests should be favored rather than discouraged because they represent utility for both donors and donees and because the inducement to bequeath adds to the capital stock and increases the nation's long-run potential consumption. Whatever the merits of these arguments, they tend to undermine the equity arguments favoring the expenditure tax.

The equal endowment approach to equity depends critically on a lifetime perspective and emphasizes wage income as the basic com-

6. Ibid., p. 12.

ponent of endowment.[7] Several developments have increased the appeal of the life cycle approach. First, because of medical advances life is now more predictable and more structured in stages or periods than it was in the past. Planned retirement is much more widespread than heretofore and has been associated with a significant increase in private and public retirement pensions. Moreover, social security and other factors have worked to break down intrafamily compacts in which older adults either lived with their children or were maintained by them. The decline in the proportion of the population engaged in agriculture and in the importance of inherited farmland have worked to make wage income, or the returns to human capital, increasingly important. The general urbanization of society and the associated decline of the extended family have made life cycle saving more meaningful. Finally, the general increase in real income levels has enabled a growing fraction of the population to acquire significant savings.

Some equity arguments against a consumption-based system are easily countered. It is sometimes asserted, for example, that the ability of the miser to escape taxation by failing to consume proves the inequity of consumption taxation. Yet *if the miser's estate is taxed* as consumption at the time of his death, he—who consumed virtually nothing—and the person who consumes all his wage income as soon as it is received would pay the same tax calculated on a present value basis. The miser accumulated wealth at a very rapid rate and would pay a large tax at the time of death.

It is also argued that an expenditure tax would increase taxes on the young and the old. This problem would exist to the extent that the young would borrow for consumption or buy a disproportionate share of consumer durables, but it could be mitigated through averaging. Retired persons who consume their wealth would pay higher taxes during retirement than they would under an income tax, but this tax burden would be offset by the lower taxes paid during their working lives when they were accumulating capital or pension benefits.

Important arguments against consumption taxation are that people are not fully rational in the sense that they do not have lifetime perspectives and that they do not have access to efficient capital markets. Full rationality can be questioned, of course, and one of the

---

7. For the opposite view, see Richard Goode, "The Superiority of the Income Tax over the Expenditure Tax," paper prepared for the Brookings Institution Conference on Income versus Expenditure Taxation, October 1978.

more persuasive arguments for a social security system is that a large number of people act "irrationally" and do not save enough for their retirement. Similarly it can be argued that a tax on income is preferable to a tax on consumption because people prefer to pay taxes during their most productive periods. I do not find this argument very persuasive.

### Large Fortunes

If it is accepted that consumption is the appropriate basis of taxation for households that derive their income primarily from earnings or from capital accumulated out of their own savings, the remaining issue is the inheritance tax of large fortunes. Even if bequests are taxed as consumption at death, large fortunes can be passed on. In this case the family's economic life extends to more than one generation. But the taxation of large permanent fortunes on the equal endowment principle makes little sense because the consumption of the fortune is not an option if the family is to continue into the future. When all wealth is in nonhuman capital and is the only source of income there seems little basis for inheritance taxation unless the concentration of wealth is a concern. But to tax modest bequests as consumption and to exempt permanent fortunes from taxation is inequitable. The basic problem here is that large multigeneration fortunes violate the basic assumption of the life cycle model—that the correct period for taxation is one person's life, or a single lifetime.

There are two possible practical solutions to this problem. One is to tax inheritance under a special inheritance or accession tax, thus moving away from the equal endowment principle, and to tax bequests as consumption. The alternative is to tax small inheritances as consumption and to impose a supplemental wealth tax on large accumulations. The wealth tax would meet the objection that for many wealthy families consumption is an imperfect measure of ability to pay and that wealth represents utility or power beyond the potential consumption benefits associated with wealth.

The complications from compromising the simple life cycle model constitute not an argument for an income tax but an argument against a pure expenditure tax system. The accretion income tax, particularly when unrealized gains are untaxed, is a clumsy and inefficient way of taxing large fortunes, as it is less efficient and less equitable than the consumption tax for the vast majority of taxpayers. Some have argued that the combination of an expenditure tax and an inheritance tax is not superior to an income tax because there is no difference in paying fare periodically while riding a train and in paying a single fare at the end of the ride. Although this analogy may be appropriate for some taxpayers, it misses the basic point of the life cycle savings model; namely, that the income tax causes more distortions and inequities than does consumption taxation. The vast majority of taxpayers will not pay an inheritance tax, but they will be exposed to the distortions of the income tax.

## Efficiency Aspects of a Consumption-Based System

Some arguments for the superiority of an expenditure tax over an income tax rest on the fact that an income tax distorts both the labor-leisure choice and the consumption-savings choice, while a consumption tax distorts only the choice between working and not working, not the choice between consumption and saving. According to another popular view the efficiency argument for an expenditure tax evaporates if the interest rate elasticity of saving is either zero or small. I maintain in this section that both these arguments are misleading and incomplete. I assume first that the before-tax wage rate and interest rate are given and that the growth effects of tax changes are ignored; then I allow for effects of changes in the capital stock or wages.

According to a traditional argument the efficiency cost of taxes on profits is small if the supply of saving (expenditures of present consumption on future consumption) is inelastic with respect to the interest rate. Martin Feldstein has shown that this argument is fallacious.[8] His basic point is that future consumption out of savings is a multiple of price (interest rate) times a quantity (present consumption). So the failure of saving to respond to a change in the interest rate is compatible with, indeed implies, that the consumer-saver's preferred pattern of consumption is severely distorted. The cost of distortions from changes in the net-of-tax interest rate induced by the income tax may be quite substantial even though the elasticity of saving with respect to the rate of interest is small or even negative. Of course, the magnitude of the excess burden of a tax on interest income

8. Martin Feldstein, "The Welfare Cost of Capital Income Taxation," *Journal of Political Economy*, vol. 86 (April 1978), pp. S29–51.

will be larger the higher the interest rate elasticity of savings. Feldstein calculated the differential welfare cost of a tax system of equal yield that exempts capital income for the special case where the uncompensated savings and labor supply elasticities are both assumed to be equal to zero and found the differential cost to be approximately equal to 2 percent of net after-tax wages.

The preceding case, in which the utility function is weakly separable between leisure and other consumption goods, is of special interest. Atkinson and Stiglitz have shown that in such a case, all commodities should be taxed at the same rate, that is, future consumption should not be taxed at a rate higher than present consumption.[9] In dealing with the efficiency effects of direct and indirect taxes, Meade found that a uniform tax should apply in the three-commodity case (which I reinterpret as leisure, current consumption, and future consumption) if there is no substitutability (compensated) between leisure and either first- or second-period consumption or if the substitutabilities between each commodity and leisure are the same.[10] In neither case is there any gain from shifting from uniform consumption taxation to differential taxation, where future consumption is taxed at a higher rate. In the latter case the distortion of incentives (the demand for leisure) is as great from taxing one commodity as from taxing the other. To restate this condition—the role of an optimal tax on income from capital (future consumption) is to serve as an instrument to reduce the excess burden created by the tax on the income from labor.

These general theoretical results tend to strengthen the case for a consumption-based tax system, but it is important to remember that in general the optimal tax on capital income will not be zero. Even when the demand for future consumption is quite elastic with respect to price, the optimal tax on capital income will not be zero as long as the primary work disincentive effect is the substitution of leisure for first-period consumption.

9. A. B. Atkinson and J. E. Stiglitz, "The Design of Tax Structure: Direct vs. Indirect Taxation," *Journal of Public Economics,* vol. 6 (July-August 1976), pp. 55–76. This result is a generalization of the results obtained much earlier by the precursors of optimal taxation. See W. J. Corlett and D. C. Hague, "Complementarity and the Excess Burden of Taxation," *Review of Economic Studies,* vol. 21 (April 1953), pp. 21–30; and J. E. Meade, *Trade and Welfare,* vol. 2 (Oxford University Press, 1955), *Mathematical Supplement,* pp. 24–33.

10. Meade, *Trade and Welfare,* vol. 2, p. 117.

Although for the special case of separability (Cobb-Douglas) the differential excess burden of a general income tax relative to a consumption tax is substantial, Atkinson and Sandmo have demonstrated that while the optimal tax on capital income may well be below that of a tax on wages, the magnitude of the optimal tax is quite sensitive to the estimates for the suppy of labor.[11] So as in all second-best problems, the issue of how heavily capital income should be taxed relative to labor is an empirical question that in this case hinges on the supply elasticities of labor and saving.

## Interest Elasticities of Saving

Boskin has estimated the interest elasticity of personal saving to be about +0.4, about twice the elasticity estimated by Wright.[12] Their papers are the only ones in which significant interest rate effects on savings are found.

Hymans and Howrey criticized Boskin's paper on a number of grounds, found his results to be quite sensitive to choice of sample period and to specification, and reported they could find no significant interest rate effect using an alternative definition of savings.[13] It is unlikely that further empirical work with time series will narrow the range of elasticity estimates. Furthermore, such refinements may not be very important. First, the measure of deadweight loss resulting from taxes on capital is not very sensitive to the estimates of the interest elasticity.[14] Second, the estimate of the optimal tax on capital income is more sensitive to a precise estimate of labor supply elasticities, which despite careful research are very elusive parameters. Fi-

11. A. B. Atkinson and A. Sandmo, "The Welfare Implications of Personal Income and Consumption Taxes," Discussion Papers (Bergen, Norway: Norwegian School of Economics and Business Administration, October 1977).

12. Michael Boskin, "Taxation, Saving, and the Rate of Interest," *Journal of Political Economy*, vol. 86 (April 1978), p. S16; and Colin Wright, "Saving and the Rate of Interest," in Arnold C. Harberger and Martin J. Bailey, eds., *Taxation of Income from Capital* (Brookings Institution, 1969), pp. 275–99.

13. E. Philip Howrey and Saul H. Hymans, "The Measurement and Determination of Loanable-Funds Saving," *Brookings Papers on Economic Activity, 3:1978*, pp. 655–85. See also Michael Boskin's vigorous comments on the Howrey-Hymans paper in ibid., pp. 694–700.

14. See Boskin, "Taxation, Saving and the Rate of Interest," p. S19. Boskin's estimates of welfare loss range around $60 billion a year, about 15 percent of tax receipts from individual and corporation income taxes and from social security taxes. This large amount is probably an overestimate, as Boskin uses a large estimate of savings for retirement.

nally and most significantly, theoretical advances with multiperiod life cycle models indicate that the indirect wealth effects of interest rate effects on savings are much more significant than the interest rate substitution effects as conventionally measured.

### Wealth Effects

In 1967 Tobin generalized the Modigliani-Brumberg life cycle model to allow for positive interest rate effects and a variety of demographic features in an attempt to determine whether life cycle saving can account for the U.S. capital stock.[15] Hall applied this model to compare the effects of a 25 percent income tax and a 33 percent consumption tax on welfare. More recently Summers used the multiperiod life cycle model to analyze a number of differential tax comparisons involving capital taxes and consumption and wage taxes.[16]

Each of the other studies finds interest rate elasticity of savings several times larger than that estimated for two-period models. The reason the multiperiod model yields larger estimates than the conventional two-period model is quite simple. It is the special feature of the logarithmic (Cobb-Douglas) utility function that *first-period consumption* is independent of the rate of interest and depends on wealth that is the present value of wage income. The principal difference between the two-period and multiperiod case is that for the latter an increase in interest rates with constant wages decreases the present value of wealth, decreases consumption, and increases savings in the early years. There is no such wealth effect for the two-period case.

Summers, who calculates theoretical interest elasticities of 2 or more, has pointed out that it is this wealth effect that makes empirical estimates of savings tricky.[17] Using Boskin's estimates of the wealth elasticity of savings, Summers estimates the "full effect" elasticity to be very close to his theoretical estimate.

Despite the similarities in their models and their conclusions re-

15. James Tobin, "Life Cycle Saving and Balanced Growth," in *Ten Economic Studies in the Tradition of Irving Fisher* (John Wiley, 1967), p. 237.

16. Robert Hall, "Consumption Taxes versus Income Taxes: Implications for Economic Growth," in *National Tax Association–Tax Institute of America Proceedings of the Sixty-First Annual Conference on Taxation, 1968* (Columbus, O.: NTA-TIA, 1969), pp. 125–45; and Lawrence H. Summers, "Tax Policy in a Life Cycle Model," Working Paper 302 (Cambridge, Mass.: National Bureau of Economic Research, November 1978).

17. Lawrence H. Summers, "Tax Policy in a Life Cycle Model" (manuscript, n.d.).

garding savings elasticities, Hall and Summers reach radically different conclusions about the welfare implications of capital income
taxes. Hall calculated that the substitution of a 25 percent income tax
for a 33 percent consumption tax in 1968 would have resulted in a
loss in steady state consumption of about $100 per capita relative to
per capita consumption of $2,500, or 4 percent of consumption. In
contrast, Summers calculated an increase for steady state consumption of 17 percent or more if the present system is replaced by a consumption tax.[18]

Although the multiperiod life cycle model generates the strongest
efficiency (incentive) argument for a consumption-base system, these
calculations are subject to the obvious qualification that they ignore
work-leisure distortions. Moreover, the welfare gains associated with
increased savings that in a closed economy result from increased output per worker are probably overstated if some of the increased savings displace foreign investment or flow abroad. But at the very
least the generalized form of the life cycle model implies very elastic
response in personal savings to changes in the after-tax rate of return
on capital.

### Basic Administrative Considerations

A common argument against the expenditure tax is that it would
be hard to administer. Yet recent work strongly suggests that in a
number of important respects an expenditure tax would be significantly simpler to administer than a comprehensive income tax. Most
of the administrative problems under the income tax are related to
the appropriate tax treatment of physical assets. Under the expenditure tax the most serious administrative problems concern the appropriate treatment of consumer durables.

The administrative problems of an accretion income tax are well
known. They include approximating the change in the value of un-

18. Hall concludes that the efficiency argument for a consumption tax is weak,
but his estimates imply an excess burden of 10 percent of tax revenues ("Consumption Taxes versus Income Taxes," p. 144). An excess burden of 4 percent of current
personal consumption amounts to $55 billion, which is the yield of the federal cor-
porate tax for 1978. Hall assumes a 25 percent tax on capital, while Summers and
Boskin use a current profits tax of 50 percent. Summers also assumes a positive rate
of technical progress while Hall does not. Another basic difference is that Hall does
not allow for a retirement period, while Summers assumes that one-fifth of a person's
economic life is spent in retirement. These differences should explain the differences
in conclusions on the welfare implications of tax changes.

realized capital gains, computing the services of owner-occupied homes, and determining the true value of real economic depreciation. The problems related to depreciation and capital gains are greatly compounded by inflation. Inflation also redistributes wealth between creditors and debtors in ways that are only partially moderated by changes in interest rates. Under an ideal income tax all debts as well as assets would be indexed.[19]

But indexing the income tax would significantly complicate its administration and the associated accounting rules. One of the main arguments for an expenditure tax during protracted inflation is the unlikely prospect that the income tax will be indexed. An unindexed income tax falls capriciously on income from capital during inflation.

Under a consumption-based system a whole set of practical evaluation problems related to the measurement of capital income would disappear, and tax liability would be calculated on the basis of current cash flow information. The administrative advantages of such a system relative to the income tax are fairly clear cut, unless practical problems unique to an expenditure tax can be shown to exist.

### A Proportional Expenditure Tax without Durables

To isolate the complications associated with progressivity and with the taxation of durables under the expenditure tax, I assume that all expenditures are on nondurables and are taxed proportionately. In such a situation the calculation of current consumption on the basis of current cash flow information is straightforward.[20] The first step is to calculate all cash receipts over the tax period (year), including wages, gross profits of personal business enterprises, interest and dividends, the sale of all assets, and all forms of retirement income. The second step is to allow deductions for the purchase of all income-earning assets, including real capital goods, stocks, bonds, and savings accounts. In addition various costs of acquiring income will be allowed. Other deductions, such as charitable donations, might be allowed, but they are independent of the basic identity that defines consumption.

19. The feasibility of indexing has been shown by recent work. See U.S. Treasury Department, *Blueprints for Basic Tax Reform;* and Henry Aaron, ed., *Inflation and the Income Tax* (Brookings Institution, 1976).

20. See U.S. Treasury Department, *Blueprints for Basic Tax Reform;* Andrews, "A Consumption-Type or Cash Flow Personal Income Tax," pp. 1113–88; and William D. Andrews, "Accessions Tax Proposal," *Tax Law Review,* vol. 22 (May 1967), pp. 589–633.

### A Proportional Expenditure Tax with Durables

With proportional rates, the taxation of durables is straightforward. The capital value of a durable is equal to the present value of its services plus the present value of any proceeds from resale (scrap value). The tax on the services that the consumer derives from the durable can be taxed at the moment of purchase; in other words, the tax can be "prepaid." Consider the purchase of a $1,000 car that lasts one year. If the rate of interest is 10 percent, the value of the services derived from the car is $1,000 plus $100 interest (10 percent of $1,000), or $1,100.

If a 50 percent tax is assessed on the rental value at the end of the year, the taxpayer pays $550. On the other hand, if the tax is imposed on the capital value of the durable when it is purchased, the tax is $500, the present value of which is equal to $550 payable one year later. This example illustrates a general principle that greatly simplifies the taxation of durables: consumption taxation does not require estimates of depreciation for durables, interest rates, and other information that is required under an income tax.

Consumer loans do not significantly complicate the picture. They can be treated in one of two equivalent ways. (These two ways have close analogues in the treatment of asset purchases, described below as qualified accounts treatment and tax prepayment treatment.) One way of dealing with consumer loans is to include loan proceeds in receipts at the time the loan is made, and then to allow a deduction for interest and amortization of the loan as it comes due. Alternatively and equivalently, the proceeds of the loan and subsequent interest and amortization can all be disregarded.

If the second approach is applied to the purchase of a house, the consumption tax paid will approximate a tax imposed on annual services derived if the service life of the house corresponds to the life of the mortgage. When a $50,000 house is purchased and is fully mortgaged, and if loan proceeds are excluded, with mortgage interest and amortization not deductible, a consumption tax will effectively be paid on interest and mortgage amortization.

Most consumer durables raise no serious administrative problems except those related to averaging. Complications arise with such durables as antiques and art that are purchased for investment as well as consumption. If these assets are treated as ordinary durables, it might appear that some people (particularly wealthy taxpayers) would make large tax-free gains. The tax advantage of investing in these durables depends on whether their rate of return compares favorably with that of more conventional investments. If the rate of return is comparable to that on other assets, the investor would enjoy the consumption benefits tax free.[21] In order to deal with this problem the Meade Committee proposed the retention of a residual capital gains tax on valuable consumer durables.[22] One way such a tax could be implemented would be to require that half the gains on such a durable be included in receipts under a cash flow expenditure tax. Roll-over provisions might be introduced.

A related problem is connected with owner-occupied housing. In the absence of general inflation and with constant housing prices, an expenditure tax would not create a tax incentive for people to own homes rather than to rent, and housing consumption would not be subsidized relative to other forms of consumption. However, if inflation is anticipated, if interest rates equal the real interest rate plus the anticipated inflation rate, and if houses are treated like other durables as tax-prepaid assets, there would be no tax advantage to homeownership because the real cost of housing and the real interest rate are fixed.

Like the income tax, the consumption tax gives rise to inequities in the tax treatment of housing due to unanticipated inflation or changes in the value of a particular house relative to other goods. Equity would require that the cost basis of a house be changed during inflation. But to do so would destroy the administrative simplicity in the tax treatment of housing under an expenditure tax and would also provoke serious political opposition.

If houses are treated like other durables, unanticipated real capital gains arising from ownership will go untaxed. A leaf could be borrowed from the present system in which proceeds from a house sale are taxed only if they are not invested in another principal residence. This provision, while familiar and neutral with respect to choice of residence, promotes the consumption of owner-occupied housing. No solution is administratively simple, equitable, and allocatively neutral.

---

21. During the inflationary decade 1968–78, the yield on Chinese ceramics, old masters, stamps, and the like, gross of transaction cost, was two to three times higher than the yield on bonds. See John Picard Stein, "The Monetary Appreciation of Paintings," *Journal of Political Economy*, vol. 85 (October 1977), pp. 1021–35.

22. See Meade, *The Structure and Reform of Direct Taxation*, p. 180.

The seriousness of the inequities is a matter of judgment, but it is heightened by the rapid and unanticipated recent increase in house prices. For most families, a house is their principal asset. Expenditures for housing represent 20 percent or more of total consumption. Consequently while the imperfect taxation of housing consumption under an expenditure tax is logically similar to the incomplete taxation of capital gains on owner-occupied housing under a comprehensive income tax, it is a larger defect under the expenditure tax than under the income tax. But the proposed taxation of housing is vastly simpler than the imputation method under a fully comprehensive income tax.

### Averaging and Alternative Tax Treatment of Investment Assets

If consumer durables were taxed without complicated imputations, averaging would become significant for a much larger proportion of taxpayers than it is under the present system. Families often buy houses whose capital value exceeds their annual income. Cars, boats, furniture, and other durables represent large fractions of annual expenditures for the typical household. A progressive rate structure would increase the need for averaging to prevent large one-time consumption outlays fom pushing families into high rate brackets. To the extent that durables are purchased with borrowed money and that loans are not included in receipts, the averaging or progressivity problem is largely solved.

One practical averaging scheme has been proposed for the taxation of owner-occupied homes purchased with equity. A person who purchases a $100,000 home would be allowed to deduct such an investment when the house was purchased and annually would report in receipts an amount equal to annual amortization and interest payments on a conventional mortgage. From the tax standpoint such a rule is really equivalent to actually taking out a mortgage. The generalization of this approach would allow taxpayers to "amortize" over a number of years a large expenditure on durables. For example, the cost of a car could be deducted when it was purchased, and this amount could be included in receipts over the car's useful life. The principal shortcomings of this approach are its administrative complexity and the scope for windfall gains or losses when inflation does not equal the rate implicit in the interest rate used in computing the amortization.

### Qualified Accounts Treatment and Tax Prepayment Treatment

To permit taxpayers considerable flexibility in the timing of consumption tax payments, Meade, in an unpublished memorandum, has advocated two kinds of tax payment arrangements.[23] Under the qualified accounts treatment, taxpayers would be permitted to deduct the value of an asset at time of purchase and would be required to report net income as earned, without allowance for depreciation. The tax prepayment treatment would not allow the taxpayer a deduction when the asset was purchased but would not require him to report income from it.

Under a proportional rate structure the two approaches are equivalent if the market price is predicated on a correct anticipation of income from the asset and if the market discount rate implicit in the asset's price and income flow remains constant over the life of the asset. For example, a person in the 50 percent bracket who saves $1 to purchase an asset yielding 10 percent that would yield $1.10 for consumption at the end of one year can either pay 50 cents in tax at the start of the year (the tax prepayment approach) or 55 cents at year-end. Both tax payments have a present value of 50 cents at the 10 percent discount rate.

The rationale for permitting a choice between these approaches is that it allows taxpayers desirable flexibility in the timing of tax payments. For example, a family saving for many years to pay for their children's college education could avoid a large one-time tax liability by prepaying the tax liability on assets purchased with such savings.

More generally, when tax rates are progressive the taxpayer can protect himself against large bulges in consumption by prepaying taxes on assets he holds, or if he holds few assets, by borrowing, not taking current loan proceeds into receipts, and paying the tax in later periods. If a person expects consumption expenditures to drop, he can borrow, paying taxes as he repays what he owes rather than currently.

The existence of both types of assets and loans complicates record-keeping and tax compliance for the taxpayer, but the possibility of combining different assets and loans to minimize tax liabilities is a virtue rather than a limitation since it enables the taxpayer in effect to

23. J. E. Meade, "Notes on the Feasibility of Progressive Taxation of Expenditures" (manuscript, 1976), p. 7 and app. A.

have his tax assessed on the basis of lifetime consumption rather than on the basis of a particular tax accounting period.

A number of practical considerations call for restriction on the use of both types of assets accounts and loans. For example, unless fluctuations in consumption can be anticipated accurately, ex post averaging will still be necessary because many taxpayers may lack the sophistication to do their own averaging. Sophisticated investors may manipulate the system by prepaying tax on assets that have a good chance of yielding high returns, while paying taxes only as income is received on assets with predictable normal returns. But even without asset manipulation there is the question of whether society wishes to allow people the full option, in the presence of uncertainty, to be taxed on the basis of what goes into an investment rather than on the basis of what comes out. Gold prospectors who elect prepayment would pay tax only on the cost of their supplies, not on the value of their discoveries.

Taxation under the prepayment option resembles a lottery and will offend the sense of equity of many. High-yield investments are not random because success begets further success. The general taxpayer will derive little comfort from knowing that the tax law treats the successful investor and the failure alike. He may be reminded of Anatole France's remark that the French law on trespass, with lofty indifference, prohibited rich and poor alike from sleeping under bridges.

I recommend that the qualified assets treatment be made standard for most assets and that tax prepayment be restricted in amount and to safe low-variance assets. Loans for business purposes should be reported in current receipts; consumption loans would be excluded from receipts, but amortization and interest would not be deductible.

## Issues and Problems Common to the Income Tax and the Expenditure Tax

Many problems and issues arise under both consumption and income taxation. Neither base can be truly comprehensive as a practical matter. Neither can reach the value of leisure and household production. Under neither tax should deductions be allowed for costs associated with the services of consumer durables if the value of such services is not taxed. This principle has special relevance to the deduction of mortgage interest and state and local taxes. Similarly the question of which work-related expenses and charitable contributions should be deducted are essentially the same for both the income tax and the consumption tax.

Issues of personal exemptions, accounting for family size, and the choice of appropriate unit of taxation are also very similar under both the income and the expenditure tax. The question of joint filing and related questions about taxation of the family have been widely discussed, and it is recognized that the taxation of two working persons as a household under progressive taxation and tax neutrality toward marriage are incompatible.[24] It is also recognized that joint filing under progressive taxation would have severe disincentive effects on secondary family workers, especially if the earnings of the secondary worker are low relative to the earnings of the primary worker. On the other hand, individual filing is incompatible with the notion of a unified household and creates incentives for intrafamily distributions of wealth or income to minimize tax burdens. Whatever the approach chosen, it could also apply to the income tax.

The problems of taxing insurance are similar under income and expenditure taxes. Under the latter it is irrelevant to a first-order approximation whether insurance premiums (broadly defined) are deductible and the receipts from the policies (also broadly defined) are included in cash flow receipts or whether premiums are not deductible and receipts from insurance policies are excluded from taxable receipts. Under the income tax the same general principle would apply. If contributions to a social insurance system are taxed when they are made, only the portion of benefits representing accumulated interest should be taxed. On the other hand, if contributions to insurance funds are not taxed, all proceeds would be included in taxable income. The complication under the income tax is the tax treatment of interest that accumulates on various insurance systems. This issue does not arise for the expenditure tax and represents a further administrative simplification of this tax system.

Under both the income and consumption tax similar choices must be made in the treatment of public subsidies. Whether to include public assistance, food stamps, or the value of public housing, free medical care, or free public education must be resolved under either consumption or income taxes.

If not all income is consumed the base of the income tax is broader than that of a consumption tax, and the average consumption tax rate

24. See the papers by Alicia Munnell and Harvey Brazer in this volume.

at each income bracket will be higher than that of an equal-yield consumption tax. Consequently the incentive to engage in untaxed activities or to underreport wage income will be greater under an expenditure tax than under an income tax. If all income is consumed, there is a simple relationship between expenditure tax rates $(t_c)$ and income tax rates $(t_y)$, $(1 - t_y) = 1/(1 + t_c)$. Any pair of proportional tax rates, $t_y$ and $t_c$, satisfying this relation yields the same revenue. A 50 percent income tax is equivalent to a 100 percent expenditure tax, a 33⅓ percent income tax to a 50 percent consumption tax, and so on. If all income is consumed, the income tax and the expenditure tax are, not surprisingly, fully equivalent. The incentive to produce various items in the home will be the same for both tax systems. The incentive to avoid taxes will also be the same.

If not all income is consumed, the expenditure tax rate must increase on an average to rates above the equivalent levels. If saving is not significantly greater under the expenditure tax than it is under the income tax, the increase in tax rate will be small, as gross consumption is roughly 90 percent of comprehensive income.[25]

To the extent that saving requires a higher rate under the expenditure tax than indicated above, the various incentives to avoid payment of taxes will be greater under a consumption tax than under a fully comprehensive income tax. Conversely it can be argued that the incentive to underreport investment income or to make investments where underreporting or fraud is easy is stronger under the income tax than under the expenditure tax. The point quite simply is that when investments are made in qualified accounts the taxpayer gets a tax deduction under the expenditure tax. Of course, some taxpayers may take a deduction and then try to underreport net income from the asset: as a result, the auditing of qualified accounts will have to be quite strict. On balance, the problem of tax fraud should not be more severe under the expenditure tax than it is under the income tax.

## Issues of Harmonization and Integration

In most respects the administrative problems associated with the expenditure tax are not serious, but international tax harmonization

25. See the calculations in U.S. Treasury Department, *Blueprints for Basic Tax Reform*, table 12, p. 168, where comprehensive consumption and income are estimated as $1.161 trillion and $1.270 trillion, respectively, for 1976.

and the integration of the tax with other provisions of the federal tax system pose major difficulties.

The case for adopting an expenditure tax is seriously weakened unless the corporation income tax is eliminated or significantly modified. The perpetuation of the corporation income tax, a significant tax on capital income, weakens the efficiency argument favoring the expenditure tax. Furthermore, perpetuation of the corporation income tax would continue the complicated accounting problems associated with the measurement of corporate income and would deprive the expenditure tax of a principal administrative advantage: termination of the need to measure net profits for tax purposes. In my opinion, a corporate tax also has no place in a rational, equitable comprehensive income tax because it taxes corporate-source income twice.

The international aspects of introducing an expenditure tax and eliminating the corporate tax for investment in the United States are major, and the issues raised are not mere technical details that can be resolved by compromise. The fact that most countries now tax the income of corporations on a source-of-income basis means that even if the United States repealed its corporation income tax, the income U.S. corporations earn abroad would continue to be taxed. Furthermore, a large part of U.S. taxes now levied on foreign corporations would simply be collected by foreign treasuries rather than by the U.S. Treasury. In the present situation most major industrial countries impose corporate taxes and taxes on dividends. The system of foreign tax credits negotiated by treaty allows for the crediting of foreign taxes. This system preserves approximate export and import neutrality; in other words, a capital exporter is indifferent between investment at home and abroad, and foreign investors are treated on a par with residents.

Should the United States initiate an expenditure tax and eliminate the corporation income tax, two key questions would arise: (1) whether profit taxes paid abroad would be credited under the tax imposed on households, and (2) whether the exemption of returns on savings would be extended to foreign investors. There would be strong pressure to eliminate taxes on foreign investments in the United States, as nondiscrimination between residents and nonresidents is one of the basic principles of international tax arrangements. Counteracting this discrimination criterion is the fact that the United States would lose tax revenue if foreign investment were exempt from tax.

The U.S. government might argue that if American taxes on foreigners were eliminated, foreign countries should reciprocate in kind; otherwise real resources would shift from the U.S. Treasury to foreign treasuries. But if foreigners agreed, they would be violating capital export neutrality in their countries.

It would be very much in the interest of the United States to continue to tax the incomes from foreign investments in the United States as long as other countries continue to tax U.S. subsidiaries and branches abroad. The United States simply could not adhere to the principle of nondiscrimination if it did not tax domestic profits but other countries did so. It would have to impose sizable taxes, of 40 percent or more, on the earnings of foreign subsidiaries and branch operations. Similar taxes would have to be imposed on foreigners who purchase U.S. equities or bonds.

The second general issue is whether U.S. taxpayers should be permitted credits against consumption tax liabilities for foreign profit taxes paid by American corporations. This proposal would arouse controversy, as it would directly reduce U.S. tax collection by $1 for each dollar of tax paid abroad. Nevertheless, the credit would not necessarily decrease the real income of the United States relative to the existing situation. At present foreign governments collect taxes on American profit income earned abroad and they would continue to do so. Without the credit, relative after-tax yields abroad would decline, and U.S. corporations and individuals would have a strong incentive to liquidate their foreign investments, a move that would be in the interest of neither the United States nor the countries in which American-owned investments are located.

A secondary issue concerns the treatment of American citizens living abroad under the expenditure tax. Some Americans would be tempted to accumulate wealth in the United States and to consume it in countries that do not tax consumption. In a world where most countries tax income, not consumption, a price in administrative and statutory complications would have to be paid to plug this and related loopholes.

Some of the potential simplification of tax administration made possible by an expenditure tax would be lost if the states continued to impose income taxes on individuals and corporations. The problems could be particularly vexing if states moved to adopt divergent definitions of depreciation, capital gains, or other quantities that are irrelevant for a cash flow expenditure tax but must be known under an income tax.

# Approaches to Transition, or Phase-in, of the Expenditure Tax

The most complicated technical and administrative problems associated with introducing an expenditure tax are problems of transition.

## Consumer Durables and Housing

The easiest and least controversial of these problems concerns consumer durables other than owner-occupied houses. A problem arises for people who buy consumer durables with their own equity just before the introduction of the expenditure tax. In principle one could take an inventory of durables before the effective date and levy a tax on durables. The administrative problems with such an approach would be severe. It would be best to ignore these durables but to require that the receipts from the sales of durables purchased before the effective date be included in receipts.

The issues concerning owner-occupied housing are logically identical but far larger than those concerning other durables because housing lasts longer and typically represents a larger proportion of consumption expenditures than other durables. To the extent that housing consumption is financed by debt (mortgages) there is no problem because debt repayment on loans negotiated before the consumption tax went into effect would be subject to consumption tax. The imputed income on the homeowner's equity interest would not be taxed until he sold his house. A tax on such sales would maintain horizontal equity for all households that invested in housing equity after the effective date. For households that bought their housing before the effective date, it would be more equitable to impose a consumption tax on all housing equity at the effective date. The argument that the equity was previously accumulated from proceeds net of income tax is weakened by the very favorable tax treatment of owner-occupied housing under the income tax. Indeed, the transitional problem associated with owner-occupied housing discussed here is really one of moving to the comprehensive taxation of owner-occupied housing. Essentially, the same issues would arise if the deduction of mortgage interest were eliminated and rent were imputed on the homeowner's equity under a comprehensive income tax.

### Financial Assets

The treatment of persons who have saved under an income tax expecting to consume the capital free of additional tax raises serious issues of equity. There is no major problem with respect to such tax-sheltered savings as private pensions. For other savings it would be possible to exempt some consumption out of accumulated wealth during the transition period. Such an exemption might be related to age or wealth. Alternatively, during a transition period two tax systems could coexist and taxpayers could be given a choice of filing under one system or the other. The possibilities of abuse under such a dual system are fairly obvious, and choice might be permitted only to the aged.

It might be desirable to introduce the expenditure tax quickly for the general tax-paying population but to provide some taxpayers the option of having some of their wealth taxed as under their current system during a transition. This proposal, although it introduces still a third asset, limits the duality of the tax system during the transition period; all households would file an expenditure tax, and some would file the supplementary income tax for a limited time period.

I recommend a two-stage transition. During the first stage the expenditure tax would replace the minimum tax for the wealthy, as suggested by Andrews.[26] An expenditure tax along with a high exemption level would be introduced for a period of about five years. During this experimental period administrative and statutory details could be developed and tested. If the tax proved to be successful, then the general election of a full-blown expenditure tax could be introduced along with a five- or ten-year transition period that would allow for income tax treatment of past accumulations of wealth. It would be important to announce as many of the general features of the full system at the beginning of the minimum tax stage as needed to give taxpayers maximum time to anticipate and plan for various tax adjustments.

26. Andrews, "A Consumption-Type or Cash Flow Personal Income Tax," pp. 1113–88.

## Summary

I have reviewed the main issues concerning the replacement of the income tax with a progressive expenditure tax. None of the administrative difficulties in such a change is insuperable. Most of the issues of equity, administration, and compliance are common to both the income and expenditure tax systems. Transitional problems and various aspects of international tax harmonization are the main hurdles to the introduction of expenditure taxation.

In addition to the issues of efficiency and severe administrative problems associated in tax capital income, the choice between the income and expenditure taxes seems to reduce to fundamental considerations of equity. The case for the expenditure tax on equity grounds is strong if savings are viewed from a life cycle perspective. Large fortunes transmitted from generation to generation may require special treatment.

JOHN B. SHOVEN *Stanford University*

PAUL TAUBMAN *University of Pennsylvania*

# Saving, Capital Income, and Taxation

THE PRESENT SYSTEM of taxation of capital income is needlessly complex and promotes inefficiency. It suffers from these flaws because of the separation of the corporate and personal income tax systems and because of an inappropriate definition of income. This paper addresses two basic issues. First, should capital income and savings be subject to any tax? Second, if there are to be such taxes, should their design differ from that of the current system of taxation and, if so, how?

We will focus on the treatment of corporate and noncorporate business income and propose a particular tax system integrating personal and corporate income taxation. While this plan involves some sweeping changes, it generates nearly as much revenue as the current tax system. We also will briefly summarize relevant concepts and major features of the current tax treatment.[1] Throughout, we assume that government expenditures and transfer payments are fixed and that only the financing of the budget is at issue.

## Criteria for Judging Tax Systems

In examining the design of the tax system, economists and others generally make use of a variety of criteria of which the most important

The authors wish to thank Henry J. Aaron, Boris I. Bittker, Stanley S. Surrey, Bernard Wolfman, Joseph A. Pechman, Emil M. Sunley, and Jack Bogdanski for comments on an earlier draft.

1. More detailed treatment of these issues can be found in Joseph A. Pechman, *Federal Tax Policy*, 3d ed. (Brookings Institution, 1977).

are economic efficiency, equity, and feasibility. Feasibility covers a multitude of issues, including the costs of objectively measuring the tax base and keeping records, the ease of avoiding taxes, and the costs associated with the invasion of privacy.

Efficiency is hard to measure because changes in tax rates generally make some people better off and others worse off. By altering prices, taxes induce businesses to produce and individuals to consume different combinations of goods and services.[2] Because a tax change rarely uniformly helps or hurts everyone, economic efficiency is usually operationally defined in terms of the total output of goods and services generated by a particular fiscal system. A tax system that increases output is generally regarded as more efficient because increased production permits the sum of the citizens' utilities to increase. The problems with this measure, particularly the interpersonal comparison of utilities, are obvious and are not dealt with here.

Equity, or fairness, has both a vertical and horizontal aspect. Horizontal equity is defined as treating equals equally, while vertical equity is defined as treating unequals fairly. In some sense these concepts are merely slogans unless defined specifically in terms of a social welfare function. Other than assuming that vertical equity requires average tax rates to be lower for those with low income than for those with high income, we do not discuss how unequally unequals should be taxed.

We follow tradition and provisionally define as equally well-off two people who have the same level of money income, including transfers, and who are otherwise in similar circumstances. No attempt will be made to define which other circumstances are relevant. We discuss whether consumption is a better definition of economic welfare and subsequently argue that in theory the traditional definitions of income and consumption should include the value of leisure and home-produced goods. Because of practical considerations, however, we concur in the practice of defining consumption and income in terms of market transactions. Given this practical consideration, we show that it is not obvious whether a consumption tax or an income tax creates more inefficiency.

It is possible to define money income in a variety of ways. For ex-

2. We assume here (and throughout the paper unless otherwise noted) that resources are fully employed before and after the change. Thus we are using long-run analyses.

ample, money income is the sum of its sources: returns from investments (in nonhuman capital), wages, salary payments, and transfers. Money income also equals the sum of its uses: consumption, saving, and taxes. Alternatively, because saving is the change in a person's net worth, income can be defined as the amount a person could spend on taxes plus consumption while leaving his net worth unchanged.

Money income need not equal the tax base in any corporate or personal income tax law. Thus it is customary to distinguish between "economic income" and "taxable income." This distinction is an important one for equity, efficiency, and feasibility considerations. If persons with the same economic income have different taxable incomes, then equals will pay different taxes.[3] The government creates such differences consciously to improve economic efficiency or to meet such social goals as the reduction of pollution through tax incentives for the purchase of antipollution equipment. Often, however, taxable income is defined without recourse to relevant information. For example, before 1954 little consideration was given to the rate at which various assets depreciated. Yet the divergence of economic and tax depreciation allowances has a large impact on investment.[4] Once such provisions develop a constituency, it is difficult to root them out.

The difference between taxable and economic income must arise because of preferential treatment given to some types of income or expenditures or because of variations in definitions of income, revenues, and expenses. If some types of income, such as that from mineral extraction, are taxed more lightly than others, investors will divert resources from more socially productive activities to those that produce more lightly taxed income in order to maximize personal after-tax income. If investment in physical capital is encouraged by permitting deductions for depreciation greater than actual economic depreciation or by investment tax credits, businesses will alter their production process to use more physical capital. Differences between economic and taxable income often will also lead to increased expenditures on record-keeping, lobbyists, lawyers, and accountants. For example, many firms now calculate and report different depre-

3. We realize that money income is a poor measure of economic welfare (or "equals") because, for example, it ignores differences in family size, allocation of time to nonwork activities, climate, and work conditions.

4. See, for example, Dale W. Jorgenson, "Econometric Studies of Investment Behavior," *Journal of Economic Literature,* vol. 9 (December 1971), pp. 1111–47.

ciation allowances to the Internal Revenue Service and the Securities and Exchange Commission. Moreover, there is an active business in tax shelters in which resources are spent on brokers' fees, advertising, and the like.

## Income and Consumption Taxes

Many different tax systems with different tax bases have been proposed.[5] The most widely discussed and analyzed ones are the broadly based income tax and the consumption (or expenditure) tax. As income equals consumption plus savings plus taxes, the difference between the two tax bases is the inclusion of savings under an income tax. Both tax systems would apply to wage *and* capital income. A consumption tax base is income less savings where income includes wages, interest, dividends, rents, and capital gains, as under the income tax base. It is *only income not spent on consumption* that differentiates the systems. Neither system need discriminate by income source.[6]

The major argument generally advanced against taxing savings is that such a tax distorts the choice between consumption in the present and consumption in the future, and that the cost of this distortion is large.[7] Even if corporate income were untaxed, an income tax would affect saving decisions because the tax reduces the rewards from saving.

All feasible taxes distort some decisions.[8] It is not clear that an income tax causes more or less costly distortions in the allocation of resources than does a consumption tax or any other tax with an equal revenue yield. For example, a consumption tax reduces the rewards from market labor relative to benefits of unmarketed goods and

5. See Pechman, *Federal Tax Policy*.
6. One should not incorrectly equate consumption and sales taxes. As described here, a consumption tax is a direct tax that could be collected exactly as an income tax. The issue is the deductibility of savings from taxable income.
7. Martin S. Feldstein, "The Welfare Cost of Capital Income Taxation," *Journal of Political Economy*, vol. 86 (April 1978), pt. 2, pp. 529–52.
8. See Michael J. Boskin and Joseph E. Stiglitz, "Recent Developments in Public Finance Theory," *American Economic Review*, vol. 67 (February 1977, *Papers and Proceedings, 1976*), pp. 295–301; George F. Break, "The Incidence and Economic Effects of Taxation," in *The Economics of Public Finance* (Brookings Institution, 1974), pp. 119–237; and I. M. D. Little, "Direct versus Indirect Taxes," *Economic Journal*, vol. 61 (September 1951), pp. 577–84.

services, including leisure. An income tax also excludes the home-produced income from the tax base and affects these choices but requires a lower rate than does a consumption tax yielding equal revenue.[9] The size of the tax rate affects the amount of efficiency loss. Thus if the choice between labor and leisure is more sensitive to tax changes than the choice between consumption and saving, an income tax with its lower rate may reduce efficiency less than would a consumption tax.

The available empirical evidence is insufficient for determining which tax reduces efficiency less. Because the United States now imposes an income tax, not a consumption tax, we focus on the income tax in the remainder of this paper.

## Problems with the Current System of Federal Income Taxation

The tax base of the federal income tax does not clearly resemble the usual definitions of economic income. Not only is much saving excluded from this base,[10] but about one-third of capital income is taxed twice, once because the corporate income tax (CIT) applies to profits and a second time when dividends and retained earnings are each again taxed at the personal level as dividends or as realized capital gains.[11] On the other hand, persons who own small businesses may reduce their tax liability by incorporating and by retaining earnings within the corporation to shelter them from personal income taxes.

Taxing corporate profits twice has a number of drawbacks. First, the various sectors of the economy differ in the degree to which they are incorporated and are therefore liable to pay the CIT. This variation in the taxation of capital income causes a reallocation of re-

9. This statement assumes that saving is positive, as it has been in the United States in every year since 1929, the first year covered in the national income accounts.

10. The proliferation of company pension plans, Keogh, and Independent Retirement Accounts has opened many tax-sheltered saving opportunities and has brought the tax systems somewhat closer to an expenditure tax.

11. The *Survey of Current Business* for March 1978 (vol. 58, p. 12) reported that before-tax corporate profits in 1977 were $171.6 billion, while personal income minus the sum of labor and three-quarters of self-employment income amount to $384.1 billion. Any reasonable adjustment of self-employment income would still leave corporate profits at more than one-third of capital income.

sources and a loss in economic efficiency. The static cost of this dead-weight loss has been estimated as approximately $8 billion a year.[12] This loss is in addition to the loss due to distortion of the consumption-saving decision discussed above.

Businesses in the agriculture, real estate, and crude oil and gas industries largely escape corporation income tax.[13] These businesses have either increased their share of private fixed investment or have bid up the prices of resources they use heavily. These calculations do not include the distortionary effects introduced by the reduction in the sum of corporate and personal taxes achieved by the incorporation of small businesses. To the best of our knowledge, no one has estimated the effects of this distortion.

Second, the CIT cannot be varied among owners of businesses subject to this tax according to such circumstances as income or number of dependents.[14] Thus a widow with eight children whose income consists solely of dividends from 100 shares of stock is in effect taxed at the same rate as a bachelor owner of 10,000 shares who has other sources of income.

Third, the determination of a corporate income tax base poses serious difficulties. Textbooks state that income equals revenue less costs. If firms started up, bought all their inputs, sold all their outputs, and liquidated all remaining assets and liabilities within the accounting period (say, a year), the determination of income would be simple. However, calculating the annual income of a firm whose sales and operations are continuing is more difficult.

The major accounting problem is not in computing the firm's revenues but in determining the costs of goods sold.[15] One aspect of this problem is to allocate across time the cost of the physical plant and equipment whose economic lifetimes exceed one year. Because of the

12. D. Fullerton and others, "A General Equilibrium Appraisal of U.S. Corporate Tax Integration," paper presented at the 1977 annual meeting of the Econometric Society in New York. The present value of the loss in the dynamic model exceeds $100 billion.

13. Businesses in agriculture and real estate are largely unincorporated. Those in crude oil and gas are predominantly incorporated but face very low effective corporate tax rates, owing to special provisions in the tax law.

14. Even the reduced corporate rate on the first $50,000 of profits is poorly correlated with the total income of the owners of the corporation.

15. The same problems occur in the taxation of noncorporate business income, but, as explained below, the availability of additional information on stock prices for most corporations substantially alters the situation.

lack of good markets in used capital equipment, reliable information on true economic depreciation is hard to get. Companies now may choose among several ad hoc depreciation patterns (some clearly more accelerated than economic depreciation). In fact, many firms report more depreciation on their tax returns than in their reports to stockholders in annual reports.[16]

Furthermore, in a 1962 Treasury Department study, wide variation in useful lives was found within prescribed asset classes, suggesting that true depreciation for a given type of asset varies among firms.[17] An efficient and fair tax system would require firms to deduct their *true* depreciation rather than to follow industry or economy-wide averages. It is extremely difficult to measure true depreciation for every firm, but as shown below, it is possible to tax perceived differences between true depreciation and such industry or economy-wide averages.

Another difficulty in determining the cost of goods sold is in the calculation of the cost of inventories. Several systems of inventory accounting are permitted and used. Differences among these systems cloud comparisons of business performance but, unlike the situation with depreciation, firms must use the same accounting procedure for tax purposes and for reports to stockholders.

Inflation further complicates the measurement of business income. Currently used tax accounting procedures, which are designed for a world of stable prices, can generate misleading results in a situation with significant inflation. The two aspects of this problem that have received most attention are depreciation and inventory accounting. While accelerated depreciation is permitted, the base for deduction is always original cost. When there is inflation the decline in a firm's net worth over a year is understated and its income and taxes are exaggerated. The most commonly used inventory accounting technique (first-in, first-out) also bloats income figures and hence taxes because it records the nominal appreciation of the inventoried stock as a profit, without allowing for replacement cost.

The two inflationary distortions just described artificially exaggerate both profits and taxes. Two other provisions work in the op-

16. The annual reports to shareholders normally contain a reconciliation, usually in the balance sheet or its notes.

17. Richard L. Pollock, *Tax Depreciation and the Need for the Reserve Ratio Test*, U.S. Department of the Treasury, Tax Policy Research Study 2 (GPO, 1968), p. 5.

posite direction. First, most corporations are net debtors. The Internal Revenue Service allows these firms to deduct as costs their entire interest bill, even if the debt was issued in a period of high inflation expectations and includes a large inflation premium. In fact, the real cost of this debt is much lower than indicated by the nominal interest payments, because the future payments on this obligation are made in "smaller" dollars. One way to correct the accounting procedure would be to continue to allow the full deductibility of interest costs but to require the reporting of the real depreciation of debt as income. With 10 percent interest and 8 percent inflation, this method would correctly compute the real cost of a fixed principal nominal debt as 2 percent. We would also tax the bond owner on only the 2 percent real interest rather than the 10 percent cash flow.

Another closely related adjustment to income must be made when nominal interest rates change, because of inflation or other causes. If interest rates rise, the nominal value of bonds (that is, corporate liabilities) declines. The owners of these bonds accrue a capital loss, while the equityholders, for whom the bonds are an obligation, enjoy a capital gain due to the real decline in the value of their debt. In the past twenty-five years interest rates have generally risen, making this gain on long-term liabilities a nontrivial correction to income.[18]

The points of the last two paragraphs can be illustrated simply. Consider a firm that issues a long-term bond for $1,000 at 10 percent interest. Inflation, which had been expected to be 6 percent, rises to 9 percent and is expected to stay at this new higher level. Interest rates on new issues go up, and at the end of the year the value of this company's bond has fallen to $800. The two points are that (1) the liability of the firm is in "smaller" dollars at the end of the year than initially anticipated, and (2) the bond market has reduced the valuation of the firm's debt from $1,000 to $800. Both factors decrease the value of the bondholders' position and symmetrically increase the net worth of the equityholders.

It is easy for a firm to calculate the effect of price changes on the real value of its outstanding debt. The other adjustments require more

---

18. The depreciation, inventory, and financial adjustments to income required with inflation are described and estimated in John B. Shoven and Jeremy I. Bulow, "Inflation Accounting and Nonfinancial Corporate Profits: Physical Assets" (including comments and discussion), *Brookings Papers on Economic Activity, 3:1975*, pp. 557–611; "Inflation Accounting and Nonfinancial Corporate Profits: Financial Assets and Liabilities" (including comments and discussion), ibid., *1:1976*, pp. 15–66.

information, some of which may involve a substantial burden. The method we propose below would not require complex calculations or require as much information, though our system works best when all information is available.

The current tax treatment of business income is further complicated by a variety of investment incentives. A partial list of these incentives includes the short depreciation lives granted by the asset depreciation range (ADR) method, the concentration of tax depreciation in early years, and the investment tax credit.[19] Because of these and other less important provisions, the average tax rate on corporate income is about 30 percent, although the statutory rate for most corporations would be just under 48 percent. These incentives, however, are not granted uniformly to all types of investments or to all firms. For example, in 1979 the investment tax credit applied fully only to equipment with a useful life in excess of seven years. The provisions of ADR help most those firms having assets whose actual lives greatly exceed those allowed under ADR. While we are far from convinced that there is any need to subsidize business investment, a system that rebated the same percentage of the purchase price on all investments would be preferable.

# Proposed System of Capital Income Taxation

An alternative income tax system, particularly as it would apply to business income, is described below. For practical reasons, under this system assets for which market values are available are frequently treated differently from other assets.

## Assets with Available Market Values

Owners of securities and assets with readily available market values would add to taxable income the sum of actual cash disbursements from such assets (dividends, interest, capital gain distributions, and so on) and the change in the real market value of the holdings over the accounting period. If income as computed by accountants differs

19. The differential pattern of subsidies implied by the investment tax credit and ADR causes serious problems of inequity and inefficiency. See Paul Taubman, "The Investment Tax Credit, Once More," *Boston College Industrial and Commercial Law Review*, vol. 14 (May 1973), pp. 871–90; "The Economics of the Asset Depreciation Range Problem: The Case Against ADR," *Journal of Finance*, vol. 27 (May 1972), pp. 511–24.

from the change in market value, no one actually receives the income calculated by the accountant. Thus the first advantage of our approach is that the accounting problems discussed in the preceding section have no bearing on federal taxes, because tax liability is based on market valuation which is unambiguous.[20] For typical common stocks the resulting income figure under our procedure is dividends paid plus real appreciation accrued during a calendar year. The computation of real, rather than nominal, gain would use the consumer price index.[21]

A second advantage of this method of computing business income for taxable domestic owners of marketed capital is that there would be no need for separate CIT liability. Thus much of the difference between the treatment of corporate and noncorporate capital earnings and most of the corresponding distortion in the allocation of investment would be eliminated. Third, the proposal would also eliminate the special tax adjustments now accorded to capital gains. Such gains would be taxed when accrued as ordinary income.

Under this tax system the CIT would be retained as a withholding mechanism for domestic owners. We suggest a 50 percent tax rate to be applied to taxable accounting income. Domestic taxable stockholders would claim the CIT as a cashable tax credit against personal income tax liability; foreign and tax-exempt stockholders such as pension funds, would not. For these holders of corporate stock the CIT is a crude charge for such government expenditures as police protection and the legal system that benefit the corporations whose stock they own. Domestic owners pay for these expenditures through other tax payments.

### Nonmarketed Assets

Our treatment of income of closely held firms and noncorporate businesses income resembles present practice and traditional reform proposals. Because changes in market value are not readily available, income as calculated by accountants is the only measure of business

20. Certainly an accounting of the economic performance of corporations would still prove necessary for such purposes as national income accounting and the evaluation of management performance. Therefore, in its annual report, each firm would have to justify nonstandard methods of depreciation and inventory accounting.

21. For a discussion of the issues in selecting a price index and an alternative view, see Edward F. Denison, "Price Series for Indexing the Income Tax System," in Henry J. Aaron, ed., *Inflation and the Income Tax* (Brookings Institution, 1976), pp. 233–61.

income available. We advocate the partnership method suggested by other economists whereby accounting income is imputed to the owners of the company and fully taxed whether retained or paid out.[22] Capital gains are taxed when realized, but the basis is raised by the retained earnings cumulated during the holding period. Noncorporate business income, as measured by accountants, also is added to the personal tax base. For both types of business the accounting changes we would support would adjust for inflation (as described above) and would allow firms to use any real depreciation pattern that matches their actual practice.

Durables, such as jewelry, rare paintings, and antiques require separate treatment. Changes in the estimated real value of these items would be taxed as ordinary income. The government could use insurance values in assessing the reasonableness of the owner's estimates. If the value of these assets at sale or the owner's death differs significantly from that suggested by past estimates, an explanation must be forthcoming or a tax penalty would be imposed. Either the taxpayer or the government would have the right to an assessment at any time.

Finally, we would eliminate such preferences as the investment tax credit, expensing (rather than amortizing) R&D outlays, and the excess of percentage over cost depletion. While we recognize the beneficial role of the investment tax credit as a stabilization instrument, in fact it has become a semipermanent subsidy to certain kinds of investments. Some may justify its present use as an offset for the effects of inflation and for the lack of real depreciation. With proper adjustments for inflation, it is no longer needed for that purpose.

### Changes in Revenue

The plan just outlined would lower tax receipts slightly. Eliminating the federal corporation income tax for taxable, domestic equity-holders reduces revenue about $48 billion, 81 percent of 1977 CIT receipts (see table 1, line 1). This tax reduction will show up either as retained earnings or dividends and will generate $23.6 billion in personal income tax receipts (table 1, line 2).

The proposed system would also tax the existing dividends and accrued capital gains more heavily than does the current system because people would move up the rate schedule as capital gains are

22. See Pechman, *Federal Tax Policy*, pp. 175–78.

**Table 1. Estimated Changes in Revenue Implied by Tax Reform, 1977**
(Billions of dollars)

| Reform | Revenue change |
|---|---|
| 1. Elimination of corporate income tax for taxable domestic shareholders (81 percent of 1977 federal tax liability)[a] | −48.1 |
| 2. Personal tax revenue on additional $49.3 billion in corporate income (49 percent of [1])[b] | +23.6 |
| 3. Elimination of $100 dividend exclusion[c] | +0.3 |
| 4. Tax on accrued capital gains from retained earnings not included in [2][d] | +24.3 |
| 5. Removal of tax on realized capital gains[e] | −6.2 |
| 6. Net change in tax receipts related to corporate income before elimination of current investment subsidies | −6.1 |

a. *Survey of Current Business*, vol. 56 (March 1978), p. 5. Feldstein and Frisch indicate that 19 percent of dividends do not go to individuals; see Martin S. Feldstein and Daniel Frisch, "Corporate Tax Integration: The Estimated Effects of Capital Accumulation and Tax Distribution of Two Integrated Proposals," *National Tax Journal*, vol. 30 (March 1977), p. 50, note 19.

b. Feldstein and Frisch, in "Corporate Tax Integration," calculate the average marginal tax rate on a full integration plan as 47 percent in 1973. We raise it to 49 percent to adjust for higher income levels in 1977.

c. *Tax Expenditures: Compendium of Background Material on Individual Provisions*, Committee Print, Senate Committee on the Budget, 94 Cong. 2 sess. (GPO, 1976), p. 63.

d. From *Survey of Current Business*, vol. 56 (March 1978), p. 12, before-tax profits of $171.6 less federal, state, and local profits tax of $69.1, less dividends of $61.3 yields retained earnings of 49 percent of $61.3 billion. We use 49 percent of 81 percent of $61.3 billion.

e. *Tax Expenditures*, p. 65.

treated as ordinary income. The increase in revenue from this source is not shown in the table. The $100 dividend exclusion could be repealed because it would no longer be needed to reduce double taxation of corporate income (table 1, line 3). The proposed system also taxes capital gains fully as they accrue rather than at half rate when the gain is realized (table 1, line 4). While capital gains are a particularly volatile component of income, on the average our system will generate more revenue from this source than does the current system.

On the average a competitive stock market valuation of a firm will increase in the long run dollar for dollar with its true retained earnings. We estimate real retained earnings of corporations as $61 billion in 1977.[23] If this amount is reflected in accrued capital gains for

23. For derivation of this estimate, see note d of table 1. The correction to real rather than nominal cost of debt raises the income of the equityholders but symmetrically lowers the income of the interest recipient. The average marginal personal tax rate of equityholders far exceeds that on such bondholders as pension funds, insurance companies, banks, and other such institutions. Any gain the firm experiences because of its financial liabilities is similarly matched by a loss for the holders of those obligations. The depreciation and inventory adjustments, however, do not have this feature of "the other side of the coin."

domestic taxpayers, our system would raise $24.3 billion from this source,[24] in contrast to $6.2 billion generated by the present system, which is based on realizations taxed at preferred rates. If we aggregate all the revenue adjustments discussed above and shown in table 1, the result is a net shortfall of $6.1 billion relative to present receipts. Elimination of accelerated depreciation, the asset depreciation range system, and the investment tax credit would raise additional revenues; hence the net tax loss would be less than $5 billion, or roughly the magnitude of business tax cuts enacted in 1978.

The next section shows that substantial gains in efficiency, equity, and simplicity from the introduction of this system would easily justify such a modest reduction in revenue.

## Comparison of This Proposal with Other Integration Schemes and Current Practice

Our particular plan differs from both the partial and full integration plans advanced by others.[25] Because our plan would tax both dividends and real accrued capital gains (including those arising from the retention of earnings), the plan is one of full integration. The proposed treatment of marketed securities is superior in at least four respects to the more familiar partnership method in which stockholders are taxed on their pro rata share of taxable accounting earnings.

First, assets other than corporate stock yield real capital gains, which should be treated similarly, although tax evasion on assets such as diamonds may be difficult to control. Second, the partnership method is based on taxable accounting income, which is inevitably somewhat arbitrary because depreciation is based on economy-wide or industry-wide data. As long as the stock market responds to economic income in setting stock prices, the system proposed here will tax economic income while the partnership method will not. For example, who benefits if a firm retains some part of accounting earnings, but the price of the stock fails to respond? The correct answer

24. The implied marginal tax rate of 49 percent is slightly higher than the figure obtained for 1973 by Martin S. Feldstein and Daniel Frisch, "Corporate Tax Integration: The Estimated Effects of Capital Accumulation and Tax Distribution of Two Integrated Proposals," *National Tax Journal*, vol. 30 (March 1977), pp. 37–52, because of increases in nominal income between 1973–77.

25. See, for example, Feldstein and Frisch, "Corporate Tax Integration."

seems to be nobody. The phantom earnings stem from imperfections of the accounting. Thus one major advantage of our approach is that it appeals to market valuations whenever possible. Third, in most discussions of the partnership method of allocating retained earnings, capital gains are taxed upon realization. This provision encourages people to postpone sales in order to reduce the present discounted value of the tax payment. If people postpone sales or are locked into retaining an asset with a large capital gain, they can end up with less than optimally diversified portfolios.[26] Under an accrual tax system, no such problem arises.

The system proposed here has another advantage over the partnership method. When a person sells his shares during the calendar year, the partnership system requires an estimate of profits as of the date of sale in order to credit the seller with a pro rata share of corporate profits. Because quarterly reports are generally based on unaudited data and firms often post certain changes only once a year, this task is especially difficult. In our plan the seller merely counts as his capital gain or loss the real increase or decrease in price since the past December 31.

In certain respects the system proposed here is better than both current practice and the partnership method. For example, both the current system and the partnership method cause a powerful lock-in effect that is absent from our system. Both the current law or the partnership method require retention of information on the tax basis until the gain is realized. Proposals for heirs to assume the tax basis of bequeathed stock would necessitate record-keeping for fifty or seventy-five years. Under our system all that is needed is last year's and this year's value (or purchase and sale price) for current-year computations. Our system also has other advantages relative to current practice. For instance, under present law, in the period between the declaration of a dividend and the exdividend date, a seller of a stock is reimbursed for the dividend owed to him by an increase in the price of the stock, though the buyer presumably only pays the after-tax value of the dividend. The seller thus converts a dividend into a capital gain. In our system the buyer and seller are treated fairly since capital gains and dividends are taxed identically.

26. See Marshall E. Blume, Jean Crockett, and Irwin Friend, "Stockownership in the United States: Characteristics and Trends," *Survey of Current Business*, vol. 54 (November 1974), pp. 31–32, who find that most investors have highly concentrated (nondiversified) portfolios.

## Administrative Considerations

The system of taxation proposed here has a number of administrative advantages. It requires fewer intrusions into the privacy of the taxpayer, requires less record-keeping, and is easier to enforce than the present system.

People now must report dividends received from all corporations, as well as realized capital gains. For widely traded stocks the proposed system would require additional information on last year's and this year's market value—a task we do not consider burdensome for dividend-paying stocks, as the corporation could supply end-of-year quotations on the 1099 form now used to report dividend payments. Each corporation would have to attribute taxes paid to stockholders, but since they already do the record-keeping for dividends, no extra costs are involved. Monitoring and enforcing the tax provisions for such stocks would be no more difficult than they are now.

For listed stocks paying no dividend, the need to list the change in value of the stock during the year would require more information from the taxpayer than does the present system, although some taxpayers include stock values on state personal property tax forms. The extra record-keeping for the stockholder would be minimal. Corporations would have to issue forms for each stockholder indicating taxes paid. Presumably this requirement would be a burden only for those firms who never issue 1099s and would have to set up a new computer program. Monitoring and enforcing difficulties would be minor as profit-making firms would have withheld taxes and would have to inform both the government and the stockholder. An extra report would be required for unlisted firms with losses, but it would be in the interest of the stockholders for the companies to issue 1099 forms. Indeed, it seems likely that it would be easier to enforce capital gains taxes on such stocks than under the present system.

The major problem with taxing capital gains on unlisted stock or on a noncorporate asset is establishing the price of the stock or the asset. While it would be possible to approximate capital gains from changes in retained earnings and in price earnings ratios for similar stock, the estimates would be imprecise. For such firms, we recommend the alternative partnership tax treatment, which we foresee as having no problems not present in the current law.

It is alleged that taxing accrued capital gains is undesirable because it will force some stockholders to liquidate stocks to pay their tax liability and that taxpayers may feel it unfair to be taxed before they receive their income.[27] While such situations may arise, they are not a source of difficulty, because a person's income increases by definition when his stock appreciates; and in our system he can realize such income at the cost of broker fees without raising his tax burden. It should be noted that in our system those capital gains that arise from the retention of earnings will have their liability covered by the corporation payment of the 50 percent withholding tax.

There will probably remain, however, some capital gains and losses caused by changes in expectations about sales and profits. We advocate lifetime income averaging, explained below, to reduce the severity of these fluctuations. But it will probably still be true that gains and tax payments will fluctuate over the business cycle. As for the taxpayer who owes much money because of his successful investment, we do not see why his 1 percent tax-deductible brokerage fees should deter him from paying his taxes.

Our system will also affect the stability of the economy. If capital gain taxes increase during booms, accrual taxation of capital gains will generate higher taxes and hence lower disposable economic income than does the present system. Even those economists who argue that temporary fluctuations in income have no effect on consumption admit that they affect purchases of consumer durables. The implementation of our system should strengthen the automatic stabilizers already built into the tax system and thus could improve the macroeconomic performance of the economy.

### Lifetime Averaging

The feasibility of one feature of our plan—lifetime averaging—requires some special attention. The system works in the following way. Each year a person or couple is informed by the government of the present value of his total previous taxable income,[28] present value of taxes paid for all previous years, and number of previous years in the tax system. He then adds this year's taxable income to the present value of his previous total, calculates his average taxable income by dividing the new total by number of years in the system, finds the tax on this average income, and multiplies this average tax by the number

27. Pechman, *Federal Tax Policy*, p. 106.
28. This number would be equivalent to the current balance if past income had been placed in an interest-bearing savings account. The interest rate could be set equal to the average rate on federal government debt.

**Table 2. Simplest Form of Tax Computation under Lifetime Averaging**

| Computation item | Amount |
|---|---|
| 1. Number of years in system | ———— |
| 2. Present value of past taxable income | ———— |
| 3. Present value of past tax payments calculated as if made under current law | ———— |
| 4. Current year's taxable income | ———— |
| 5. Total lifetime taxable income | ———— |
| 6. Lifetime tax obligation | ———— |
| 7. Amount owed Treasury for current year | ———— |

Notes: Line 2 is the amount shown on line 5 of last year's return multiplied by $(1 + r)$; line 5 equals line 2 plus line 4; line 6 equals line 1 taxes on (line 5/line 1); line 7 equals line 6 minus line 3.

of years in the system. From this lifetime tax liability, he subtracts previous payments to find his current tax bill. Table 2 shows the steps necessary to calculate this year's liability.

This averaging system computes the tax an individual would have owed if his income in each year were equal to the average over the period and if the same tax law applied in each year. Under these circumstances the only informational requirements are the continuously updated figures on total taxable income, total taxes paid, the appropriate discount rate, and years in the tax system.

Complications arise if the tax schedule changes, since the same constant income would have yielded a different tax in the past than under the current schedule. We propose that the person be treated as if he had paid his tax on the basis of his past actual taxable income and the current rate schedule. The necessary information then would be the number of years in the system, total taxable income in each year, and total adjusted tax payments. The adjustment would be calculated separately from each year's income. It might be thought that it would be difficult for the government to retain taxable income for long periods. The social security system has demonstrated this is not so, since it retains a continuously updated record of annual earnings for each social security number.

## Conclusion

This chapter has presented a tax reform plan that is simpler, more conducive to economic efficiency, and more equitable, both horizontally and vertically, than the present system. The proposal in aggregate generates roughly the same revenue at existing rates as the taxes it would replace.

The simplifications arise because several tax systems are collapsed into one, thereby eliminating unintended interactions between them and reducing paperwork. Moreover, the considerable time and effort spent in converting income from one tax base to another would no longer be profitable. The proposed system requires that the taxpayer refer only to last year's return in computing capital gains and in averaging income. This contrasts with the current practice that occasionally demands information from previous generations. Lastly, in terms of simplification the proposed tax system would refer wherever possible to market valuations and thus would diminish reliance on accounting. The intense periodic debates over proper depreciation and inventory accounting rules would become irrelevant.

The efficiency gains arise because differences in the taxation of income from various sources would be reduced. This change would cause resources to be reallocated toward those activities that currently are relatively heavily taxed. In addition, under the proposed scheme people would not be hampered in acquiring their desired portfolios by the lock-in effect.

Horizontal equity would be improved because people with the same economic income would pay the same tax regardless of its source. Vertical equity also would be improved because people with low earnings but modest net worth in corporate stocks would pay reduced taxes. The proposed plan would also enhance the automatic stabilizing effect of the tax system. The life cycle feature of our proposed plan would end the tax penalty faced by those whose income fluctuates severely from year to year.

# PART FOUR

# The Tax Treatment of the Family

HARVEY E. BRAZER  *University of Michigan*

# Income Tax Treatment of the Family

AS THE PROPORTION of wives working outside the home nears one-half, clearly one of the major unresolved issues in income tax policy is how to treat married couples relative to single people. Practice varies widely among developed countries. At one extreme, Australia and Canada assess husband and wife separately, treating each as an individual when income exceeds a modest threshold. At the other extreme, France and the Netherlands aggregate the incomes of husband, wife, and dependent children and apply tax rates that vary inversely at each level of taxable income with family size. The United Kingdom occupies an intermediate position, permitting each spouse to be taxed as an individual, but only on earned income.[1]

In the United States married couples may aggregate their incomes, and if they do, they are taxed at lower rates than single people are.[2] As a consequence of this and other features of the tax law, marriage

I am grateful to Boris I. Bittker, Marjorie C. Brazer, Meredith Edwards, Alan R. Prest, Harvey S. Rosen, Emil M. Sunley, Stanley S. Surrey, and the editors for helpful comments on an earlier draft.

1. Property income is always attributed to the husband for tax purposes, even when ownership interests accrue exclusively to the wife. A recent publication of the Organisation for Economic Co-operation and Development, Committee on Fiscal Affairs (*The Treatment of Family Units in OECD Member Countries under Tax and Transfer Systems* [Paris: OECD, 1977]), came to my attention too late to make use of it in this paper.

2. Single people who have one or more dependents may qualify for an intermediate status, head of household, subject to a rate schedule that is somewhere between the schedule for married couples and that for single people. See 26 U.S.C. 33.

or its dissolution may give rise to major increases or decreases in tax liabilities. The change depends largely on the distribution of income between those affected. Single adults pay the same tax whether they live alone or together, but their taxes are substantially different from those of married couples. Thus the U.S. income tax emphasizes equal treatment of married couples having the same total income.[3] It is not neutral toward marriage. Whether marriage increases or decreases a couple's combined tax obligation depends on aggregate income, its distribution between husband and wife, whether or not they itemize deductions, how medical expenses and capital losses are distributed between them, their eligibility for the earned income credit and the child care credit, and some other minor features of the law.

The present income tax law, therefore, through its definition of the basic units for taxation is capricious in its determination of the relative tax liabilities of people who differ only in their formal marital status. But a progressive income tax poses a difficult choice. It is possible to tax equally a two-earner married couple and two cohabiting single persons when each pair has the same aggregate income. It is also possible to tax equally one- and two-earner married couples having the same income. But it is not possible to do both. Until 1969 income taxation in the United States favored marriage, but since then two single earners, depending on their circumstances, may or may not pay less in income tax than a married couple with equal earnings.

In this paper I outline the conflicting objectives of tax policy that are at issue, trace the relevant changes in the tax law since 1969, and present some illustrative calculations of the impact of marital status on income tax liabilities. My principal conclusion is that the traditional view that the family is the appropriate taxable unit, long an article of faith among tax authorities, is inconsistent with the growing tendency for women to participate actively in the labor force for most of their adult lives and with the increasing number of people who opt for a life-style that does not include formal marriage. These changes suggest the enhanced importance of tax neutrality toward marital status, as opposed to equality among married couples, and point to the imposition of the income tax on the individual as the taxable entity.

3. Boris Bittker refers to legally married couples as a "crisply defined and readily verified group" in "Federal Income Taxation and the Family," *Stanford Law Review*, vol. 27 (July 1975), p. 1399.

## Policy Objectives

The objectives of any aspect of tax policy can generally be stated in terms of equity and economic efficiency. Equity is an elusive concept. Virtually no one now pretends to define vertical equity in a way that can have relevance for tax policy, and Musgrave sounds a deeply pessimistic note on both vertical and horizontal equity:

In the absence of vertical equity norms, the case for horizontal equity is reduced to providing protection against malicious discrimination, an objective which might be met more simply by a tax lottery. Vertical equity in turn cannot be defined without horizontal equity norms, as it must deal with differential treatment of people who, to begin with, have been grouped on horizontal equity grounds.[4]

Surely, however, this position goes further than necessary, at least concerning horizontal equity. Granted that the old orthodoxy, calling for the equal treatment of equals, with equality defined in reference to income and subject to adjustment for number of dependents and some other circumstances, is less than perfect. Nonetheless, it does have a fundamental intuitive appeal to one's sense of justice that makes its outcomes preferable to Musgrave's lottery and to the norms of the "new public finance," for which horizontal equity requires only that all people face the same tax schedules (*provided* they all have the same utility functions—that is, the same tastes and abilities). In these circumstances people of equal income (and thus utility) are taxed equally and utility orderings remain unchanged.[5] If on the other hand, utility functions differ among people, horizontal equity can be achieved only if tax schedules are appropriately matched to utility functions. Because analysts can hardly pretend to know what people's various utility functions are, however, horizontal equity eludes their grasp.[6]

4. Richard A. Musgrave, "ET, OT, and SBT," *Journal of Public Economics*, vol. 6 (July-August 1976), p. 4.

5. Martin Feldstein, "On the Theory of Tax Reform," ibid., pp. 82–87.

6. Feldstein's argument in ibid., p. 95, is developed in the context of the theory of tax reform when he stipulates that "*if two individuals would have the same utility level if the tax remained unchanged, they should also have the same utility level if the tax is changed*" (emphasis in the original). Accepting this line of reasoning is to adopt a criterion for justifying tax policy changes even more stringent than the Pareto optimality rule, for the latter, while demanding that no one be made absolutely worse off, permits some being made relatively better off. It is thus difficult to imagine any changes in the tax code being justifiable on equity grounds under

The choice, then, would seem to lie between Musgrave's lottery (ex ante) and the old orthodoxy position, as most forcefully and uncompromisingly set forth in Henry Simons's *Personal Income Taxation*.[7] I opt for the latter, partly because of my view that people's utility functions probably do not differ very much, at any rate not enough or in sufficiently specifiable ways to warrant differences in their tax schedules or tax treatment. A second reason for this preference lies in a lack of faith in the power of imperfect markets to achieve appropriately compensating adjustments.

There remains, however, the basic question of whether the criterion "equal treatment of equals" is properly applied to the individual, to the household irrespective of formal marital relations between adults, or to the couple if married and the single person otherwise. It may be argued that the welfare of the individual is a function not simply of his or her income but of the aggregate income of the group that constitutes a household by reason of its pooling the income of its members and sharing collectively in consumption decisions and enjoyment. In this view the horizontal equity criterion would apply to the household, presumably with appropriate allowance for variation in size. Marriage is neither a necessary nor a sufficient condition for the establishment of a household; that economic union may be just as real and just as enduring whether the people in it are brothers, sisters, mother and daughter, friends, or spouses. The difficulty, though, is that if a progressive income tax were to be applied to household income, it is impossible to imagine acceptable means of avoiding incentives to create households in some instances and to avoid their disclosure in others. Thus the marital unit is resorted to as the readily identifiable "group" and everyone else is treated as a single person. An evenhanded approach to the objective of horizontal equity would avoid this burden on (or benefit to) marriage and treat everyone alike—as individuals. Given progression, therefore, the objective of horizontal equity suggests that entry into or departure from a marriage should not affect a person's tax liabilities, that the tax laws should realize neutrality with respect to marital status. This marriage

---

Feldstein's rule; whatever is, must and should remain. Even if that conclusion were supportable in equity terms, it is not acceptable from the standpoint of efficiency. It is rejected here on equity grounds as well because the point of departure, what is, may be wrong, and losses are not compensated through perfect market adjustments.

7. Henry C. Simons, *Personal Income Taxation: The Definition of Income as a Problem of Fiscal Policy* (University of Chicago Press, 1938).

neutrality is achieved if the individual is designated as the unit for taxation.

Vertical equity need be of no concern here, except perhaps at some peripheral points, because society can achieve its distributional objectives whatever the choice of the basic unit of taxation, whatever the role of marital status in the determination of tax liabilities, and whatever choices are made regarding the various elements of the tax law that apply to individuals and married couples. If, however, the graduated rate schedules were replaced by a single uniform rate applicable to total net income, with no personal exemptions, deductions, or credits, the choice of a unit for taxation and marital status would become irrelevant.

Efficiency as an objective of tax policy connotes the avoidance of reductions in income or utility due to tax-inspired changes in people's behavior. An income tax, no matter how the taxable unit may be defined, is intrinsically inefficient because it is unneutral between work and leisure, consumption and saving, and high- and low-risk occupations and investments. The choice of taxable entity may exacerbate this unneutrality; it cannot, quite obviously, eliminate it. In the present context, therefore, the policy goal is to choose the alternative that minimizes inefficiency, that yields a pattern of behavior as close as possible to what would have emerged under a tax that is neutral among available options.

A progressive tax on the aggregate income of couples cannot be efficient, because secondary earners among married couples, given the same labor market opportunities, face higher marginal tax rates than do single people, the first earner, or the worker in one-earner married couples. Thus the ratio of net to gross wages will vary among people in otherwise identical circumstances, and decisions on labor market entry, investment in human capital, occupation, and risk-taking will be distorted. Welfare losses result when people choose alternatives offering higher net-of-tax rewards in lieu of those that yield higher gross-of-tax returns.[8] Most clear, perhaps, is the inefficiency caused by the high marginal tax rates facing second earners (still typically wives). Because the elasticity of the supply of labor of

8. Thus, for example, a person may face the alternatives of working as a research analyst for $8 an hour, $4.80 net of tax, or replacing the housekeeper who earns $5 an hour. The gain to the person is 20 cents an hour plus the saving of nondeductible costs of working outside the home; the loss to society is $3 an hour. The implied tax rate is 40 percent. At, say, 30 percent there remains a monetary incentive to stay with the research job.

married women is substantially higher than that of married men or single people,[9] the "inverse elasticity" rule would clearly suggest that for economic efficiency they should be taxed at lower, not higher, marginal rates, irrespective of the choice of taxable unit.

Thus efficiency considerations would call for lower marginal income tax rates for married women than for others in the labor force. If the married couple is chosen as the unit for taxation on equity grounds, a trade-off between efficiency and equity would be involved. The efficiency losses from high tax rates on secondary workers would be reduced if the individual were the taxable entity, because marginal tax rates on such workers would be the same as those for all other workers. And if a decision to favor secondary workers were made to attain greater efficiency, smaller reductions in marginal tax rates would be needed than if the couple were the taxable entity. I find, therefore, that on efficiency grounds the individual is superior to the married couple as the unit for taxation.

On equity grounds, the choice is harder. If income is seen essentially as a means to consumption, or if the income tax were converted to a consumption tax, treating the group that shares in consumption as the taxable unit has some appeal, but not if the arbitrary line around the group is drawn by the ties of formal marriage. Nor does this approach retain its attraction if one keeps clearly in mind that the taxable object is income and that the use to which that income is put is best regarded in terms of both equity and efficiency as being of no concern to the tax laws and their administrators. Hence on both counts the case for defining the individual as the taxable unit seems strong.

I now take a closer look at the current U.S. personal income tax provisions that permit tax liabilities to depend in greater or lesser degree on marital status.

## Impact of Income Tax Provisions[10]

Until 1948 the taxable unit under the personal income tax was the individual. The Revenue Act of 1948 provided for aggregation of the income of married couples together with income splitting and the

9. On this point see Michael J. Boskin and Eytan Sheshinski, "Optimal Tax Treatment of the Family: Married Couples," *Journal of Public Economics,* 1980, forthcoming.

10. This section refers to the tax law as it stood after the passage of the Tax Reduction and Simplification Act of 1977 (P.L. 95-30) but before congressional action on President Carter's proposals of January 1978.

continued use of one tax rate schedule. In 1951 Congress extended approximately one-half of the benefit of income splitting to people who maintain a home for one or more dependents and who thus qualify to file tax returns as heads of households.

Thus the tax law penalized single people and favored married couples in which only one partner had income. But it taxed equally couples with income equally divided between the spouses and single people with incomes equal to half that of such couples. Marriage, except that between people with substantially equal incomes, typically was rewarded with a tax cut. With the partial exception of those recognized as heads of households, however, that tax advantage accrued only to legally married partners. Given contemporary mores, the personal income tax seems an inappropriate instrument for penalizing those who do not choose heterosexual wedlock blessed by civil or religious authority.

The Tax Reform Act of 1969 brought some relief to single taxpayers who had long complained that they paid more tax than couples with the same income—3.6 percent more when the taxable income of both was $1,000, 25.2 percent more at $12,000, and 42.1 percent more at $28,000. Beyond $28,000 of taxable income the absolute amount of the discrepancy continued to grow, but the percentage difference declined.[11] The act provided that single people should not incur tax liabilities greater than 120 percent of those of married couples with equal taxable incomes.

### The Rate Schedule

With the passage of the 1969 act, it was no longer possible to generalize about the effect of marital status on tax liabilities. Before the act, marriage would always reduce or leave unchanged the aggregate tax liability of the couple. After 1969 marriage could either increase or decrease tax liability depending on the combined taxable income of the partners and on its distribution between them. Table 1 shows the distribution of income at selected levels of taxable income, ranging from $5,000 to $200,000, at which marriage leaves tax liabilities unaffected. As combined taxable income rises, so must the proportion of income that accrues to one of the partners if the marriage is neither to incur a tax penalty nor confer a tax benefit. A marriage penalty occurs for families with equally divided income

---

11. For a more detailed history of income tax treatment of the family, see the chapter by Alicia Munnell in this volume.

**Table 1. Break-Even Distributions of Taxable Income between Marriage Partners and the Marriage Penalty when Distribution Is 50/50 at Selected Levels of Income, 1978**

| Aggregate taxable income (dollars) | Break-even distribution, husband/wife or wife/husband[a] (percent) | | Marriage penalty when distribution is 50/50 (dollars) | |
|---|---|---|---|---|
| 5,000 | 60/40 to 40/60 | | 0 | |
| 8,000 | 50/50 | | 0 | |
| 12,000 | 61/39 | | 40 | |
| 20,000 | 73/27 | | 200 | |
| 30,000 | 80/20 | | 840 | |
| 40,000 | 82/18 | | 1,680 | |
| | Property income[b] | Earned income[c] | Property income[b] | Earned income[c] |
| 60,000 | 88/12 | 83/17 | 3,520 | 3,280 |
| 100,000 | 93/7 | 82/18 | 4,800 | 3,480 |
| 200,000 | 96/4 | 84/16 | 4,800 | 3,480 |

a. The break-even distribution is the one at which marriage or its dissolution does not change the combined tax liabilities of the partners by reason of the impact of the tax rate schedules for joint returns and single people who are not heads of households. For heads of households tax rates lie roughly halfway between those for single people and those filing joint returns. When income is more concentrated than the indicated ratio, marriage reduces taxes and its dissolution increases taxes. When income is less concentrated, marriage increases taxes and its dissolution decreases taxes. At combined incomes below $8,000 marriage reduces tax liability however income is divided.
b. Tax rates extend to a maximum of 70 percent.
c. Maximum marginal tax rate is 50 percent.

when income exceeds $8,000. The fraction of income that must be received by one spouse if no marriage penalty is to result rises to 84 percent at $200,000 if all income is earned (96 percent if all income is unearned).[12] A marriage penalty results if income is more equally divided than the critical ratios in table 1. This tax penalty reaches its maximum when the taxable incomes of the pair are equal.[13]

12. For single people who are not heads of households the 50 percent maximum marginal tax rate applies to earned taxable income in excess of $32,000. For joint returns the 50 percent rate limit applies to taxable income in excess of $44,000. On property income marginal tax rates continue to rise beyond 50 percent, reaching 70 percent on taxable income of about $100,000 for single people and $200,000 for joint returns of married couples.

13. Readers familiar with the Internal Revenue Code realize that the calculations underlying table 1 and the numbers presented in the text take some liberties with the law. Because of the "zero rate" bracket, or standard deduction, $2,200 for single persons and $3,200 for married couples filing joint returns in 1978, two taxable incomes of, say, $6,000 do not become an aggregate taxable income of $12,000 when those earning them marry. Rather, because marriage reduces the standard deduction by $1,200, two $6,000 incomes become one $13,200 taxable income. I prefer, however, to treat the impact of the rate schedule on the taxation of single versus married people separately from that of the deductions, including the standard deduction (to continue terminology rendered obsolete by the Revenue Act of 1977).

Marriage offers a tax bonus to couples when one spouse receives a larger proportion of the aggregate taxable income than the break-even distribution. For example, if one spouse received income of $30,000 and the other nothing, the tax liability would be $9,390 before and $7,880 after marriage, for a saving of $1,510, or 16 percent.[14]

Thus marriage or divorce may substantially increase or decrease taxes depending on how income is distributed. That the swing is large by any conceivable standard, even at the modestly high income of $30,000, may be seen in the fact that marriage may cost as much as $840 or save $1,510. A difference among couples with equal taxable incomes of as much as $2,350 at the extremes seems unconscionably large. And the dollar dimensions of the problem are larger at higher incomes.

One may argue that married couples with twice the income of a single person have more than twice as much ability to pay taxes because they enjoy economies of scale in the operation of the household and because the value of the household services of the nonworking spouse are not taxable. This argument supports larger taxes on a one-earner couple than on two people who maintain separate households, each with half as much income, and suggests that the schedules of the pre-1969 act were defective. On the other hand, the inconsistency and unevenness in the impact of the present tax rate schedules, even in terms of this argument, are not justified. The inconsistency, if not capriciousness, of the effect of these rate schedules arises, of course, because almost half of all wives work, some have property income as well, and the proportion of the income of married couples attributable to the wives varies so widely. Moreover, households of two or more people who are not formally and legally married will similarly pay amounts of tax that are different from the tax of married couples because of the rate schedules. And any case that can be made for taxing married couples more heavily than single people may just as forcefully be made for any two-adult household relative to one-adult households.

Even the "virtue" of the current law in taxing married couples with equal taxable incomes equally becomes a flaw once the untaxed home-

14. At a taxable income level of $60,000 the corresponding figures are $26,390, $22,300, $4,090, and 15.5 percent, and at $100,000 they are $53,090, $45,180, $7,910, and 15 percent, assuming that the 50 percent maximum marginal tax rate does not apply.

makers' services in one-earner households and the extra work-related expenses in two-earner households are recognized.

### Personal Deductions

In addition to the rate schedule, several major structural elements of the personal income tax influence tax liabilities by affecting the size of an individual's or married couple's taxable income.

STANDARD DEDUCTION. The Tax Reduction and Simplification Act of 1977 was another chapter in the rapidly changing story of the percentage standard deduction and the low-income allowance. It created a "zero rate bracket" of $2,200 for single people and $3,200 for married couples, replacing the previous fixed standard deduction. These zero-rate brackets constitute a threshold that itemized personal deductions must exceed before a taxpayer is better off itemizing medical expenses, charitable contributions, state and local taxes, interest paid, casualty losses, and a miscellaneous bag of other nonbusiness expenses.

The zero-rate bracket is larger for two single people than for a couple—$2,200 for each single person or a total of $4,400, versus $3,200 for the couple, a reduction of $1,200 should the two single people marry. Thus apart from the impact of the rate schedules, for two single people, each of whom has income at least equal to the personal exemption of $750 plus $2,200 and does not itemize deductions, marriage would add $1,200 to their joint taxable income and at least $170 to their tax bill. At the top of the income scale this feature of the current tax law could cost as much as $840.[15] Conversely, divorce may reduce taxes in the same circumstances by $170 to $840 a year.

This feature of the code is clearly not neutral toward marital status, nor can it be justified as a means of attaining equality in the taxation of married couples with equal incomes. It does, however, exempt from tax individuals and families with incomes below the poverty line. The zero-rate bracket of $2,200 for single people and $3,200 for married couples, combined with personal exemptions, comes very close to official poverty thresholds. On the other hand, a marriage-neutral exclusion of $2,200 for individuals and *each* of the marriage partners would be overly generous to the latter relative to the poverty line. But surely this is a bit of sophistry in circumstances in which

15. The tax payable by a married couple on the first $1,200 of taxable income is $170; $840 is the top marginal tax rate of 70 percent multiplied by $1,200.

social security taxes are paid on the first dollar of earned income and indirect taxes burden the lowest incomes.

MEDICAL EXPENSES. A floor of 3 percent of adjusted gross income applies to medical expenses that may be taken as an itemized personal deduction, and drugs are counted as medical expenses only to the extent that they exceed 1 percent of AGI. Suppose two single people each have an AGI of $10,000 and that one incurs $600 in medical expenses each year, $300 of which is deductible. If they marry, their combined income is $20,000 and deductible medical expenses are zero.

In this illustration the floors on medical deductions impose only a minor tax charge on marriage. At higher levels of income, however, when both parties have substantial incomes (or could share incomes through alimony payments following divorce) and medical expenses are incurred largely by one of them, the reduction in deductible medical expenses due to marriage will always be equal to 4 percent of the other partner's AGI.[16] If that income amounts to $100,000, for example, the reduction will be as much as $4,000, and the medical-expense marriage penalty may reach $2,800. As long as medical expenses are deductible only when they go beyond a floor or threshold expressed as a percentage of the taxable unit's AGI, treating the married couple as the unit for taxation makes this tax penalty on marriage inevitable.

### *Personal Credits*[17]

Personal credits against income tax that vary in amount with the marital status of the taxpayer include the earned income credit, the general tax credit, and the credit for employment-related expenses, commonly known as the child care credit.[18]

16. Three percent for medical expenses other than drugs and 1 percent for drugs, assuming that the expenses of the other partner for both categories exceed the 3 percent and 1 percent of his or her AGI.

17. Although possibly affected by marital status, the investment tax credit, the jobs tax credit, the credit for expenses of work incentive programs, and the credit for the elderly are not dealt with here. The first of these is affected by marital status primarily through the $25,000 limit on its full deductibility against tax due; the second has a $100,000 a year limit; the third is fully deductible up to $50,000 a year; and the fourth generally applies only to those not eligible for social security or railroad retirement benefits. Thus the total number of taxpayers involved in tax penalties on marriage via these credits would seem far too small to warrant their discussion here. For the relevant limitations see 26 U.S.C. 53, 83, 41.

18. 26 U.S.C. 47, 46, 50, respectively.

EARNED INCOME CREDIT. The earned income credit was designed to offset the social security tax on low-income wage earners. People who maintain a home for themselves and one or more dependent children are eligible for it. In 1978 the credit was 10 percent of earned income up to $4,000, reduced by 10 percent of the AGI of the taxpayer in excess of $4,000, thus reaching a maximum of $400 and declining to zero at $8,000 of AGI (or earned income if it is greater than AGI). If the credit exceeds the tax liability, the difference is refundable. In this respect the earned income credit is unique.

Married couples can claim the credit only if they file joint returns. Thus the marriage of two people, each of whom earns $4,000 and supports one or more dependent children, results in the loss of the two $400 refundable credits against income tax. This $800 loss, 10 percent of their joint income, occurs even though the marriage in no way affects the aggregate income of the two people or their social security tax obligations. If they were to form a common household without the sanction of a marriage ceremony, or if they were of the same sex, they would be $800 a year better off than if married because of the earned income credit alone.[19]

GENERAL TAX CREDIT. In 1978 a tax credit was allowed on all returns equal to the greater of $35 per exemption claimed or 2 percent of up to $9,000 of taxable income, that is, $180. As a result of this feature of the tax code, marriage may either increase or decrease tax liability. At one extreme, if neither partner itemizes deductions and each had taxable income before marriage that totaled less than $9,000, the total excluded by reason of the zero-rate bracket declines by $1,200 with marriage, increasing taxable income by this amount; in those cases marriage may increase the general tax credit by as much as 2 percent of $1,200, or $24. At the other extreme, if two single people entitled in total to five or fewer exemptions and reporting $9,000 or more of taxable income decide to marry, the total credit available is reduced $180 by marriage, other things constant, from $360 to $180.

19. It is of interest to note that the tax credit for political contributions equal to 50 percent of eligible contributions is subject to a maximum of $25 for single people and $50 for married couples filing joint returns, so that it does not involve a marriage penalty (26 U.S.C. 45). Similarly, the additional first-year depreciation allowance for small business permitted for any one year is limited to depreciable property costing $10,000 for a single person and $20,000 for a married couple filing joint returns.

CHILD CARE CREDIT. The child care tax credit is 20 percent of employment-related expenses, defined as those incurred for household services and for the care of a dependent child under the age of fifteen, of any other dependent who is incapacitated, or of the spouse of the taxpayer if that spouse is incapable of self-care, provided that the expenses are incurred to enable the taxpayer to be gainfully employed. The deduction for allowable expenses may not exceed $2,000 when one person requires care and $4,000 when two or more require care, subject to the further limitation that such expenses may not exceed a single person's earned income or the smaller of the earned incomes of the partners to a marriage. Thus the credit is limited to $400 or $800.

Marriage reduces the amount of this credit under several circumstances. If one partner does not work outside the house, marriage renders the couple ineligible for the credit. For two single people, each with dependent children or incapacitated elderly dependent parents and each with earnings of at least $4,000 a year, marriage can reduce their tax credit for child and other dependent care expenses by as much as $800. An even larger reduction may occur if, although both spouses are gainfully employed before and after marriage, the earned income of one of them after marriage falls to less than $4,000. Conversely, divorce increases the credit.

### Capital Loss Offsets

Losses during a year on the sale or exchange of capital assets may be offset in general against gains and if a net capital loss is incurred, it may be offset against up to $3,000 of ordinary taxable income. A net short-term loss is deductible on a dollar-for-dollar basis, but long-term losses must be reduced by 50 percent before being offset against income.[20] Such losses in excess of $3,000 may be carried forward and offset against capital gains in succeeding years, or to the extent that they exceed realized gains, against ordinary income in the amount of $3,000 a year until they are exhausted.[21]

The provision for capital loss offsets penalizes marriage because single people and married couples (whether or not they file joint returns) are subject to the same $3,000 limit. Hence if a husband and wife incur losses on jointly owned property or if each has realized losses, they can double the amount chargeable against taxable in-

20. 26 U.S.C. 676.
21. 26 U.S.C. 677.

**Table 2. Marriage Penalty for Couples with Various Incomes and No, Two, or Four Dependents**

Dollars

| Aggregate adjusted gross income[a] | Annual penalty | | | Present discounted value of annual penalty over 30 years (3 percent discount rate) | | |
|---|---|---|---|---|---|---|
| | Couple, no dependents[b] (1) | Couple, two dependents[c,d] (2) | Couple, four dependents[b,c] (3) | Couple, no dependents[b] (4) | Couple, two dependents[c,d] (5) | Couple, four dependents[b,c] (6) |
| 5,000 | 0 | 200 | 200 | 0 | 3,920 | 3,920 |
| 8,000 | 195 | 920 | 800 | 3,822 | 18,032 | 15,600 |
| 12,000 | 604 | 654 | 400 | 11,839 | 12,819 | 7,840 |
| 20,000 | 866 | 370 | 612 | 16,974 | 7,252 | 11,995 |
| 30,000 | 1,203 | 750 | 1,972 | 23,579 | 14,700 | 38,652 |
| 40,000 | 1,917 | 1,430 | 2,766 | 37,574 | 28,029 | 54,215 |
| 60,000 | 3,522 | 3,380 | 4,784 | 69,032 | 66,249 | 93,769 |
| 100,000 | 6,176 | 6,994 | 8,750 | 121,052 | 137,085 | 171,504 |

Source: Author's calculations. For further detail on the derivation of numbers in this table, see appendix tables.

a. Income is assumed to be equally divided between the partners.

b. No capital loss carry-over; personal deductions not itemized for incomes up to $12,000. For incomes of $20,000 and above, capital loss carry-over is at least $6,000, income is measured before offset for capital loss, and itemized deductions equal 20 percent of adjusted gross income including $1,200 of medical deductions (divided $1,000 and $200 between the partners).

c. Two dependents each generate the maximum credit for child and dependent care.

d. No capital loss offsets or medical deductions at any income level.

come by divorce or legal separation. The gain could be as much as $3,000 a year multiplied by the couple's marginal tax rate, or up to $2,100 a year.

*An Overview: Some Illustrations*

The personal income tax generally penalizes marriage in many ways. Couples can escape these penalties by avoiding formal marriage or by legal dissolution of the marriage. These penalties derive from the rate schedules; the zero-rate brackets; the medical expense deduction floors; the earned income, general tax, and child care credits; and the capital loss offset against ordinary income. For a minority of two-earner couples the income tax encourages marriage.

How do the features of the tax code that penalize marriage interact with one another? Of course, for any one couple they are unlikely all to apply at once. For example, people who are eligible for the earned income credit seldom have capital loss carry-overs or sufficient medical expenses to justify itemizing them. Initially I will compare the combined tax liability of a nonaged couple with equally divided income (before any adjustment for capital losses but after the deduction or addition of alimony payments or receipts).

Table 2 presents the differences between tax liabilities incurred by single and married pairs of individuals with no, two, or four dependents and with income ranging from $5,000 to $100,000. The table takes into account the appropriate tax rate schedules and, where reasonably applicable, the influence of the earned income and general tax credits, the maximum capital loss offset, and the 3 percent floor for deductible medical expenses.[22] Observe that at all income levels above $5,000, where tax liability is zero, the married couple pays a substantially larger annual tax bill. At $8,000 the tax difference is 10 percent of income or more with two or four dependents. The absolute value of the marriage penalty tends to increase with income, although its size relative to income declines.[23] Columns 2 and 3 report the marriage penalty when dependents are present and the taxpayer uses the dependents' care deduction. Column 2 differs from columns 1 and 3 in that the couple is assumed not to have capital

22. Further details may be found in the appendix tables.
23. The drop in the marriage penalty for the couple with two dependents as income moves from $12,000 to $20,000 occurs because at $20,000 the married couple is assumed to itemize deductions, while single persons do not; at $12,000 no one itemizes.

losses or medical deductions. Table 2 illustrates the very large number of alternative circumstances couples and their dependents actually confront.

Columns 4, 5, and 6 show the present value of annual tax penalties over thirty years discounted at 3 percent.[24] In some cases the penalty may considerably exceed one year's income. Moreover, it would take only a modest bit of tax planning by unmarried couples to reduce their tax bill and thus increase the tax price of marriage. Particularly in the $12,000 to $30,000 income range considerable savings could be effected if one partner incurred as large a proportion of deductible expenses as possible, while the other used the zero-rate bracket, thus adding, in the extreme, $2,200 to income not subject to tax.

On the whole I find that in its income tax policy, a society that generally blesses love *and* marriage rather perversely appears to reward those who by preference or otherwise avoid marriage. This finding applies only to those cases in which each of the parties receives a substantial proportion of the couple's aggregate income. As table 1 and the related discussion show, marriage can yield tax advantages if all or, at taxable income levels above $20,000, three-quarters or more of that aggregate income is attributable to one partner. It is possible, therefore, for some people to be generously rewarded by the tax code upon marriage while others are heavily penalized. Even under such circumstances couples can engineer profitable divorces if they agree to alimony that divides income more equally between themselves.

## Alternative Approaches

Aggregation of the income of husband and wife, the recognition of the marital unit as the basic unit for taxation, and the differential treatment of single people and married couples achieve equal treatment of one- and two-earner married couples at the expense of neutrality concerning marital status. Moreover, the fact that the marginal tax rates applicable to the earnings of married people depend not only on each person's own income but on that of their spouses creates additional costs. "Secondary" earners face a marginal tax rate higher than that encountered by the single worker or investor to a degree that

24. The 3 percent rate is chosen as an approximation to a "real" rate. Market rates are higher but include an inflation premium. The use of a real rate is justified because no allowance is made for the impact of inflation on absolute tax liabilities and on the marriage penalty.

varies directly with the income of the primary earner. This reduction in the secondary earner's net wage rate and rate of return on investment, coupled with the exclusion of the value of household services, discourages saving and investment and reduces the rate of participation in the labor force and the number of hours worked. The effect on labor force participation is likely to be especially severe because at the point of decision the high marginal tax rate presents a negative substitution effect without the offsetting positive income effect encountered by individuals already committed to working outside the home. Because the elasticity of labor supply of married women has been found to be much higher than that of married men and of single men and women, high marginal tax rates on their earnings discourage their labor supply more than high rates applied to other groups in the labor force.[25]

If the U.S. tax code were to revert to tax schedules under which married couples paid tax equal to twice that imposed on a single person with half their taxable income, and if the various credits and deductions discussed in the preceding section were all twice as large for married couples as for single people, the marriage penalty would vanish in nearly all cases. In this event marriage would offer major tax gains to almost all couples and by the same token large tax penalties would be imposed on unmarried people.

Few students of taxation have abandoned their support for the choice of the marital unit as the basic unit for income taxation. Groves, for example, found that "students of public finance with few exceptions regard the family rather than the individual as the proper unit for income taxation."[26] Vickrey had earlier put the matter even more strongly; he concluded that "it is neither possible nor, in fact, desirable to attempt to consider each individual as an independent unit for tax purposes" and that "the fact of marriage is of sufficient importance in itself to support a fairly substantial tax differential."[27]

25. For a discussion of efficiency or optimal taxation aspects of income tax treatment of the family, see Boskin and Sheshinski, "Optimal Tax Treatment of the Family"; and Harvey S. Rosen, "Applications of Optimal Tax Theory to Problems in Taxing Families and Individuals," in U.S. Department of the Treasury, *OTA Papers: Compilation of OTA Papers,* vol. 1 (Government Printing Office, 1978).

26. Harold M. Groves, *Federal Tax Treatment of the Family* (Brookings Institution, 1963), p. 69. He found a "consensus" of "lay and expert" opinion in favor of the proposition that "two couples with equal taxable incomes pay the same tax regardless of the technical legal division of the income" (ibid.).

27. *Agenda for Progressive Taxation* (Ronald Press, 1947; Augustus M. Kelley, 1972), pp. 274, 291.

Goode, Pechman, and Prest support this position, although Goode
and Pechman express concern about the position of the single person.[28] Pechman proposes to achieve equality between married couples
with equal taxable incomes and to eliminate the difference in tax liability between single people and married couples "either by extending
the rate advantages of income splitting to single people or by requiring married couples to use the same tax rate schedule as single people."[29] In order to avoid the pre-1948 problem stemming from community property laws in eight states, Pechman favors subjecting all
taxpayers to the same rate schedule, but married couples would aggregate and split their incomes and their taxable income brackets
would be half as wide as those for single people. This seemingly
complex arrangement is aimed entirely at the community property
problem; the combination of income splitting and halved taxable
income bracket sizes obviously produces the same tax liabilities as
aggregation without splitting coupled with tax rate schedules and
brackets identical for all taxpayers.

Pechman clearly recognizes that his plan would impose a tax
penalty on marriage between two people who both receive income.
He also acknowledges that the one-earner married couple is better
off than the two-earner couple because the imputed income from
housework is untaxed in the first case, and many of the costs incurred
by the second earner are not deductible. In addition he is concerned
about the adverse effect on labor supply of the high marginal tax rate
applicable to the earnings of the second spouse. To alleviate these
problems he proposes that two-earner married couples be allowed a
deduction from income of 25 percent of the earnings of the spouse
with the lower earnings, up to a maximum of $2,500. Alternatively,
he has suggested a 10 percent of earnings tax credit, up to $1,000.
The deduction would produce effective marginal tax rates equal to
$m(1 - e)$ on income up to $10,000, where $m$ is the statutory rate and
$e$ is the percentage allowed as a deduction. For second earners with
earnings of more than $10,000 the effect of the deduction at the
margin would be nil and the problem of adverse efficiency effects
would remain unsolved. The credit of 10 percent up to $1,000 would

28. Richard Goode, *The Individual Income Tax*, rev. ed. (Brookings Institution,
1976); Joseph A. Pechman, *Federal Tax Policy*, 3d ed. (Brookings Institution,
1977); and A. R. Prest, *Public Finance in Theory and Practice*, 5th ed. (London:
Weidenfeld and Nicolson, 1975).
29. Pechman, *Federal Tax Policy*, p. 95.

reduce marginal rates less than the deduction and also would do nothing at the margin for couples in which the lesser earner receives more than $10,000.

Either the deduction or the credit would reduce the tax penalty on marriage between two people with earned income. It would not, however, do anything in the cases where one or both spouses have property income, and as table 2 indicates, deductions or credits of the amounts proposed would perpetuate the marriage penalty on upper-middle-income and high-income married couples.

Nevertheless, the Pechman plan would be a major improvement over present law.[30] In an area of tax policy where there is no unequivocally "correct" solution and compromise is unavoidable, the Pechman plan obviously is highly attractive. Its merits, when compared with those of an approach that treats the individual as the basic unit for taxation, rest in large part on how one views the importance of marital status for tax purposes.

### Marital Status and Taxation

Proponents of the marital unit as the taxable entity have held that pooling economic resources within the family makes combined resources the best measure of "ability to pay." Sixty-five years ago when the income tax originated in the United States, most households consisted either of married couples and their dependents or single people —widows, widowers, bachelors, and spinsters—commonly sharing the home of parents or other relatives. Women typically lived with their parents until married and seldom worked after marriage. Divorce was rare. Single women seldom shared living quarters with other single women and even more seldom with single men. The nuclear family usually contained one breadwinner and his dependent wife and children. Under these circumstances it would have seemed strange to argue that the individual should be the taxable unit.

But social mores have changed, as have the status and role of women. Young and not-so-young people commonly form households in which marriage plays no part. Divorce is common. A large proportion of women now plan to work outside the home for as much of

---

30. It has the further important advantage of enjoying the support of Senator Edward M. Kennedy, who proposed its adoption, with some modifications, in his statement, "The Path to Fundamental Tax Reform," of July 1, 1977, presented on the floor of the Senate. See *Congressional Record,* daily edition (July 1, 1977), p. S11413.

their lives as do men. The married woman is therefore no longer clearly distinguishable from her unmarried sister, nor is she of necessity a dependent of her husband, any more than he is a dependent of hers.

One might argue that the taxable unit should simply be broadened to include all persons in the household. But if tax liabilities turned on household arrangements not certified by law, inspection and audit of life-styles and dwelling units would become a necessary and burdensome part of the tax collector's job and the taxpayer's life. Furthermore, many of the difficulties encountered under present law would continue. People's marginal tax rates would depend on the economic position of other people with whom they shared quarters, and the income tax would not be neutral toward the formation or dissolution of households.

### The Individual as the Basic Unit

The one obvious alternative left is to make the adult individual the basic unit for taxation. This approach has two major virtues. It is neutral regarding marital status and it meets my efficiency objective. It fails, however, to achieve equal treatment of married couples and other two-or-more-adult households with equal taxable incomes. The one-earner couple (regardless of sex or marital status) would pay higher total tax than the two-earner couple. In general one may well accept this outcome because the first couple, enjoying the untaxed imputed income from the housework of the otherwise unemployed partner who can avoid commuting, restaurant meals, extra clothing, and other costs of working outside the home, is obviously better off. It will also be accepted by those who view the income tax as a tax concerned only with the size of one's income and not with the division or disposition of that income among persons or objects of expenditure. Some will object, of course, that less than perfect justice will be done. This is so, but the same may be said of the deductions or credit offered in the Pechman proposal.

The proper treatment of property income poses hard problems because spouses can divide it among themselves and others and thus reduce tax liability.[31] Because earned income does not provide the same opportunities for tax avoidance, a major problem of horizontal

31. The community property laws are ignored in the perhaps naive view that Congress can and would override state laws with respect to both earned and property income in this area as it has with respect to assets under the federal estate tax.

equity enters. The solution to this problem is not obvious. The taxing authorities might ignore transfers between spouses, but wily taxpayers could devise avoidance devices. The British practice of taxing all the couple's property income to the husband, even though it may belong entirely to the wife, while the wife is taxed separately on her earnings, is one alternative. It is an approach to the problem that is distinctly contrary to the spirit of treating the individual as the taxable entity, and it is demeaning to women as well. It does, however, have the merit of reducing the marginal tax rate for the earnings of married women who own income-yielding property. Another perhaps somewhat less unattractive alternative is to tax the couple's property income to the partner with the higher taxable income. This approach would place a tax penalty on marriage in those instances in which one party to the marriage owned property while all or most of the earnings accrued to the other. A fourth alternative is to allocate property income equally between husband and wife, irrespective of the distribution of ownership. Like each of the other "solutions," however, this alternative involves imposing tax liabilities on people for income they do not own or control. Perhaps the Canadian approach is best. It allows free rein to those married couples who wish to transfer property between them.

Similar problems arise concerning income from unincorporated businesses and closely held corporations and the allocation of deductions between spouses. The appropriate answer is no more readily forthcoming in these areas either. This array of problems for which there are no good solutions in sight must dull the gloss of the case for shifting to the individual as the taxable unit. But almost any conceivable tax policy change must involve trading some losses in order to acquire gains.

### Treatment of Dependents

Finally, in dealing with the impact of the income tax on the family, there remain the problems relating to children and other dependents. These tend to center on earnings, property income, and personal exemptions or allowances.

In order to avoid the use of transfers of income-yielding property to children as a tax avoidance device it would seem necessary to tax income from property held by dependent children to the parent with whom the dependent lives or, if he or she lives with both parents, to the parent with the higher taxable income. Earned income, on the other hand, in the interests of efficiency, should be charged to the earner.[32]

The dependents' exemption may be allowed to either parent. The case for converting it to a credit is stronger if the individual is to be the taxable entity. The value of the exemption would depend on the distribution of income between spouses and on which spouse claimed the exemption. A credit would not create these problems.

## Summary and Conclusions

With a progressive rate schedule it is impossible simultaneously to achieve equal taxation of households (not necessarily narrowly defined as legally recognized married couples) with equal incomes, neutrality with respect to marital status, and efficiency (defined as confronting a person with a tax rate that depends entirely on his or her own income rather than on the economic position of a second person).

The U.S. personal income tax achieves the first goal but fails to achieve the second and third. Its multiple tax rate schedules and various structural elements combine to impose vastly different tax liabilities on pairs of people with equal incomes, varying with the distribution of income between the partners and their marital status. Perhaps capriciousness is the term that best describes the impact on marriage of the present law. For some taxpayers marriage can reduce tax liabilities, while for others it produces a huge increase. Under present law the income tax causes far more economic inefficiency than it needs to.

Alternative solutions seem to have at least one feature in common: reversion to a single tax rate schedule. Although the Pechman plan has merit and is preferable to existing law, it would continue to impose a penalty on some marriages and inordinately high marginal tax rates on second earners.

One is led, therefore, to the virtues of making the individual the unit for income taxation. This approach is neutral regarding marital status and more conducive to efficiency. It would sacrifice equal tax-

32. The practice of reducing the allowance or exemption by the amount of, or by half the amount of, a dependent child's earnings (as in Canada), has the effect of taxing that income to parents at high marginal rates and therefore seems inappropriate.

ation of married couples with equal taxable income. I do not, however, regard this as a major loss, if indeed it is a loss at all. For if lifestyles, social mores, and the stability and desirability of marriage are changing or have changed as much as appearances and some data would suggest, then equal taxation of married couples would seem to be very much diminished in importance as a goal of income taxation. If this view is accepted, then efficiency and neutrality with respect to marital status clearly become the dominant objectives. Because they can be attained as a practical matter only if the individual. is the taxable entity, this approach, although not without its difficulties and unsatisfactory compromises, has far more appeal than retaining the family as the taxable entity.

# Appendix: Tables Illustrating the Tax Liabilities of Couples, Married and Single

The tables in this appendix show how the data in table 2 were derived. In each case they are based on author's calculations.

**Table A-1. Illustrative Tax Liabilities of Married Couples and Pairs of Single Persons, No Dependents, Selected Levels of Income, 1978[a]**
Dollars

| Aggregate adjusted gross income | Tax liability | | Difference in tax liability[b] (3) | Present value of difference, life expectancy of 30 years[c] (4) |
| | Married couple, joint return (1) | Two single persons (2) | | |
| --- | --- | --- | --- | --- |
| 5,000[d,e] | 0 | 0 | 0 | 0 |
| 8,000[d,e] | 431 | 236 | 195 | 3,822 |
| 12,000[d,e] | 1,101 | 497 | 604 | 11,839 |
| 20,000[f,g] | 2,105 | 1,239 | 866 | 16,974 |
| 30,000[f,g] | 4,328 | 3,125 | 1,203 | 23,579 |
| 40,000[f,g] | 7,193 | 5,276 | 1,917 | 37,574 |
| 60,000[f,g] | 14,230 | 10,708 | 3,522 | 69,032 |
| 100,000[f,g] | 31,246 | 25,070 | 6,176 | 121,052 |

a. Each single person receives half the pair's aggregate income.
b. Column 1 minus column 2.
c. Computed using an interest rate of 3 percent a year.
d. No capital loss carry-over.
e. Personal deductions not itemized.
f. Capital loss carry-over available of more than $6,000. Adjusted gross income is before offset of capital loss.
g. Itemized deductions equal to 20 percent of adjusted gross income, including medical expenses of $1,200, of which $1,000 is incurred by one of the pair. Deductible medical expenses decline to zero for married couples at an AGI of $40,000 and for a single person with $1,000 of such expenses, at $33,333.

Table A-2. Illustrative Tax Liabilities of Married Couples and Pairs of Single Persons, Two Dependents, Selected Levels of Income, 1978[a]
Dollars

| | Tax liability | | | |
|---|---|---|---|---|
| Aggregate adjusted gross income | Married couple, joint return, two dependents (1) | Two single heads of house-holds, one dependent each[b] (2) | Difference in tax liability[c] (3) | Present value of difference, life expectancy of 30 years[d] (4) |
| 5,000[e] | −300 | −500 | 200 | 3,920 |
| 8,000[e] | 120 | −800 | 920 | 18,032 |
| 12,000[e] | 822 | 168 | 654 | 12,819 |
| 20,000[f] | 2,330 | 1,960 | 370 | 7,252 |
| 30,000[f] | 4,520 | 3,770 | 750 | 14,700 |
| 40,000[f] | 7,310 | 5,880 | 1,430 | 28,029 |
| 60,000[f] | 14,380 | 11,000 | 3,380 | 66,249 |
| 100,000[f] | 31,420 | 24,426 | 6,994 | 137,085 |

a. Differs from table A-3 in that (1) the two (rather than four) dependents are children under fifteen years of age for whom there is no child care, (2) there is no capital loss carry-over, and (3) no medical expenses are included in itemized deductions.
b. Each single person receives half the pair's aggregate income.
c. Column 1 minus column 2.
d. Computed using an interest rate of 3 percent a year.
e. Personal deductions not itemized.
f. Itemized deductions equal to 20 percent of adjusted gross income. At $20,000 married couples itemize, single people do not.

Table A-3. Illustrative Tax Liabilities of Married Couples and Pairs of Single Persons, Four Dependents, Selected Levels of Income, 1978[a]
Dollars

| | Tax liabilities | | | |
|---|---|---|---|---|
| Aggregate adjusted gross income | Married couple, joint return, four dependents (1) | Two single heads of house-holds, two dependents each (2) | Difference in tax liability[b] (3) | Present value of difference, life expectancy of 30 years[c] (4) |
| 5,000[d,e] | −300 | −500 | 200 | 3,920 |
| 8,000[d,e] | 0 | −800 | 800 | 15,680 |
| 12,000[d,e] | 0 | −400 | 400 | 7,840 |
| 20,000[f,g] | 612 | 0 | 612 | 11,995 |
| 30,000[f,g] | 2,642 | 670 | 1,972 | 38,652 |
| 40,000[f,g] | 5,262 | 2,496 | 2,766 | 54,215 |
| 60,000[f,g] | 11,946 | 7,162 | 4,784 | 93,769 |
| 100,000[f,g] | 28,745 | 19,995 | 8,750 | 171,504 |

a. Each single person receives half the pair's aggregate income. Dependents are either children under fifteen years of age or other dependents who are incapacitated, so that all qualify for the child care or other dependent care credit. The full allowable amount of this credit is assumed.
b. Column 1 minus column 2.
c. Computed using an interest rate of 3 percent a year.
d. No capital loss carry-over.
e. Personal deductions not itemized.
f. Capital loss carry-over available of more than $6,000. Adjusted gross income is before offset of capital loss.
g. Itemized deductions equal 20 percent of adjusted gross income, including medical expenses of $1,200 of which $1,000 is incurred by one of the pair. Deductible medical expenses decline to zero for married couples having an AGI of $40,000 and for single persons with $1,000 of such expenses, at $33,333.

ALICIA H. MUNNELL  *Federal Reserve Bank of Boston*

# The Couple versus the Individual
# under the Federal Personal Income Tax

WHEN imposing income taxes, all governments must choose among the following highly appealing but logically inconsistent goals:

1. *Equal taxation of couples with equal incomes,* which implies that married couples should be considered as economic units, with their taxes based on the amount of joint income, not on its distribution between spouses. For example, a couple with each spouse earning $10,000 should pay the same tax as a couple in which one spouse earns the full $20,000.

2. *Marriage neutrality,* which implies that there should be no penalty for marriage and none for being single. For example, a man and a woman each earning $10,000 should pay the same amount in taxes whether single, married, or divorced.

3. *Progressivity,* which implies that a single person earning $20,000 should pay more tax than two single people earning $10,000 each.

Each of these three principles has widespread appeal. The principle of equal taxation of couples with equal incomes was established in 1948 with the introduction of income splitting. Advocates argue that

The author would like to thank Sharon Spaight for excellent research assistance and Anna Estle for secretarial help. Henry J. Aaron, Carolyn Shaw Bell, Roger E. Brinner, Peter A. Diamond, Emil H. Sunley, Stanley S. Surrey, and James W. Wetzler, as well as colleagues at the Boston Federal Reserve Bank have all provided useful comments. Finally, Joseph A. Pechman, while strongly disagreeing with almost every aspect of this paper, significantly improved its quality.

because spending decisions are made jointly by the husband and wife, economic well-being and taxable capacity depend on their combined income. Therefore, couples with identical incomes should pay equal taxes.[1] While marriage neutrality has always been viewed as a desirable goal, it has received greater attention as a result of the changing status of women. With the increased likelihood that both the husband and wife are employed, the avoidance of any tax increase due to marriage has become an increasingly important issue. Progressivity is an old and widely accepted principle of income taxation in the United States. An often quoted rationale for progressive rates is that with the declining marginal utility of income, taxpaying ability increases more than proportionately with income.[2]

The logical impossibility of attaining these seemingly desirable goals simultaneously is demonstrated in figure 1. All tax systems must sacrifice at least one of these goals. The history of the U.S. income tax contains a series of attempts to correct for inequities to married or single people by abandoning one of the principles.

Considerable controversy has surrounded the choice of the appropriate unit of taxation since the establishment of the federal personal income tax in 1913. Before 1948 the tax was levied on individuals, and personal exemptions were used to differentiate for family size. Married persons who lived in community property states, however, were allowed to divide their income evenly between husband and wife and to file separate returns. This option, combined with a progressive rate structure, lowered taxes for married couples in community property states, but until World War II rates were so low that the tax differential mattered little. After World War II the much-increased tax rates led several more states to institute community property provisions in order to obtain for their married residents tax advantages that had become significant.

1. Some have argued that two married persons with a given income have greater ability to pay than if they were single, owing to the economies of living together, and that they therefore should pay a higher tax than two single persons. Unmarried people also have the opportunity, however, to join together with others to enjoy economies of scale. Therefore, experts recently have suggested that such economies should not be considered for tax purposes. See Boris I. Bittker, "Federal Income Taxation and the Family," *Stanford Law Review*, vol. 27 (July 1975), pp. 1422–24.

2. For a criticism of this simplified explanation and a full discussion of the economic basis for progressive taxation, see Richard A. Musgrave and Peggy B. Musgrave, *Public Finance in Theory and Practice*, 2d ed. (McGraw-Hill, 1976), pp. 215–19.

**Figure 1. The Conflict among the Principles of Federal Personal Income Taxation**

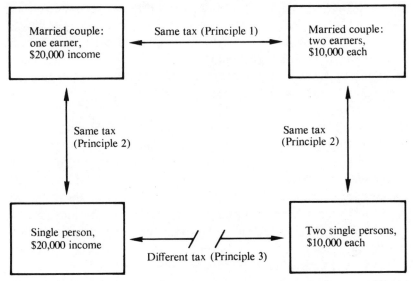

Source: U.S. Treasury Department, Office of Tax Analysis, "Federal Income Tax Treatment of Married and Single Taxpayers" (OTA, September 13, 1977), p. 2.

To restore geographic equity Congress extended the benefit of income splitting to all couples. The married couple became the basic unit of taxation and half of the couple's income was attributed to each spouse. To implement this scheme the rate schedule for married couples was given income brackets twice as wide as those for single individuals. Income splitting, however, produced a substantially larger tax burden on single people than on married people with the same income. Pressures on Congress to treat single people more liberally resulted in the adoption of a lower rate schedule for single taxpayers in 1969 that limited their tax liability to no more than 120 percent of that for a couple with the same taxable income.

Despite the repeated revisions, three major problems surrounding the treatment of married and single people persist under the current law.[3] First, as a result of the 1969 reduction in the rate schedule for the unmarried, marriage may significantly increase the tax liability of two workers. Second, an inequity exists between one-earner and two-

3. These problems have been discussed extensively by Grace Blumberg in "Sexism in the Code: A Comparative Study of Income Taxation of Working Wives and Mothers," *Buffalo Law Review*, vol. 21 (Fall 1971), pp. 49–98.

earner families. Under income-splitting provisions couples with equal total income pay equal taxes, but no adjustment is made for the additional work-related expenses or for the loss of services or leisure incurred by the second earner. Finally, taxing on a family basis means that the earnings of the "secondary" worker are subject to high rates of taxation. Because women are usually regarded as the second worker, such high marginal tax rates may discourage women's participation in the labor force.

The problems under the current law are evident to most observers and have led to some ad hoc adjustments. The substantial liberalization of child care provisions in the 1970s can be viewed as an attempt to alleviate the tax burden for workingwomen with children.[4] The Carter administration seriously considered a broader reform, as part of the 1978 tax reform proposal, that would have introduced a new deduction for married couples equal to 10 percent of the first $6,000 of wages of the spouse with the lower income.

The most comprehensive and realistic reforms have been proposed by Joseph A. Pechman.[5] He continues to treat the family as the basic unit of taxation and advocates the elimination of income splitting and the use of the same rate schedule for individuals and married couples. This proposal completely restores marriage neutrality between a single person and a married couple with one earner. To reduce the marriage penalty and the severe work disincentives of aggregating a couple's income without income-splitting provisions, he proposes tax relief for two-earner couples through a special deduction or credit based on the earnings of the spouse earning the least. For example,

4. The child care deduction was liberalized under the Revenue Act of 1971 (85 Stat. 518). Previously the deduction, which was enacted in 1954, was available only to single persons and married couples with incomes of less than $6,000. They were allowed to deduct up to $600 for the cost of the care of one child and $900 for two or more. The 1971 legislation expanded the deduction to $400 a month for taxpayers with adjusted gross incomes of up to $18,000 and was reduced by one-half of this amount after $18,000 so that no deduction could be claimed by those whose income exceeded $27,600. The Tax Reduction Act of 1975 (89 Stat. 32) raised the limit at which the phaseout started to $35,000. The original justification for the deduction was that child care expenditures were a necessary expense incurred by many taxpayers to earn a livelihood. In this light it is difficult to rationalize the provision in the Tax Reform Act of 1976 (90 Stat. 1563) that replaced the child care deduction with a credit of 20 percent of child care expenditures of up to $2,000 for one child and up to $4,000 for two children.

5. Joseph A. Pechman, *Federal Tax Policy,* 3d ed. (Brookings Institution, 1977), pp. 94–97.

two-earner couples would be allowed a deduction of 25 percent of the lesser earnings up to a maximum deduction of $2,500 or, alternatively, a 10 percent tax credit up to $1,000.

This paper explores the case for an alternative approach—namely, taxation on the basis of the individual rather than the family. Such a procedure would prevent any increase in taxes when two single earners married, would differentiate between one-earner and two-earner families, and would greatly reduce the higher tax rates on the "secondary" earnings of married women. A similar tax distribution could be achieved with deductions and credits under family income taxation, so that the choice between the two approaches must rest on philosophical considerations and the administrative feasibility of a system of individual taxation.

As a prelude to developing the arguments for individual taxation, the first section presents the history of the treatment of the family under the personal income tax and summarizes the provisions of the current code that create inequities between single and married taxpayers as well as between one-earner and two-earner families. The history is instructive for two reasons. First, it highlights the difficulties created by community property laws and indicates that unless these state laws were overruled for federal income tax purposes, individual taxation would cause geographic inequities. Second, the history reveals numerous changes in both the taxable unit and the relative burden of single and married taxpayers since the advent of the federal income tax.

The second section summarizes various social changes in the United States during the 1960s and 1970s that justify reconsideration of the appropriate taxable unit.[6] The dramatic increase in two-earner

6. Generally it has been accepted that the married couple should be retained as the basic taxpaying unit and that relief should come from some type of earned income credit or deduction for the second earner. (See ibid., pp. 93–94; and James W. Wetzler, "Marriage and the Federal Income Tax" [January 1978], pp. 27–28.) Michael J. McIntyre and Oliver Oldman proposed that the taxation of the family should return essentially to the 1948–69 situation in "Treatment of the Family," in Joseph A. Pechman, ed., *Comprehensive Income Taxation* (Brookings Institution, 1977), pp. 205–34. Income splitting is extended beyond the couple to include children, based on the application of the "benefit principle," that is, the person who benefits from the income should pay the taxes. While various income-splitting formulas could be developed, McIntyre and Oldman advocate retention of deductions for children for the sake of simplicity. This approach effectively allocates some portion of total income to the children and taxes it at a zero rate. Recently, however, two

families, the increased independence of women, and the rise in divorce suggest the need to reexamine the contention that couples typically pool their incomes and therefore should be taxed jointly. In the contemporary environment it may be more reasonable to assume that each spouse has a proprietary interest in his or her own income and would prefer to be taxed individually. The trend toward cohabitation also raises questions about a tax code that differentiates among individuals on the basis of legal marital status.

The second section also addresses the impact of joint taxation on economic efficiency. Married women frequently are secondary workers with considerable discretion over their labor force activity. Yet, under a system that aggregates a couple's income, these workers are subjected to the highest marginal taxes on their earnings. Raising the same amount of tax revenue with individual filing would reduce the economic loss suffered as a result of the distortion in labor force activity of married women.[7]

The third section presents the results of a Treasury Department simulation of one possible form of individual taxation. In the simulation, married couples may file separate returns for earned income and all taxpayers are taxed under the rate schedule applicable to single persons. This procedure, which results in a small decrease in aggregate tax revenues, substantially shifts tax burdens from two-earner couples to both one-earner couples and single people. Couples with only one earner, particularly those with incomes between $20,000 and $50,000, experienced large tax increases. This shift can be considered a tax on the greater leisure or imputed services of the nonemployed spouse. This section also addresses one of the most frequent criticisms of individual taxation: that the tax burden for a couple depends on the distribution of earnings between the spouses. This

economists have advocated individual taxation. See comments on the McIntyre and Oldman paper by Harvey E. Brazer in Pechman, *Comprehensive Income Taxation,* pp. 237–40, and his remarks in *American Families: Trends and Pressures, 1973,* Hearings before the Subcommittee on Children and Youth of the Senate Committee on Labor and Public Welfare, 93 Cong. 1 sess. (Government Printing Office, 1974), pp. 204–13; and Harvey S. Rosen, "Is It Time to Abandon Joint Filing?" *National Tax Journal,* vol. 30 (December 1977), pp. 423–28.

7. A recent study concluded that by eliminating the work disincentives for married women through moving from joint to individual filing, the same amount of income tax revenue could be collected, with 30 percent less loss of economic welfare. See Harvey S. Rosen, "A Methodology for Evaluating Tax Reform Proposals," *Journal of Public Economics,* vol. 6 (July-August 1976), pp. 112–15.

inevitable result of individual taxation under a progressive rate schedule appears inequitable only if the couple rather than the individual is accepted as the relevant unit of comparison.

The final section examines the legal and administrative problems of implementing individual taxation in the United States. Ample precedents exist for Congress to override state community property laws to avoid the chaos of the pre-1948 situation. Individual taxation, however, might still meet with strong political resistance from the community property states. The allocation of unearned income could be subject to explicit regulation to prevent intrafamily transfers designed to minimize taxes; or more realistically, individual taxation could be limited to earned income. An appropriate method could also be devised for the distribution of itemized deductions between spouses. The feasibility of introducing a system of individual taxation is supported by the fact that eleven states, as well as the District of Columbia, and fourteen of the twenty-four nations of the Organisation for Economic Co-operation and Development (OECD) have adopted such a plan.

In fairness, however, little evidence exists on how effectively these systems are administered. Initially the transition from the couple to the individual as the taxable unit would involve some administrative turmoil. But in view of the expanded labor force participation of married women and the frequency of divorce and unmarried cohabitation, individual taxation would greatly increase both the equity and efficiency of the federal income tax.[8]

## History of the Taxable Unit

The tax treatment of single and married persons has gone through three phases: the pre-1948 system, which taxed according to title; the 1948–69 provisions of income splitting; and the post-1969 income splitting with a reduction in the rate schedule for single persons.

8. Between 1940 and 1978 the labor force participation rate of married women more than tripled, from 14.7 percent to 47.6 percent. The divorce rate doubled, from 2.5 to 5.1 per 1,000 population between 1966 and 1978. During the 1970s the total number of couples cohabitating has more than doubled; for those under forty-five years of age, the number of cohabitating couples has increased almost sevenfold. (U.S. Bureau of the Census, *Current Population Reports,* series P-20, no. 336, "Population Profile of the United States: 1978" [GPO, 1979], pp. 1, 19, 37.)

## 1913–48: The Individual

Before 1948 single persons and married couples were taxed under the same rate schedule but received different exemptions. Under this system the goals of progressivity and marriage neutrality took precedence over equal taxation of families. Married couples could aggregate their incomes and file joint returns if they wished, but with progressive rates such a move would only increase the couple's tax liability to match that of a single person with the same total income. The tax burden for married couples depended not only on the distribution of income between the two spouses but also on the state in which the couple resided. This anomaly occurred because nine states in the West and Southwest had community property laws that treated marriage as a partnership and vested each spouse with half of the couple's income.[9] As a result, married couples with incomes unequally divided between the spouses paid less tax in these states than in others.[10]

9. These states were Arizona, California, Colorado, Idaho, Louisiana, Nevada, New Mexico, Texas, and Washington. Their property law is derived from Spanish law in contrast to that of other states and the federal government, which is based on English law. Ownership in these states was individualistic, depending on the active role of each spouse in acquiring income or property. See Harold M. Groves, *Federal Tax Treatment of the Family* (Brookings Institution, 1963), pp. 60–62.

10. Tension was evident from the beginning because individualism is expressed in the federal code, which refers to "the net income of each individual," but the property laws of the southwestern and western states give the wife "a present interest" in one-half of the community income while vesting her husband with the exclusive right to manage the property. Until 1930 the Treasury was responsible for resolving the obvious conflict. Until 1919 the Treasury required the husband to report all community income in his name, a decision based on his power to manage all property. In 1919 the Treasury retreated slightly from this position by permitting the couple to split unearned income on separate returns, but it continued to require the husband to report all the couple's earned income.

The new position, in turn, was abandoned in the face of the 1920 and 1921 rulings by the attorney general that stated that each spouse could report one-half of the couple's combined income for federal income tax purposes since all the community property states except California give the wife a vested interest in half the community income. California was treated differently because the wife had only "a mere expectancy" rather than a "vested interest" under the state's property law. The exception of California paved the way for reexamining the entire community property controversy, resulting in 1930 in a series of Supreme Court rulings that the married residents of community property states were each taxable on one-half of the community income regardless of which spouse earned it. See *Poe* v. *Seaborn*, 282 U.S. 101 (1930); *Goodell* v. *Koch*, 282 U.S. 118 (1930); *Hopkins* v. *Bacon*, 282 U.S. 122 (1930); *Bender* v. *Pfaff*, 282 U.S. 127 (1930); and Bittker, "Federal Income Taxation and the Family," pp. 1405–08.

Initially this geographic inequity mattered little because federal tax rates were low and progressivity was mild.[11] During the 1930s and particularly during World War II, however, the rates and progressivity of the federal income tax increased dramatically, creating obvious and inequitable advantages for the taxpayers in community property states.

In the early 1940s several states moved to enact community property laws in order to provide their residents with the advantages of income splitting.[12] The community property epidemic forced Congress to act.[13] Earlier options of mandatory joint returns or taxing wages and salaries to the earner would have met with strong resistance from both the old and new community property states. By en-

11. The following table (prepared by Richard Goode in *The Individual Income Tax,* rev. ed. [Brookings Institution, 1976], p. 4) reveals the limited applicability of the federal income tax before World War II:

| Year | Percentage of population covered | Tax as percentage of personal income |
|---|---|---|
| 1913 | Less than 1.0 | 0.1 |
| 1918 | 7.7 | 1.8 |
| 1926 | 4.2 | 0.9 |
| 1939 | 5.0 | 1.2 |
| 1945 | 74.2 | 10.0 |
| 1950 | 58.9 | 8.1 |
| 1960 | 73.1 | 9.8 |
| 1970 | 80.8 | 10.4 |

The underlying personal income estimate for 1913 is the average for 1912–16; that for 1918 is the average for 1917–21.

12. Oklahoma began the stampede in 1939 by authorizing optional community property provisions, and Oregon followed in 1943. In 1944, however, the Supreme Court ruled (*Commissioner* v. *Harman,* 323 U.S. 44 [1944]) that community property laws were not applicable for federal income tax purposes if individuals could "opt in." As a result, Oklahoma and Oregon changed their optional law to a mandatory one. Hawaii, Nebraska, Michigan, and Pennsylvania followed, and by 1948 community property laws were under consideration in New York and Massachusetts. See Bittker, "Federal Income Taxation and the Family," pp. 1411–12.

13. This "epidemic" came only after the defeat in 1941 of legislation to eliminate the tax advantages of community property states. Before 1941 the Treasury tried unsuccessfully to overturn these provisions through the courts. In 1941 the House Ways and Means Committee recommended mandatory joint returns, which would have eliminated the disparity between community property and common law states. This proposal met a storm of protest because it would have substantially increased taxes for married couples in community property states as well as for those couples in other states in cases where both spouses received income. Even the Senate Finance Committee's proposal to tax wage and salary income to the spouse who earned it and unearned income to the spouse entitled under state law to manage and control it was rejected.

acting income splitting, Congress paradoxically produced the same results that would have been realized had the movement to enact community property laws proceeded unhindered.

### 1948: Income Splitting

The 1948 legislation established the principle that a couple should pay the same tax as two single people each of whom have half the couple's income. The income brackets for couples under the new rate schedule were twice as wide as those for single taxpayers. This method of determining the relative burdens of single persons and married couples remained in effect until 1970. Residents of community property states experienced no change in their tax burdens, but married couples in all other states received a significant tax reduction.

The 1948 income-splitting provisions ensured that the goal of equal taxes for couples with equal income was fully satisfied. In the process, however, the goal of marriage neutrality was completely abandoned, as single persons paid substantially more tax than a married couple with the same income. For example, between 1965 and 1970 a couple in which the husband had a taxable income of $32,000 and the wife had no income would pay $8,660 in taxes if they used a joint return. But if the husband had been taxed as a single person, he would have paid $12,210 or 41 percent more.[14]

The large differential in the tax burdens imposed on married and single people was initially seen as allowance for differences in family responsibilities. Single taxpayers with family responsibilities found income splitting unfair, however. In response, Congress passed legislation in 1951 that established a special tax rate schedule for single people maintaining a home for dependents. The new "head of household" (HOH) schedule produced a tax liability about halfway between the liability of a single person and that of a married couple filing a joint return.

The question of the appropriate taxation of single persons with dependents surfaced again in 1954. Although the House proposed to extend the full benefits of income splitting to any "head of family,"[15]

14. Commerce Clearing House, Inc., *1965 U.S. Master Tax Guide* (CCH, 1964), pp. 7, 9. The calculation ignores any surcharges effective during the period.
15. *Internal Revenue Code of 1954*, H. Rept. 1337, 83 Cong. 2 sess. (GPO, 1954).

the final bill only expanded the HOH provisions to include dependent parents (even if living separately) and extended the full benefits of income splitting to a surviving spouse with dependent children for two years after the spouse's death.

These special provisions affected relatively few single taxpayers; most continued to face a large tax penalty based on their marital status.[16] Not until the Tax Reform Act of 1969 did Congress respond to public criticism of these disparities by reducing rates for unmarried people. The new schedule, which became effective in 1971, ensured that a single person's tax would never exceed 120 percent of that for a married couple on the same income. This change represented a significant reduction from the more than 40 percent differential under the old schedule, but was achieved only at the expense of introducing a "marriage penalty" on some married couples.

### Current Law

The Tax Reform Act of 1969 technically abolished income splitting as instituted under the 1948 legislation. While couples still may aggregate their income and divide it equally between the spouses, they no longer may use the single-person rate schedule. Under current law if two workers with identical incomes marry, they will experience an increase in their tax liability. The marriage penalty arises because a couple with equal incomes receives no advantage from income splitting but suffers the disadvantage of forgoing the lower single rate schedule. In contrast, when one spouse earns all the income, the benefit of income splitting outweighs the loss of the single person's rate schedule, which only provides about half the benefit of income splitting. Because two offsetting effects are at play—the advantage of income splitting and the advantage of the single individual's lower rate schedule—the existence and size of the marriage penalty depends on the distribution of income between the spouses.

Actually the situation is even more complicated because other provisions of the income tax law, such as the standard deduction and the low-income allowance, which were replaced in 1977 by the zero bracket amount, have exacerbated the penalty on marriage. Before the Tax Reduction Act of 1975 this problem was particularly serious

16. Of the 86 million returns filed in 1977, 6 million were filed by heads of households and 35 million by single persons. See U.S. Department of the Treasury, Internal Revenue Service, *Statistics of Income—1977, Individual Income Tax Returns,* Preliminary Report, Publication 198 (6-79) (GPO, 1979), pp. 1, 22, 24.

because both provisions applied the same terms to married and single taxpayers. Those taxpayers unable to itemize deductions were allowed an optional standard deduction of 15 percent of adjusted gross income up to a maximum of $2,000 or the low-income allowance of a flat $1,300.[17] Under these provisions if two low-income workers married, their combined low-income allowance would decline from $2,600 to $1,300, and for those eligible for the maximum standard deduction the reduction due to marriage would be $2,000.

The Tax Reduction Act of 1975 and the Revenue Adjustment Act of 1975 made some progress toward eliminating this inequity by distinguishing between single and married taxpayers in both the maximum standard deduction and the low-income allowance. In 1977 a single provision replaced the two provisions. It established brackets of income exempt from taxation (zero bracket amount) for both married and unmarried individuals. These amounts equal $2,200 for single persons and $3,200 for married couples, implying that a married couple receives a standard deduction of $1,000 more than one single person but $1,200 less than two single people.

The general tax credit, first enacted in 1975, also increases the marriage penalty. This credit equals the greater of $35 per personal exemption or 2 percent of taxable income in excess of the zero bracket amount up to a maximum of $9,000. Should the first option be chosen, the general tax credit is twice as large for a married couple as for a single person. For those who use the 2 percent variant and have a taxable income in excess of $12,200, the size of the credit is exactly the same, $180, for a single person as for a married couple with the same taxable income. For taxpayers with combined incomes between $5,700 and $12,200, however, the credit is larger for two single people than for married couples.

Marriage can also reduce the benefits of certain itemized deductions such as medical expenses. Medical expenses are deductible only to the extent that they exceed 3 percent of adjusted gross income and the costs of medicine and drugs only insofar as they exceed 1 percent. In cases where most or all of such expenses are incurred by one spouse, the deduction may be substantially larger if that spouse has income and can file as a single taxpayer.

17. The choice between the standard deduction and the low-income allowance hinged on the taxpayer's income level. With an adjusted gross income of up to $8,667, the low-income allowance exceeded the standard deduction.

Table 1 summarizes the overall impact of the rate schedules, the standard deduction, and the general tax credit. The tax burden resulting from marriage varies not only by income level but also with the division of income between spouses. At middle- and upper-income levels, the marriage penalty surfaces as soon as the lower-wage earner contributes as much as 20 percent of total income. At lower levels the second earner must contribute about 40 percent of total income before the marriage penalty arises.

The current law is clearly a compromise between the three principles of income taxation presented at the beginning of this paper. The tax is progressive, and no distinction is made on the basis of whether married couples include one or two earners. The law, however, violates the principle of marriage neutrality. A single person generally pays more tax than a married couple with the same income; and a married couple may pay more or less than they would if they were single. The following section will examine whether adherence to the goal of equal taxation of couples with equal income justifies the serious resulting violations of marriage neutrality.

## The Taxable Unit and Social Trends

Considerable debate has surrounded the question of whether the family or the individual constitutes the appropriate tax unit. A summary of the opposing positions is contained in the reports of the official commissions in Canada (1966) and Australia (1975) that addressed this problem. The Canadian Royal Commission on Taxation reported:

We believe firmly that the family is today, as it has been for many centuries, the basic economic unit in society. Although few marriages are entered into for purely financial reasons, as soon as a marriage is contracted, it is the continued income and financial position of the family which is ordinarily of primary concern, not the income and financial position of the individual members. Thus, the married couple itself adopts the economic concept of the family as the income unit from the outset. In western society, the wife's direct financial contribution to the family income through employment is frequently substantial. It is probably even more true that the newly formed family acts as a financial unit in making its expenditures.[18]

18. *Report of the Royal Commission on Taxation* (1966), vol. 3, p. 123.

Table 1. Income Tax Marriage Penalty (−) or Bonus (+) under 1977 Law

| Adjusted gross income of the couple (dollars) | Share of combined income of lesser-earning spouse (percent) | | | | | |
|---|---|---|---|---|---|---|
| | 0 | 10 | 20 | 30 | 40 | 50 |
| 0 | 0 | 0 | 0 | 0 | 0 | 0 |
| 3,000 | 0 | 0 | 0 | 0 | 0 | 0 |
| 5,000 | +278 | +199 | +118 | +43 | 0 | 0 |
| 7,000 | +351 | +232 | +113 | −5 | −118 | −183 |
| 10,000 | +460 | +240 | +49 | −141 | −194 | −204 |
| 15,000 | +758 | +353 | −33 | −176 | −256 | −277 |
| 20,000 | +1,102 | +451 | −32 | −263 | −423 | −463 |
| 25,000 | +1,534 | +592 | −10 | −381 | −610 | −701 |
| 30,000 | +1,934 | +682 | −50 | −599 | −920 | −1,019 |
| 40,000 | +2,769 | +887 | −274 | −1,163 | −1,662 | −1,852 |
| 50,000 | +3,710 | +1,086 | −674 | −1,930 | −2,640 | −2,870 |
| 100,000 | +8,694 | +3,045 | −910 | −3,575 | −5,164 | −5,700 |

Source: James W. Wetzler, "Marriage and the Federal Income Tax" (January 1978), p. 5.

On the other hand, the Asprey Committee in Australia concluded that the adoption of a compulsory family unit basis must be rejected on grounds of general social principle. The right to be taxed as an individual has always been accorded in Australia. At a time when women are playing an ever greater role in the economic and other affairs of society, the withdrawal of this right would certainly be regarded as a retrograde step. And objections would come not only from women: men too might take exception to a universal and compulsory commingling of their tax affairs with those of their wives. This would, in the Committee's view, make a change in this direction politically unacceptable irrespective of whether married women (or married men) paid more or less tax after the change than they do now: social attitudes to the separate status of the sexes, rather than purely economic considerations, are involved here.[19]

Clearly both arguments have merit. Therefore, the selection of the taxable unit involves a value judgment that presumably reflects a nation's social norms.

In 1948, when Congress adopted income splitting, husband and wife families constituted almost 80 percent of households. Generally the husband was the breadwinner and the wife did not work outside the home. Thus the one-earner married couple was the appropriate norm to adopt as the taxable unit. Since 1948, however, the composition of households has changed, and both the labor force participation of women (especially married women) and the divorce rate have increased dramatically with important implications for tax policy.

### Labor Force Participation of Women

The labor force participation of all women has increased, and that of married women who live with their spouses most of all. Between 1940 and 1978 the overall female labor force participation rate doubled, from 27.4 percent to 49.1 percent, but the rate for married women more than tripled, from 14.7 percent to 47.6 percent.[20] Over the course of married life a far greater fraction of women work. The significant increase in the fraction of married women in the labor force and the prevalence of two-earner couples seriously undermines the principle that couples should pay the same tax however earnings are divided between the spouses. The issue involves considerations of both equity and efficiency.

19. Taxation Review Committee, *Full Report* (January 31, 1975), p. 134.
20. These figures refer to married women with husband present. See Bureau of the Census, *Statistical Abstract of the United States, 1979* (GPO, 1979), p. 400.

Table 2.  Distribution of Households by Type of Family, 1940–78, and Projections, 1980–90

Percentage of total household

| Year | Total households (thousands) | Families | | | | Single persons |
|------|------|------|------|------|------|------|
| | | Husband-wife | | | | |
| | | Zero or one-earner | Two-earnerᵃ | Male head | Female head | |
| 1940 | 34,949 | 64.8 | 11.2 | 4.3 | 9.8 | 9.9 |
| 1947 | 39,107 | 62.6 | 15.7 | 2.9 | 8.2 | 10.6 |
| 1950 | 43,554 | 59.7 | 18.6 | 2.7 | 8.3 | 10.8 |
| 1955 | 47,874 | 54.7 | 21.0 | 2.8 | 8.7 | 12.8 |
| 1960 | 52,799 | 51.6 | 22.7 | 2.3 | 8.4 | 15.0 |
| 1965 | 57,436 | 47.4 | 25.2 | 2.0 | 8.7 | 16.7 |
| 1970 | 63,401 | 41.7 | 28.8 | 1.9 | 8.7 | 18.8 |
| 1975 | 71,120 | 36.7 | 29.3 | 2.1 | 10.0 | 21.9 |
| 1978 | 76,030 | 32.7 | 29.6 | 2.1 | 10.6 | 25.1 |
| 1980ᵇ | 79,356 | 31.1 | 30.1 | 2.0 | 10.8 | 26.1 |
| 1985ᵇ | 87,188 | 26.8 | 31.5 | 2.0 | 11.0 | 28.7 |
| 1990ᵇ | 94,270 | 22.8 | 32.7 | 2.0 | 11.2 | 31.3 |

Source: U.S. Bureau of the Census, *Statistical Abstract of the United States, 1978* (GPO, 1979), tables 655, 656, p. 404; *Current Population Reports*, Series P-20, no. 313, "Households and Families by Type, March 1977 (Advance Report)" (GPO, 1977), p. 6; and *Current Population Reports*, series P-20, no. 336, "Population Profile of the United States: 1978" (GPO, 1979), pp. 18, 42. Figures are rounded.

a. The percentage of two-earner husband-wife families was obtained by multiplying the labor force participation rate of married women with husband present by the number of intact husband-wife families. The figures for the years 1975 and 1978, 29.3 and 29.6, differ from Census Bureau estimates that the 30.8 and 30.8 percent of households are composed of two-earner husband-wife families. The difference is attributable to the various samples employed by the Census Bureau, their variability, and the dates of the samples. The figures, however, are consistent with the often quoted statistics that over 50 percent of married women aged twenty-five to sixty-four work. Data presented in the table also include those families in which the employed wife is younger than twenty-five or older than sixty-four.

b. Projections were based on Census Bureau estimates of the total number of households. Its estimates of the number of husband-wife families and single persons were not employed, as the figures did not reflect the continuing decline in the number of intact families and the dramatic increase of single persons. Instead, the average percentage decline in the number of intact families in the Census Bureau projections was applied to the 1978 data to obtain figures for 1980, 1985, and 1990. Future labor force participation rates for married women with husband present were based on the assumption that by 1990 their rate would equal the 1978 participation rate for single women of 58.9 percent. This is consistent with the current experience of women aged twenty to thirty-four. Again the increase was assumed to be linear.

EQUITY CONSIDERATIONS. If all couples contained one worker, the choice of the unit of taxation—individual or couple—by definition could not raise any questions of equity involving the relative tax burdens of couples. During the early 1940s only 15–20 percent of all couples contained two earners, and one-earner couples constituted a majority of all households (see table 2).

By 1978 the household composition of the American population had shifted dramatically. Two-earner couples were nearly as numerous as one-earner couples, and according to Census Bureau projections, they will become far more numerous. Moreover, only about one-third of all households were one-earner couples, and that fraction is projected to drop to about one-quarter.

With roughly similar numbers of one- and two-earner couples, some important questions come to the fore. How should the tax system treat work-related expenses required when both spouses work? And what account, if any, should be taken of home services and leisure forgone when both spouses work?[21] While it would be administratively impossible to estimate accurately the value of such work and leisure, to disregard it entirely for tax purposes systematically benefits one-earner couples relative to two-earner couples.

In addition, to allow no deductions for such work expenses as commuting, meals, and so on, is particularly burdensome for the two-worker family. Ideally these expenses should be deducted from a worker's earnings to determine net income from employment, but Congress has disallowed them for administrative reasons.[22] If every household had only one earner, this inequity created by improperly defining income would be uniform. A two-earner couple, however, incurs approximately twice the amount of work expenses as a one-earner couple with the same income and therefore is particularly disadvantaged.

The rise in the labor force participation of women also makes the marriage tax, which emerged from the 1969 reduction in the single rate schedule, increasingly recognizable and objectionable. If all married couples had only one earner, adjusting the tax rates on individuals relative to those for couples would only affect the burdens of the two groups. With the proliferation of the two-earner family and the growth of female earnings, however, the marriage tax falls ever more heavily on a large number of married workers.

EFFICIENCY CONSIDERATIONS. The movement of married women into employment outside the home has increased the impact of high marginal tax rates on work incentives. If the wife is the family's "secondary" worker, then taxing a married couple via a joint return

21. It is important to consider leisure as well as services because two-earner couples may receive the same amount of imputed services by substituting housework for leisure time.

22. Congress authorized earned income deductions for all workers during the periods 1924–31 and 1934–43. See Bittker, "Federal Income Taxation and the Family," p. 1435.

implies that the first dollar earned by the wife is taxed at the marginal rate on the last dollar earned by the husband.

In the absence of taxation and if people could work exactly as much as they wished, individuals would work up to the point where the wage from an extra hour of employment just exceeds the value of an additional hour of leisure. In competitive markets, firms pay workers a wage equal to the value of additional product produced through that worker's effort, the worker's marginal product. Thus without taxes an economically efficient solution is achieved: workers work up to the point where the value of additional output they could produce just exceeds the value of additional leisure time.

Income taxes reduce the worker's after-tax wage below the worker's marginal product to the firm. Such a reduction creates both an "income" and a "substitution" effect. The income effect promotes work activity because the wage reduction will encourage individuals to increase work effort in order to maintain their previous consumption. The substitution effect will discourage work or, in other words, encourage leisure because the cost of leisure in forgone wages has declined. Because it is impossible to predict logically whether an increase in taxes will raise or lower work effort, the effect must be measured empirically.

Available evidence suggests that the labor supply of primary earners, male or female, is less sensitive to variations in the net wages than that of secondary workers, wives, and teenagers. Studies of the labor force activity of males generally have concluded that factors other than money play the most important role in work motivation and that the labor force participation of males is affected little by the income tax.[23] These findings should not be surprising, as healthy males in the United States generally are considered to be responsible for supporting themselves and their families and therefore are expected to work. In the current social context, the labor force participation of married women is viewed as discretionary. For all these

23. See Marvin Kosters, "Effects of an Income Tax on Labor Supply," in Arnold C. Harberger and Martin J. Bailey, eds., *The Taxation of Income from Capital* (Brookings Institution, 1969), pp. 301–24; Clarence D. Long, *The Labor Force under Changing Income and Employment* (Princeton University Press, 1958); George F. Break, "Income Taxes and Incentives to Work: An Empirical Study," *American Economic Review*, vol. 47 (September 1957), pp. 529–49; and T. A. Finnegan, "Hours of Work in the United States: A Cross-Sectional Analysis," *Journal of Political Economy*, vol. 70 (October 1962), pp. 452–70.

reasons the labor supply of married women is more sensitive than that of their spouses to high taxes on earnings.

The fact that the proportion of married women who work has been rising does not contradict the assertion that their decision to work is highly sensitive to taxes. While currently 47 percent of married women are in the labor force, the issue is whether participation rates and the number of hours worked would be substantially greater under an alternate tax structure. Econometric studies generally indicate that an increase in the net hourly wage for married women would result in a substantial increase in hours worked. One study suggests that a 10 percent increase in the net hourly wage rate would lead to a 16 percent increase in the number of hours worked by married women per year.[24] Other studies reach similar results.[25] Because the labor supply of wives is more sensitive to variations in net wages than that of their spouses or of single workers, a shift to individual taxation would reduce the distortion in the labor supply caused by taxes. A recent study concluded that by moving from joint to individual filing, the same amount of revenue could be collected with 30 percent less loss of economic welfare.[26] Efficiency considerations, therefore, support individual taxation.

### Divorce

The divorce rate, after remaining relatively constant between 1940 and 1965, has doubled in the last decade, from 2.5 per 1,000 population in 1966 to 5.1 in 1978.[27] Furthermore, the divorce experience of young adults has already exceeded that of older adults when they were of comparable age. The Census Bureau estimates that more than one-third of the married persons between twenty-five and thirty-five years old in 1975 will end their first marriage in divorce. The prospects for successful second marriages is even poorer. About 40

24. Harvey S. Rosen, "Taxes in a Labor Supply Model with Joint Wage-Hours Determination," *Econometrica*, vol. 44 (May 1976), pp. 485–507.

25. Michael J. Boskin and Eytan Sheshinski, "Optimal Tax Treatment of the Family: Married Couples," *Journal of Public Economics*, 1980, forthcoming; and Robert E. Hall, "Wages, Income and Hours of Work in the U.S. Labor Force," in Glen G. Cain and Harold W. Watts, eds., *Income Maintenance and Labor Supply* (Rand McNally, 1973), pp. 102–62.

26. Rosen, "A Methodology for Evaluating Tax Reform Proposals," p. 113.

27. Bureau of the Census, *Current Population Reports*, series P-20, no. 336, "Population Profile of the United States: 1978" (GPO, 1979), p. 1.

percent of the second marriages of previously divorced persons between twenty-five and thirty-five will probably end in divorce.[28]

The prevalence of divorce raises serious questions about joint filing. The rationale for employing the couple as the basic unit of taxation involves a presumption that couples do pool income and jointly meet financial obligations out of a common budget. If the couple were a stable and permanent unit, this might be a legitimate assumption. In view of the dramatic increase in the likelihood of divorce, however, for many couples the long-term economic welfare of each spouse may depend more on his or her own earnings than on the couple's combined income. The prospect of divorce suggests that the taxing authorities should not presume that income will be pooled.

Second, the rise in divorce has already contributed to a significant increase in single-parent families—a trend that is projected to continue. This development will lead to increased dissatisfaction with a tax system that taxes the income of a parent-child family more heavily than it does the income of a one-earner couple. In both cases the income of the wage earner must support two people, but the parent-child family does not receive the imputed services provided by the nonemployed spouse in the single-earner couple. Furthermore, without some child care deductions, the taxable income of the single parent would overstate the net earnings of the single-parent family, because part of this income must be allocated for the care of the child while the parent is working. No rationale seems to exist for applying a higher rate schedule to single-parent families than to married couples. As the number of single-parent families increases, the inequity will become increasingly burdensome.

### Cohabitation

With the increase in divorces and the decline in marriages has come dramatic growth in the number of unrelated adults sharing two-person households. In 1978, more than 2 million persons lived in the 1.14 million households with an unrelated adult of the opposite sex. The number of such households almost doubled between 1970 and 1978; those under age forty-five living in these households showed an almost sevenfold increase during the same period.[29] While the pro-

28. Ibid., no. 307, "Population Profile of the United States: 1976," p. 15.
29. Ibid., series P-20, no. 338, "Marital Status and Living Arrangements: March 1978" (GPO, 1979), p. 4.

portion of adults of the opposite sex sharing living quarters remains low—only about 9 percent of all primary individuals and 2 percent of all household heads—cohabitation without marriage is clearly growing. If this trend continues, it will make it increasingly difficult to justify taxing people on the basis of their legal marital status. Under the current tax laws unmarried couples with one earner are denied the advantages of income splitting—a tax incentive for marriage—while those with two earners escape the marriage penalty—an incentive for staying single. With individual taxation, married and unmarried couples would pay the same tax.

*Summary*

The demographic and economic patterns that made the couple seem the proper taxable unit in 1940 no longer prevail in the 1970s. The married one-earner couple now represents only one-third of all households, down from two-thirds in 1940. Almost as many couples have two earners as have one, a fact that undermines the case for equal taxation of families with equal income. The aggregation of the earnings of two-worker families discourages married women from working. It also results in a "marriage penalty" when two employed persons marry.

Finally, the increase in the number of unmarried persons who live together erodes the foundations of a tax system that discriminates on the basis of legal status. In short, the changes in life-styles during the 1960s and 1970s indicate that the individual has become a fairer and more efficient taxable unit than is the couple.

# Distribution of the Tax Burden under Individual Taxation

In 1976 the Treasury prepared a simulation that highlights the shifts in relative tax burdens involved in moving from the couple to the individual as the unit of taxation. The Treasury study examined only one of many possible forms of individual taxation and gives only a rough indication of which groups would gain and lose under such a change. The specific proposal applied the single-person rate schedule to all persons, introduced a $1,000 marriage deduction, and allowed one spouse to file a separate return for earned income only, using one personal exemption and the per capita or taxable income credit up to

Table 3. Estimated Revenue Effect at 1976 Income Levels of Using Single-Person Rate Schedule Only, $1,000 Marriage Deduction, and Option for One Spouse to File a Separate Return for Earned Income Only

| Adjusted gross income (thousands of dollars) | Returns with tax decrease (thousands) | Amount of tax decrease (millions of dollars) | Returns with tax increase (thousands) | Amount of tax increase (millions of dollars) | Net tax change (millions of dollars) |
|---|---|---|---|---|---|
| 0–6[a] | 1,375 | 142 | 327 | 24 | −118 |
| 6–10 | 9,425 | 1,110 | 752 | 58 | −1,053 |
| 10–20 | 9,483 | 1,145 | 2,514 | 131 | −1,014 |
| 20–25 | 5,731 | 949 | 4,491 | 564 | −385 |
| 25–30 | 4,497 | 1,691 | 4,653 | 1,552 | −139 |
| 30–50 | 1,422 | 1,328 | 1,527 | 1,321 | −7 |
| 50–100 | 397 | 1,007 | 419 | 946 | −61 |
| 100 and over | 86 | 371 | 98 | 538 | +167 |
| Total | 32,417 | 7,744 | 14,783 | 5,133 | −2,611 |

Source: Unpublished data provided by the Joint Committee on Internal Revenue Taxation.
a. Includes individuals with negative income.

$90. All remaining exemptions, deductions, and credits remained with the "basic" return. The results of the simulation are limited in two respects. First, all taxpayers are assumed to take the standard deduction and, as just noted, no attempt is made to attribute any of the deduction to the spouse filing separately. Second, the comparison of tax liabilities of single persons and married couples pertains only to earned income so that it is not possible to discern the effect of aggregating unearned income. This limitation may, in fact, be quite realistic since the possibility of manipulation of unearned income to minimize taxes may make it preferable to retain the couple as the taxable unit for unearned income.

Table 3 presents the estimated revenue effects at 1976 income levels of the proposed changes by income class. The proposal reduces tax revenues by $2.6 billion or about 2 percent. Most of the returns with tax decreases are clustered in the $6,000–$20,000 range, while most increases occur between $20,000 and $50,000. The comparison of the tax liability of single persons and married couples with one and two earners presented in table 4 indicates the shift in tax burdens among different types of households.

The reduction in the marriage tax is evident by comparing the relative tax burden on a couple in which each spouse accounts for

Table 4. Ratio of Tax Liabilities of a One-Earner Married Couple (Couple A), a Two-Earner Married Couple (Couple B), a Single Person with Income Equal to Couple A or B (Individual C), a Single Person with Income Equal to One-Half That of Couple A or B (Individual D)[a]

| | 1976 law | | Individual taxation proposal | | | |
|---|---|---|---|---|---|---|
| Total wage income (dollars) | Individual C to couple A or B (1) | Couple A or B to two individual D's (2) | Individual C to couple A (3) | Individual C to couple B[b] (4) | Couple A to two individual D's (5) | Couple B to two individual D's (6) |
| 10,000 | 1.40 | 1.30 | 1.46 | 1.68 | 1.26 | 1.09 |
| 15,000 | 1.28 | 1.16 | 1.24 | 1.38 | 1.20 | 1.08 |
| 20,000 | 1.31 | 1.13 | 1.21 | 1.37 | 1.22 | 1.08 |
| 25,000 | 1.30 | 1.20 | 1.16 | 1.39 | 1.34 | 1.12 |
| 30,000 | 1.28 | 1.26 | 1.13 | 1.41 | 1.43 | 1.14 |
| 40,000 | 1.25 | 1.27 | 1.09 | 1.47 | 1.45 | 1.08 |
| 50,000 | 1.23 | 1.28 | 1.08 | 1.50 | 1.46 | 1.05 |

Source: U.S. Treasury, Office of Tax Analysis, "Task Force on Single and Married Taxpayers" (OTA, September 30, 1978), tables 1 and 8, pp. 3, 13.

a. Current, 1976 law: minimum standard deduction of $1,000, single, and $2,100, joint; standard deduction of 16 percent and $2,400 and $2,800 ceiling; tax credit of $35 per capita or 2 percent of taxable income up to $9,000. A proposed alternative individual taxation proposal is $1,000 marriage deduction and optional separate return for earned income, spouse filing a separate return for earned income only can use one personal exemption and the per capita or taxable credit up to $90. The remaining exemptions, deductions, and credits remain with the "basic" return. This treatment of the standard deduction, which was used for simplicity, may result in depriving the separate return of some standard deduction. However, about one-half the loss is offset by the larger taxable income credit.

b. For two-earner couples each spouse is assumed to earn one-half the total amount in column one.

half of the family's earnings and two individuals with the same earnings. Column 2 of table 4 shows that the couple pays 13 to 30 percent more than two individuals under current law—the marriage tax. Under the proposed alternative shown in column 6 the marriage tax would run from 5 to 14 percent, less than half that under current law at most incomes.

Similarly, the extra tax paid by an individual in comparison with a one-earner couple would also be reduced. At present the individual pays 23 to 40 percent more than the couple (column 1). Under the proposed alternative (column 3) the difference would diminish in all except the lowest income brackets.

A comparison of the tax burdens of one-earner and two-earner couples (column 3 versus column 4) indicates that the proposed alternative system would tax the one-earner couple more heavily than a two-earner couple (13 percent more heavily at $20,000, 39 percent more heavily at $50,000). Under current law couples with equal incomes pay equal taxes; taxing each spouse individually reduces the taxes on the two-earner couple relative to the couple with one earner. Differentiation is desirable because the one-earner couple benefits from the untaxed services or greater leisure of the nonemployed spouse who does not incur work-related expenses. The increasing differential as income rises reflects the decreasing importance of the additional deductions as well as the progressivity in the rate structure. Whether the large differential at high-income levels is appropriate or excessive would need to be studied closely.

While the simulation cannot answer all questions, the results indicate which groups would gain and which would lose. For the purposes of summarizing the effects for the various types of taxpayers, the small net revenue effect, which is a result of the specific provisions of the Treasury proposal, can be ignored. Several conclusions emerge. First, two-earner couples would experience a tax reduction and their burden relative to one-earner couples would be substantially reduced. Second, individuals would not experience a change in their tax burden, as the single rate schedule was adopted for all taxpayers. Third, taxes on married couples with one spouse working would increase, especially those earning between $20,000 and $50,000. Finally, the head-of-household category (not shown in table 4) would be eliminated and those formerly in this category would pay slightly higher taxes because they would become subject to the single-person rate schedule. Heads of households, however, would experience a reduction in liability relative to married couples since the proposal would treat these two groups equally (except for the $1,000 marriage deduction).

All these changes are consistent with the criteria suggested earlier. A similar pattern would result if couples and single persons were taxed under a single rate schedule and two-earner couples were eligible for a credit or deduction. The choice between the two schemes depends on one's views of the appropriate unit of taxation.

While individual taxation accomplishes many desirable goals, the tax burden of a married couple will vary with the distribution of earnings between the spouses (see table 5). Such variations in tax burden among the two-earner couples based on the distribution of earnings has been criticized often as one of the major deficiencies of individual taxation. If the couple whose earnings are divided 80–20 worked fewer hours than the couple whose earnings are divided 50–

Table 5. Aggregate Tax Liability of Married Couples Filing as Two Single Persons

| | Adjusted gross income[a] (dollars) | | |
|---|---|---|---|
| Income ratio | 10,000 | 20,000 | 50,000 |
| 100–0 | 1,222 | 4,007 | 17,815 |
| 80–20 | 810[b] | 2,872[b] | 13,857[b] |
| 60–40 | 566 | 2,482 | 11,890 |
| 50–50 | 557 | 2,444 | 11,660 |

Source: Author's calculations.
a. All income is assumed to be earned.
b. Approximates liability for married couple filing jointly under 1977 law.

50, the extra tax paid by the "80–20" couple may be justifiable recognition of its lower wage expenses, of extra time for household services, or of additional leisure time. But if the secondary wage earner in each case is engaged in full-time employment, the tax differential is harder to justify.

This criticism of individual taxation begs the central question, however. It is based on the assumption that the aggregate tax paid by the couple is the relevant basis of comparison. If the individual is the appropriate taxable unit, then the fact that the tax burden varies according to the division of income between two people who decided to marry should not be of great concern. Nevertheless, this phenomenon, which is the natural consequence of taxing on an individual basis under a progressive rate schedule, should not be ignored in policy discussions since it represents a source of concern to most tax experts.

## Problems of Implementation

While levying taxes on individuals rather than taxing couples jointly would alleviate many inequities and reduce inefficiencies caused by current law, such a change involves numerous legal, administrative, and economic problems.

### Legal

The most obvious question is whether it would be possible to tax individuals without recreating the chaos of the pre-1948 situation. Both to avoid geographical inequities and to forestall mass adoption of community property laws, Congress would have to override state property laws for federal income tax purposes. Congress nearly did so in the Revenue Act of 1921. The House version of that bill contained a provision requiring that income be taxed to the spouse having management and control over the community property. The Senate Finance Committee accepted this provision, but the full Senate deleted it after a brief debate and the House-Senate Conference dropped it.[30]

In 1941 the Senate Finance Committee proposed that in community property states wages be taxed to the spouse who earned them and investment income to the spouse who controlled the asset.[31] Although this proposal was rejected by the Senate, it reveals that Congress at least considered making the community property states conform to the intent of the federal tax law at that time. In contrast, the ultimate adoption of aggregation and income splitting in effect changed the federal tax code to conform to the states' community property law.

As recently as 1972 Congressman Edward J. Koch introduced a bill in the House to establish "a uniform tax rate schedule for all taxpayers, whether they be married, widowed, divorced or single" that "would be applied to an individual's taxable income, regardless of his or her marital status."[32] The bill was cosponsored by 158 members of the House, indicating considerable political support for a shift from joint to individual taxation.[33]

While income tax legislation that overrode community property provisions was never passed, the Revenue Act of 1942 reduced estate tax advantages of community property.[34] This legislation substituted economic origin of property for legal ownership as the criterion of taxability. It required the inclusion of all property in the estate of the first spouse to die, unless such property was attributable to the surviving spouse's personal services or separate property. Although this

30. This historical note was uncovered by James Wetzler. See "Marriage and the Federal Income Tax," p. 6, note 6.

31. *Revenue Bill of 1941*, S. Rept. 673, 77 Cong. 1 sess. (GPO, 1941), pt. 1, pp. 9–12, 36.

32. *Tax Treatment of Single and Married Persons where Both Spouses Are Working*, Hearings before the House Committee on Ways and Means, 92 Cong. 2 sess. (GPO, 1972), p. 96.

33. For list of cosponsors, see ibid., p. 97.

34. Revenue Act of 1942 (56 Stat. 942). Similar changes were made in the gift tax (56 Stat. 943).

procedure openly defied community property law, the Supreme Court held the amendments constitutional.[35] Boris Bittker has argued that these rules for the estate tax might have become the prototype of changes in the income tax law.[36] Instead, Congress repealed them in 1948 when it authorized income splitting for married couples and concurrently enacted marital deductions for estate and gift taxes. Nevertheless, the precedent remains and might provide the legal basis for the federal taxation of income according to economic origin. Whether enough political support could be mustered to override the opposition of community property states and whether the Supreme Court would affirm such an approach remain open questions.

### Administrative

The two major administrative problems in individual taxation revolve around the splitting of unearned income and the allocation of itemized deductions. Using the individual as the taxpaying unit also would double the number of computations on tax returns of two-earner couples who now file jointly.

While many of the arguments for taxing earned income on the basis of the individual also apply to unearned income, administrative difficulties associated with taxing unearned income to individuals are more serious. In the absence of stringent and arbitrary allocation rules, taxing married people as individuals would enable couples to reduce their taxes by transferring assets to the spouse with the lower income. Such incentives would be particularly strong for high-income families.[37]

To reduce opportunities for tax avoidance through the transfer of assets, arbitrary allocation rules would be required. For example, all unearned income could be attributed to the spouse with the higher earnings. Alternatively, unearned income could be allocated in pro-

35. *Fernandez* v. *Wiener,* 326 U.S. 340 (1945), p. 941.
36. Bittker, "Federal Income Taxation and the Family," p. 1411, note 60.
37. Whether married couples would take full advantage of this opportunity is unclear. With a high probability of divorce, spouses may be reluctant to surrender ownership and assets. Even before the dramatic rise in the divorce rate, a Treasury study of 1957 and 1959 returns revealed that high-income individuals did not take full advantage of transfers to minimize their liability under federal estate and gift taxes. Intrafamily transfers of assets have not been a major problem in Canada where individual taxation has been in effect for many years. For a discussion of the Treasury study, see Carl S. Shoup, *Federal Estate and Gift Taxation* (Brookings Institution, 1966).

portion to earned income. Finally, unearned income could be divided equally between the spouses. The first two rules would result in substantially higher taxes than the third. The third alternative is equivalent to retaining income splitting for unearned income and taxing only earned income individually.

Each of these allocation rules is arbitrary and would be difficult to enforce. Although taxing the couple for unearned income would violate the principle of individual taxation, the administrative difficulties probably outweigh the desirability of individual taxation in this area. Moreover, unearned income accounts for only about 10 percent of adjusted gross income and therefore for most of the population would not present a serious deviation from individual taxation.[38]

The second major administrative problem concerns the allocation of itemized deductions. Under a system of individual taxation, deductions should be attributed to the spouse legally entitled to them. Difficulties would arise, however, when the deductible expenditures represent joint obligations and are paid out of joint funds. A rule for allocating deductions between the spouses is necessary both for administrative simplicity and to prevent unwarranted attribution of deductions to the spouse with the higher income. Itemized deductions could be split evenly between the spouses, prorated according to total income, or prorated according to earned income.

The administrative problems of taxing individuals under a common rate schedule are real, but surmountable, as indicated by the fact that most OECD members and several states in this country have adopted such a scheme.

The trend toward individual taxation among developed nations has been especially pronounced during the 1970s. In 1977 individual taxation was allowed in fourteen of the twenty-four OECD countries and was compulsory, at least for certain income groups, in thirteen countries (see table 6). The adoption of the individual as the taxable unit reflects "the desire to promote greater equality between the sexes, to encourage wives to take up employment and to protect the privacy of the individual."[39] While individual taxation of earned in-

38. Internal Revenue Service, Preliminary Report, *Statistics of Income: 1977*, p. 1.

39. "How Direct Taxes Affect Individuals and Couples: Old Values and New," *OECD Observer*, no. 85 (March 1977), p. 28.

Table 6. Treatment of Family Earnings in OECD Countries, 1977

| *Individual taxation adopted before 1970* | *Individual taxation adopted since 1970* | *Joint taxation* | *Family taxation* |
|---|---|---|---|
| Australia | Austria (1973) | Germany | France |
| Canada | Belgium (1976) | Iceland | Netherlands |
| Greece | Denmark (1970) | Ireland | |
| Japan | Finland (1976) | Luxembourg | |
| New Zealand | Italy (1977) | Norway | |
| Portugal[a] | Sweden (1971) | Spain | |
| Turkey | United Kingdom (1972)[b] | Switzerland | |
| | | United States | |

Source: Organisation for Economic Co-operation and Development, Committee on Fiscal Affairs, *The Treatment of Family Units in OECD Member Countries under Tax and Transfer Systems* (Paris: OECD, 1977), pp. 15–17.

a. Portugal's schedular taxes are levied on the individual. Its global taxes are levied on joint income of the spouses. This feature makes Portugal unique among OECD countries.

b. This applies to earned income only.

come has become widely accepted, investment income of the family is almost invariably aggregated in OECD countries, regardless of the unit adopted for the taxation of earnings. Aggregation is usually considered necessary to forestall tax avoidance by artificial splitting of income.[40]

In this country, eleven states and the District of Columbia have income taxes that assess married couples individually under a common progressive rate schedule (see table 7).[41] While separate filing for married couples is optional in all these states, most of the instruction booklets indicate that if both spouses have income, couples can reduce their tax liability by filing separate returns. Generally the states have ignored the possibility of abuse in the attribution of unearned income, as the receipts from an investment are taxed to the spouse who owns the asset. The states also offer considerable flexibility in terms of distributing itemized deductions. Three states and the District of Columbia allow the couple to allocate the deductions as they wish. Another three states stipulate that the party legally

40. OECD, Committee on Fiscal Affairs, *The Treatment of Family Units in OECD Member Countries under Tax and Transfer Systems* (Paris: OECD, 1977), p. 8.

41. Other states also allow optional individual filing for married couples but do not merit inclusion because they employ separate schedules, do not have progressive rate schedules, or insist that the couple file in the same manner as under the federal income tax, which effectively precludes individual taxation at the state level.

Table 7. Treatment of Selected Provisions under Income Tax Laws of States Permitting Individual Returns for Married Couples[a]

| State | Number of tax forms to be filed | Allocation of: Unearned income | Allocation of: Itemized deductions |
|---|---|---|---|
| Alabama | 2 | Title | Shared equally or proration[b] |
| Arkansas | 1 | Title | Proration[b] |
| Colorado | 1 | Title | No arbitrary rule |
| Delaware | 1 | Title | Same as federal |
| District of Columbia | 1 | No arbitrary rule | No arbitrary rule |
| Kentucky | 1 | Title | Legal entitlement or proration[b] |
| Maryland | 1 | Title | Legal entitlement[c] |
| Minnesota | 1 | Title | No arbitrary rule |
| Montana | 1 | Title | Legal entitlement |
| North Dakota | 2 | Title | Legal entitlement or proration[b] |
| South Carolina | 1 | Title or proration[d] | Legal entitlement[c] |
| Wisconsin | 1 | Title | No arbitrary rule |

Source: Individual state income tax forms, 1977.

a. Other states that allow married couples to file as two separate individuals were not included for one of two reasons: (1) some states have proportional tax rate structures and their experience is not applicable to the federal income tax; (2) other states require taxpayers to file as they did for federal purposes. Since married couples would pay substantially more tax using the "married, filing separately" schedule, the vast majority of couples in these states are prohibited from filing individually.

b. Joint obligations are shared equally.

c. Itemized deductions are attributed to husband and wife in line with the ratio of their individual income to total income.

d. Unearned income is allocated between spouses according to the ratio of each person's earned income to total earned income.

entitled to the deduction must claim it, while two offer the additional option of proration. Two states arbitrarily divided the deductions either evenly or prorated by the ratio of each spouse's income to the total, and the remaining states' rules follow the federal code. In general, if one spouse itemizes, the other must also. This provision would be useful at the federal level as well.

The state forms generally contain a separate column for the income of each spouse, terminating in a single slot for the net refund or tax due. Couples desiring separate payments or refunds must file two forms. The additional work required of the taxpayer is quite manageable; instead of adding together two salaries, they simply must write down the numbers separately. For those employing the standard deduction, one additional set of calculations would be required to determine taxable income and liability. Those taxpayers who itemize their deductions would determine their total deductions jointly, as under current law, but then would be required to allocate them to each spouse on the basis of some rule.[42] The Internal Revenue Service would be faced with an increase in the number of calculations to audit, but the actual number of checks for payments or refunds need not increase very much because most couples would probably be satisfied with filing on the same return.

### Economic Considerations

Individual taxation under a uniform rate schedule does not provide differentiation among people with diverse family responsibilities through deductions or exemptions. Any differentiation between the taxes paid by a single person and those paid by a one-earner couple with the same income will violate the principle of marriage neutrality but may be a desirable compromise to reflect the economic reality that the income of the one-earner couple must support two people. Many OECD countries offer a marriage allowance, and all levy lower taxes on a one-earner couple than are imposed on a single person with the same income.[43] A deduction of approximately $1,000 would ensure that the couple paid somewhat less tax than the single person does. The differential would be greatest at low-income levels where income is used to meet necessary expenses; at high-income levels the tax liabilities of single people and one-earner couples would be approximately the same. A marriage allowance, however, would also reduce the taxes of two workers with equal incomes who marry, but it could be justified by the additional work expenses of the second earner. For instance, commuting expenses are not deductible, because decisions about how far to live from work are considered discretionary. But when both spouses work it may not be possible to live near both people's place of employment.

Exemptions for children are necessary because children make real claims on the taxpayer's income that should be reflected in lower taxable income. Whether additional child care deductions should be available when both spouses work is more difficult. If married women

42. In 1977 only 26 percent of all returns contained itemized deductions. *(Statistics of Income, 1977—Individual Income Tax Returns, p. 3.)*

43. OECD, Committee on Fiscal Affairs, *The Treatment of Family Units,* pp. 38–41. Calculations were made for earnings of the typical production worker. At wages of half the typical worker's, the differential in favor of the married couple increases; while in the case of an income twice the typical production worker's wage the differential is reduced, and in several countries the tax on single and married taxpayers at the same income levels is roughly equal.

were taxed as individuals and if the marriage allowance were transferred to them once they took up employment in order to reflect additional work-related expenses, then further deductions for child care would seem unwarranted. Whether to have children or to work is now a voluntary choice for most people, and federal subsidies beyond those already discussed appear expensive and unnecessary.

## Conclusions

The current federal income tax significantly increases the tax liability of two workers who marry, discriminates against two-earner couples, and creates a work disincentive for married women by subjecting their earnings to high marginal rates. These problems have been widely recognized, and many reforms have been proposed to mitigate some of the obvious inequities. They generally have taken the form of making offsetting adjustments through additional deductions for work expenses of the second earner and provisions for child care.

The problems in the current law arise because the couple is the unit of taxation and the earnings of the spouses are aggregated for calculating tax liability. In 1948, when one-earner couples represented two-thirds of households, levying taxes on couples did not create serious inequities. Social patterns have changed dramatically as women have moved from the home into offices, stores, and factories, as the divorce rate has doubled, and as other forms of living arrangements have gained favor. Other developed countries have recognized these changes by shifting from the couple to the individual as the basic unit of taxation. Adoption of a similar procedure in the United States would achieve marriage neutrality, differentiate between one-earner and two-earner families and reduce taxes on married women. These desirable results would be achieved at the expense of variation in a couple's tax liability based on the distribution of earnings between the spouses. This objection to individual taxation remains the most serious. Allocation rules could be developed to solve the administrative problems of abuse through shifting of assets or deductions between spouses to minimize tax liability.

Society has changed. The federal government should follow the lead of the fourteen OECD countries, eleven states, and the District of Columbia that have adopted the individual as the basic unit of taxation and should recognize these social changes in its tax structure.

# PART FIVE

# Investment Neutrality

DAVID F. BRADFORD *Princeton University*
*and National Bureau of Economic Research*

# Tax Neutrality
# and the Investment Tax Credit

THIS PAPER concerns the question of how the rules for calculating the investment tax credit and the associated rules for calculating depreciation allowances for tax purposes should be structured to assure the "appropriate" relationship between the subsidy granted to long-lived assets and that to short-lived assets. Under the U.S. federal income tax a credit is allowed against tax liability equal to a certain fraction of the cost of qualifying investments. The fraction depends on the durability of the asset, as measured by its "useful life." For assets with useful lives of less than three years no credit is allowed; assets with lives of between three and five years qualify for a credit of $3\frac{1}{3}$ percent; those with lives of between five and seven years, $6\frac{2}{3}$ percent; and those with lives of seven or more years, 10 percent.[1] This credit against tax is ignored in the calculation of tax allowances for depreciation, which are based on the historical cost of the asset.[2]

The author would like to acknowledge helpful discussions with Seymour Fiekowsky, Harvey Galper, and Roger Gordon on the subject of this paper. Any opinions expressed are those of the author and not of Princeton University or the National Bureau of Economic Research.

1. This description neglects the extra credit that is allowed, contingent on employer contributions to a qualifying employee stock ownership plan.

2. The Long Amendment (named for the chairman of the Senate Finance Committee, Senator Russell B. Long), a part of the original investment credit enacted in 1962 but subsequently repealed with retroactive effect, required subtraction of the investment credit from the purchase price of the asset in the calculation of depreciation allowances.

Both of these features of the tax rules have a bearing on the choice by an investor between long- and short-lived assets. The increasing rate of tax subsidy under the investment credit favors long-lived assets by comparison with a flat-rate credit, while the neglect of the credit in calculating depreciation allowances favors short-lived assets (for which the depreciation allowance is a more important element in the cash flow). There is considerable confusion about which of these two biases in the rules is the right one.[3] In reviewing the literature on this issue Sunley focused on the question of whether the investment credit should vary with the durability of the asset purchased.[4] He concluded that neutrality requires a subsidy rate increasing with the useful life of the asset in a way qualitatively similar to that prescribed in present U.S. law.

This paper develops Sunley's discussion through the use of simple formal models of the yield from investment. A principal conclusion is a qualified confirmation of Sunley's view that neutrality requires the rate of credit to increase with asset life. Furthermore, if tax rules are otherwise fundamentally correct, the cost basis for depreciation allowances should be net of investment tax credit.[5] Even with this condition, however, it is not possible in general to present a neutral rule for calculating the investment credit independently of the rate of interest and of the detailed pattern of returns from the asset.

The essential principle underlying the conclusions of this paper is that efficiency requires equality of the before-tax and before-subsidy rates of return on investments in assets of various durabilities. To obtain an efficient allocation, subsidy and tax rules must be appropriately related to the durability of the assets. Although it may be possible to design such a relationship in the case of the investment credit applied to assets within some limited class of durability characteristics (for example, within the class of assets that lose a constant fraction of their value every year), no simple rule will give appropriate results for all classes. In particular, the cases examined il-

3. It is sometimes argued that the increasing subsidy for longer-lived assets is justified primarily as a rough offset to the failure to use as the basis for depreciation the true effective cost to the investor, namely, the after-tax credit cost.

4. Emil Sunley, Jr., "Tax Neutrality between Capital Services Provided by Long-Lived and Short-Lived Assets," in U.S. Department of the Treasury, *OTA Papers,* vol. 1: *Compilation of OTA Papers* (Government Printing Office, 1978).

5. That is, the Long Amendment is necessary. It is not suggested that the depreciation rules available under U.S. law are correct; they certainly are inadequate in a time of inflation.

lustrate the way simple rules relating investment credit to the single dimension, "asset life," go wrong as the actual pattern of returns varies from exponential decay to point output, to constant flow output.[6]

The analysis takes up in turn three special models of investment opportunities: point input, exponentially declining output; point input, point output; and point input, constant flow output. The first is perhaps the most familiar to economists. Exponential decay is much the most convenient depreciation assumption to make in models of economic growth. It has also been common in the tax literature.[7] The very analytical convenience that makes exponential depreciation attractive, however, may lead to neglect of the question of how conclusions are affected by it. Hence a section of the paper is devoted to the alternative investment models mentioned.

For the most part I assume that taxpayers use true "economic" depreciation in calculating income subject to tax. This assumption is important because it assures that if the investment subsidy can be made "neutral," the income tax system, whether proportional or progressive, will influence investment only via its effect on savings and not via the composition of the capital stock.[8] It is necessary in this context to be clear about the definition of economic depreciation, an issue that calls for a digression on "recapture" and the treatment of secondhand assets.

## Taxes and Investment Credit in an Exponential World

The model of investment made familiar by Jorgenson is most naturally interpreted as a world in which the quantity of capital consists of a number of identical physical units (for example, shovels

6. Such shortcomings of simple approximating rules need not imply the procedures should be changed. The relative performance of different rules of thumb is the issue. It does appear that for purposes of subsidizing investment a partial write-off for tax purposes would be both simpler and superior to present practices from the point of view of neutrality. This point is developed more fully by Harberger in this volume.

7. See, for example, Robert E. Hall and Dale W. Jorgenson, "Tax Policy and Investment Behavior," *American Economic Review,* vol. 57 (June 1967), pp. 391–414.

8. See Paul A. Samuelson, "Tax Deductibility of Economic Depreciation to Insure Invariant Valuations," *Journal of Political Economy,* vol. 72 (December 1964), pp. 604–06.

or machines).[9] Each machine produces a fixed output per period. As a result of physical deterioration, a fixed proportion of the stock of machines disappears each period.

In this world the quantity of capital of any particular type is readily understood. Whereas in a more general case it may not be obvious what quantity of capital I own when I have a one-year-old machine, it is clear how many units I own if they consist of a fraction of the previous year's stock of identical machines.

The "rental cost of capital," $c$, also has a ready interpretation in this model: it is the price paid for the use of one machine for one period. In a competitive system this price will clear the market for machine services, equating the quantity supplied by capitalists to the quantity demanded by firms for use in production.

Particular interest attaches to the relationship in equilibrium between the rental cost of capital, the market rate of interest, $i$, and the price, $q$, of a newly produced machine. Under my assumptions, in the absence of taxes the capitalist receives a cash flow from a machine, $c \cdot \exp[-\delta s]$, where $\delta$ is the fractional rate at which machines disappear and $s$ is the age of the machine. The capitalist able to borrow and lend at the market rate of interest, $i$ (I neglect uncertainty throughout), will be indifferent about purchasing another machine when

$$q = c \int_0^\infty \exp\left[-(i + \delta)\xi\right] d\xi$$

or

$$c/q = i + \delta.$$

If an income tax is imposed at proportional rate, $u$, the capitalist will evaluate net-of-tax cash flows at his after-tax rate of return from lending, $(1 - u)i$.[10] The cash flow from purchasing a machine will also be affected by (1) any investment tax credit assumed equal to $k$ per unit invested, and (2) depreciation allowances assumed granted

9. See Hall and Jorgenson, "Tax Policy and Investment Behavior."

10. The analysis that follows is most easily understood as applying to direct investment by individuals. It will apply to corporations as well if it is assumed that the same marginal rate of tax applies to shareholder equity returns and the bond interest of those shareholders. For a fully satisfactory treatment, however, one would have to resolve analytical problems (for example, the existence of many different shareholder tax rates) beyond the scope of this paper.

at rate $D(s) \cdot q$, where $s$ is asset age.[11] Equilibrium with wealth maximization now implies[12]

$$(1 - k)q = (1 - u)c \int_0^\infty \exp\left[(-\delta - i(1 - u))\xi\right] d\xi$$

$$+ uq \int_0^\infty \exp\left[-i(1 - u)\xi\right] D(\xi) \, d\xi$$

or

$$c/q = [i(1 - u) + \delta][1 - k - uZ(i(1 - u))]/(1 - u)$$

where

$$Z(r^a) = \int_0^\infty \exp\left[-r^a\xi\right]D(\xi) \, d\xi$$

is the present value to the taxpayer of the tax-allowed depreciation deductions on one unit of tax basis if $r^a$ is the taxpayer's after-tax return. For easier comparison with the equilibrium condition without taxes this can alternatively be written as

(1) $$c/q = (r^a + \delta)[1 - k - uZ(r^a)]/(1 - u).\text{[13]}$$

When the depreciation schedule, $D(s)$, is applied to the effective purchase price, $(1 - k)q$, rather than the nominal historical price, $q$, the equilibrium relationship between $c$ and $q$ (expression 1) is replaced by

$$c/q = (r^a + \delta)[1 - uZ(r^a)](1 - k)/(1 - u).$$

11. This roughly describes present law.

12. These formulas apply for an investment held forever. Hence it is not necessary to be concerned about the proceeds of sale of the asset. This will only be wealth maximizing appropriate tax rules, even in the steady state with constant $c$, $q$, $u$, and $i$, as is discussed further below.

13. As the derivation indicates, because tax rates and hence after-tax rates of return vary among taxpayers, the supply price of machine services may vary from taxpayer to taxpayer. This variation is incompatible with equilibrium in the market for machine services. Such inconsistency may be resolved by sorting out asset types by the tax brackets of their owners, as occurs in tax shelter situations. In what follows, to avoid having to deal with this, assume $u$ is the same for all taxpayers. For an analysis of how opportunities for profit are eliminated when taxpayers face different rates, see David F. Bradford, "The Tax System, Saving, and Capital Formation," in George von Furstenberg, ed., *Capital Investment and Saving*, vol. 2: *The Government and Capital Formation* (Ballinger, 1980).

## True Depreciation: A Conceptual Problem

What is the rate of economic or true depreciation experienced by investors under either of these systems? There is a certain ambiguity about this question arising out of the subsidy, $k$, and the possible tax advantage or disadvantage due to the difference between the depreciation allowed in calculating the tax and that actually occurring.

As far as the replacement cost of the asset is concerned, the matter is clear. Under the exponential decay assumption the pattern of physical depreciation is described by

$$(2) \qquad\qquad D^*(s) = \delta \exp(-\delta s).$$

Because in this case the actual decay takes the form of a reduction in the number of identical physical machines, the decline in replacement cost value (the price paid by the buyer before receiving any credit) must follow this pattern as well. The replacement cost of a machine of age $s$ and of type $\delta$ must be given by $q \exp(-\delta s)$, and the instantaneous loss at that age is given by $D^*(s) \cdot q$.

This would describe the path of the demand price of the asset if a purchaser of the used asset could obtain the same tax and subsidy treatment as if he had purchased the same number of identical but newly produced machines. The value to the original purchaser of the asset will generally be less than this amount because tax and credit advantages will have already been realized. Special rules are required to prevent, for example, the buyer of a new machine from obtaining the investment credit and then immediately reselling his asset to another purchaser, who in turn receives the same credit. The "recapture" rules of the U.S. tax system, applicable to the investment credit and certain forms of accelerated depreciation, as well as special rules for the treatment of used assets, are designed to moderate such tax-motivated transactions.[14] To avoid complexity, I assume that these rules are perfect so that the tax system has no influence on the desired time-since-acquisition structure of a capitalist's stock of machines.[15]

ECONOMIC DEPRECIATION TO THE HOLDER. What is the path of asset value to the holder of one of the machines who plans to keep it

14. See Gerard M. Brannon and Emil M. Sunley, Jr., "The 'Recapture' of Excess Tax Depreciation on the Sale of Real Estate," *National Tax Journal*, vol. 29 (December 1976), pp. 413–21, for an interesting and surprising discussion of recapture rules in the U.S. income tax.

15. Recall that the assumption is that all machines having the same durability coefficient, $\delta$, are identical, regardless of the time since construction.

perpetually? I refer to the rate of decrease of asset value along this path as "economic depreciation." It will in general depend on the tax rules, including the depreciation allowances. Hence to use economic depreciation for tax purposes requires finding a fixed point: economic depreciation is a function of tax depreciation; a rule is sought that will make tax depreciation equal economic depreciation.

Let $v(s)$ denote the value of a machine as a function of the time, $s$, since original construction and purchase, and let $H(s)$ represent the schedule of depreciation allowances—as distinguished from the schedule of depreciation rates, $D(s)$, against basis—for tax purposes. Then the cash flow from the asset at $t$ is

(3) $$(1 - u)c \exp(-\delta t) + uH(t),$$

so that

(4) $$v(s) = (1 - u)c \int_0^\infty \exp(-\delta\xi) \exp[-r^a(\xi - s)] \, d\xi$$

$$+ u \int_s^\infty H(\xi) \exp[-r^a(\xi - s)] \, d\xi.$$

The expression for depreciation is found by differentiating expression 4 to obtain

$$-v'(s) = (1 - u)c \exp(-\delta s) + uH(s) - (1 - u)cr^a \int_s^\infty \exp(-\delta\xi)$$

$$\exp[-r^a(\xi - s)] \, d\xi + ur^a \int_s^\infty H(\xi) \exp[-r^a(\xi - s)] \, d\xi$$

$$= \text{cash flow at } s - r^a v(s).$$

If the value of depreciation in this sense is used for tax purposes (call this schedule $H^*(s)$), then using $-v'(s) = H^*(s)$:

$$(1 - u)H^*(s) = (1 - u)c \exp(-\delta s) - r^a v(s).$$

Differentiating,

$$(1 - u)H^{*\prime}(s) = -\delta(1 - u)c \exp(-\delta s) + r^a H^*(s).$$

This equation has a solution:

(5) $$H^*(s) = [\delta(1 - u)c \exp(-\delta s)]/[r^a + \delta(1 - u)]$$

$$= [\delta c \exp(-\delta s)]/(i + \delta)$$

$$= [\delta/(i + \delta)](\text{before-tax cash flow at age } s).$$

Note that this user depreciation schedule is not related to the purchase price of the asset. Such a relationship will be a derived consequence of market equilibrium. The sum of all depreciation allowances according to this formula is given by

$$(6) \qquad v(0) = \int_0^\infty [\delta c \exp(-\delta\xi)]/(i + \delta)\, d\xi = c/(i + \delta).$$

The right-hand side is the purchase price, $q$, if $q(i + \delta) = c$, the equilibrium relationship in the absence of taxes. And in this case the economic depreciation to the holder is equal to replacement cost depreciation, given by expression 2. If this relationship does not hold, the depreciation allowances will sum to a total different from the purchase price.

THE PROBLEM OF THE INVESTMENT CREDIT. This reasoning and the calculations that went before it are based implicitly on the mathematical assumption that $v(s)$ is a differentiable function. This assumption seems safe enough for all the features of the tax system except the investment tax credit. Thus expression 3 correctly describes the cash flow except at the moment of purchase, when there is an additional lump sum accumulation (an infinitely high cash flow for an instant) equal to the rebated investment tax credit. Similarly expression 4 is correct for $s$ greater than zero, but $v(0)$ does not correctly describe the value of a new asset to the holder. That value depends on the investment subsidy and its tax treatment.

One may think of the purchaser of an asset at price $q$ as receiving with the asset a coupon good for $kq$ in cash. Neglecting the question of whether there is enough tax liability to collect $kq$ (because under present U.S. law the credit is only usable to pay taxes), there are two ways of viewing this coupon. First, it may be ignored for tax purposes, in which case presumably the decline in asset value that takes place when the owner tears off the coupon and cashes it will also be disallowed as a deduction, even though it reflects a real fall in asset value to the holder.[16] Second, the coupon value may be taken into taxable receipts, in which case the associated decline in asset value will also be recognized for tax purposes.

Both approaches have the same effect on the net-of-tax cash flow of the purchaser of the asset. Therefore let $V$ denote the value to the holder when the true depreciation to the holder is used for tax pur-

16. This is the treatment under the Long Amendment (see note 2).

poses, and when either of the treatments above is applied to the tax credit. Then

$$V = kq + v(0),$$

and, using expression 6, equilibrium implies

(7)                                     $$V = q$$

$$(1 - k)q = v(0)$$

$$c/q = (1 - k)(i + \delta).$$

Hence from expression 5, in equilibrium

$$H^*(s) = (i - k)\delta \exp(-\delta s).$$

Several conclusions may be drawn from this exploration of economic depreciation to the holder, none perhaps wholly unexpected. First, in equilibrium the "basis" for tax depreciation purposes, $v(0)$, is the net of credit price to the buyer, $(1 - k)q$, either because the subsidy is not taken into taxable receipts and not allowed as an immediate write-off or because the subsidy is taken into taxable receipts and immediately deducted. Either approach accurately reflects the path of asset value to the owner and leads to a sum of depreciation allowances equal to the appropriate cost of the asset. Second, given this use of true depreciation, the tax rate has no effect on the equilibrium relationship between the rental cost of capital, $c$, and the price of a newly produced machine, $q$, except as it may influence the rate of interest, $i$. Third, the investment credit does enter the equilibrium condition in such a way as to influence the durability of assets emerging, even though the "correct" basis for depreciation is used. This conclusion brings me back to the principal concern of this paper.

### Efficiency and the Durability of Assets

What is the requirement of efficiency in the allocation of investment at a given instant among machines of different durabilities? For simplicity I concentrate on steady states where the relevant marginal productivities can be regarded as constant over time. The question can then be rephrased: how should investment be allocated so as to obtain the highest sustainable flow of net output?

To answer this question, consider the perpetuity obtainable by sacrificing a unit of consumption to purchase an asset of type $\delta$ and subsequently reinvesting sufficient amounts of the proceeds to keep net output constant. The way to do this is to reinvest the replacement cost depreciation from the gross yield. By doing this it is possible to maintain a steady flow of $(c_\delta/q_\delta - \delta)$ where $c_\delta$ is here interpreted as the consumption-good flow of output from the new machine, and $q_\delta$ is taken to be the consumption-good cost of a machine of type $\delta$.[17] (Note the shift from price to real productivity and cost concepts.)

Thus at least if attention is confined to constant net output "steady state" paths, efficiency in the allocation of each instant's investment requires

(8) $$c_\delta/q_\delta - \delta = c_{\delta'}/q_{\delta'} - \delta'$$

if both types $\delta$ and $\delta'$ are employed.

THE INVESTMENT TAX CREDIT AND EFFICIENCY WITH TRUE HOLDER'S DEPRECIATION. In order to assess the efficiency implications of various rules for the investment credit, it is necessary to consider the relationship between the marginal productivity of machines, $c_\delta$, and the marginal consumption good cost, $q_\delta$, of the immediately preceding analysis and the rental price of machines, $c$, and the market price, $q$, of a machine in competitive equilibrium. To keep the analysis within manageable bounds I make the usual growth-model assumption that the production process generates output that is either immediately consumable or convertible to machines of various types (identified by $\delta$) on fixed terms (depending possibly on the stock or

---

17. To demonstrate this proposition, let $I(t)$ be the amount reinvested in asset type $\delta$ at time $t$, where the whole process is regarded as starting at time 0. $I(t)$ will be the difference between the gross yield from the initial investment plus subsequent reinvestment and $c_\delta/q_\delta - \delta$. It will thus satisfy

$$I(t) = \int_0^t I(\xi) \frac{c_\delta}{q_\delta} e^{-\delta(t-\xi)} \, d\xi + \frac{c_\delta}{q_\delta} e^{-\delta t} - \left(\frac{c_\delta}{q_\delta} - \delta\right).$$

One may quickly verify by substitution that the solution to this integral equation is given by

$$I(t) = \delta.$$

That is, the program of constantly reinvesting the depreciation flow maintains gross output constant and thus maintains net output at $c_\delta/q_\delta - \delta$. To obtain any higher net output flow would require at least for some finite time accepting a lower net output flow.

rate of production of the machine type in question). This means that both $c$ and $q$ can be regarded as measuring correctly the consumption opportunity cost of, respectively, the use and the construction of a machine. Since I am now concerned with machines of different durabilities, furthermore, I refine the *price* notation, and let $c_\delta$ and $q_\delta$ represent, respectively, the rental price of a unit of type $\delta$ machine services, and the price of one new type $\delta$ machine.

Under these conditions efficiency in investment can be identified with the equating of the before-tax rate of return (internal rate of return) from investment. This internal rate of return on type $\delta$ is given by

$$r_\delta = c_\delta/q_\delta - \delta.$$

Condition 7 shows that when $k = 0$ this requirement is satisfied in equilibrium, regardless of the proportional tax rate, $u$.[18]

When $k$ is not zero, condition 7 says that $c_\delta/q_\delta - \delta = (1 - k)i - k\delta$. While $i$ is the same for all asset types, $\delta$ obviously is not.

Consider now the question of the relationship between asset durability and investment credit needed (when all assets display exponential capacity decay) to obtain efficiency in the presence of the credit. Because efficiency requires $c_\delta/q_\delta - \delta$ to be the same for all $\delta$, formula 7 can be used to express the requirement for $k$:

$$(9) \qquad c/q - \delta = (1 - k)i + (1 - k)\delta - \delta = r,$$

where $r$ is the internal rate of return common to all investments in an efficient program. Let $k(\delta)$ be the relationship between tax credit and durability required for efficiency. Then, solving formula 9 for $k(\delta)$ explicitly,

$$k(\delta) = 1 - (r + \delta)/(i + \delta)$$

is obtained.

As expected, the subsidy must increase with durability (decline with $\delta$) in order to obtain neutrality, with a zero subsidy for a zero life asset ($\delta = \infty$). The "right" subsidy for each durability cannot, however, be specified in advance unless one can correctly anticipate the equilibrium interest rate.

18. This is the point established in Samuelson, "Tax Deductibility of Economic Depreciation."

## Point Input, Point Output, and Related Investment Models

To explore the effect of varying the exponential decay assumption I consider in this section the cases of (1) point input, point output and (2) point input, constant flow output production.

### Point Input, Point Output

The assumption here, as it was implicitly in the previous section, is a homogeneous output that can either be consumed or invested. In this case, however, one cannot naturally associate units such as "number of machines" with investment. Consequently it will be simpler to consider a unit investment of type $d$ as costing one unit of consumption and yielding $y_d$ units of consumption $d$ time units later. This is to be understood as the entire return, liquidating the investment.

EFFICIENCY AND EQUILIBRIUM. The efficiency condition in this model, corresponding to condition 8 in the exponential decay model, may be derived by noting that the time pattern of an investment with returns after, say, two periods can be reproduced by investment in a one-period project together with reinvestment of all proceeds for a further period. Generalizing, this requires for all $d$ and $d'$ representing investments actually undertaken in positive amounts

$$(10) \qquad y_d = (y_{d'})^{d/d'}.$$

The internal rate of return, $r_d$, associated with an investment in form $d$ is given by

$$(11) \qquad \exp(r_d d) = y_d$$

or

$$r_d = \ln y_d / d.$$

It will be immediately verified from formula 10 that efficiency implies equalizing the internal rate of return on investment opportunities pursued. In the absence of taxes, wealth maximizing capitalists will equate the internal rate of return at all investment margins to the rate of interest;

$$(12) \qquad i = r_d$$

for all $d$, thus satisfying necessary condition 10 for efficiency.

THE EFFECT OF AN INVESTMENT CREDIT. It will simplify the analysis of the effect of an investment tax credit if one takes for granted the proposition that if correctly calculated economic depreciation is used for tax purposes, tax rates do not upset the efficiency of market equilibrium in the sense of condition 10. The effect of a credit at percentage rate $k$ is then to change the market equilibrium in condition 12 to

(13)  $$i = r_d^a,$$

where $r_d^a$ is the after-credit rate of return from investment in asset type $d$, given by

(14)  $$r_d^a = ln\ [y_d/(1 - k)]/d$$

$$= r_d - [ln(1 - k)]/d.$$

If expression 14 is used, equilibrium condition 12 can be rewritten:

(15)  $$r_d = i + [ln(1 - k)]/d.$$

As in the previous model, the rate of credit, $k$, must be varied with the durability of assets (interpreted here as the time, $d$, between point investment and point return) to assure satisfaction of efficiency condition 10. Unlike the previous case, there is in this model a method for doing this independently of the equilibrium rate of interest: $k$ need simply be varied to maintain the constancy of $ln(1 - k)/d$.

An explicit expression for the schedule, $k(d)$, of credits necessary to assure a given common before-subsidy rate of return, $r$, can be obtained by solving expression 15 to obtain

$$k(d) = 1 - exp\ [(r - i)d].$$

### Point Input, Constant Flow Output

In the last special investment model I assume that in return for a point input of one dollar of forgone consumption a constant flow of output at rate $x_T$ can be generated from the instant of investment until a time $T$ periods later, at which point the investment is exhausted.

To analyze the efficiency conditions for a program of investments of different durabilities it will be convenient to assume that the point input, point output opportunities are also available. Since a point input, flow output pattern can be reproduced by an appropriate mixture of point input, point output projects, efficiency requires that the cost of the two methods of obtaining the same effect be the same. In particular, by undertaking $x_T/y_d$ units of type $d$ point input, point output investment for all $d$ between 0 and $T$, a steady output flow of $x_T$ per period is produced over the interval. This investment program costs

$$(16) \qquad \int_0^T (x_T/y_\xi) \, d\xi,$$

and efficiency requires this to equal 1. Let $r$, defined as in expression 11, denote the common internal rate of return on all point input, point output projects in an efficient program. Then, using expression 16, efficiency in the point input, constant flow output case requires

$$(17) \qquad x_T \int_0^T \exp(-r\xi) \, d\xi = 1$$

for all "durabilities," $T$, in use. This is precisely the requirement that the internal rate of return, $r_T$, defined in expression 18 also equal $r$ for all $T$ employed.

$$(18) \qquad x_T \int_0^T \exp(-r_T\xi) \, d\xi = 1.$$

In the absence of investment subsidies, wealth maximization will lead to the equating of all investment returns to the market rate of interest, by the usual arguments. Let $r_T^a$ denote the after-subsidy internal rate of return, defined by

$$x_T \int_0^T \exp(-r_T^a\xi) \, d\xi = 1 - k.$$

Equilibrium now requires

$$(19) \qquad\qquad\qquad i = r_T^a$$

for all durabilities, $T$, employed.

It will not in general be true that the before-subsidy internal rate of return associated with this equilibrium will be the same for all $T$, as required for efficiency. Suppressing the associated algebra, one can write the variation in $k$ with $T$ required to assure satisfaction of expression 17 as

$$k(T) = 1 - \{[1 - \exp(-iT)]/i\}/\{[1 - \exp(-rT)]/r\}$$

$$= 1 - (r/i)[1 - \exp(-iT)]/[1 - \exp(-rT)],$$

where $r$ is the common social rate of return on real investment and $i$ is the market rate of interest, which by expression 19 also equals the rate of return to the investor.

As in the two previous models, efficiency requires the subsidy rate to increase with the life of the investment. Further, as in the exponential decay model, but not as in the point input, point output case, it is necessary to know the equilibrium situation—that is, to know $i$—in order to obtain the rule for the efficiency-preserving relationship between credit and asset durability.

## Summing Up

The foregoing analysis gives a formal demonstration of two general principles: (1) that a credit varying with the durability of the investment is required for neutrality of the subsidy with respect to this aspect of investment choice; and (2) that a different structure of such credits will in general be necessary for different patterns of returns. Table 1 suggests the importance of these principles as a practical matter. This table illustrates the structure of credits required to induce a common before-credit rate of 8 percent on investments of various types and durabilities while providing the investors with a common 10 percent after-credit (before income tax) rate of return in every case.

Unfortunately it is difficult to relate these illustrative figures to actual tax practice or to draw policy guidance from them beyond what emerges from the qualitative argument of the theory. Indeed, the theoretical argument is less than satisfactory. Apart from their being cast in a steady state framework, the theoretical conclusions have the shortcoming of being based on the assumption that the market cost of investments correctly measures the consumption goods forgone.[19] But presumably the relative market prices of various investment and consumer goods are influenced by the investment tax credit.

This issue is too complicated to do more than suggest the nature of the problem here. Suppose, for example, that a machine of some type can be produced either directly by conversion of consumption goods or indirectly by the machine itself. The higher the investment credit,

19. All of this assumes that the second-best rules call for production efficiency. Even this rule may not hold under some circumstances; see J. E. Stiglitz and P. Dasgupta, "Differential Taxation, Public Goods, and Economic Efficiency," *Review of Economic Studies*, vol. 38 (April 1971), pp. 151–74.

**Table 1. Illustrative Schedule of Durability-Neutral Investment Tax Credit[a]**
Rates in percent

| Exponential depreciation[b] | | Point input, point output[c] | | Point input, constant flow output[d] | |
| --- | --- | --- | --- | --- | --- |
| Durability parameter $\delta$ | Neutral investment credit rate[e] $k(\delta)$ | Durability parameter $d$ | Neutral investment credit rate[f] $k(d)$ | Durability parameter $T$ | Neutral investment credit rate[g] $k(T)$ |
| 1 | 1.8 | 1 | 2.0 | 1 | 1.0 |
| 1/2 | 3.3 | 2 | 3.9 | 2 | 1.9 |
| 1/3 | 4.6 | 3 | 5.8 | 3 | 2.8 |
| 1/4 | 5.7 | 4 | 7.7 | 4 | 3.7 |
| 1/5 | 6.6 | 5 | 9.5 | 5 | 4.5 |
| 1/7 | 8.2 | 7 | 13.1 | 7 | 6.1 |
| 1/10 | 10.0 | 10 | 18.1 | 10 | 8.2 |
| 1/15 | 12.0 | 15 | 25.9 | 15 | 11.1 |
| 1/20 | 13.3 | 20 | 33.0 | 20 | 13.3 |
| 0 | 20.0 | ∞ | 100.0 | ∞ | 20.0 |

a. Under various assumptions about form and duration of return patterns, entries show investment credit required to generate a rate of return ($i$) of 10 percent to the investor when the common underlying rate of return ($r$) is 8 percent.
b. This can be interpreted as assuming the asset disappears at rate $\delta e^{-\delta s}$, where $s$ is the time since construction.
c. A unit investment at time 0 yields $y_d$ at time $d$.
d. A unit investment at time 0 yields a steady flow $x_T$ of output until time $T$.
e. $k(\delta) = 1 - (r + \delta)/(i + \delta)$.
f. $k(d) = 1 - \exp(r - i)d$.
g. $k(T) = 1 - (r/i)[1 - \exp(-iT)]/[1 - \exp(-rT)]$.

the lower will be the equilibrium rental price of machines. As a result, machines will increasingly be produced by other machines rather than by direct conversion of consumption goods. The outcome is a tax-induced inefficiency in the production of machines. If the machine-produced machine differs from the directly-converted-from-consumption-goods machine with respect to durability, it may be possible to offset this inefficiency through appropriate useful life discrimination in the credit rules.

There is another shortcoming in the theoretical argument that appears in many efficiency analyses: the absence of guidance on how much difference mistakes make. Remedying this defect seems out of the question, however, as it would require a knowledge of the elasticities of substitution of each machine type for others in production, as well as of the production conditions of the machines themselves. (Remember that the term "machine" is used here to represent all forms of investment.)

**Table 2. Illustrative Schedule of Neutral Investment Credit under "Plausible" Depreciation Assumption**

| Durability parameter[a] $\delta$ | Useful life (years) | Neutral investment credit rate (percent) | Present U.S. law credit[b] (percent) |
|---|---|---|---|
| 2/3 | 3 | 2.7 | 3.3 |
| 2/5 | 5 | 4.0 | 6.7 |
| 2/7 | 7 | 5.1 | 10.0 |
| 1/5 | 10 | 6.5 | 10.0 |
| 1/6 | 12 | 7.3 | 10.0 |
| 2/15 | 15 | 8.4 | 10.0 |
| 1/10 | 20 | 9.9 | 10.0 |

Source: Based on Emil Sunley, Jr., "Tax Neutrality between Capital Services Provided by Long-Lived and Short-Lived Assets," in U.S. Department of the Treasury, *OTA Papers*, vol. 1: *Compilation of OTA Papers* (GPO, 1978), p. 15. Investor obtains 10 percent return (before tax) on all asset classes; before-credit return is 8 percent on all assets. For details of assumptions see text.
a. Exponential decay rate.
b. Neglects extra credit for employee stock ownership plan.

If these technical problems are overlooked, practical difficulties in using the figures in table 1 remain. For one thing, it is not clear how one should associate the various durability parameters of the table to the concept of "useful life" in U.S. tax law. Does an asset exponentially decaying at 10 percent a year (average life, ten years; half life, seven years) have a longer or shorter useful life than one producing all its output exactly ten years after construction or one producing a constant flow output for, say, fifteen years? Second, allowance must be made for the fact that the figures in the table are based on requiring a deduction of investment credit from the basis for depreciation and using true economic depreciation for tax purposes.

Basing his calculations on an unpublished paper by T. Nicholaus Tideman, Sunley derived the investment credit schedule required for neutrality (in the sense analyzed here) assuming (1) original purchase price used as the basis for depreciation; (2) exponential decay of assets; (3) sum-of-years method of depreciation for tax purposes, interpreting $2/\delta$ as the useful life of an asset decaying at rate $\delta$; and (4) a marginal tax rate of 0.48 (needed because tax depreciation is different from economic depreciation).[20] Sunley's neutral credit schedule is shown in table 2. It is interesting and somewhat surprising

20. See Sunley, "Tax Neutrality between Capital Services Provided by Long-Lived and Short-Lived Assets"; and T. Nicolaus Tideman, "Refinements in the Formula for the Price of Capital Services and Their Application to Tax Neutrality" (1975).

how similar the neutral credit rates are under the more realistic assumptions made by Sunley and those for exponential decay in table 1. The fit of both of these with present law also appears better than might have been expected, and it looks even better if one measures useful life by the average or expected life of the asset, $1/\delta$, instead of $2/\delta$.

On the other hand, under the exponential depreciation assumption there is clearly a bias in present law against the long-lived assets, and there is no way of assessing the importance of other patterns of investment returns. These are but two relatively unimportant reasons for a substantial revision in the way capital income is measured and taxed. But this is the subject of another paper.[21]

21. The results of this paper and those of Arnold Harberger's paper in this volume are complementary. I show that if depreciation is allowed on the net price of a capital good—the purchase price less the investment tax credit—then a neutral investment credit depends on the pattern of true economic depreciation and rises with durability. Harberger shows that if depreciation is allowed on $100 (1 - k/t)$ percent of the purchase price of a capital good (where $k$ is the investment credit rate and $t$ is the income tax rate), then a constant investment tax credit is neutral. To illustrate, if the tax rate is 40 percent and the credit is 10 percent, then the credit is neutral with respect to durability if the firm is permitted tax depreciation equal to true economic depreciation on 75 percent of the value of the capital good; if the firm can depreciate any larger fraction of the value, and in particular if it can depreciate 90 percent as under the Long Amendment, then a constant credit favors short-lived capital goods and a neutral credit must rise with durability.

ARNOLD C. HARBERGER *University of Chicago*

# Tax Neutrality in Investment Incentives

IN THIS PAPER various alternative schemes of tax incentives for investment are examined with respect to a criterion of neutrality.[1] Obviously when a society gives such incentives it expects additional investment projects to be undertaken—ones that would not have come into existence without the tax incentive. I define as neutral an investment tax incentive that does not induce new "covered" investments with low rates of social yield, while failing to induce other "covered" investments with higher rates of social yield.

The only differences between private and social yield that I shall consider are taxes and tax offsets (for example, credits). In these circumstances the social rate of yield of an investment is the internal rate of return of its before-tax cash flow. The private rate of yield is the internal rate of return of its after-tax cash flow.[2]

To take a numerical example, suppose that in the absence of a tax incentive, corporate investments at the margin typically yielded a 20 percent rate of return gross of tax and a 10 percent rate net of tax. The introduction of a tax incentive would cause more investments to become "interesting" from the private standpoint. Neutrality requires

---

1. The basic ideas in this paper developed out of my work for the Fiscal Reform Mission to Bolivia in 1976. An early version of them is set out in "Tax Incentives to Investment in Bolivia," in Richard A. Musgrave, ed., *Fiscal Reform in Bolivia* (Cambridge: Harvard International Tax Program, 1977), chap. 22.

2. I consider only "normal" investment projects, that is, those whose cash flow starts with an "investment" sequence of one or more periods of negative net flows followed by a number of periods with positive net flows.

299

that an investment stimulus would make acceptable all investments with gross-of-tax yields above a critical level (say 18 percent), but not any with gross-of-tax yields less than that level. Making the incentive more generous would admit all investments with gross-of-tax yields of, say, 17 percent or more, but none with yields of less than 17 percent. For each level of stimulus, then, neutrality requires some social rate of return, such that all independent investment projects meeting that rate will tend to be privately accepted, while no project failing to meet that rate will be privately accepted.

The next section shows that the investment tax credits, fixed-period (for example, four-year) accelerated write-offs, and accelerated depreciation over half the normal economic life of an asset all fail to meet my neutrality test. The following section shows that the neutrality criterion is fully met by an alternative scheme, permitting the immediate expensing of a given fraction, $\alpha$, of the investment outlays of a project, while the remaining fraction $(1 - \alpha)$ is required to be written off following the normal pattern of true economic depreciation of the asset.

## Tax Credits and Accelerated Depreciation

The 30 percent investment tax credit that I encountered in Bolivia during my work there in 1976 served to underscore the wisdom of the dictum "If you want to quickly see the fundamental effects of a given type of disturbance, assume that the disturbance is *big*." A 30 percent tax credit clearly reveals the fundamental conceptual weakness of the tax credit idea—a weakness that would be harder to discern if the tax credit were one of 5 or 7 percent.

Table 1 compares two investment projects under the assumption that the private discount rate used for comparing investments is 10 percent. The first project summarized in table 1 entails investment of 1,000, with returns of 300 a year for the next three years. The internal rate of return of the before-tax cash flow of this sequence is almost exactly $-5$ percent and its net present value (at $r = 10$ percent) is $-100$. If the project is undertaken, however, the government puts up 30 percent of the funds, and in addition the project later generates tax losses that reduce tax liabilities on income from other sources. The result is an after-tax cash flow profile with an internal rate of return of 17 percent and a net present value (at 10 percent) of 89. If the private after-tax discount rate is 10 percent, the project

Table 1. Comparison of Privately Acceptable and Unacceptable Projects, Each with 30 Percent Tax Credit

| Item | Year | | | |
|---|---|---|---|---|
| | 0 | 1 | 2 | 3 |
| *Privately acceptable project*[a] | | | | |
| Gross-of-tax cash flow | −1,000 | 300 | 300 | 300 |
| Tax credit | 300 | 0 | 0 | 0 |
| Depreciation | 0 | 333 | 333 | 334 |
| Taxable income | 0 | −33 | −33 | −34 |
| Tax at 50 percent (cash flow) | 0 | −16 | −17 | −17 |
| Private cash flow | −700 | 316 | 317 | 317 |

| | Year | | | | | |
|---|---|---|---|---|---|---|
| | 0 | 1 | 2 | 3 | ... | ∞ |
| *Privately unacceptable project*[b] | | | | | | |
| Gross-of-tax cash flow | −1,000 | 120 | 120 | 120 | ... | 120 |
| Tax credit | 300 | 0 | 0 | 0 | ... | 0 |
| Taxable income | 0 | 120 | 120 | 120 | ... | 120 |
| Tax at 50 percent (cash flow) | 0 | −60 | −60 | −60 | ... | −60 |
| Private cash flow | −700 | 60 | 60 | 60 | ... | 60 |

a. Internal rate of return: social, −5 percent; private +17 percent. Private net present value at 10 percent is 89.

b. Internal rate of return: social, 12 percent; private 8$\frac{4}{7}$ percent. Private net present value at 10 percent is −100.

will undoubtedly be undertaken. A project that is worse than worthless from the social yield point of view has been brought into existence solely because of a tax credit.

The second project in table 1 has a *much* higher social yield than the first; yet it would be rejected by private investors even in the presence of a 30 percent tax credit. In this case the investment of 1,000 yields 120 annually in perpetuity, gross of tax. This project, in spite of its social rate of return of 12 percent, would be rejected by private investors because its private yield, 8.57 percent, is less than the private after-tax discount rate.

The fact that private investors would choose to accept the first project, which has a social yield of −5 percent, and reject the second, with a social yield of 12 percent, demonstrates that the investment tax credit fails to meet the neutrality criterion.

### Four-Year Accelerated Depreciation

One type of accelerated depreciation that has been used with some frequency consists of permitting assets to be written off over a pre-specified, usually quite short, period. I shall use a four-year period to

**Table 2. Comparison of Privately Acceptable and Unacceptable Projects, Each with a Four-Year Write-off**

| Item | Year | | | | | | | | |
|---|---|---|---|---|---|---|---|---|---|
| | 0 | 1 | 2 | 3 | 4 | 5 | 6 | ... | 50 |
| *Privately acceptable project*[a] | | | | | | | | | |
| Gross-of-tax cash flow | −1,000 | 130 | 130 | 130 | 130 | 130 | 130 | ... | 130 |
| Depreciation | 0 | −250 | −250 | −250 | −250 | 0 | 0 | ... | 0 |
| Taxable income | 0 | −120 | −120 | −120 | −120 | 130 | 130 | ... | 130 |
| Tax at 50 percent (cash flow) | 0 | −60 | −60 | −60 | −60 | 65 | 65 | ... | 65 |
| Private cash flow | −1,000 | 190 | 190 | 190 | 190 | 65 | 65 | ... | 65 |

| Item | Year | | | | | |
|---|---|---|---|---|---|---|
| | 0 | 1 | 2 | 3 | 4 | 5 |
| *Privately unacceptable project*[b] | | | | | | |
| Gross-of-tax cash flow | −1,000 | 350 | 320 | 290 | 260 | 230 |
| Depreciation | 0 | −250 | −250 | −250 | −250 | 0 |
| Taxable income | 0 | 100 | 70 | 40 | 10 | 230 |
| Tax at 50 percent | 0 | −50 | −35 | −20 | −5 | −115 |
| After-tax cash flow | −1,000 | 300 | 285 | 270 | 255 | 115 |

a. Internal rate of return: social, approximately 13 percent; private, approximately 10.5 percent. Private net present value at 10 percent is 200.
b. Internal rate of return: social, 15 percent; private, 8 percent. Private net present value at 10 percent is −37.

illustrate the nonneutrality of this procedure, but similar results could be obtained for any other period that is significantly shorter than the normal economic life of many investments.

The first investment project in table 2 has a fifty-year operating lifetime and a 13 percent social rate of yield. With a four-year write-off of the investment cost, it is made acceptable from the private point of view, using any after-tax discount rate below 10.5 percent. The second project of table 2 has a 15 percent social rate of return. But it would be rejected by private investors using a 10 percent after-tax discount rate because its private rate of yield is only 8 percent. The examples in table 2 demonstrate that fixed-period accelerated depreciation does not meet the neutrality criterion that I have imposed.

### Depreciation over Half the Normal Life of Assets

This particular incentive scheme is representative of a broad class characterized by a general shortening of depreciation periods without distorting the ordinal ranking of asset lives. That is, the long-lived assets end up with longer depreciation periods than do the short-lived assets.

Cutting in half the depreciable life of assets appears to distort the process of project selection significantly less than do the two schemes already discussed. Nonetheless, it is still possible to find examples that violate my neutrality criterion. The pair of projects shown in table 3 is a case in point. The first project, with a $16\frac{2}{3}$ percent social rate of return, would be privately acceptable, while the second project, with a 17 percent social rate of return, would be rejected at a 10 percent private after-tax discount rate.

## A Neutral Incentive Scheme

This section is a report of a neutral incentive scheme, discovered on the basis of key clues offered by Paul A. Samuelson and Richard A. Musgrave. I shall first summarize their contributions and then show how the incentive scheme suggested here really amounts to a linear combination of two neutralities that I characterize as "Samuelson neutrality" and "Musgrave neutrality."

### Samuelson Neutrality

In a brief but important contribution in the mid-1960s, Samuelson showed that a proportional income tax left undistorted the choice

**Table 3. Comparison of Privately Acceptable and Unacceptable Projects, Each with Depreciation over Half the Normal Life of the Project**

|  | Year | | | | | | | | |
|---|---|---|---|---|---|---|---|---|---|
|  | *0* | *1* | *2* | *3* | ... | *20* | *21* | ... | *40* |
| *Privately acceptable project*[a] | | | | | | | | | |
| Gross-of-tax cash flow | −1,200 | 200 | 200 | 200 | ... | 200 | 200 | ... | 200 |
| Depreciation | 0 | 60 | 60 | 60 | ... | 60 | 0 | ... | 0 |
| Taxable income | 0 | 140 | 140 | 140 | ... | 140 | 200 | ... | 200 |
| Tax at 50 percent | 0 | −70 | −70 | −70 | ... | −70 | −100 | ... | −100 |
| Private cash flow | −1,200 | 130 | 130 | 130 | ... | 130 | 100 | ... | 100 |

|  | Year | | | | | | |
|---|---|---|---|---|---|---|---|
|  | *0* | *1* | *2* | *3* | *4* | *5* | *6* |
| *Privately unacceptable project*[b] | | | | | | | |
| Gross-of-tax cash flow | −1,200 | 524 | 470 | 400 | 148 | 100 | 77 |
| Depreciation | 0 | 400 | 400 | 400 | 0 | 0 | 0 |
| Taxable income | 0 | 124 | 70 | 0 | 148 | 100 | 77 |
| Tax at 50 percent | 0 | −62 | −35 | 0 | −74 | −50 | −39 |
| Private cash flow | −1,200 | 462 | 435 | 400 | 74 | 50 | 38 |

a. Internal rate of return: social, approximately 16⅔ percent; private, approximately 10.3 percent. Private net present value at 10 percent is 53.
b. Internal rate of return: social, 17 percent; private, 9.2 percent. Private net present value at 10 percent is −23.

among projects or assets of different economic lives and time profiles so long as taxable income was calculated by deducting from the gross income accruing to capital the true economic depreciation (TED) of the assets in question.[3] Samuelson took monetary income as a measure of real income (that is, he did not address the question of indexing for inflation), and I shall follow him in that assumption.

Samuelson showed that the ranking of investments using a discount rate of $r = \rho(1 - t)$ to evaluate the after-tax returns, where $r$ is the after-tax and $\rho$ the before-tax rate of return on the project, is the same as it would be if one used the rate $\rho$ as the discount rate for the gross-of-tax flows, *provided that* true economic depreciation has been allowed for in determining the gross-of-tax flows.

Samuelson's point becomes intuitively clear if one imagines that the alternative "projects" are different financial instruments (notes, bonds, mortgages, and the like). In a steady-state equilibrium with a constant before-tax interest rate, $\rho$, the market value of each asset that paid interest at this rate on the unpaid balance would fall in each period by exactly the amount of amortization. In this case the true economic depreciation of the instrument *is* the amortization payment of the period, the before-tax income is the interest (equal to $\rho$ times the outstanding balance) and an equal percentage tax on these interest payments will be neutral among assets.

Suppose, however, that in the same economy there is some asset whose stated interest rate is different from $\rho$. For such assets the true income in a period would be the cash payment received minus the fall in the market value of the asset. In the extreme case of a note that simply promises to pay $1,000 at the end of $n$ years, with no stated interest or annual payment at all, the market value of the note at the beginning of a period $k$ years after the note is issued would be $1,000 $(1 + \rho)^{k-n}$, and its rise in value during the period would be $\rho$ times this figure. True economic depreciation is here negative, and Samuelson's principle of neutral taxation would call for tax to be paid on the appreciation of value—that is, $1,000 \rho (1 + \rho)^{k-n}$.

For corporate investment projects like those reviewed in the preceding sections, Samuelson's proposition holds simply that with an after-tax rate of discount of 10 percent and a tax rate of 50 percent,

3. Paul A. Samuelson, "Tax Deductibility of Economic Depreciation to Insure Invariant Valuations," *Journal of Political Economy,* vol. 72 (December 1964), pp. 604–06.

only projects with gross-of-tax yields equal to or greater than 20 percent would pass the private test, so long as taxable income was computed using true economic depreciation. Anomalies like those presented in the preceding section (where an independent project with a low yield would be accepted while another with a higher yield would be rejected) would not exist.[4]

### Musgrave Neutrality

In his classic treatise, *The Theory of Public Finance,* Musgrave discusses the case of instantaneous depreciation (immediate expensing) of capital outlays.[5] He rightly concludes that with full and immediate loss offsets, an income tax would be totally neutral among assets or projects with different economic lives and differently shaped time profiles of net benefits. "It is a perfectly neutral solution—so neutral, in fact, as to be a zero tax."[6]

With a 50 percent tax rate, the government in effect becomes a 50 percent partner in the venture. It puts up half of the amount invested, either as an offset to taxes that the company would otherwise pay or as a direct payment in the case the capital outlays exceed other taxable income. And as a stream of gross income is generated the government takes exactly half of it, period by period. The time profile of net costs and benefits that is relevant for the government is in this case absolutely identical with that facing the private owners of the company. In general, with a tax rate, $t$, the government pays a fraction $t$ of costs and gets the same fraction $t$ of benefits; for the private owners the corresponding fractions are $(1 - t)$. The profiles facing the government and the private owners are identical in shape and differ only by a constant multiple.

4. I emphasize independent projects because it is easily possible for a lower-yield project to be accepted and a higher-yield project to be rejected when they are alternatives. For example, a high dam costing $2 billion and giving a perpetual stream of benefits of $500 million has a net present value at 20 percent of $0.5 (=$2.5 minus $2.0) billion. A low dam on the same site costing $1 billion and giving a perpetual stream of benefits of $280 million has a net present value of $0.4 billion ($1.4 billion minus $1.0 billion). If 20 percent is the "right" discount rate, the larger dam is the right choice even though its yield is lower (25 percent versus 28 percent). Net present value, not yield, is the relevant general criterion, but for independent projects the two come down to the same thing. All independent projects with yields greater than the relevant opportunity cost of capital should be undertaken, so if the two dams were on different rivers, each being of the best economic design for its site, both should be undertaken.

5. Richard A. Musgrave, *The Theory of Public Finance: A Study in Public Economy* (McGraw-Hill, 1959), p. 343.

6. Ibid.

In these circumstances the internal rate of return of the private profile must be identical with that of the gross-of-tax profile. In the numerical example, assuming the private after-tax rate of discount still to be 10 percent, investment projects would be undertaken up to the point where for marginal investments the before-tax yield was exactly equal to 10 percent.

## A Neutral Investment Incentive

From what has just been said it should be evident that Samuelson neutrality and Musgrave neutrality are two quite different things. Samuelson neutrality occurs when the government is truly taxing; Musgrave neutrality comes when the government is in effect a true partner in the enterprise. But the interesting point is that a combination of expensing part of the investment and depreciating the rest (using true economic depreciation) is also neutral. In particular, the immediate expensing of a fraction $\alpha$ of investment outlays, while the remaining fraction $(1 - \alpha)$ is left to be depreciated over the full lifetime of the asset according to the pattern of true economic depreciation—the actual deduction each year being $(1 - \alpha) \cdot (\text{TED})$—preserves neutrality as I have defined it.

I showed above (1) that with a 10 percent after-tax discount rate and a tax of 50 percent, all independent projects yielding 20 percent or more, and none yielding less than 20 percent, would be undertaken; and (2) that if full expensing of investment outlays were allowed, the criterion rate for projects would become 10 percent. I show here that if a fraction $\alpha$ of investment outlays is allowed to be expensed, with normal depreciation of the remainder, the criterion rate will lie somewhere between 10 and 20 percent, its precise location being, in this example, $20(1 - 0.5\alpha)$ percent.[7]

Consider an investment whose yield is precisely 16 percent and suppose that 40 percent of the investment can be expensed ($\alpha = 0.40$). Of 1,000 invested, 400 is expensed, leading to a tax credit of 200. Divide the entire investment profile into two parts, in the proportions 60/40. On the 600 that was not expensed consider the re-

7. The general formula, defining $\rho_o$ as the required gross-of-tax yield of an investment without any special incentive, and $r$ as the required after-tax yield of all investment, is

$$\rho_\alpha = \alpha r + (1 - \alpha)\rho_o = \alpha r + \frac{(1 - \alpha)r}{(1 - t)} = \frac{r(1 - \alpha t)}{(1 - t)}.$$

Here $\rho_\alpha$ is the criterion gross-of-tax rate of return on an investment for which the fraction $\alpha$ of investment outlays is allowed to be expensed.

quired gross-of-tax yield to be 20 percent and the full tax to be applicable. On the 40 that was expensed consider the government to be a 50 percent partner and the required yield to be 10 percent. In that event the project as a whole must yield 16 percent to be undertaken.[8] The first part will be precisely sufficient to provide a 20 percent yield on the 600 that is hypothetically subject to "Samuelson tax treatment," while the second part will provide a 10 percent yield on the 400 that is hypothetically subject to "Musgrave tax treatment."

The division is apparent for the cases of perpetuity and a one-year investment. For both cases the 1,000 of investment is broken into two parts, 600 and 400. For the perpetuity the yield of 160 a year may be divided into a perpetual flow of 120, which gives a 20 percent return on 600 of investment, and another perpetual flow of 40, which gives a 10 percent yield on 400 of investment. For the one-year project the profile of −1,000, +1,160 is divided into two parts, (1) −600, +720, and (2) −400, +440. Again there is a 20 percent return on the first part and a 10 percent return on the second.

The demonstration for a one-year project is critically important because any multiyear project profile can be decomposed into a sequence of one-year profiles. Thus the two-year investment profile of −1,000, +560, +696, which has an internal rate of return of 16 percent, can be decomposed into

|        |   | Year    |       |       |
|--------|---|---------|-------|-------|
|        |   | 0       | 1     | 2     |
|        | a. | −1,000 | +1,160 |      |
|        | b. |         | − 600 | +696  |
| Total  |   | −1,000  | + 560 | +696  |

Similarly a three-period project whose profile is −1,000, +560, +196, +580 can be broken down into

|        |   | Year    |        |       |      |
|--------|---|---------|--------|-------|------|
|        |   | 0       | 1      | 2     | 3    |
|        | c. | −1,000 | +1,160 |       |      |
|        | d. |         | − 600  | +696  |      |
|        | e. |         |        | −500  | +580 |
| Total  |   | −1,000  | + 560  | +196  | +580 |

8. The required yield of 16 percent can be derived from the relation in footnote 7:

$$\alpha = 0.4, r = 0.1, \rho_o = 0.2; \text{ hence } \rho_\alpha = 0.16.$$

The original projects $(-1,000, +560, +696)$ and $(-1,000, +560, +196, +580)$ each had an internal rate of return of 16 percent. They have been broken down into sequences of one-year projects—(a, b) and (c, d, e) respectively—each of which also has an internal rate of return of 16 percent.

In a similar fashion, *any* multiyear profile can be broken down into a sequence of overlapping one-year profiles, each of which has the same internal rate of return as the original project. This fact makes it possible to use the proof presented above for the case of a one-year project as the basis for a general statement concerning the neutrality of the incentive scheme under review.

## Tax Neutrality in the Presence of Debt

Up to now the analysis has dealt with investments that included only equity capital. In this section the analysis is broadened to accommodate cases where debt as well as equity capital is present, either in fixed proportions between debt and equity or in variable proportions, with optimizing behavior on the part of equity owners.

### Fixed Proportions between Equity and Debt Capital

The assumption that debt and equity are used in fixed proportion makes little economic sense but has the great virtue of simplifying an otherwise knotty set of problems; for this reason it has become almost the standard assumption in empirical analyses of the efficiency effects of corporation income taxes (as well as other taxes on the income from capital).[9]

In empirical applications this assumption boils down to combining interest payments along with gross-of-tax profits (and possibly other

9. Arnold C. Harberger, "The Corporation Income Tax: An Empirical Appraisal," in *Tax Revision Compendium: A Compendium of Papers on Broadening the Tax Base*, Committee Print, House Committee on Ways and Means (Government Printing Office, 1959), pp. 231–50; Arnold C. Harberger, "Efficiency Effects of Taxes on Income from Capital," in Marian Krzyzaniak, ed., *Effects of Corporation Income Tax: Papers Presented at the Symposium on Business Taxation, Wayne State University* (Wayne State University Press, 1966), pp. 107–17; John B. Shoven, "The Incidence and Efficiency Effects of Taxes on Income from Capital," *Journal of Political Economy*, vol. 84 (December 1976), pp. 1261–83; and Don Fullerton, John B. Shoven, and John Whalley, *General Equilibrium Analysis of U.S. Taxation Policy*, 1977 Conference on Tax Research, Office of Tax Analysis, U.S. Treasury Department (GPO, 1978).

taxes falling on capital, such as property taxes) into one global gross-of-tax return to capital for each industry or sector being analyzed. The corporate (and possibly other) tax payments made by the industry or sector are then expressed as a fraction of this total, the resulting fraction being the effective tax rate striking the income from capital in that sector.

In this framework, even though the only tax being dealt with is the corporation income tax and even though its nominal rate as a fraction of taxable profits is uniform, substantial differences arise in effective tax rates on income from capital. These differences depend principally on differences in debt-equity ratios but also on differences in nominal interest rates paid, or in profit rates earned across industries and sectors. Typically, however, the applications assume that the net-of-tax return to equity and to debt capital is the same (so that net income accruing to capital can be used as a measure of the amount of capital itself). Thus it could be true that in an industry with 100 percent equity the effective tax rate would be 50 percent, while in another with 75 percent equity it would be 37.5 percent, and in yet a third with 25 percent equity the effective tax rate would be only 12.5 percent.

In these circumstances the corporation income tax would not itself, even within the corporate sector, meet the neutrality criterion used in this paper. Projects in industry three could have a 12 percent yield and could pay a 12.5 percent effective tax rate and still be acceptable at a 10 percent after-tax discount rate, while projects in industry two would have to be rejected, using a 10 percent after-tax rate, even if they yielded as much as 15 percent before tax.

If the real world comes close to approximating the model of debt-equity ratios that differ among industries and activities but are more-or-less fixed for each such industry or activity, then what can be said for the "neutrality" of the investment incentive scheme presented above?

It certainly does not restore a "neutrality" that was not there in the first place. There still is an element of rationality about the "neutral investment incentive," however, that is not shared by the investment tax credits, fixed-period accelerated depreciation, or accelerated depreciation over a specified fraction of each asset's normal life. The easiest way to describe this element of rationality is as follows:

If $\tau$ is the general rate of corporation income tax, $\beta_i$ is the (fixed) ratio of equity to total capital in industry or activity $i$, and $\tau_i'$ is the effective rate of corporation income tax in the absence of any tax incentive scheme, then $\tau_i' = \beta_i \tau$. By comparison, if $\alpha_i$ is the fraction of investment costs in industry or activity $i$ that can be immediately expensed (with the remainder being depreciated over the normal pattern and normal life of the asset), and $\tau_i^*$ is the effective rate of corporation income tax in the presence of such partial expensing, then $\tau_i^* = (1 - \alpha_i)\tau_i' = (1 - \alpha_i)\beta_i \tau$.

What it all amounts to is this: the investment tax incentive by itself does nothing to modify, correct, or ameliorate the "favoritism" toward debt-intensive activities that is implicit in a fixed rate of corporation income tax in the presence of different, fixed debt-equity ratios among activities and equal rates of after-tax return to all forms of capital. What it does is to cause a "shrinkage" of the effective tax rate, whatever it may be, the degree of shrinkage being proportional to $\alpha_i$, the fraction of investment costs that can be expensed.

Perhaps the best adjective to apply to the $\alpha$-incentive scheme is that it is *calibrated*. The incentive reduces the effective tax rate that would have prevailed in the absence of the incentive $(\tau_i')$ by exactly the fraction $\alpha_i$. If one grants a constant incentive, $\alpha$, to all industries and activities, the result is a radical reduction of the vector of distortions $(\beta_i \tau)$ introduced by the corporation income tax $(\tau)$. Thus it can be said that for any set of investments for which $\tau_i'$ and $\alpha_i$ are the same my criterion of neutrality is fully satisfied.

### Variable Ratios of Equity and Debt Capital

Needless to say, the assumption that debt-equity ratios are fixed for each industry or activity but differ among them is a gross oversimplification. Its convenience as an assumption lies in the fact that it permits one to treat the corporation income tax as a tax on the income from capital employed in an activity, rather than as a tax that falls just on the income from equity capital. Under this simplification the distorting effects of the corporation income tax are principally of two kinds, the first stemming from an expansion of noncorporate activities at the expense of (actual or potential) corporate ones, and the second arising out of the substitution of labor for capital within corporate-sector activities.

In fact, the corporation income tax is a tax on the earnings of corporate *equity* capital. For that reason there is, in addition to the effects just mentioned, a third: a shift from equity to debt financing in the corporate sector.

If one thinks in terms of "welfare triangles," the simplified measure is

$$\tfrac{1}{2} \sum_i \tau'_i \rho_i \Delta K_i,$$

where $\tau'_i$ is the effective rate of tax on capital in activity $i$, $\rho_i$ its rate of marginal productivity in the presence of the tax, and $\Delta K_i$ the tax-induced change in the amount of capital in activity $i$. The more subtle measure is

$$\tfrac{1}{2} \sum_i \tau \pi_i \Delta E_i,$$

where $\tau$ is the rate of corporation income tax, $\pi_i$ is the rate of profit on equity in the presence of the tax, and $\Delta E_i$ is the tax-induced change in the amount of equity capital in activity $i$. $\Delta E_i$ includes the three main components listed above: less equity is used in sector $i$ (1) because of a reduction in the level of the sector's output, (2) because of a decrease in its capital intensity, and (3) because of its greater reliance on debt financing.[10]

The assumption of variable debt-equity ratios has encountered difficulties in studies of the efficiency effects of taxation when it comes to measuring or somehow estimating the quantitative effect of the substitution of debt for equity. Happily for my present purpose there is no need to estimate such an effect. All that is required is an assumption of optimizing behavior by (or on behalf of) the owners of equity. This assumption leads to the notion of a debt-equity ratio that is optimal from the point of view of the owners of the firm. At the margin they should be indifferent between financing a small increment to their real capital stock by way of increased debt or by the use of additional funds of their own. If, then, their "required" after-tax rate of return on their own funds is 10 percent a year and if the tax rate is 50 percent, the required rate of gross-of-tax yield will be 20 percent a year if an increment of investment is financed by equity. Optimization requires that if the "true" marginal cost of debt financing is less than

10. If there is a change in the rate at which income flows are capitalized, the change in the value of preexisting equity capital stemming from this source is *not* a part of $\Delta E_i$. No welfare cost is generated by a simple revaluation, which could occur even in a world where completely inelastic supply or demand functions precluded any *real* change, hence any real welfare cost.

this, debt financing must be increased until the point is reached where its marginal cost is also 20 percent a year.

Once this point is reached a tax incentive permitting the expensing of 30 percent of investment costs will reduce the required gross-of-tax yield of an incremental investment from 20 to 17 percent a year, *regardless* of the particular level of the optimal debt-equity ratio. Thus a 30 percent expensing provision will have the same effect on the criterion rate of return on an incremental investment, regardless of whether the optimal debt/equity ratio is 50 percent, 20 percent, or 80 percent. Unlike the result obtained when each activity was assumed to have its own *fixed* debt-equity ratio, the required gross-of-tax rates of return here do not differ (to a first approximation) among different activities within the corporate sector.[11]

Thus, perhaps paradoxically, it turns out that an investment incentive of the form here recommended—the expensing of a fraction $\alpha$ of investment costs, together with the depreciation of the remaining fraction $(1 - \alpha)$ over the normal lives of the different assets involved —looks even better under the microscope of a more subtle approach (variable debt-equity ratios) than it does under the cruder assumption of debt-equity ratios that are fixed for each activity but vary among them.[12]

11. At a second level of approximation, issues associated with differential "security" or "risk" of different activities could lead to a situation in which activity A has a gross-of-tax criterion rate of return of 20 percent, while, say, activity B has one of only 18 percent. This could come about because different people were the equity-holders in the two activities, or because those who simultaneously held positions in both had preferences such that they equated (in terms of their own utility) a 10 percent after-tax yield in activity A with a 9 percent after-tax yield in activity B.

12. See note 21 of David Bradford's paper in this volume, which relates my findings to his complementary results.

# PART SIX

# Issues in Fiscal Federalism

GEORGE F. BREAK *University of California at Berkeley*

# Tax Principles in a Federal System

A GOOD FEDERAL TAX SYSTEM is not basically different from a centralized tax system, but it is considerably more complicated. The complications arise from the special need in a federal system for an intricate set of rules defining the treatment each level of government is to give to the taxes levied by other levels. These rules set forth which taxes are to be deductible and which are not, which are to be creditable and to what degree, and which are to be taken account of—and in what ways—by policymakers at each level of government.

This paper focuses on the deductibility question. This topic, although narrow, has long been a prolific source of controversy because there is no general agreement on the basic rationale for deductibility. On the one hand, deductibility of tax payments made to one level of government from income subject to tax by another level lowers the risk that independently operating levels might impose excessively high tax rates on certain groups of people and also moderates the economic inefficiencies created by large interregional tax burden differentials. According to this rate-limiting rationale, the deductibility under the federal individual income tax of state and local nonbusiness taxes (federal deductibility) is not part of the measure of an individual's ability to pay federal income tax and hence is considered a tax expenditure. Indeed, federal deductibility is included in official estimates of federal tax expenditures, and in fiscal 1980 its budgetary impact is estimated to be $19 billion.[1]

1. Property taxes on owner-occupied homes are estimated to reduce 1980 federal tax revenues by almost $7 billion, and the effect of all other state and local non-

The alternative rationale for tax deductibility is that in a multi-level system of government, deduction of taxes paid to one level of government is an indispensable part of any measure of an individual's ability to pay taxes to at least one other level of government. Under this view tax deductibility is not seen as a tax expenditure but rather as central to calculation of the tax base.

This chapter is an attempt to clarify the circumstances under which one rationale rather than the other provides the better basis for tax reform policy.

Joseph A. Pechman has pointed out that the deductibility feature of the federal income tax may convert a proportional or progressive state income tax into a regressive tax and that state deductibility of federal income taxes accomplishes little more for taxpayers at a substantial cost to the state.[2] These conclusions are the logical product of the rate-limiting rationale. Under the tax-base-measure rationale, as can be seen below, Pechman's first proposition is generally not valid but the second is.

# Redistributive Finance in a Multilevel Government System

One of the basic policy problems in a federal system is choosing the level of government responsible for making desired changes in the distribution of income. A strong case has been made for lodging this responsibility in the central government.[3] In such a world, as Musgrave has noted, state and local governments would use benefits-received taxes and user charges to finance their activities, and there would be no need for intergovernmental tax deductibility of any kind.[4]

---

business taxes is placed at $12 billion. These estimates, strictly speaking, should not be added. See *Special Analyses, Budget of the United States Government, Fiscal Year 1980*, pp. 208–11.

2. *Federal Tax Policy*, 3d ed. (Brookings Institution, 1977), pp. 256–57. Similar views are expressed in Richard A. Musgrave and Peggy B. Musgrave, *Public Finance in Theory and Practice*, 2d ed. (McGraw-Hill, 1976), pp. 281–82.

3. See Richard A. Musgrave, *The Theory of Public Finance: A Study in Public Economy* (McGraw-Hill, 1959), pp. 181–82; and Wallace E. Oates, "The Theory of Public Finance in a Federal System," *Canadian Journal of Economics*, vol. 1 (February 1968), pp. 45–48.

4. *The Theory of Public Finance*, p. 180. User charges and benefit taxes are not logically deductible in computing a person's ability-to-pay tax base because their burdens are presumed to be offset by the public benefits received in return.

In the real world, of course, this sharp separation of functions does not exist. State and local government officials and state and local taxpayers are preoccupied with ability-to-pay, not benefits-received, tax policies. They consistently stress the progressivity or regressivity of state and local tax burdens in relation to income (the ability-to-pay test), rather than the proportionality of tax burdens to the value of state and local public services (the benefits-received test).

One interpretation deplores this emphasis as conducive to inefficient economic behavior, which tax reformers at all levels of government should work to remedy. Another interpretation finds in the great variation existing from one state to another a clear indication of interregional preferences for different degrees of income redistribution.[5] Adherents of the latter view hold that responsibility for adjusting the distribution of income should not be vested solely in the federal government but should be shared jointly by all three levels. It is here that intergovernmental tax deductibility plays a basic role.

The precise nature of that role is hard to define. The first step is to identify the part to be played by each level of government in the redistributive process; as Buchanan emphasizes, determining the nature of those roles is an empirical problem whose answers are uncertain now and probably will change over time.[6] Take, first, the national distribution of income and wealth. Few states are likely to believe that their own tax-transfer policies significantly influence that distribution; and yet in the aggregate all state tax-transfer policies, working together, clearly do. If income, property, general sales, and death taxes can be regarded as the main ability-to-pay levies used in this country, there is considerable significance in the fact that state and local governments raise nearly as much revenue from those taxes as does the federal government.[7] Of course, the federal share has stronger redistributive effects and is more explicitly directed at fulfilling that purpose. The federal government, then, may be said to be both the primary and the final arbiter of the national distribution of

5. See especially Mark V. Pauly, "Income Redistribution as a Local Public Good," *Journal of Public Economics*, vol. 2 (February 1973), pp. 35–58.

6. James M. Buchanan, "Who Should Distribute What in a Federal System?" in Harold M. Hochman and George E. Peterson, eds., *Redistribution Through Public Choice* (Columbia University Press in cooperation with the Urban Institute, 1974), pp. 22–42.

7. In 1975, for example, federal revenues from those taxes were $168 billion and state and local revenues were $136 billion. See Pechman, *Federal Tax Policy*, p. 2. Even if some portion of general sales and property tax revenues were assigned to a benefits-received category, the state-local share would remain significant.

income and wealth. Having these responsibilities, it should base its calculation of needs and capabilities on private incomes *net* of all state and local ability-to-pay taxes. If this view is accepted, federal deductibility is a fundamental requirement of an equitable multi-level tax system; the main policy question consequently centers on which state and local levies should be deductible.[8]

What redistributive role, then, should be played by state and local governments? The answer depends entirely on whether or not people are satisfied with the way the federal government is dividing the pie. If a given region prefers a different degree or kind of income redistribution, and if it regards the regional, as distinct from the national, distribution as important, then that state or locality should seek to counteract or to supplement federal policies. In the absence of such differences in preference, the federal government should establish redistributive policies to satisfy all regions, local adjustments then being unnecessary.

Differences in regional taste in these matters cannot easily be incorporated in tax policy. One obvious problem comes from the danger of provoking movements of capital or labor that would offset the effects of regional redistributive policies. This hazard can be circumvented only if taxpayers can be attracted to high-redistribution jurisdictions in spite of their higher taxes and, simultaneously, if transfer recipients can be attracted to low-redistribution areas in spite of their lower benefits. Success in regions with higher taxes could be achieved only to the extent that the public benefits to be realized there offset the private burdens, and success in regions with lower transfer payments only to the extent that transfer payment recipients found their lesser private benefits offset by personal preferences for less redistributive public policies.[9] In a world in which only private burdens and benefits

8. Compare Musgrave, *The Theory of Public Finance*, p. 181.
9. For a normative analysis of these issues see Pauly, "Income Redistribution as a Local Public Good." His stress is entirely on the public benefits enjoyed by taxpayers who prefer communities with more equal distributions of income. It appears, however, that transfer recipients might also recognize some public benefits from redistribution policies that would burden them privately. They might, for example, prefer to live in a less redistributive community, though it provided lower level transfers than were available elsewhere, because it conformed to their own conceptions of economic and social justice, particularly if they expected to move into the taxpayer category in the future.

The importance of the public benefits of income redistribution, of course, is an empirical question. Like Pauly, empirical analysts stress the public benefits enjoyed

count, as the Musgraves put it, "fiscal redistribution . . . must be uniform within an area over which there is a high degree of capital and labor mobility."[10]

Given the right conditions and attitudes, then, state and local governments can to a degree be the final arbiters of their own distributions of income, and the question that remains is whether they should then tax residents' income net or gross of federal income taxes. In other words, should they regard state deductibility as part of an equitable, ability-to-pay state or local tax? The answer depends very much on what the federal government does.

## Federal Deductibility

Suppose, first, that the federal government in its role of final arbiter of the national distribution of income allows full deduction of all state and local ability-to-pay taxes in the computation of the federal income tax base. If a state then levies a proportional income tax on its residents at rate $s$, two separate effects may be distinguished: (1) an incremental income tax burden on state taxpayers at income level $i$ equal to $s(1 - f'_i)$, where $f'_i$ is the marginal federal income tax rate; and (2) an interaction effect, operating through $i^{th}$ level taxpayers and reducing federal income tax revenues, equal to $sf'_i$.

The total state tax rate, $s$, is composed of these two parts, the first varying inversely with each taxpayer's marginal federal tax rate and the second varying directly. That is, $s = s(1 - f'_i) + sf'_i$. The second component is an implicit unrestricted federal grant channeled to the state through its own resident taxpayers.[11]

For present purposes, however, the important component of the state tax rate is the first. Given a shared responsibility for income redistribution, states are presumably interested in the vertical distri-

---

by taxpayers. See, for example, Larry L. Orr, "Income Transfers as a Public Good: An Application to AFDC," *American Economic Review*, vol. 66 (June 1976), pp. 359–71.

10. Musgrave and Musgrave, *Public Finance in Theory and Practice*, p. 623.

11. Whether the burdens of this grant fall on federal taxpayers because federal taxes are higher than they otherwise would be, on federal program beneficiaries because federal expenditures are lower, or on diverse other groups because federal debt sales or money creation are higher cannot readily be determined. What is reasonably certain, however, is that few states are likely to take these burdens into account when deciding where to set their own income tax rates.

bution of the incremental income tax burdens placed on their residents in relation to their incomes net of federal income taxes. With full federal deductibility, this relation is $IBR = s(1 - f'_i)/(1 - f_i)$, where $IBR$ is the incremental burden ratio and $f_i$ is the average federal tax rate at income level $i$. It will be recognized that the ratio by which the nominal state tax rate, $s$, is multiplied in this expression is the measure of residual income progression, that is, the income elasticity of disposable income.[12] This being the case, two propositions may be stated concerning the relation between the nominal state tax rate and the incremental burden ratio:

1. Since $(1 - f'_i)/(1 - f_i)$ is less than unity for a progressive income tax, the nominal rate, $s$, is greater than the incremental burden ratio.

2. If residual income progression were constant over the entire income range, the incremental burden ratio would be proportional, progressive, or regressive as the nominal rate structure, $s_i$, was proportional, progressive, or regressive. Under these conditions, in other words, federal deductibility would not convert a proportional state tax into a regressive one nor could it convert a progressive tax into a proportional or regressive one.

The residual income progression of the federal individual income tax, then, is a critical element in the formulation of intergovernmental ability-to-pay tax policies. Long regarded simply as one of several equally good measures of the degree of tax progression,[13] residual income progression was recently selected by Jakobsson as the only logical measure of progression when the purpose of income taxation is to redistribute personal incomes.[14] He also shows that a proportional increase in all incomes before tax leaves the redistributive effect of the tax system unaffected if, and only if, the tax schedule is one of constant residual progression.

Constant residual income progression, then, may be a desirable structural goal for the federal individual income tax, though that whole question is too complex to be discussed here. What can be noted, however, are the important advantages that such a federal tax

12. R. A. Musgrave and Tun Thin, "Income Tax Progression, 1929–48," *Journal of Political Economy,* vol. 56 (December 1948), pp. 498–514.

13. See, for example, Musgrave and Musgrave, *Public Finance in Theory and Practice,* pp. 285–87.

14. Ulf Jakobsson, "On the Measurement of the Degree of Progression," *Journal of Public Economics,* vol. 5 (January-February 1976), pp. 161–68.

has for a federal system that assigns joint responsibility for income redistribution to two or more levels of government. Though one of the relevant policy instruments is federal deductibility, critics stress its potentiality to distort the appearance of state and local income taxes, making proportional levies regressive and reducing the progressivity of redistributive state taxes, if not actually making them proportional or regressive. These distortions, however, would not exist if federal residual income progression were constant.[15] Such a federal tax structure, then, has important attractions.

The adoption of constant federal residual income progression and federal deductibility as desirable principles for the U.S. tax system would raise two federal income tax reform issues. The first is whether state and local ability-to-pay taxes should remain as itemized personal deductions or be moved "above the line" on income tax forms, becoming "adjustments to income." Logically this is what should be done. Proponents of tax simplicity, however, might argue for the status quo on the grounds that the standard deduction, now called the zero bracket amount, extends the privileges of federal deductibility to taxpayers who do not itemize and does it in a way that reduces their compliance costs. We already have full federal deductibility, in other words, because if state and local tax deductions were moved above the line, the size of the standard deduction would be reduced correspondingly, and nonitemizers as a group would be no better off. Be this as it may, it seems clear that taxpayer attitudes toward changes in state or local income tax rates would be different under explicit deductibility from what they are now under implicit deductibility.

The second tax reform issue concerns the state and local taxes that should qualify for federal deductibility. It seems clear, for example, that income taxes should qualify as deductible ability-to-pay levies but that gasoline taxes should not. The Revenue Act of 1978 implemented this rule by eliminating the deductibility of nonbusiness gasoline taxes beginning in 1979. The proper treatment of the other two

15. Variable residual income progression creates distortions, some of which are the opposite of those usually attributed to federal deductibility. If the federal income tax had a regressive rate structure or if it were a single-rate, credit income tax, for example, the steady decline in residual progression at higher income levels would, by raising the value of the ratio $(1 - f'_i)/(1 - f_i)$, convert a proportional state tax into a progressive one, in terms of its incremental burden ratio. The familiar kind of distortion occurs, of course, when residual income progression increases as incomes of federal taxpayers go higher.

currently deductible state and local taxes, however, is unclear. Is the distribution of the benefits of state services similar to the distribution of expenditures on commodities subject to the retail sales tax? If so, the sales tax is a benefits-received levy that should not be deductible. Or does the state sales tax exist because state voters wish to give less weight than the federal tax system gives to personal saving and expenditures on nontaxable goods as components of ability to pay? If so, the sales tax should be deductible.

The local property tax also combines benefits-received and ability-to-pay elements, but like the sales tax, it is almost universally evaluated on an ability basis. Both levies are sharply criticized as regressive in relation to family income, and the widespread use of exemptions, circuit breakers, and income tax credits indicates the strength of public desire to convert them into better ability taxes. As long as these views are paramount, federal deductibility should continue to apply to state and local income, retail sales, and residential property taxes.

The deductibility rules just proposed can be applied to any state and local tax that is clearly either a benefit or an ability levy, but what about those that are neither? There are, of course, numerous taxes that are imposed mainly because they are convenient ways of raising money without much political opposition, and all of them do affect the distribution of income in the society. Since these effects are incidental and haphazard, however, federal deductibility is not justified on equity grounds for such taxes.

All things considered, federal deductibility should be restricted to broad-based taxes that are closely related to one of the three measures of personal ability to pay—namely, income, consumption, and net wealth.[16] To restrict the application of deductibility to, say, the income tax alone, would be to favor that measure of ability over the other two. Neutrality among the three ability measures requires full deductibility for either all or none of the state and local taxes based on them. Choosing none, however, would simply shift the intergovernmental deductibility question to the state level.

## State Deductibility

Even if both state and federal levels of government continue to assume some responsibility for the shape of the vertical distribution

16. For a discussion of the differential incidence of property and net wealth taxes see Musgrave and Musgrave, *Public Finance in Theory and Practice,* chap. 19.

of private incomes, federal deductibility *alone,* as noted, may be all that is needed to enable each level of government to base its income tax on the proper ability-to-pay base. By its existence, federal deductibility explicitly recognizes the right of state and local governments to influence the distribution of disposable income in their own chosen ways.

If federal deductibility is repealed, states will have to adopt deductibility and base their income tax burdens on incomes net of federal taxes. If a state levies a proportional income tax, each taxpayer's incremental burden will be $s/(1 - f_i)$—as it should be. For the federal income tax, the same two effects discussed under "Federal Deductibility" will exist, although opposite in nature: (1) an incremental income tax burden on the $i^{\text{th}}$ federal taxpayer equal to $f_i(1 - s)$, and (2) an interaction effect equal to $sf_i$, representing an implicit state grant to the federal government.

Though logically sound as a solution to the intergovernmental tax problem in a federal system, state deductibility alone is not consistent with the acknowledged primary responsibility of the federal government for the country's distribution of income and wealth. For the reasons already given, federal deductibility is the preferable policy.[17]

## Conclusions

In a federal system, intergovernmental tax deductibility may be viewed either as a method of preventing excessive tax rates or as a fundamental component of the rules by which the taxpayer's ability to pay is measured. In the former case federal or state deductibility is a tax expenditure whose continued use requires proof that its benefits are valuable and cannot be obtained by some alternative means, such as a tax credit, which would sacrifice tax equity less.

The opposing view is that income redistribution can be a state or local objective as well as a federal one and that therefore intergovernmental tax deductibility is an inherent part of an equitable and efficient ability-to-pay tax system in any multilevel government. Whether or not income redistribution is a subnational objective is an empirical question that each society and perhaps each generation must answer for itself. As I argue above, if that answer is yes, full

17. A more complicated intergovernmental problem, which cannot be discussed here, would be created if federal deductions for state and local ability-to-pay taxes were converted into tax credits.

federal deductibility for all state and local ability-to-pay taxes is both a necessary and a sufficient component of the equitable multilevel tax system. Only if federal deductibility did not exist would state deductibility be desirable.

If this structural view of the rationale for federal deductibility is accepted, several propositions for federal tax reform follow. First, federal deductions for state and local ability-to-pay taxes should not be converted into credits. Second, federal deductions for state and local taxes should be moved from the "itemized deductions" category on federal income tax forms to the "adjustments to income" category. Third, only state and local taxes based on ability to pay should qualify as such adjustments to income. Fourth, state and local taxes that qualify for "above the line" deductibility (income adjustment) should be removed from official tabulations of federal tax expenditures. Finally, as a standard of vertical equity for the federal individual income tax, constant residual income progression has important intergovernmental, as well as equity, advantages over other competing standards.

CHARLES E. McLURE, JR. *National Bureau of Economic Research*

# The State Corporate Income Tax: Lambs in Wolves' Clothing

CORPORATION income taxes have accounted for roughly 8 percent of state tax revenues and some 4.5 percent of all state and local tax revenues over recent years.[1] Although they are clearly less important to state or local governments than to the federal government, where they have accounted for over 20 percent of tax collections, corporation income taxes are an important source of state revenue. Moreover, revenues from state corporate taxes have risen substantially faster over the past quarter-century than have those from the federal tax.[2]

The increased yield of the state corporation income taxes results in part from corporate growth. But some 60 percent of the increase in yield from 1975 to 1976 has been attributed to rate changes, extensions of the tax base, and administrative actions,[3] and there is little reason to believe that that period is atypical. Though there is no way

This paper was originally written under a contract from the Office of Tax Analysis of the U.S. Department of the Treasury. The author wishes to thank Michael Boskin, Gary Hufbauer, Peggy Musgrave, and Wayne Thirsk for comments on an earlier draft but not to implicate them or the Office of Tax Analysis in any errors or views expressed here. The paper has not been reviewed by the Board of Directors of the National Bureau of Economic Research.

1. See Advisory Commission on Intergovernmental Relations, *Significant Features of Fiscal Federalism*, vol. 2: *Revenue and Debt*, 1976–77 ed. (Government Printing Office, 1977), p. 10.
2. Ibid., p. 9.
3. Ibid., p. 52.

such things can be known with certainty, it seems safe to surmise that part of the attractiveness of the state corporate income tax can be traced to the belief that the tax adds significantly to the progressivity of the state tax system.

In an earlier paper I asserted that state corporation income taxes levied on multistate firms have essentially the same effects as discriminatory state taxes on corporate payrolls, property, or sales (at origin or destination, as the case may be) if the profits of the firm are allocated among the states for tax purposes on the basis of formulas that include payrolls, property, or sales (at origin or destination).[4] This paper provides a more rigorous justification for this assertion, describes the circumstances under which (or the extent to which) it is accurate, and reviews the implications of this analysis for public policy toward state corporation income taxes—especially the need to replace the taxes with federal revenues.

I assume initially that the state corporation income tax applies only to economic profits. Later I modify this unrealistic assumption to recognize alternatively (1) that the tax may apply as well to the normal return to equity capital and (2) that a national corporate income tax may have no effect on the cost of capital at all. No explicit account is taken of the deductibility of state taxes in calculating federal income tax liabilities. But in general such deductibility should not affect the qualitative analysis, as the "federal offset" should roughly halve any effect that would otherwise occur.

In this analysis I take the point of view of one taxing state; taxes in other states are taken as given. I have not asked a different (and important) question: what is the effect of the system of corporation income taxes levied in the United States?[5] In this regard the analysis

4. Charles E. McLure, Jr., "Revenue Sharing: Alternative to Rational Fiscal Federalism?" *Public Policy,* vol. 19 (Summer 1971), p. 472. For a description of state practices in the field of corporation income taxation and recent efforts to gain uniformity, see Charles E. McLure, Jr., "State Income Taxation of Multi-State Corporations in the United States of America," in United Nations, *The Impact of Multinational Corporations on Development and on International Relations,* Technical Papers: Taxation (New York: United Nations, 1974), pp. 58–111. Whether all states use the same allocation formula and definition of income for tax purposes is largely immaterial for the argument made here, but it is convenient to assume uniformity. Finally, references to sales are to gross receipts rather than to retail sales to consumers.

5. For a further discussion of this approach, see Charles E. McLure, Jr., "The Interstate Exporting of State and Local Taxes: Estimates for 1962," *National Tax Journal,* vol. 20 (March 1967), especially pp. 51–52. State corporation income taxes perhaps constitute even less of a system than do local property taxes.

resembles Mieszkowski's analysis of the excise effects of the property tax.[6] Mieszkowski correctly notes that any local change in property taxes will primarily affect the real incomes of locally specific factors and consumers, and will have little effect on the return to capital; in contrast, a nationally uniform change in property tax will alter the returns of owners of capital and have few other important effects.[7] By the same token a change in any one state's corporation income tax can be expected to have the effects postulated here, even though in the aggregate, state corporation income taxes are indeed income taxes.[8]

## Tax on Economic Profits

Suppose that a given multistate corporation has total economic profits, $\pi$, where $\pi = S - R - W$, and $S$ is total sales, $R$ is payments to owners of property (including the normal return to equity invested in the firm), and $W$ is the firm's total wage bill. For convenience it is assumed that the firm has no other expenses.

Under a three-factor allocation formula that includes sales, payrolls, and property, state $i$ would levy a tax on the basis of the firm's sales, use of property, and wage payments occurring in state $i$, respectively $S_i$, $R_i$, and $W_i$. Profits attributable to state $i$, $\pi_i$, are commonly computed as follows:

$$\pi_i = [(S_i/S) + (R_i/R) + (W_i/W)]\pi/3.[9]$$

6. Peter Mieszkowski, "The Property Tax: An Excise or a Profits Tax," *Journal of Public Economics*, vol. 1 (April 1972), pp. 73–96.

7. For an elementary exposition of how these apparently conflicting results can be reconciled, see Charles E. McLure, Jr., "The 'New View' of the Property Tax: A Caveat," *National Tax Journal*, vol. 30 (March 1977), pp. 69–75.

8. Again, following Mieszkowski, one can use the analysis presented here for deviations from the average rate of state income taxation, the average being borne like a nationwide income tax.

9. The text relation is similar to the Massachusetts formula, which employs the capital stock rather than payments to capital in the property component. Little is lost and some simplification is gained by using the return to capital as the measure of property. If there are any rents resulting from such assets as patents and mineral deposits owned by the firm, they can be thought of as being included in $\pi$. No distinction is made between sales at origin and sales at destination since the mathematics does not require it. If the profits tax is based on a formula that includes sales at destination, the sales portion of the tax resembles a conventional destination principle sales tax. If the formula includes sales at origin, the resemblance is to a tax on sales at origin, or production.

Letting $t_i$ denote the tax rate and $T_i$ the revenue yield of state $i$, one could also write

$$T_i = t_i\pi_i = t_i[(S_i/S) + (R_i/R) + (W_i/W)]\pi/3.$$

The state "profits" tax could also be characterized as being composed of three separate smaller taxes, each levied at one-third the statutory rate, on $\pi S_i/S$, $\pi R_i/R$, and $\pi W_i/W$. For simplicity I shall focus on $T_{is}$, the sales-related portion of the profits tax. In state $i$

(1)                               $T_{is} = t_i'\pi(S_i/S) = t_i'a\pi,$

where $t_i'$ is one-third the statutory corporate tax rate in state $i$ and $a$ is state $i$'s share in the total sales of the firm. The object will be to compare explicitly the effects of the sales-related portion of the state corporate profits tax with the effects of both a true income tax and a simple gross receipts tax on corporate output, and by analogy, the payroll and property-related portions of the "profits" tax to a true income tax and to taxes levied directly on corporate payrolls and property.

The following simple exercise demonstrates clearly that state income taxes based on formula allocation are not truly taxes on income arising in the state. Assume that some exogenous event changes a firm's profits truly attributable to the taxing state but not its sales in either the taxing state or the rest of the nation. In such a case tax receipts from the sales-related portion of the "profits" tax change, not by the product of the tax rate and the change in the profits truly attributable to the taxing state, as under a true income tax, but by only the fraction $S_i/S$ times that much.[10] Because of formula allocation the change in profits truly attributable to a given state is effectively divided among the states in proportion to sales, rather than entering solely and entirely the tax base of the state in which, by assumption, it actually occurs.[11]

10. Differentiating equation 1 with respect to $\bar\pi_i$, profits truly attributable to the taxing state, reveals that

$$dT_{is}/d\bar\pi_i = t_i'(d\pi/d\bar\pi_i)(S_i/S) = t_i'S_i/S.$$

This result might occur, for example, if the firm discovered mineral deposits in state $i$ that increased profits but not sales in state $i$.

11. It should be noted that strictly speaking, the formulas given in footnotes 10 and 12, and therefore the statements in the text, are completely accurate only if the taxing state's share of the firm's total sales does not change when profits change. Otherwise the sales allocation factor changes and an additional term, $t_i\pi d(S_i/S)/d\bar\pi_i$, must be added to the right-hand side of the expression in note 10. (In the equation

In contrast, consider an increase in profits generated by cost savings, none of which was truly attributable to the taxing state. The state would tax its share of changes in the total national tax base regardless of whether profits truly attributable to the state change.[12]

It is also true that the sales-related portion of the profits tax is likely to affect corporate decisions in much the same way as a tax on corporate gross receipts in (from) the taxing state. As a preliminary step, recall that the result of traditional analysis is that a national tax on economic profits of the corporation has no effect on price and output decisions of a profit-maximizing firm. Either with or without the tax, a profit-maximizing firm expands sales until marginal cost equals marginal revenue.[13] This result does not hold for a state tax on corporate profits, as usually imposed.

To see this, I begin by differentiating the definition of profits, $\pi$, with respect to $Q_i$, the quantity of sales in state $i$, and setting the result equal to zero:

$$d\pi/dQ_i = dS/dQ_i - dR/dQ_i - dW/dQ_i = 0.$$

In the absence of a state income tax profits are maximized by setting marginal revenues resulting from sales in a given state equal to the marginal capital and labor costs associated with those sales. But this result does not hold when state $i$ imposes a sales-related corporate profits tax. Subtracting equation 1 from profits, $\pi$, yields profits net of this part of the state corporation tax, $\pi_n$, where[14]

(2)    $\pi_n = \pi - T_{is} = \pi(1 - t_i'S_i/S) = (S - R - W)(1 - at_i').$

---

in note 12, $d\pi$ would replace $d\bar{\pi}_i$ in the additional term.) Of course, it is not possible for profits to increase with neither an increase in sales nor a decrease in labor or capital costs. Thus it is only approximately true that an increase in profits truly attributable to the taxing state (or to the rest of the nation) is allocated among the states in proportion to their shares in sales, payroll, and property.

12. Differentiating equation 1 with respect to $\pi$, the firm's total (national) profits yields

$$dT_{is}/d\pi = t_i'S_i/S.$$

13. Presuming that the slope of the marginal cost curve exceeds that of the marginal revenue curve.

14. This equation and the conditions for profit maximization are based on the assumption that there are no corporate taxes in other states, and they would be different if indeed other states levied corporate income taxes. But if one impounds other taxes in ceteris paribus, the *differences* in conditions for profit maximization with and without a corporate tax in state $i$ are as indicated here. Alternatively, if one were examining a national system of state corporate income taxes, this analysis would be appropriate for differentials from the national average tax rate.

Thus the sales-related part of the state corporation tax causes marginal revenue to exceed marginal cost at the sales level that maximizes profits.[15]

The nature of the sales-related portion of the state corporate tax appears most clearly if one assumes that the firm sells only a small fraction of its output in the taxing state but that the change in sales under analysis occurs principally in the taxing state. In that case $a$ is approximately zero and $dS/dS_i$ is near unity. In that event the deviation of marginal revenue from marginal cost at an output that maximizes profits is

(3)     $dS/dQ_i - dR/dQ_i - dW/dQ_i \cong (t_i'\pi/S)(dS_i/dQ_i)$.[16]

From this it is easily seen that the divergence between marginal cost and marginal revenue arises from the sales-related portion of the corporation income tax.[17]

15. This conclusion can be shown formally by differentiating equation 2 with respect to $Q_i$ and setting the result equal to zero:

$$d\pi_n/dQ_i = (dS/dQ_i - dR/dQ_i - dW/dQ_i)(1 - at_i')$$

$$- t_i'(\pi/S)[(dS_i/dQ_i) - a(dS/dQ_i)] = 0.$$

Of course, $dS/dS_i$ is determined by the interplay of supply conditions and characteristics of demand in the taxing state and elsewhere. But if an increase in sales to the taxing state also represents an increase in total sales rather than a reduction in sales in other states (that is, if $dS/dQ_i = dS_i/dQ_i$), algebraic manipulation of the expression above produces the following equation:

$$dS/dQ_i - dR/dQ_i - dW/dQ_i = [(1 - a)/(1 - at_i')](t_i'\pi/S) \, dS_i/dQ_i.$$

Of course, if the firm either has no profits ($\pi = 0$) or has sales only in the taxing state ($S_i = S$ and $a = 1$), marginal cost equals marginal revenue. But in the case that is of interest here, that of a profitable multistate corporation, marginal revenue exceeds marginal cost for the profit-maximizing firm. One is tempted to go on from this result to say that the tax reduces sales in the taxing state, increases the prices of goods sold there, and is passed on in part to consumers. That is more than need be said at this point, however, and more than can be said without a more detailed examination of conditions in the industry, including the market interaction of corporate firms of various degrees of profitability, unincorporated firms, and consumer demand. The point I want to make here is that the sales-related portion of the profits tax should affect corporate behavior in roughly the same way as a corporate sales tax levied at differential rates on different firms. The further repercussions of such a sales tax are discussed further below.

16. This equation is derived from the second equation in note 15 under the stated assumptions. As noted in equation 1, $t_i'\pi/S = T_{is}/Si$.

17. Since a profits tax represents a different fraction of sales for various firms in a given state, the sales-related part of the corporate tax is not a uniform flat-rate sales tax. This point is considered further below.

Equation 3 is quite similar to the expression showing the output at which profits would be maximized if the firm faced a tax levied on gross receipts at the rate $t_s$.[18] In that case net profits, $\pi_n$, are given by

(4)                    $\pi_n = S - R - W - t_s S_i.$

Differentiating equation 4 with respect to $Q_i$ and setting the result equal to zero yields

(5)      $d\pi/dQ_i = dS/dQ_i - dR/dQ_i - dW/dQ_i - t_s dS_i/dQ_i = 0$

or

(5a)      $dS/dQ_i - dR/dQ_i - dW/dQ_i = (T_s/S_i)(dS_i/dQ_i).$

Comparison of equations 3 and 5a for a given revenue yield from the taxed firm shows that the divergence between marginal costs and revenues is almost identical in the two cases. Thus for a state constituting a small fraction of the national market for a firm's products, the sales-related portion of the state corporation income tax under a formula allocation rule is essentially equivalent to a simple gross receipts tax levied on the corporation's sales in that state, though at rates that differ between firms. Thus it is likely to have roughly the distributional effects of a tax levied on the firm's sales in the state and will not simply reduce profits by the amount of the tax as a general income tax does. Similar procedures would establish analogous results for the payroll and property-related portions of the state corporation income tax.

Because no state accounts for a zero fraction of the sales of a firm actually selling in the state, the corporate profits tax is not fully equivalent to a gross receipts tax. Table 1 shows the percentage of the sales-related part of the profits tax that is equivalent to a sales tax.[19] Except for very high tax rates the value of $(1 - a)/(1 - at'_i)$ is very near the value of $(1 - a)$. Since state corporate tax rates in the United

18. For ease of comparison this sales tax rate is defined here as a percentage of the tax-inclusive price rather than of the tax-exclusive price, which is more common in the United States.

19. In particular, table 1 shows the proportion of a sales-related profits tax that results in a divergence between marginal costs and marginal revenues. Table 1 is based on $dS/dS_i = 1$. Adjustment for other cases is straightforward.

The Economics of Taxation

**Table 1. Proportion of the Sales-Related Part of the State Corporation Income Tax That Is Equivalent to a Sales Tax, for Selected Values of $t_i'$ and $S_i/S$[a]**

| Percent of corporate sales occurring in the taxing state, $a = S_i/S$ | Values of $t_i'$ (percent) | | |
|---|---|---|---|
| | 1 | 5 | 10 |
| 5 | 95.0 | 95.2 | 95.5 |
| 10 | 90.1 | 90.5 | 90.9 |
| 20 | 80.2 | 80.8 | 81.6 |
| 50 | 50.3 | 51.3 | 52.6 |
| 80 | 20.2 | 20.8 | 21.7 |

a. The values in this table are calculated from the relation $[(1 - a)/(1 - at_i')]$. Data are rounded.

States typically fall within the range of 5–8 percent,[20] only the first two columns of table 1 are relevant. Unless firms operate predominantly within one state, most of the sales-related part of the profits tax is equivalent to a sales tax. While the equivalence is not total, it is quite strong for multistate corporations. Finally, to the extent that payrolls and property are more concentrated in a few states than are sales, the payroll and property-related portions of the state profits tax are more nearly true profits taxes than is the sales-related portion— but only for the states in which production is concentrated.

## Modification of the Analysis

The results presented in the previous section apply strictly only to monopolistic firms and perhaps to firms operating in oligopolistic industries because in competitive industries there are no economic profits except as a transitory phenomenon. Moreover, it might be objected either ( 1 ) that the results presented thus far depend on the unrealistic assumption that corporation income taxes are levied only on economic profits or ( 2 ) that recent theoretical analyses suggest that corporate income taxes are basically lump-sum taxes and have no effect on the cost of capital or investment decisions. The remainder of this section demonstrates that the results presented above are generally valid and that these objections are misplaced.

20. ACIR, *Significant Features of Fiscal Federalism*, pp. 219–22. Recall that $t_i'$ is only one-third the statutory rate and is further reduced by federal deductibility. Higher values of $t_i'$ would be relevant, however, if formula allocation were adopted in an international context.

## Tax on Accounting Profits[21]

Define taxable corporate profits for a nationwide tax, $\pi_t$, to include the normal return to equity capital, $N$. Then $\pi_t = \pi + N = S - W - R + N$, and net economic profits, $\pi_n$, are shown as $\pi_n = (S - R - W)(1 - t) - tN$.

Differentiating this equation for net profits with respect to $Q$ shows that profits are not maximized when marginal revenue equals marginal cost but at a lower level where marginal revenue exceeds marginal cost.[22] Thus

(6) $\quad d\pi_n/dQ = (dS/dQ - dR/dQ - dW/dQ)(1 - t) - tdN/dQ = 0$

or

(6a) $\quad dS/dQ - dR/dQ - dW/dQ = [t/(1 - t)]\,dN/dQ.$

If one differentiates the equation for net profits with respect to $Q_i$ rather than with respect to $Q$, it is seen that there is no qualitative difference in the results:

(6b) $\quad dS/dQ_i - dR/dQ_i - dW/dQ_i = [t/(1 - t)]\,dN/dQ_i.$

The result is quite different if taxable profits are defined to include the normal return to capital but are apportioned among the states according to formula. Net profits, taking account of only the sales-related portion of the profits tax in state $i$, are then

$$\pi_n = (S - R - W)[1 - t'_i S_i/S] - (t'_i S_i)N/S.$$

21. The analysis presented here is essentially short run, abstracting from the intersectoral repercussions described by Arnold C. Harberger in "The Incidence of the Corporation Income Tax," *Journal of Political Economy,* vol. 70 (June 1962), pp. 215–40. The point is that the state corporation income tax will have effects more like those of a state tax on corporate sales, property, or payrolls than like those of a tax on corporate profits in the short run, and hence even if long-run general equilibrium interactions are taken into account.

22. The part of the tax levied on economic profits does not distort economic decisions, but the part levied on normal profits does. Suppose the tax were levied *only* on normal profits. Thus $\pi_n = (S - R - W) - tN$. Differentiating, the result is $dS/dQ - dR/dQ - dW/dQ = tdN/dQ$. The component $dN/dQ$ can also be written as $(dN/dS)\,(dS/dQ)$, the product of the normal profit margin on marginal sales and marginal revenue. Employing $m = dN/dS$, equation 6a can be rewritten as

$$dS/dQ[1 - mt/(1 - t)] = dR/dQ + dW/dQ.$$

The divergence between marginal cost and marginal revenue thus depends on the profit margin and the tax rate.

Differentiating this equation with respect to the quantity of sales in the taxing state and setting the result equal to zero yields the following:

(7) $d\pi_n/dQ_i = (dS/dQ_i - dR/dQ_i - dW/dQ_i)(1 - t'a)$
$- (t'\pi/S)[(dS_i/dQ_i) - a(dS/dQ_i)]$
$- t'_i[adN/dQ_i + (N/S)\{(dS_i/dQ_i) - a(dS/dQ_i)\}] = 0.$

As before, this can be rewritten for the special case of $dS = dS_i$, this time as follows:

(7a) $dS/dQ_i - dR/dQ_i - dW/dQ_i = [t_i\pi_i(1 - a)/S(1 - t'_ia)] dS/dQ_i$
$+ [t'_ia/(1 - t'_ia)] dN/dQ_i.$

The comparison of equation 7a with equation 6b shows that in the former there is an extra component in the divergence between marginal cost and marginal revenue due to the formula allocation of taxable profits, and that this extra term is analogous to the right side of the second equation in note 14. Moreover, the component corresponding to the divergence in equation 6b is now $[t'_ia/(1 - t'_ia)]$ $(dN/dQ_i)$ rather than simply $[t/(1 - t)]$ $(dN/dQ_i)$. This component vanishes for small values of $a$, the taxing state's share of the firm's total sales. As before, for small values of $a$ (if $S_i/S$ is small) the difference between marginal cost and marginal revenue approaches $(t'_i\pi_i dS_i/dQ_i)/S$, and the sales-related portion of the profits tax is merely a disguised gross receipts tax. Similar comments apply to the property and payroll-related portions of the tax on profits defined to include the normal return.

### State Taxes and the Cost of Capital

One of the important theoretical developments of recent years is the demonstration by Stiglitz that under certain conditions the corporation income tax would have no effect on marginal decisions.[23] This result occurs because in the presence of the corporate tax all marginal investment is debt-financed and the optimal amount and nature of debt-financed investment is independent of the tax. Does this result carry over to state corporate income taxes and must the results developed so far in this paper be modified by the Stiglitz analysis?

23. See Joseph E. Stiglitz, "Taxation, Corporate Financial Policy, and the Cost of Capital," *Journal of Public Economics*, vol. 2 (February 1973), pp. 1–34.

These questions are most easily answered by considering the decision of a firm with national profits $\pi_o$ and sales $S_o$, all attributable to no-tax states, which is considering whether or not to expand into a state with a corporate income tax levied at rate $t_i$. Suppose, following Stiglitz, that any required investment would be debt financed. The firm's total potential base for state corporate income taxes is $\pi_o$, and its base for the sales-related portion of the tax $\pi_o/3$. If the firm sells $S_i$ in the taxing state but does not increase its profits it incurs sales-related tax liability of $t_i \pi_o S_i / (S_o + S_i) 3$. Thus the state tax is likely to affect marginal decisions on the location of economic activity, and the analysis presented in earlier parts of this paper is applicable in the Stiglitz world.

## Tentative Thoughts on Incidence

Yet another way to see the similarity between the sales-related portion of the state corporation income tax and an ordinary sales tax in the case of $dS = dS_i$ and values of $a$ near zero is to rewrite equations 3 and 5 as

(8) $$MR_i(1 - \pi t_i'/S) = MC_i$$

and

(9) $$MR_i(1 - t_s) = MC_i.$$

It is useful at this point to distinguish between sales-related profits taxes and sales taxes that are based on destination of sales and those based on origin of sales. In equations 8 and 9 the marginal costs $(MC)$ and marginal revenues $(MR)$ are marginal in the sense that they give the incremental costs and revenues of sales to state $i$ for destination-based taxes. For origin-based taxes the incremental costs and revenues would relate to sales from state $i$.

One can expect reactions to the sales-related part of the profits tax that are similar to reactions to gross-receipts taxes. This is most clearly seen in the monopoly case. We begin with a destination-based tax. Figure 1 shows the marginal cost $(MC_i)$, demand $(D_i)$, marginal revenue $(MR_i)$, and net marginal revenue $(MR_i')$ of a monopolistic firm that sells a small proportion of its output in the taxing state. The difference between $MR_i$ and $MR_i'$ is due to the sales-related part of the corporate income tax. This tax affects the cor-

**Figure 1. Effect of a Sales-Related Profits Tax on a Monopoly**

Price in state $i$, $P_i$

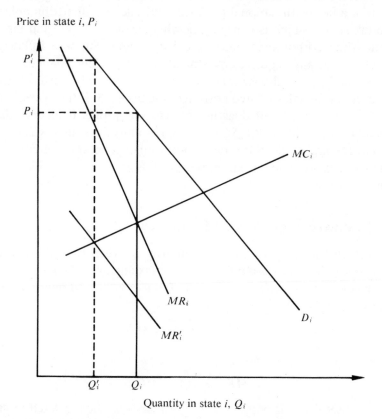

Quantity in state $i$, $Q_i$

porate decision on prices and output in much the same way an equal-yield sales tax does.[24] It reduces the marginal revenue curve as seen by the firm from $MR_i$ to $MR'_i$, where $MR'_i = (1 - t'_i \pi/S)$ $MR_i$ (compared with $(1 - t_s)$ $MR_i$ for the sales tax case) and results in a fall in the profit-maximizing output from $Q_i$ to $Q'_i$ and a rise in price from $P_i$ to $P'_i$. Two points bear emphasis.[25]

24. In order to draw figure 1 the operations attributable to sales in state $i$ are treated as separable from those in other states, though they will generally not be separable.

25. The discussion that follows goes back to Charles E. McLure, Jr., "An Analysis of Regional Tax Incidence, with Estimation of Interstate Incidence of State and Local Taxes" (Ph.D. dissertation, Princeton University, 1965), pp. 79–86, but incorporates analysis from Mieszkowski, "The Property Tax," and McLure, "The 'New View' of the Property Tax."

First, in the case of a destination-based tax, it is useful to characterize the $MC_i$ curve not merely as the marginal *production* cost of selling in the taxing state, but as the *opportunity* cost of doing so. For nationally marketed goods sold in a small state, the $MC_i$ curve is likely to be quite flat, because the firm has the alternative of selling in other states. For that reason the sales tax equivalent of the corporation income tax will cause a maximum effect on price in the taxing state. The $MC_i$ curve for "home goods" (those with primarily a local market) should have a greater slope than the $MC_i$ curve for goods produced for national markets by multistate producers, so that more of the burden would be borne by factor owners. Because capital is mobile between states, land and immobile labor are likely to bear a substantial part of the tax. But in either of these cases the tax would be borne in part from economic profits.

Second, an origin-based tax is most usefully seen as a tax on production. By analogy with the argument presented above for destination-based taxes, the relevant marginal revenue curve for goods with national markets is quite flat, because the national market can be served from other states. As a result, the origin-based tax on nationally or regionally marketed goods would be borne in large part by immobile factors. On the other hand, for "home goods" substantially more forward shifting is to be expected.

It seems likely that results for oligopolistic industries will also be similar to those for a true gross receipts tax, though the analysis required to demonstrate it is not so clear-cut. Two considerations are relevant. First, for a given firm the tax falls somewhere in the spectrum between a true profits tax and a sales tax, depending on the firm's value of $a$. Second, for the interstate firm the effective sales tax rate depends on the firm's profitability in the nation as a whole. Because various firms have different values of $a$ and different profit margins, and therefore different effective sales tax rates, the likely degree of shifting for a given industry is not clear, even if one ignores the usual complexities of market interaction that plague the analysis of incidence of taxes in oligopolistic industries. It seems reasonable to believe, however, that for destination-based taxes levied on national industries dominated by interstate firms, the high-profit firms selling relatively small fractions of their output in a given state are likely to hold a price umbrella over the less profitable firms and/or intrastate firms for whom the tax is more truly a profits tax. Thus it seems quite likely, especially for the smaller states, that this sales-related portion of the state profits tax is shifted in roughly the way one would expect a true state sales tax to be.[26] Oligopolistic interaction merely strengthens this supposition. For taxes on profits of oligopolistic firms producing primarily for local markets—firms that are likely to be basically intrastate firms—this conclusion of forward shifting is less certain; burden on profits seems somewhat more likely.

The arguments of the previous paragraph apply, strictly speaking, only to a state tax levied on economic profits. But there is little reason to believe that the result would be much different for a tax on accounting profits, except that burdens on capital are even less likely than if the tax were on economic profits.

Next, consider briefly the case of pure competition, for the destination-based tax on accounting profits. (In long-run equilibrium there would be no profits in the competitive case, and therefore no tax if economic profits were the tax base.) Though the analysis would again be tricky, it seems likely that the tax would be reflected in higher prices. By how much the price would rise, however, is unclear, as firms would pay different tax rates, and there is less presumption of price umbrella effects.[27]

Except for one important analytical difference, factor-related profits taxes and origin-based sales-related profits taxes are usefully considered together. As with any tax on the use of a factor, rather than on sales, the property and payroll-related portions of the corporate income tax are not easily portrayed using the partial equilibrium diagram of figure 1, except in the case of complete impossibility of factor substitution.[28] But in the cases of both monopoly and pure competition the property and payroll portions of the tax on economic or accounting profits are almost certainly borne, at least in part, by owners of immobile factors, land and perhaps labor, located in the taxing state.[29] The real analytical problems involve the oligopolistic

26. If the apportionment formula employs sales at destination, the shifting would be to consumers. If it includes sales at origin, backward shifting to immobile factors, land and perhaps labor, is more likely.

27. Long-run competitive equilibrium, however, would seem to require that all firms have identical ratios of sales to accounting profits and equal fractions of their sales in given states.

28. For a further discussion of this problem, see Charles E. McLure, Jr., "General Equilibrium Incidence Analysis: The Harberger Model after Ten Years," *Journal of Public Economics*, vol. 4 (February 1975), pp. 125–61.

29. See also McLure, "The 'New View' of the Property Tax." For a discussion of this issue in a slightly different context, see Charles E. McLure, Jr., "The Relevance

sector. Here it seems quite possible that both origin-based sales-related profits taxes and the factor-related portions of state profits tax are shifted in part to consumers of taxed products throughout the nation via price umbrella effects rather than reflected in lower factor returns, especially if production is dominated by a few firms and geographically centered in the taxing state.[30]

## Concluding Remarks: Implications for Policy

The analysis presented here has important implications for tax policy. But as in the case of Peter Mieszkowski's analysis of the incidence of the property tax, the implications depend on whether one takes the point of view of one state or the nation as a whole. Nonetheless, the most important implication of both points of view is that the corporation income tax is an unsatisfactory source of revenue for state governments and should be replaced by other forms of state or federal taxation.

### State Tax Policy

The upshot of this analysis for state tax policy is clear. Economists have long recognized that state and local governments have little business engaging in redistributional taxation implemented through corporate income taxes and progressive personal income taxes because geographic mobility is likely to doom such efforts.[31] My analysis suggests that the prospects are even worse than usually supposed. Rather than being the potentially progressive tax that it appears to be, the state corporation income tax is actually levied, in effect, on two bases that would usually be agreed to lead directly to regressive taxation: sales and payrolls. Moreover, recent analysis of the incidence of the property tax suggests that the property-related portion is likely

---

of the New View of the Incidence of the Property Tax in Less Developed Countries," in Roy W. Bahl, ed., *The Taxation of Urban Property in Less Developed Countries* (University of Wisconsin Press for the Committee on Taxation, Resources and Economic Development, 1979), pp. 51–76. To the extent that locational monopoly rents exist, the tax may be borne in part by owners of the firm (or other owners of the economic interest in the assets generating rents).

30. For the use of such an assumption, see McLure, "The Interstate Exporting of State and Local Taxes."

31. See, for example, Richard A. Musgrave, *The Theory of Public Finance* (McGraw-Hill, 1959), pp. 181–82; and Wallace E. Oates, "Theory of Public Finance in a Federal System," *Canadian Journal of Economics*, vol. 1 (February 1968), pp. 37–54.

to be regressive as well.[32] Thus the state corporation income tax does not do what many would seem to intend it to do, and it works only very clumsily and possibly at considerable cost. Therefore, any single state would seem to be well-advised at least to replace the corporation income tax with a tax levied directly on corporate sales, payrolls, and property (or whatever else happens to be in its present allocation formula). The only real changes would be (1) the use of a standard rate of tax instead of one that depends on the firm's national profit performance and (2) a considerable simplification of tax administration and compliance. Moreover, unless there is a clear reason for preferring to discriminate against the corporate form of organization, it would seem even better to levy the sales, payroll, and property tax on all economic activity, not just that in the corporate sector. Finally, the portions of the substitute tax based on payrolls, property, and sales at origin could probably be replaced by a more general source-based state tax, such as an origin principle value-added tax, and that on sales at destination could be replaced by a destination principle value-added tax or absorbed into the (perhaps newly enacted) state retail sales tax or personal income tax.[33] I submit that this kind of replacement of the corporation income tax would make economic and administrative sense for any state.

### The National Perspective

There are at least three good reasons why state governments should not employ corporation income taxes, in addition to the two already

32. Recall that I am dealing with the tax as seen from the vantage point of individual states, so it is "excise effects" that are relevant. As noted earlier, what is true for each state is not true for all states acting together. That is, if all states levied the same corporation income tax, corporate profits *would* be burdened (if the Harberger-type shifting to owners of noncorporate capital is ignored). But this is largely irrelevant to decisions made in any statehouse because any deviations from that uniform tax would have the effects described here.

33. One real problem with state personal income taxes is the difficulty of including corporate-source income, especially retained earnings. This is one possible justification for not taking the final step to replacing the state tax on sales at destination with a state personal income tax. On the other hand, allowance can be made for family circumstances under the personal income tax, but this is difficult under the present corporate profits taxes and flat-rate payroll and property taxes. Similarly, retail sales taxes allow exemption of key items, which does not occur under state corporation income taxes. If the corporate and personal income taxes were integrated at the federal level, it would be substantially easier to obtain the information necessary to tax personal income at residence at the state level.

presented (that states have no business levying taxes such as this that are supposedly progressive and that the tax, as seen by any one state, is not really an income tax anyway).

First, even as a federal levy, the corporation income tax makes no sense, except as a withholding device. Second, it is generally logically impossible to tax accurately the corporate profits originating in any particular state of a multistate firm. Third, the locational allocation of resources is distorted by differentials in the corporate profits taxes levied in various states.

The first of these is beyond the scope of this paper and has been discussed elsewhere.[34] But the analysis of this paper is directly germane to the second and third.

Like overhead, neither economic nor accounting profits can be accurately allocated to any one state. That is the fundamental reason why it is necessary to employ such an arbitrary and unsatisfactory approach as formula apportionment to allocate the national profits of a firm among states. Nor is the use of separate accounting (the practice under which a firm's activities in each state are treated as constituting a separate business) much better. As experience with section 482 of the U.S. Internal Revenue Code has demonstrated in the international sphere, joint costs and problems of transfer pricing render separate accounting as arbitrary as formula apportionment.[35] Because

34. For a detailed discussion of the lack of rationale inherent in a separate tax on corporation income, see Charles E. McLure, Jr., "Integration of the Personal and Corporate Income Taxes: The Missing Element in Recent Tax Reform Proposals," *Harvard Law Review,* vol. 88 (January 1975), pp. 532–82. Administrative difficulties of integration and divided relief are the subject of Charles E. McLure, Jr., *Must Corporate Income Be Taxed Twice?* (Brookings Institution, 1979).

35. For discussions of problems of section 482 see, for example, M. L. Hamlin, "Correct Allocations under Section 482 Are Still Difficult Despite New Regs," *Journal of Taxation,* vol. 43 (December 30, 1975), pp. 358–63; and Lawrence C. Phillips, "The Current Status of the Application of Section 482 to Foreign Related Corporations," *Taxes,* vol. 48 (August 1970), pp. 472–78.

In recent years there has been some interest in the use of formula apportionment to replace the separate accounting approach found in the tax treatment of multinational firms by national governments. As evidence of this, see United Nations *The Impact of Multinational Corporations.* For an expression of preference for formula apportionment in the international field, see Peggy B. Musgrave, "International Tax Base Division and the Multinational Corporation," *Public Finance,* vol. 27, no. 4 (1972), pp. 394–413. The present criticism of formula-apportioned income taxation should not be interpreted as a preference for separate accounting. Which of these approaches is a superior way of allocating the unallocable is beyond the scope of this paper.

accurate state taxation of corporate income is often a logical impossibility, it seems best to abandon this tax as a source of state revenue.[36] One way to encourage this abandonment would be to disallow the deduction of state corporate income taxes in the calculation of income for federal tax purposes.

In discussions of state taxation of multistate corporations, relatively little has been said about the extent to which differential rates of profit taxation distort investment and other decisions, except in the context of specialized discussions of the effects of taxes and tax incentives on industrial location. This inattention contrasts markedly with the considerable attention focused on the consistency of various systems of international taxation with worldwide efficiency, that is, the neutral allocation of resources (primarily capital), among nations.[37]

36. The basic problem is jointness or indivisibility of the firm's operations, and the same principles that apply to public goods in the literature on fiscal federalism seem to apply here also. The allocation of responsibility for the provision of various public goods among levels of government should depend on the area over which benefits extend. Similarly taxation of the multistate firm should be imposed by the jurisdiction most nearly congruent with the area the firm's activities cover. If the decision units are smaller than optimal, problems arise. Among the problems are the locational effects discussed below.

37. This difference in emphasis almost certainly reflects the different principles on which state and national income taxes are based. State corporation income taxes are based essentially on a territorial principle. That is, states ostensibly attempt to tax only profits whose source lies within their borders, independently of the legal site of residence of the corporation or its owners. On the other hand, many nations (but not all of even the important industrial nations) apply a worldwide principle under which all profits of resident firms are subject to profits tax, wherever earned.

Under the territorial or "source" principle the net return to investment (assuming the corporation income tax actually is levied on profits produced in a given area instead of through formula apportionment) depends on where capital is invested, unless effective tax rates are the same in all jurisdictions. Thus the territorial principle inherently interferes with worldwide or nationwide efficiency. By comparison, the achievement of worldwide efficiency is at least generally consistent with the worldwide or "residence" principle. Nations applying this approach, however, almost always also tax all profits originating within their borders. For an excellent background discussion of various methods of relieving the double taxation that results from overlapping taxes being levied on the same income, and other issues relevant to the material covered in this section, see Mitsuo Sato and Richard M. Bird, "International Aspects of the Taxation of Corporations and Shareholders," *International Monetary Fund Staff Papers,* vol. 22 (July 1975), pp. 384–455. I take as given continued state reliance on the territorial principle because corporate taxation at residence does not have the appeal in the interstate context that it has in the international sphere.

It is usually thought to be necessary for the achievement of locational efficiency that the tax levied on a given amount of profit be invariant with regard to the geographic source of that profit.[38] In the present context—and inevitably where analysts are concerned with taxes levied in an open economy—one cannot generally identify the geographic source of profits, as noted above. But it seems reasonable to argue more generally that locational efficiency requires that the tax levied on a given amount of profit should be invariant with respect to where property is located.[39]

Naturally enough the property-related portion of the total corporate tax of the firm is invariant to the location of property only if the tax rate in all jurisdictions is the same (or if the firm earns no profits).[40] Formula apportionment is generally nonneutral (if profits are positive), as it tends to discourage investment in high-tax states.

Concern with locational efficiency of resource allocation thus suggests that states should not use formula-apportioned corporation income taxes, or at least that rates should be uniform across states.[41] If the tax continues to be used, this last conclusion has important ramifications for intergovernmental fiscal relations. First, it suggests that the Multistate Tax Commission (MTC), or something like it,

38. See, for example, Peggy B. Musgrave, *United States Taxation of Foreign Investment Income: Issues and Arguments* (Harvard Law School, International Tax Program, 1969).

39. Concern with locational effects on investment is most analogous to concern about equal taxation of profits, which is essentially a matter of the locational allocation of capital.

40. Of course, if tax rates are uniform, many systems of taxation are locationally neutral. In order to show that formula apportionment does not generally result in locational efficiency, I write the following expression for the property-related portion of the profits tax on a firm collected in state $i$ and in all other states (lumped together as $j \neq i$):

$$T = [bt_i + (1 - b)t_j]\pi$$

or

$$T = [t_j + b(t_i - t_j)]\pi,$$

where $t_j$ is the weighted average of tax rates in all states other than $i$. Differentiating, with respect to $b$, the fraction of total property of the firm located in state $i$, the result is

$$dT/db = (t_i - t_j)\pi.$$

41. It is ironic, but natural, that the property-related portion of the state tax is both the culprit most responsible for adverse locational effects and perhaps the most natural choice as the best single apportionment factor in the Massachusetts formula.

should concern itself with rate differentials as well as with the definition of income and apportionment formulas.[42] This may be a large
order indeed, since membership in the MTC is voluntary, and some
member states do not currently levy corporation income taxes. Elimination of differentials would require either elimination of all state
corporate taxes or, as a first step, the imposition of corporation income taxes in the states now abstaining from using this source of
revenue. But I have argued above that this is an inferior form of state
tax, regardless of whether it is appraised from the state or the national
point of view. Thus any federal requirement that all states levy state
corporate income taxes so that rates could be equalized is hardly a
clear step forward. A more sensible approach would be to prohibit
state use of this tax and make up the lost revenues through federal
taxation and grants to the states.[43] A surcharge on the federal corporation income tax might be the obvious choice since it is more or
less equivalent to a uniform state tax. But given the faults that an
unintegrated corporation income tax has, even at the federal level,
one might hope that a better source of revenue could be found.[44]
Though this is not the place to go into that question, logical candidates might be a value-added tax, the personal income tax, or a progressive tax on personal expenditures.

42. For descriptions of the MTC and its activities, see McLure, "State Income
Taxation of Multistate Corporations"; "Taxation of Multi-Jurisdictional Corporate
Income: Lessons of the U.S. Experience," in Wallace Oates, ed., *The Political Economy of Fiscal Federalism* (Lexington Books, 1977), pp. 241–59, and especially
Eugene F. Corrigan, "Interstate Corporate Income Taxation: Recent Revolutions
and a Modern Response," *Vanderbilt Law Review,* vol. 29 (March 1976), pp.
423–42.

43. This suggestion might seem to be inconsistent with my questioning of the role
of unconditional grants in "Revenue Sharing: An Alternative to Rational Fiscal
Federalism," pp. 474–76. But I argued there that state corporation income taxes have
no place in a rational system of fiscal federalism, whereas unconditional grants may
be more or less equivalent to broad-based general taxes, such as sales and personal
income taxes, and therefore acceptable.

44. Moreover, if this tax were used, there might be a natural tendency to assume
that grants to states should be based on corporate income originating in the states.
But such an assumption would resurrect the insurmountable problems of income
measurement that lead me to suggest that the states should not use the corporate
income tax.

# PART SEVEN

# Other Topics

E. CARY BROWN  *Massachusetts Institute of Technology*

# Reflections on Fiscal Policy

THE REPUTE and apparent effectiveness of fiscal policy have both fallen a long way from peaks reached in the mid-1960s. Policymakers no longer regard fiscal policy as an effective device for fighting inflation, and analysts have questioned its overall effects. The present economic structure seems profoundly different from that of earlier decades and much less receptive to the macroeconomic policies that worked then. Indeed, some write off fiscal policy completely as of no consequence for stabilization policies.

It would be delightful to put forth a solution to these difficulties— an overlooked synthesis, a new fiscal instrument. This chapter, how- ever, is merely a review of some of the major steps that brought fiscal policy to its present stage and a consideration of some of the major criticisms of fiscal policy.

## Major Developments in Fiscal Policy

Before World War II the economic profession disagreed about the capacity of expansive fiscal action to increase income and employ- ment. Policy discussion mirrored that confusion. Many regarded budget deficits as contractive, not the other way round. Wartime ad- vances in national-income accounting coupled with advances in macrotheory, particularly the discussion of the balanced-budget mul- tiplier, clarified the difference between the impact of taxes on national

349

income and that of government purchases, effectively eliminating the budget deficit as a determinant of income.[1]

## The Early Postwar Period

A second major step in the postwar development of fiscal policy theory was the incorporation of automatic stabilizers into the analysis.[2] Ultimate acceptance of automatic stabilizers for policy purposes depended on the observed fact that resources in the postwar economy were being reasonably fully employed, not seriously underemployed as in the prewar period.[3] Full-employment fluctuations rather than stagnation seemed the major stabilization problem, and automatic stabilizers could contribute to solving such a problem.

During the Korean War fiscal policy was timely and effective. Tax policy was implemented so rapidly that large budget surpluses arose in the first year of war mobilization. Three major tax bills passed Congress within a year and a half of the opening of hostilities. In contrast with World War II when, to be sure, the degree of resource mobilization was many times greater, fiscal policy during the Korean War carried the major burden of stabilization, with some backup from direct controls.[4]

By the end of the war the economics profession with few exceptions agreed on the efficacy of fiscal policy. Economists no longer feared a recurrence of the depression and stagnation that bedevilled the 1930s. Nevertheless, no U.S. administration had yet changed taxes, without making a similar change in purchases, solely for stabilization purposes.[5]

    1. See Walter S. Salant, Bent Hansen, and Paul A. Samuelson, "Origins of the Balanced-Budget-Multiplier Theorem," *History of Political Economy*, vol. 7 (Spring 1975), pp. 3–55.
    2. The Committee for Economic Development and associated economists led this advance. See Herbert Stein, *The Fiscal Revolution in America* (University of Chicago Press, 1969), pp. 220–32. A related and important emphasis of this group was on the use of taxes rather than government purchases for stabilization purposes.
    3. E. Cary Brown, "The Policy Acceptance in the United States of Reliance on Automatic Fiscal Stabilizers," *Journal of Finance*, vol. 14 (March 1959), pp. 40–51.
    4. John Kenneth Galbraith, in *A Theory of Price Control* (Harvard University Press, 1952), characterized economic policy in World War II as "the disequilibrium system."
    5. E. Cary Brown, "Federal Fiscal Policy in the Postwar Period," in Ralph E. Freeman, ed., *Postwar Economic Trends in the United States* (Harper, 1960), pp. 139–88.

## The 1964 Tax Cut

The 1964 tax cut has been regarded rightly as one of the great successes in the use of fiscal policy to stabilize the economy.[6] But the administration's incorporation of major tax reform proposals into the proposed stabilizing tax reduction caused long drawn out debate. Only a stripped-down version of the original program providing for tax reduction and virtually no tax reform eventually passed, and even that came only at President Johnson's special request following the assassination of President Kennedy.

The sluggish enactment of the 1964 legislation pointed up again the potentially long lag in the operation of fiscal policy. The dangers of such delay had been known for some time.[7] Some students of the fiscal process attributed the delay to the attempts to achieve several objectives with one piece of fiscal legislation: reform of the tax system *and* changes in total taxes; adjustments in the distribution of income *and* modification of aggregate demand. Some analysts argued that Congress could act promptly if simple temporary fiscal changes, whose form had been agreed upon in advance, were requested for stabilization purposes alone. Others proposed to reduce or eliminate this inside lag by requesting Congress to authorize the executive to vary tax rates around a permanent rate structure.[8] President Kennedy asked for such authority, but Congress ignored his request.[9]

President Johnson did not resubmit this Kennedy proposal; instead, he asked Congress to examine its procedures to see if rapid fiscal action could be achieved.[10] The Joint Economic Committee asked for the development of a standby tax program that could be

6. Walter W. Heller, *New Dimensions of Political Economy* (Harvard University Press, 1966), pp. 70–79; Arthur M. Okun, *The Political Economy of Prosperity* (Brookings Institution, 1970), pp. 44–61; and James Tobin, *The New Economics One Decade Older* (Princeton University Press, 1974), pp. 24–27.

7. Especially important were the two papers of A. W. Phillips, "Stabilisation Policy in a Closed Economy," *Economic Journal,* vol. 64 (June 1954), pp. 290–323; and "Stabilisation Policy and the Time-Forms of Lagged Responses," ibid., vol. 67 (June 1957), pp. 265–77.

8. Commission on Money and Credit, *Money and Credit: Their Influence on Jobs, Prices, and Growth* (Prentice-Hall, 1961), pp. 136–37.

9. *Economic Report of the President, January 1962,* p. 18, and ibid., *January 1963,* p. xxi.

10. Ibid., *January 1965,* p. 11.

rapidly implemented by congressional and presidential action.[11] Its Subcommittee on Fiscal Policy held hearings in 1966 and issued a report that called for enactment of standby tax changes in the form of uniform percentage increases or decreases in income tax liabilities, unconstrained in amount or time.[12] When the situation called for tax changes, Congress could vote on a particular percentage change without having to debate the distribution of it. The groundwork had been laid for prompt congressional response to presidential requests for fiscal action.

### The 1968 Surcharge

The debate on the tax surcharge of 1968, a proposal designed to cut back aggregate demand, was a turning point in the postwar discussion of fiscal policy. The administration proposed a tax surcharge in 1967 precisely in the form recommended by the Joint Economic Committee's subcommittee as the least controversial for prompt enactment. Ironically, it was not until mid-1968 that Congress enacted the surtax, and it did so then only after combining the surtax with legislation limiting certain expenditures.[13]

What went wrong? The proposed tax increase was presented in a form designed to forestall arguments over other kinds of tax changes and, implicitly, over the distribution of income. Instead, an unforeseen argument arose over the best use of society's resources. Some opposed the surtax because they feared it advanced a repugnant war effort.[14] Others opposed it because they thought the surtax would per-

11. *Report of the Joint Economic Committee, Congress of the United States, on the January 1966 Economic Report of the President, with Minority and Supplemental Views*, H. Rept. 1334, 89 Cong. 2 sess. (GPO, 1966), p. 5.

12. *Tax Changes for Shortrun Stabilization*, Committee Print, Subcommittee on Fiscal Policy of the Joint Economic Committee, 89 Cong. 2 sess. (GPO, 1966).

13. Okun, *The Political Economy of Prosperity*, pp. 86–89; and Tobin, *The New Economics*, pp. 34–36. For a detailed discussion of the administration's struggle with Congress, see Lawrence C. Pierce, *The Politics of Fiscal Policy Formation* (Pacific Palisades, Calif.: Goodyear Publishing, 1971), chap. 7.

14. "Many of us questioned the surcharge as a device to fight inflation on a number of grounds, some political-economic, some frankly political. . . . We felt that the main forces pushing toward inflation were the government expenditures for the war." Robert Eisner, Comments and Discussion of Arthur M. Okun, "The Personal Tax Surcharge and Consumer Demand, 1968–70," *Brookings Papers on Economic Activity, 1:1971*, p. 207. (Hereinafter, *BPEA*.) See also Eisner, "Fiscal and Monetary Policy Reconsidered," *American Economic Review*, vol. 59 (December 1969), pp. 897–905.

mit the continuation or expansion of Great Society programs that they regarded with distaste. The latter group scored a complete victory, combining expenditure limitations that excluded war outlays with the surtax legislation. This debate was not over stabilization at all, although it sometimes masqueraded as such, but it delayed the tax bill at a time crucial for successful stabilization policy.

The 1968 experience contrasts sharply with that during the Korean War. Mobilization in the Vietnam War was not as great, and tax increases were slower and smaller than during the Korean War. As a result, the federal budget was in deficit during the Vietnam buildup while it had been in surplus during similar stages of the Korean War.[15] Thus sharp increases in demand added to price inflation and to the inflationary expectations that have plagued us ever since.

The Vietnam surtax was not only slow in coming but also temporary. The effectiveness of temporary taxes was argued then and has received much attention since. In addressing this important issue one should not lose sight of the congressional failure to act promptly on urgent stabilization legislation.

## Effect of Temporary versus Permanent Tax Changes

The inadequate response of consumer demand to the tax surcharge of 1968 raised questions: did consumers view the tax change as temporary or permanent? If temporary, how did it affect their spending decisions?[16] Many recent studies have addressed these important

15. Government purchases for national defense represented 4.8 percent of GNP in the third quarter of 1950 and 7.5 percent in the first quarter of 1966. They rose to a peak of 13.5 percent of GNP during the Korean War and 9.1 percent in the Vietnam War. By the second quarter of 1951 they had nearly doubled to 9.2 percent, yet the budget surplus in that quarter was 2.6 percent of GNP. In the comparable period of four quarters in 1966, national defense purchases had risen to 8.4 percent and the budget deficit was 0.8 percent of GNP. (U.S. Department of Commerce, Bureau of Economic Analysis, *The National Income and Product Accounts of the United States, 1929–74 Statistical Tables*, a supplement to the *Survey of Current Business* [GPO, 1977].)

16. Some writers had warned of this possibility but may have been too casual in treating all earlier tax changes as permanent. For example, Albert Ando and E. Cary Brown ("Personal Income Taxes and Consumption Following the 1964 Tax Reduction," in Albert Ando, E. Cary Brown, and Ann F. Friedlaender, eds., *Studies in Economic Stabilization* [Brookings Institution, 1968], p. 126) wrote: "In an earlier article [Ando and Brown, "Lags in Fiscal Policy," pt. 2 of "Lags in Fiscal and Monetary Policy," in Commission on Money and Credit, *Stabilization Policies* (Prentice-Hall, 1963)], we tentatively concluded that the responses of consumers to

issues for fiscal policy.[17] On balance this quantitative work supports the view that the temporary surtax of 1968 (and similar changes) had a noticeable effect, but about half that expected from permanent tax changes. Some have expressed the view that such results largely eliminate temporary income tax changes from consideration as stabilization devices and require their replacement by temporary changes in consumption or investment taxes. My own view, however, would be that this finding only indicates the need for twice as large a swing in so-called temporary income taxes, not an abandonment of their use, when they have other desirable stabilizing characteristics.[18] This general conclusion requires a number of qualifications.

Dogmatic conclusions about consumer response to tax changes seem unwarranted because tax changes have been few and small, particularly since 1954.[19] In this period income taxes were reduced in 1964, 1965, 1970, 1975, and 1978 and were increased in 1968. This is sparse evidence on which to base conclusions about the effects of tax changes on consumer expectations.

---

changes in disposable income consequent upon tax changes do not differ materially from those consequent on changes in income before tax. This conclusion is restricted to tax changes which consumers believe to be permanent. We cannot say anything about temporary, short-run tax changes simply because there has not been any experience with them." Eisner, in "Fiscal and Monetary Policy," was one of the first to spell this issue out, although he initially confused consumption and consumer expenditure.

17. See Michael R. Darby, "The Permanent Income Theory of Consumption—A Restatement," *Quarterly Journal of Economics*, vol. 88 (May 1974), pp. 228–50; Alan S. Blinder and Robert M. Solow, "Analytical Foundation of Fiscal Policy," *The Economics of Public Finance* (Brookings Institution, 1974), pp. 3–115; Arthur M. Okun, "The Personal Tax Surcharge and Consumer Demand, 1968–70" *BPEA*, *1:1971*, pp. 167–204; William L. Springer, "Did the 1968 Surcharge Really Work?" *American Economic Review*, vol. 65 (September 1975); Arthur M. Okun, "Comment," and W. L. Springer, "Reply," *American Economic Review*, vol. 67 (March 1977), pp. 166–72; and Franco Modigliani and Charles Steindel, "Is a Tax Rebate an Effective Tool for Stabilization Policy?" *BPEA*, *1:1977*, pp. 175–209.

18. Such as separation of public-private-resource-allocation and income-distribution questions. See Tobin, *The New Economics*, pp. 76–83.

19. This warning applies with special force to studies based on data beginning in 1954 or later, such as those of Okun, Modigliani and Steindel (although they were primarily interested in the tax changes of the 1970s), and to an earlier study of Modigliani, "Monetary Policy and Consumption: Linkages via Interest Rate and Wealth Effects in the FMP Model," in Federal Reserve Bank of Boston, *Consumer Spending and Monetary Policy: The Linkages*, Conference Series 5 (Federal Reserve Bank of Boston, 1971), pp. 9–84. Other studies, such as those of Springer, Darby, and Ando and Brown, began with data from 1947 or 1948.

The standard practice of treating all income tax changes as the equivalent of negative income may never have been wholly satisfactory. Furthermore, the use of an adaptive expectation model to arrive at estimates of long-run disposable income implied that consumers were forming their expectations about income and taxes in the same way. Whether or not this assumption is valid should surely be tested.[20] The most recent major study of the effects of temporary taxes by Modigliani and Steindel has the merit of separating income and taxes, making it possible to detect a difference in consumer expectations about them.[21]

While this separation of taxes from income is a desirable step in analysis, drawing a sharp division between *temporary* and *permanent* taxes is unsatisfactory because such a division is nonexistent. So much of the recent discussion operates in an unrealistic binary world where tax changes are either temporary and treated one way by consumers or permanent and treated in another way.[22] Even the discussion of the reasons for separating income and taxes in as sophisticated a discussion as that of Modigliani and Steindel echoes this binary view:

This traditional approach implicitly assumes that consumers form expectations about future tax liabilities by using the same distributed lag of past tax liabilities that they use to estimate permanent gross income from past gross income. It implies that they respond to a change in income resulting from a *permanent* tax change in the same way they respond to variations in before-tax income, which presumably are partly transient. It is clearly a very questionable assumption.[23]

This dichotomy is fictional. Surely Congress can extend, and has extended, "temporary" legislation. It can also modify "permanent" legislation annually if it so desires. The issue comes down to expectations of consumers about taxes, not those of members of Congress or

20. For an earlier test of this hypothesis, see note 16.
21. Modigliani and Steindel, "Is a Tax Rebate an Effective Tool for Stabilization Policy?"
22. For example, Robert Eisner has asked "What may we really expect, in the light of the 'permanent-income theory,' from a *temporary* change in income tax rates such as those of the surcharge enacted in 1968?" ("What Went Wrong?" *Journal of Political Economy,* vol. 79 [May-June 1971], p. 632, emphasis added.) And in "Is a Tax Rebate an Effective Tool for Stabilization Policy?" (p. 179) Modigliani and Steindel remarked: "Tax withholding was reduced . . . in a change that was legislated as temporary but that many expected to be permanent."
23. Modigliani and Steindel, "Is a Tax Rebate an Effective Tool for Stabilization Policy?" p. 190.

of economists and especially not those of economists formed after the fact. Therefore, there must surely be a changing component in taxes, just as there is in income, that requires some kind of adaptive adjustment similar to the adjustment to income before taxes.[24] Okun has provided a number of examples of the difficulty of sorting out permanent and temporary fiscal changes,[25] and I would like to add some more.

The case could be made that a permanent rate structure was enacted in 1944 *that continued unchanged through 1963,*[26] and that all intervening changes were temporary deviations from that rate structure, expressed as percentage reductions or additions to it.[27] In 1944 and 1945 this rate structure was fully applicable. It was reduced by 5 percent in 1946 and 1947, by about 12 percent in 1948 and 1949,[28] and by about 4 percent in 1950. Tax liabilities computed under this rate structure were increased by about 2 percent in 1951 and 11 percent in 1952 and 1953. In 1954 through 1963 this rate structure was again fully applicable. It is hard to believe that consumers considered each of these tax changes as permanent ones, especially in the early part of the period, although each was embodied in "permanent" legislation. Yet the analysis of this period would be profoundly affected by treating these tax changes as temporary adjustments to a permanent rate structure rather than as permanent changes.

On the one hand, since the rate structure remained on the statute books for nineteen years the deviations (expressed as percentages) from it enacted in 1945, 1947, 1950, and 1951 could have appropriately been called temporary. Something of the order of one-fourth of 1 percent of GNP in 1946–47 and of 1 percent of GNP in 1947–49 would have been treated as temporary tax reduction under this as-

24. Experience in following tax legislation makes me wary of any legislative changes described as either permanent or temporary, regardless of their form.

25. See Okun's, "Comment," pp. 168–69; "The Personal Tax Surcharge and Consumer Demand," pp. 176–79; and Modigliani and Steindel, "Is a Tax Rebate an Effective Tool for Stabilization Policy?" pp. 208–09.

26. Revenue Act of 1943 (58 Stat. 21), as modified by the Individual Income Tax Act of 1944 (58 Stat. 231).

27. These remarks apply only to the rate structure. Substantial changes in the tax base were provided in the Revenue Act of 1945 (59 Stat. 556) and the Revenue Act of 1948 (62 Stat. 110). In the former case the victory tax was also eliminated. In the latter, exemptions were increased from $500 to $600 and income splitting was permitted for all married couples.

28. The 1948–49 decrease was provided by a three-bracket percentage reduction system, varying inversely from 17 to 10 percent with the size of tax liabilities.

sumption. (The reader may be reminded that the order of magnitude of the latter at the present time would be a $20 billion temporary tax reduction.) The tax structure would have been considered much less expansionary than it in fact appeared to be. The 1950 rate structure was 4 percent below the permanent structure (one-fourth of 1 percent of GNP), and the 1951–53 structure about 11 percent above the permanent structure (about 1 percent of GNP). Both would have been considered less deflationary than nominal tax receipts would indicate.

On the other hand, the public, conditioned by the depression and World War II—periods in which temporary changes became permanent and vice versa—may have regarded each new tax structure as about as permanent as any other. An agnostic view would have treated each change as a continuing one until further notice, adjusting expenditure each time on the assumption of continuity. Earlier studies found such an assumption to be a reasonable explanation of consumer behavior in this period.[29]

There are other interesting fiscal puzzles that have not been sufficiently noticed. The temporary tax increase of 1968 was effective for twenty-one months at a 10 percent rate and was later extended for twelve months more at one-quarter the rate.[30] The Revenue Act of 1951 provided the equivalent of a surcharge of 11 percent for twenty-six months,[31] a shorter period of time than in 1968–70. Although monetary policy was essentially permissive at that time in contrast to the later period, consumers appeared to respond more fully to the 1951 change than to the 1968 change. Apparently the public in 1951 continued to believe that temporary legislation might not mean temporary taxes, as in World War II.

Finally, how does one deal with legislation of future tax reduction, such as the step increases in exemptions enacted in 1969 and the increases in capital gains taxes enacted in 1976 to be effective at a future date? Do consumers react to them immediately? Those who

29. See, for example, Ando and Brown, "Lags in Fiscal Policy."

30. The surtax extension to June 30, 1970, has been described as for six months at a 5 percent rate. Since individual income tax returns are not filed semiannually, and since most taxpayers are on a calendar year basis, the extension was for twelve months at a 2.5 percent rate.

31. Had Congressman Daniel A. Reed, the new Republican chairman of the Ways and Means Committee, been successful, the cutoff date would have been moved back half a year. Again, the effective date would have been the same, but the rate would have been halved.

are interested in consumer response to tax manipulation are obliged to answer these questions. They cannot be solved theoretically, and the solutions must explain consumer response to an uncertain future.

## Taxes on Outlays

Faced by the problems of implementing stabilization policies through income tax changes, some have shifted their attention to taxes on consumer and business expenditure.[32] Temporary changes in such taxes are designed to induce consumers or business firms to change the timing of expenditures in a way that contributes to the stability of the economy. If taxes on, say, durable goods are temporarily raised now, and if consumers believe the tax increase will be temporary and expect durable goods prices after the tax returns to its former level to be lower than at present including the tax increase, they are likely to postpone or at least to slow down purchases of the commodity. This view lay behind some of the modest excise taxes enacted in World War II and the Korean War and also behind the manipulation of the investment tax credit. Notice that economic units must expect the tax increase to be temporary and, if temporary, that prices will be lower after the tax is rescinded. How could they be expected actually to respond when faced by such increases? They would certainly have to take into account the history of "temporary" excise tax changes.

Temporary excise taxes in World War II, such as on durable goods and luxuries, continued into the postwar period despite provision for automatic repeal at the termination of hostilities. The initial purpose of the auto excise, for example, was to shift demand from the war to the postwar period. After the war, however, shortages appeared and the tax was continued. Congress *raised* it "temporarily" in the Korean War with a terminal date of March 31, 1954, but extended it annually thereafter at the higher rate until 1965 when provision was made for its phasing down to 1 percent over a four-year period. But in 1966 these downward steps were eliminated in the face of the Vietnam War mobilization. Congress repealed the tax in 1969, with

32. Even Eisner's critique, "Fiscal and Monetary Policy," pp. 904–05, contains these well-known proposals. See also Modigliani and Steindel, "Is a Tax Rebate an Effective Tool for Stabilization Policy?" p. 201; and Tobin, *The New Economics*, chap. 5.

an effective date in 1974, later rolled back to 1971. The reader is asked to decide whether this tax was permanent, temporary, or both at different times (and, if both, when it was regarded as permanent and when temporary).

For maximum economic effect from temporary taxes on expenditures, one would want in general to impose taxes on goods with substantial potential intertemporal substitution—durable goods, typically. The targeted industries are generally averse to becoming economic counterweights and inhibit flexibility and timing through intense lobbying pressure. It is difficult for them to understand why reductions in demand should be forced on their products to make way for booming demands in other industries. Nevertheless, the broader the tax base, the smaller the opportunity for intertemporal substitution among expenditures and the larger its income effect becomes. In the extreme case, the aggregate fiscal consequences of an expenditure tax differ from those of an income tax only to the extent that savings decisions are affected by the choice. If an expenditure tax is temporary, moreover, it raises the current cost of necessities and is likely to be viewed as inequitable.

Finally, one should not gloss over the technical problems connected with spending-tax manipulations. Congress must enact any tax change proposed by the executive and such enactment takes time. During such delays, transient speculative demand counters the intent of the fiscal change. The delay may be brief or protracted. Certainly manipulation of commodity tax rates, if believed to be desirable policy, should be a strong candidate for limited presidential discretion.

A second set of technical problems stems from the lengthy production and delivery process of many goods, especially custom durables, and from the desire to deal fairly yet effectively with the decisions of economic units. To what extent, for example, should existing contracts be modified by tax changes? These problems are manifest in starting and stopping the investment tax credit.[33] If it is desirable to reduce pressure on demand, increased taxes should be imposed on *orders,* not on *deliveries,* but orders can be readily manipulated.

33. For a thorough discussion of these issues, see John Lintner, "Do We Know Enough to Adopt a Variable Investment Tax Credit?" in Federal Reserve Bank of Boston, *Credit Allocation Techniques and Monetary Policy,* Conference Series 11 (Federal Reserve Bank of Boston, 1973), pp. 113–35.

Imposing tax changes on deliveries, on the other hand, is easier but arguably unfair because it arbitrarily changes a price previously agreed to. To avoid such inequities Congress usually permits the taxpayer tax reductions on all deliveries but imposes tax increases only on deliveries ordered after the tax increase. For the usual consumer goods the production process would not be as lengthy and the difficulties would be considerably less than for the investment tax credit, yet the stabilization problems are qualitatively the same.

## Conclusions

These reflections lead to the following conclusions:

First, temporary income tax changes remain viable instruments for stabilization. The weight of evidence supports the view that they are about half as effective as permanent tax changes. To achieve a given effect, therefore, temporary rate changes must be roughly twice as large as permanent tax changes.

Second, we are a long way from knowing how consumers form expectations about taxes and incorporate them into their expectations of permanent disposable income. Research is difficult because tax changes are infrequent. But there is substantial room for improvement in the modeling of consumer behavior with existing information.

Finally, should it be desirable to use taxes on spending to stabilize the economy, a number of difficulties would have to be overcome. Narrow-based taxes, while more effective in shifting demand, are limited in the timing and amount of rate change because of pressures from the targeted industries; broad-based taxes are politically limited in the extent of rate change because of hardship cases. Spending taxes are most effective in causing consumers to defer expenditures if they are believed to be temporary; unfortunately temporary excise taxes have frequently turned out to be permanent.

RICHARD A. MUSGRAVE *Harvard University*

# Theories of Fiscal Crises:
# An Essay in Fiscal Sociology

MANY OBSERVERS over the past century have theorized that the growth of the fiscal system carries the seeds of its own destruction and that of the capitalist system. This group has included both Marxist and conservative critics of liberal social policies. In this paper, I describe these theories, point out their similarities and differences, and demonstrate that their predictions have been contradicted by events. I also show that the Marxian emphasis on class struggle casts rather little light on the struggle for fiscal influence and power in contemporary America. A pluralistic approach based on income, producer, and consumer groups offers a far better insight.

## The Marxist Tradition

Marx's own writings contain only scattered references to fiscal matters. Viewing taxation as an instrument of class struggle, he noted its use as a means of exploitation, and he pointed to excessive tax burdens as a major cause of social unrest in France.[1] He recommended "a heavy progressive or graduated income tax" as a means of

---

1. Karl Marx, "The Class Struggles in France, 1848 to 1850," in Karl Marx and Friedrich Engels, *Basic Writings on Politics and Philosophy,* ed. Lewis S. Feuer (Anchor Books, 1959), p. 297; and Karl Marx, "The Eighteenth Brumaire of Louis Bonaparte," ibid., pp. 331, 342.

overcoming the capitalist order.[2] Moreover, he noted the role of public debt in relation to capital accumulation, thus foreshadowing the later emphasis of Marxist writers on state indebtedness as a source of fiscal decline.[3]

### Goldscheid and Schumpeter

The first full-fledged effort at analyzing the fiscal role of the state in Marxist terms was undertaken by the Austrian socialist Rudolf Goldscheid.[4] Writing at the close of World War I and confronted by his country's fiscal collapse, he hoped to develop a science of "fiscal sociology." This science was to explain the fiscal crisis by examining the "social conditioning of the public household, and the fiscal conditioning which it in turn imposes upon society."[5] Placing the fiscal process at the center of state activity, Goldscheid saw fiscal sociology as the very key to an understanding of social change. The need for financial support of communal activity led to the creation of state-like organization. Goldscheid interpreted fiscal history from the Middle Ages to World War I as the decline of the state from power and wealth to poverty and debt. Throughout antiquity and the Middle Ages the typical state was based on large property holdings of the lord, who was both proprietor and ruler. His needs were met by sharing in the produce of his land and in the labor of his serfs. The princes and monarchs who followed continued to rely on these sources until the rising claims of war finance and the wasteful maintenance of the royal courts rendered them inadequate. At the same time, expansion of markets and the development of trade created new potential sources

2. Karl Marx and Friedrich Engels, "Manifesto of the Communist Party," in Marx and Engels, *Basic Writings,* p. 28.

3. Karl Marx, *Capital,* vol. 3: *The Process of Capitalist Production as a Whole* (New York: International Publishers, 1967), chaps. 28 and 29; and Marx, "The Class Struggles in France," p. 283.

4. Rudolf Goldscheid and Joseph Schumpeter, *Die Finanzkrise des Steuerstaats: Beiträge zur politischen Ökonomie der Staatsfinanzen,* ed. Rudolf Hickel (Frankfurt: Suhrkamp, 1976). The Hickel edition contains Goldscheid's major writings. For excerpts see Rudolf Goldscheid, "A Sociological Approach to Problems of Public Finance," in Richard A. Musgrave and Alan T. Peacock, eds., *Classics in the Theory of Public Finance* (Macmillan for the International Economic Association, 1958), pp. 202–13.

5. Rudolf Goldscheid, "Staat, Öffentlicher Haushalt und Gesellschaft," in Goldscheid and Schumpeter, *Die Finanzkrise des Steuerstaats,* p. 254.

of revenue. Taxation replaced income from state property as the principal source of state revenue.

But whereas the propertied state had been free to use and waste its resources as it wished, the emerging separation of ownership and state moved the state into dependency on the private sector. Property holders resented being burdened by taxation over which they had little control, and the struggle of the bourgeoisie to control the public purse came to play a central role in the move toward popular control. Taxation became a prime issue in the rise of modern democracy.

The new fiscal state, with its reliance on tax revenue, contained a flaw. It was compelled to preserve the health of the private economy on which it depended. Taxation, therefore, could not interfere with savings and investment, a constraint that limited the taxation of profits and the use of progressive income taxation. At the same time, the revenue requirements of the state were rising, owing to increasing demands of war finance and a growing need for social programs. To meet these needs the state borrowed increasingly and thereby opened itself to exploitation by its private creditors. Far from exploiting the private sector, according to Goldscheid, the state itself came to be exploited.[6] Although the people gained control over the state, they inherited only a debt-ridden and impoverished state.

Here Goldscheid's story ends. His solution was to return property to the state through a capital levy sufficient to create a public-enterprise sector that would yield enough income to finance necessary social services. In proposing state capitalism as a solution, Goldscheid criticized both the right and the left for rejecting a well-funded state, the former for considering only the interest of private property and the latter for its preoccupation with a far-off classless society where no state would be needed. As he saw it, the root cause of capitalist contradiction was to be found in the separation of property from the state, rather than in Marx's separation of property from wage labor.[7] With state property restored, a mixed economy would exist and social progress would evolve.

6. Ibid., p. 266; and Joseph Schumpeter, "Die Krise des Steuerstaats," in ibid., p. 329. Also in Goldscheid, "A Sociological Approach to Problems of Public Finance."

7. Goldscheid, "Staat, Öffentlicher Haushalt und Gesellschaft," p. 280; also in Goldscheid, "A Sociological Approach to Problems of Public Finance," p. 209.

Fascinated by Goldscheid's grand design, Joseph Schumpeter undertook a similar investigation.[8] He again viewed the development of the fiscal system as a key to understanding the sociology of the state and as an important indicator and source of social change. A state only comes into existence, Schumpeter asserted, when the public and the private sectors are distinct. No state in this sense existed in the feudal system, where public and private property were both vested in the rights of the lord, nor will it exist in the communal setting of an advanced socialist society. With the decline of feudalism, distinct public and private sectors emerged. Property once held by the state came to be held by the private sector. With the development of markets, taxation became the dominant form of state revenue and new tax forms emerged with changing patterns of economic institutions and organization. The rise of the "tax state" and the rise of capitalism were integral parts of the same process. The emergence of the income tax in particular reflected the increasing use of money and the importance of income as an index of social stratification.

Following Goldscheid, Schumpeter assigned key importance to the resulting dependence of the state on the private sector but his solution to such dependence differed. He argued that because the private sector is interested only in production for private gain, taxation will interfere with economic incentives. When revenue requirements become excessive—and, Schumpeter held, sooner or later they must—this interference will become unsupportable and the tax state will collapse. As economic abundance is reached and "the circle of social sympathy expands," society outgrows private enterprise and economic development comes to be replaced by other concerns.[9] A different form of social organization will then be needed.

Here the similarity to Goldscheid ends. Capitalism, according to Schumpeter, should be permitted to complete its task of establishing that abundance on the basis of which the new society can be built. This prescription, ironically, parallels Marx's call for the preservation of incentives until the socialist transition to communism has been

8. Joseph A. Schumpeter, "The Crisis of the Tax State," trans. W. F. Stolper and R. A. Musgrave, *International Economic Papers*, no. 4 (Macmillan, 1954), pp. 5–38. For the original version see Schumpeter, "Die Krise des Steuerstaats." A further "continental" treatment of fiscal sociology may be found in Herbert Sultan, "Finanzwissenschaft und Soziologie," in Wilhelm Gerloff and Fritz Neumark, eds., *Handbuch der Finanzwissenschaft*, vol. 1 (Tübingen, Germany: Mohr, 1952), pp. 66–98.

9. Schumpeter, "Die Krise des Steuerstaats," p. 370.

completed, at which time economic issues lose their importance.[10] While fiscal mismanagement might produce a premature collapse of the tax state, Schumpeter saw no immediate and unavoidable cause for fiscal crisis. The breakdown of Austria's finances after the First World War was not irreparable, and the historical moment for replacing the tax state had not as yet come. Moreover, the public-enterprise state would offer no solution since, according to Schumpeter, the taxable capacity of public enterprises would differ little from that of private firms.[11]

### Subsequent Marxist Views

Goldscheid's vision of a public-enterprise-financed welfare state, of course, was inconsistent with more orthodox Marxist interpretations of the fiscal crisis. If, as orthodox Marxists held, the basic flaw of the capitalist system was in the institution of wage labor, a partial transfer of property to the state could hardly correct it; and if, in fact, "the executive of the modern State is but a committee for managing the common affairs of the whole bourgeoisie,"[12] as asserted in the *Manifesto of the Communist Party,* state action could hardly be expected to defend the interests of the working class. While Marx conceded that state policies may at times clash with the immediate interests of the propertied classes,[13] apparent social reform will soon turn out merely to strengthen the underlying order of production relations and to sustain capitalist domination.[14] The reformist fiscal state, it is argued, cannot solve the contradictions of capitalist society for the simple (somewhat circular?) reason that it is part thereof.

As suggested by Paul Baran and Paul Sweezy, attempts to absorb surplus production through deficit spending can offer a temporary solution only.[15] Expenditures on civilian programs can only be pushed

10. Karl Marx, "Critique of the Gotha Program," in Marx and Engels, *Basic Writings,* pp. 114–20.

11. Schumpeter argues that the proceeds from public enterprises would not be a larger source of finance for public services than the taxation of private firms. This is an interesting observation but overlooks the fact that public and private enterprises differ in their need for "investment incentives." "Die Krise des Steuerstaats," p. 351.

12. Marx and Engels, "Manifesto of the Communist Party," p. 9.

13. See Marx's discussion of legislation to limit the length of the working day in *Capital,* vol. 1, chap. 10, sec. 6.

14. See Paul M. Sweezy, *The Theory of Capitalist Development: Principles of Marxian Political Economy* (Oxford University Press, 1942), chap. 13.

15. Paul A. Baran and Paul M. Sweezy, *Monopoly Capital: An Essay on the American Economic and Social Order* (Monthly Review Press, 1966), chap. 6.

so far before they run into business opposition based on fears that markets will be preempted. Other limitations apply to military expenditures. Due to the increasingly advanced technological nature of military hardware, Baran and Sweezy hold that military expenditures flow into profits and high salaries rather than into wages, and thus add little to demand.[16] Strangely enough they ignore the alternatives of tax reduction or transfer payments. According to this line of argument the fiscal crisis is a by-product of the capitalist crisis at large. It is a derived phenomenon rather than generated by its own dialectic, as in the Goldscheid-Schumpeter models. The latter and more interesting approach has been resumed in recent neo-Marxist writings.

James O'Connor, like Goldscheid, holds that the fiscal crisis occurs because a structural gap has developed between rising expenditure requirements and the limited ability of the state to raise revenue.[17] Both sides of the gap derive from the structure of the capitalist system and the role that the state must play. The state fulfills two conflicting functions according to O'Connor. The first, like the one described by Goldscheid, is to use expenditure policies to preserve profitable accumulation by monopoly capital, a sector that is defined to include not only large-scale industry and finance but also big union labor. The second function is to secure the necessary revenue to finance these outlays without hurting this very sector. The two objectives are incompatible and give rise to the structural gap.

In line with the first function, the state must provide both social investment and social consumption. Social investment, such as outlays on roads and education, is needed to maintain the conditions for profitable accumulation. In Marxist terms such investment increases the productivity of labor by adding to the stock of constant capital. Social consumption, such as outlays on social insurance and public health, adds to the stock of variable capital, thereby reducing the employer's cost of providing for the reproduction of labor. Both forms of social capital tend to increase surplus value and to raise

16. Ibid., p. 214.

17. James O'Connor, *The Fiscal Crisis of the State* (St. Martin's Press, 1973); see in particular p. 221. In a note on page 11, I am cited as a prime example of a fiscal theorist who places excessive faith in the manipulative omnipotence of the state, while disregarding the social structure that determines actual behavior. Having contributed to an early translation of Goldscheid and Schumpeter, I plead not guilty. Moreover, in my view, the state (while not omnipotent) can contribute to a resolution of social and economic problems, and the economist, through the conduct of normative analysis, can be helpful in this task.

profits. Also in line with the first function, the state must undertake social expenses such as welfare. These expenses do not add to productivity, but they are needed to secure the sufficient social harmony for monopoly capital to function and to legitimize the capitalist system.

The need for all these expenditures expands relative to the gross national product.[18] Social capital formation rises in response to the needs of, or demands by, the monopoly capital sector. Publicly provided investment goods cover more and more of its costs. State expansion, far from displacing monopoly capital, adds to its profits and becomes necessary for its survival. As a rising part of the population becomes proletarianized (moves into the status of wage labor) and hence alienated, the need for legitimization and resulting appeasement expenses similarly increases. Miscellaneous private interests accelerate the growth of state expenditures by pushing for a multiplicity of self-serving and frequently contradictory programs and fighting over them in an administratively incoherent and inefficient budget process.

Although expenditures rise, the revenue base does not. Outlays for social capital, constant and variable, are productive, but the gains accrue to monopoly capital. Recouping them through profit and progressive income taxation is limited because big business and unions will not permit sufficient taxes on profits or income to cover the increased outlays. Hence the state is driven to inflationary finance. Conceivably the state and monopoly capital—an "industrial-social complex"—could ally to bridge this impasse, but major and unlikely social and political changes would be needed to permit such an alliance. The realistic prospect is fiscal crisis and collapse.

## Critique and Restatement

Marxist fiscal sociology, like Marxist theory, comes in many versions. Depending on which of the traditional tenets of Marxist theory (such as the labor theory of value, wage determination by reproduction cost of labor, surplus production and declining rate of profits) are retained or relaxed, different views of the fiscal state and its sociology emerge. With the orthodox versions of Baran and Sweezy on one extreme, O'Connor's position (with surplus production and re-

18. While O'Connor does not talk explicitly about a rising *share*, I assume this to be the intent.

production-cost-determined wages still a central ingredient) may be placed in the middle, flanked on the other side by the more relaxed and only mildly Marxist positions of such writers as Ian Gough and Duncan Foley.[19] No single critique can cover all, nor would it be helpful to flog what economic history has shown to be dead horses.

Certain propositions run through most of these writings, however, and may be singled out for examination. The first is the assertion that the development of the fiscal system should be interpreted within the framework of overall social, economic, and political change. The second is that the class struggle defined as the dichotomy between capital and wage labor is the key to this interpretation. A third common tenet is the claim that fiscal control is basically (if not in all specific actions) in the hands of the capitalist class. Finally, and most interestingly, it is held that the tax state carries its own seeds of collapse, as rising expenditures outpace lagging revenue capacity.

These propositions lead to the conclusion happily shared by Marxists and libertarians that the fiscal system in a mixed economy carries the seeds of its own destruction and is doomed to failure.

### Interaction of Fiscal and Social Change

There is nothing wrong with the Goldscheid-Schumpeter tradition of viewing fiscal development in the context of the broader pattern of social change. It is evident that economic, political, and ideological forces all had their impact on the fiscal system.

Goldscheid and Schumpeter showed how economic forces stemming from the decline of feudalism and the rise of capitalism created the tax state with its dependence on the private sector. The revenue structure reflected changing modes of production and the related changes in the structure of industry and financial organization. Landholding and livestock, once meaningful measures of ability to pay, gave way to income, and the progressive income tax became the central tool of taxation. With the rise of the corporation, the income concept became more complex and an appropriate measure of taxable capacity became increasingly difficult to implement. Develop-

---

19. Ian Gough, "State Expenditure in Advanced Capitalism," *New Left Review*, no. 92 (July-August 1975), pp. 53–92; and Duncan K. Foley, "State Expenditure from a Marxist Perspective," *Journal of Public Economics*, vol. 9 (April 1978), pp. 221–38. For an orthodox critique of Gough, see Ben Fine and Laurence Harris, " 'State Expenditure in Advanced Capitalism': A Critique," *New Left Review*, no. 98 (July-August 1976), pp. 97–112.

ment of representative democracy similarly affected the decision process, creating a new framework for the determination of tax and expenditure policies, the budget system.

Philosophical currents that emerged with the rise of rationalism and of egalitarian ideology also influenced that fiscal development. What Schumpeter called the "widening circle of social sympathy" (basic as it was to the rise of the welfare state) cannot be explained solely as the grudging concessions of an increasingly beleaguered capitalist class. Ideologies respond to economic circumstances, but they also have their own dynamics and in turn affect the economic setting. Indeed, the most important impact of Marxism in the Western world, and certainly its lasting appeal to the young, has been its call for social justice; and this appeal has existed despite Marx's scathing treatment of this very concept.[20] Surely these forces must be taken into consideration when explaining the rise of the progressive income tax, defective though it may have turned out to be.

The fiscal system in turn also influenced events beyond its immediate sphere. Fiscal change contributed to the decline of the feudal system and later to the consolidation of dukedoms into national states. Resentment against taxation without representation, first on the part of vassals and then by the middle classes, contributed to the decline of absolute power and thus aided the subsequent rise of democracy and the private economic sector. Moreover, the tax system had its effect on forms of financial and business organization, just as public purchase patterns affected the structure of markets.

These interactions, which were of major importance in the past, will continue to operate. In the process the institutions of the tax state will change. But the pattern of this change is not predetermined, just as there is no fixed pattern governing the development of the private sector. At the same time, some likely trends may be detected. With increasing international trade and investment, the international aspects of taxation will gain in importance, both for the taxpayer who becomes subject to several jurisdictions and for the taxing jurisdictions that must divide up common bases of revenue. As capital and labor become increasingly mobile the widening gap between high- and low-income countries will become increasingly unacceptable, thus adding an international dimension to fiscal redistribution.

20. See Allan W. Wood, "The Marxian Critique of Justice," *Philosophy and Public Affairs,* vol. 1 (Spring 1972), pp. 244–82. One wonders whether Marx, in his inner heart, was really a Marxist in this respect!

*Fiscal Interest Groups*

There is much to be said for the Marxist tradition of emphasizing the importance of social groups, rather than isolated individuals, as forces that determine fiscal change. But it is incorrect and misleading to formulate the issue in terms of a two-class, capital-labor model. While it is not surprising that this dichotomy dominates Marxist fiscal sociology, the outcome is unfortunate because the two-class model, whatever its strength or weakness for general social analysis, is inappropriate for interpreting fiscal conflict. Closer consideration of the fiscal process, especially in its modern setting, shows that many groupings must be considered and that most of them cut across the Marxist class division. Moreover, the groupings interact, so that few problems can be understood correctly as bilateral conflicts.

Stratification by *income level* is central to fiscal analysis, yet it is not adequately allowed for by the distinction between capital and labor income. Although the distribution of capital income is less equal than that of wage and salary income (the top 20 percent receives about 70 percent of the former and 40 percent of the latter), most inequality stems from inequality in the distribution of earned income. The inequality of earnings dominates simply because earnings account for over 75 percent of total income.

On the tax side of the fiscal equation, grouping by income level (independent of source) is of most obvious importance under the global income tax. Exemptions, standard deductions, and the rate schedule are all related to total income. To be sure, various income sources pose different problems in income tax treatment, so that interest groups form by type of income. For instance, issues of income definition differ between earners of capital gains and wage income. Nevertheless, the battle lines are essentially by income level. Capital income forms a larger share of the total of high incomes, and the higher the income, the greater the potential benefit to be derived (under a progressive rate schedule) from the preferential treatment of capital gains.

Income level once more affects attitudes toward taxes on products. High-income households tend to share the same tastes, regardless of whether their income is received from wages or capital. High-income rentiers, executives, and professionals alike will join to oppose the taxation of luxury products, while low-income groups find it in their interest to oppose the taxation of necessities. It is appropriate, therefore, that the study of the distribution of the tax burden, pioneered by Joseph A. Pechman, focuses on the distribution of income among income-size groups rather than between capital and labor.

Much the same holds for the expenditure side of budget policy. Program benefits are frequently aimed specifically at low-income or high-income households but seldom specifically at recipients of capital income or wage income. Welfare programs and low-cost housing projects favor low incomes; commuter services to suburbs, such as San Francisco's rapid transit system, benefit higher-income groups. The focus is on level of income, not on whether it derives from labor or capital sources.

Stratification by *taste* is also relevant to fiscal alignment. While the budget patterns of households at any one income level share common characteristics, the patterns are not uniform. Taste differences remain that cut across income groups and are independent of income source. Thus smokers with both high and low wage and capital income join in opposing tobacco taxes. And fanciers of big cars oppose gasoline taxes. On the expenditure side conservationists (regardless of income source or income level) combine in supporting national parks; and devoted motorists (regardless of income source or income level) join in favoring highway expenditures.

After income level, the most important grouping is by the source of income. But contrary to the Marxist mold, the strategic distinction is not between capital and labor but between the *industries* from which the income (be it wages or profits) is derived. On the tax side capital and labor in the automotive industry both oppose automotive taxes; both restaurant employees and owners oppose tightening expense accounts. And on the expenditure side capital as well as labor in the automotive and construction industries support highway programs. Grouping by industry is clearly a dominant factor in the politics of expenditure decisions. In even starker contrast to the Marxist model, U.S. labor and foreign capital have a common interest in opposing tax benefits to capital outflow (that is, deferral of taxes on foreign profits), and U.S. capital and foreign labor share an interest in their support.

Next, consider the role of interest groups based on *age*. Expenditures on education benefit the young and draw support from their families. Such expenditures are of less immediate concern to the elderly and the unmarried, a factor of major importance in considerations of municipal finance. Old age benefits draw support from the retired and those soon to retire, a factor of increasing significance as the ratio of retired population to working population increases. As the influence of parent-teacher associations declines, that of Gray Panther-type organizations increases.

Finally, there are interest groupings based on *region*. Because some industries are geographically concentrated, some product taxes fall disproportionately on particular regions or states. Similarly, public purchases of private output support the economies of particular regions. Because members of Congress represent particular states or districts, regional interests are a major factor in the way they determine fiscal policy. Washington state representatives are preoccupied with defense outlays, Texas representatives attend carefully to the tax treatment of oil, New York representatives pay close attention to urban programs. Only the president can transcend these interests.

This catalog of relevant interest groups may be readily extended to include other groups—the healthy versus the sick (of major importance in the debate over national health insurance) and male versus female (for example, child care programs or the financing of abortions). Such extension may be passed over, however, as by now the multidimensional structure of fiscal interest grouping should be clear. The labor-capital dichotomy is only one, and hardly the most important. In fact, each household belongs to a set of interest groups involving (1) its sources, as well as its level, of earnings; (2) its pattern, as well as its level, of expenditures; and (3) its preferences for, and hence benefits derived from, public services. To understand the sociology of fiscal politics all these fiscally relevant groupings must be considered. They must be allowed for in predicting the voting behavior of constituents and their representatives. In short, the fiscal game is vastly more complex than the capital-labor dichotomy suggests.

### The Fiscal State

Not all Marxist theory sees the state as a pure instrument of capitalist domination. Allowance may be made for its operation in the context of balancing political powers, with some independence of state action.[21] Contemporary Marxist writers even recognize the existence

21. See for instance, Friedrich Engels, *The Origin of the Family, Private Property and the State* (Pathfinder Press, 1972), pp. 392–94.

of a state based on popular vote and reflecting the public interest. But this view is conditional only, as capital will tolerate such a state only because the image of "public interest" is needed to dampen alienation and to legitimize capitalist institutions.[22] In the end it is essential for Marxist theory to contend that the state must serve the interest of the capitalist class.

In fact, the contest for fiscal control is an open game with many players. Capital has no exclusive control over the outcome, which (à la Schumpeter) may well be to its disadvantage. Moreover, the fiscal process is not a zero-sum game marked only by conflict. It also involves cooperation and mutual gain. By the very nature of social goods, the free-rider problem renders their private provision unfeasible. Hence collective action is needed to provide them, and all or most gain from such cooperation. How then do the major fiscal actors— the public, elected representatives, and appointed officials—share in the fiscal powers of the state?

Final voting power rests with the public. In most cases this power is not exercised in a town meeting, where individual voters directly make decisions, but by elected representatives who cannot depart too far from voter preferences if they wish to stay in office. But politicians do more than merely reflect the views of their constituents; they also try to shape these views, either from self-interest (for example, re-election even if on false positions, or power, or pocketbook) or to project their own conception of the public interest. They may risk defeat because of commitment to a public-minded program. Balancing popular approval and likelihood of winning against his or her perceived value of proposed programs, the candidate engages in risk-taking, much as the investor does when choosing among alternative assets. While it is naive to hold that all politicians are altruistic, it is equally mistaken to hold that all seek power for its own sake.

Once more it is important to allow for the role of interest groups, as distinct from that of individual voters, both in the election of representatives and the positions they espouse thereafter. Such powerful interest groups as corporations, unions, realtors, or the Sierra Club enter into the decisionmaking process by public education, advertising, campaign contributions, or other lobbying devices. As some

22. See Ralph Miliband, *The State in Capitalist Society* (London: Weidenfeld and Nicolson, 1969); and Nicos Poulantzas, *Political Power and Social Classes,* trans. Timothy O'Hagan (London: New Left Books, 1973).

groups are better organized and more affluent than others, the outcome will not be a finely balanced reflection of voter position. But periodic elections provide a check, so that state policies cannot wander too far from the wishes of the voting majority. While consumers as an interest group have been underrepresented, recent developments (both inside and outside the government) suggest that this pattern is changing.

Governmental staff also have an independent influence on public policy. Some officials come close to the Weberian image of the public servant.[23] Acting as technical expert, such staffs present decision-makers with the consequences of alternative measures; acting as administrator, they implement programs as decided upon by the legislator. At the other end of the scale are the self-serving bureaucrats concerned mainly with enlarging their bureaus and perpetuating their program functions, thereby enhancing their own salary, status, and power. They will push policies that serve their purpose; but even dedicated staffers, be they technicians or administrators, cannot avoid introducing their own judgment.

As Emanuel A. Goldenweiser observed to me when I first came to Washington in 1938, it is difficult to give technical advice in a neutral fashion, nor should the professional suppress his own view. The very scale chosen in a chart will determine its visual impact, and the choice of econometric model affects the outcome. Moreover, time never permits all issues to be examined, and the very process of selection involves the "technician" in a judgment as to what matters.

Much the same holds for the staffer involved in administration. Legislation is bound to be general; regulations and guidelines, and their daily interpretation, reflect the exercise of important judgments. Thus public employees (I am using this neutral expression to avoid the value-laden terms "public servant" and "bureaucrat") are policy-makers. They cannot avoid inserting their own choices, choices that may reflect financial or status position, or which may serve what they consider to be the public interest.

Control over the fiscal structure thus does not rest in the hands of any particular agent or group. The interests of capital and labor enter, but so do others. In the end the fiscal process reflects the interaction

23. Max Weber, *From Max Weber: Essays in Sociology,* ed. and trans. H. H. Gerth and C. Wright Mills (London: Kegan Paul, Trench, Trubner, 1947), chaps. 8–9.

of pluralistic interests and interest groups. This plurality renders fiscal decisionmaking complex and difficult to predict, which is unfortunate; but it is hardly a reason for adopting an oversimplified model that gives ready but frequently mistaken answers.

## The Structural Gap Reconsidered

My final issue concerns the inevitability of fiscal crisis and collapse. According to Marxist writers, fiscal measures will not only fail to overcome the tendencies toward breakdown inherent in the private sector, but while they are trying to do so, rising expenditures will outrun taxable capacity, leading to the collapse of the tax state itself.

### Wagner's Law—the Marxist Version

The idea that public expenditures inevitably rise is not a new one. A century ago Adolph Wagner argued that the public expenditure share must rise because social progress requires expanding social services and because interdependence of economic activity requires increasing public sector involvement.[24] "Wagner's law" has been discussed ever since, and the Marxist diagnosis is a variant. However, the specifics of causation differ. The ratio of public expenditure to gross national product, according to the Marxist view, must rise to absorb overproduction by the private sector, to provide "monopoly capital" with increasing amounts of free inputs, and to dampen rising alienation with increasing attention to social services. It remains to be seen whether or not these hypotheses are supported by the facts.

Table 1 shows the pattern of U.S. public expenditure growth during this century; a similar pattern may be observed in other countries. Four main features emerge from this table. First, the overall expenditure ratio rose from 7.7 percent in 1902 to 11.8 percent in 1927. It nearly doubled during the Great Depression and continued to climb in each successive decade, reaching 36.5 percent in the seventies.

Second, only during the forties and fifties did national defense con-

---

24. For a recent discussion see Richard E. Wagner and Warren E. Weber, "Wagner's Law, Fiscal Institutions, and the Growth of Government," *National Tax Journal,* vol. 30 (March 1977), pp. 59–68. The authors find that the "law" does not uniformly apply, but their conclusions are based on only about a twenty-year period of observation. For a longer perspective see Richard A. Musgrave and Peggy B. Musgrave, *Public Finance in Theory and Practice,* 2d ed. (McGraw-Hill, 1976), chap. 6.

Table 1. Public Expenditures by Type and Function, Selected Years, 1902–77

| Item | Percent of gross national product | | | | | | | Percentage point change | | | |
|---|---|---|---|---|---|---|---|---|---|---|---|
| | 1902 | 1927 | 1940ᵃ | 1950ᵃ | 1960 | 1970 | 1977 | 1902–40 | 1940–50 | 1950–77 | 1902–77 |
| **Total** | **7.7** | **11.8** | **20.4** | **24.6** | **28.2** | **34.2** | **36.5** | **12.7** | **4.2** | **11.9** | **28.8** |
| Defenseᵇ | 1.4 | 1.3 | 2.1 | 5.4 | 10.2 | 8.9 | 6.5 | 0.7 | 3.3 | 1.1 | 5.1 |
| Civilian | 6.3 | 10.6 | 18.4 | 19.2 | 18.1 | 25.4 | 30.0 | 12.1 | 0.8 | 10.8 | 23.7 |
| **Total by type** | **7.7** | **11.8** | **19.3** | **22.1** | **28.2** | **34.2** | **36.5** | **11.6** | **2.8** | **14.4** | **28.8** |
| Purchases | n.a. | n.a. | 14.2 | 13.5 | 19.8 | 22.3 | 20.9 | n.a. | −0.7 | 7.4 | n.a. |
| Defense | n.a. | n.a. | 2.2 | 4.9 | 9.1 | 7.8 | 5.3 | n.a. | 2.7 | 0.4 | n.a. |
| Civilian | n.a. | n.a. | 12.0 | 8.6 | 10.7 | 14.5 | 15.6 | n.a. | −3.4 | 7.0 | n.a. |
| Net interest | n.a. | n.a. | 1.2 | 1.5 | 1.4 | 1.2 | 1.2 | n.a. | 0.3 | −0.3 | n.a. |
| Transfers | n.a. | n.a. | 2.7 | 6.3 | 5.7 | 7.9 | 10.7 | n.a. | 3.6 | 4.4 | n.a. |
| Otherᶜ | n.a. | n.a. | 1.2 | 1.0 | 1.4 | 2.8 | 3.7 | n.a. | −0.2 | 2.7 | n.a. |

| Civilian by function | 6.3 | 10.6 | 18.4 | 19.2 | 18.1 | 25.4 | 30.0 | 12.1 | 0.8 | 10.8 | 23.7 |
|---|---|---|---|---|---|---|---|---|---|---|---|
| General government[d] | 2.4 | 2.6 | 3.7 | 4.9 | 3.0 | 3.9 | 4.7 | 1.3 | 1.2 | −0.2 | 2.3 |
| Net interest | 0.4 | 1.4 | 1.6 | 1.7 | 1.4 | 1.2 | 1.2 | 1.2 | 0.1 | −0.5 | 0.8 |
| Economic development | 1.7 | 3.4 | 7.2 | 4.9 | 4.8 | 5.5 | 6.0[e] | 5.5 | −2.3 | 1.1 | 4.3 |
| Transportation | 0.9 | 2.2 | 2.6 | 1.6 | 2.7 | 2.7 | 2.2 | 1.7 | −1.0 | 0.6 | 1.3 |
| Other | 0.8 | 1.2 | 4.7 | 3.3 | 2.1 | 2.8 | 3.8 | 3.9 | −1.4 | 0.5 | 3.0 |
| Human resources | 1.7 | 3.1 | 5.8 | 7.8 | 8.9 | 14.7 | 18.1 | 4.1 | 2.0 | 10.3 | 16.4 |
| Education | 1.2 | 2.4 | 2.8 | 3.4 | 3.7 | 5.9 | 6.2 | 1.6 | 0.6 | 2.8 | 5.0 |
| Social insurance[f] | ... | 0.1 | 1.0 | 2.4 | 2.8 | 4.4 | 6.4 | ... | 1.4 | 4.0 | ... |
| Welfare[g] | 0.2 | 0.2 | 1.3 | 1.0 | 1.4 | 2.9 | 3.8 | 1.1 | −0.3 | 2.8 | 3.6 |
| Health and hospitals | 0.3 | 0.5 | 0.7 | 1.0 | 1.0 | 1.5 | 1.7 | 0.4 | 0.3 | 0.7 | 1.4 |

Sources: Percentages based on expenditure data and GNP: for 1902, 1927, and for breakdown by function for 1940 and 1950, U.S. Census Bureau, *Historical Statistics of the United States: Colonial Times to 1970*, bicentennial edition, H. Doc. 93-78 (GPO, 1976), pt. 1: series F 1-5, p. 224, and pt. 2: series Y 533-566, pp. 1120–21; for 1960, 1970, and for breakdown by type for 1940 and 1950, U.S. Department of Commerce, Bureau of Economic Analysis, *The National Income and Product Accounts of the United States, 1929–74, Statistical Tables*, supplement to the *Survey of Current Business* (GPO, 1977), tables 1.1, 3.2, 3.4, 3.14, pp. 2–3, 96, 108, 135, 142, 324, 340–41; for 1977, *Survey of Current Business*, July 1978, tables 1, 3.14, pp. 1, 44. Figures are rounded.

n.a. Not available.

a. Breakdown by type for 1940 and 1950 does not correspond to other categories for those years owing to different source using different accounting procedure.

b. Includes national defense, foreign military aid, and veterans' services.

c. Federal grants-in-aid to state and local governments, and subsidies.

d. Central administration and management, international affairs, civilian safety, and postal services.

e. Includes $8.3 billion in general revenue sharing.

f. Old age, survivors, and disability insurance, medical and unemployment insurance.

g. Public assistance, relief, and other welfare services.

tribute significantly to the rising overall expenditure ratio; between 1950 and 1960, in fact, the civilian ratio declined. During the sixties and seventies the defense ratio declined, while the civilian ratio rose dramatically. Over the century until 1977, defense accounted for less than one-fifth of the increase in the ratio of expenditures to gross national product.

Third, the rise in the expenditure ratio from 1940 to 1947 was due mainly to a rise in government purchases and a rise in transfers.

Finally, before 1950 the three functional civilian expenditure categories (general government, economic development, and human resources) broadly shared in the causes of expenditure growth. Thereafter, more than half of the increase in the civilian ratio was from increased expenditures on human resources, with social insurance and welfare accounting for the largest part. In contrast, the proportion of gross national product devoted to economic development as well as that spent on general government shows only a slight gain.

The evidence reveals overall expenditure growth, but it is important to note that this increase has been decelerating.[25] While the ratio of expenditure to gross national product need not rise at an increasing rate to generate a crisis (a simple increase is all that is needed), the declining rate nevertheless suggests an abatement of the crisis potential. More important, the pattern of growth hardly supports the Marxist prognosis. To begin with, defense expenditures have clearly not been the driving force. From the beginning of the century to date, defense contributed only 5.1 percentage points to the rising overall ratio, whereas civilian outlays have contributed 23.7 points. From 1960 on, the defense ratio has in fact declined. These data lend no support to the hypothesis that capitalist societies must spend ever-increasing shares on defense to absorb surplus output. If war finance has been a major factor, it has been by raising the threshold of acceptable taxation, thus permitting a step-up in postwar civilian outlays.[26] Table 1 also shows that interest payments caused by debt

25. This conclusion is strengthened by a more detailed analysis allowing for the fact that the prices of public services have risen more rapidly than prices in the private sector so that the ratio of public services in real terms (using the respective deflators) has risen less rapidly than that in money terms.

26. See Alan T. Peacock and Jack Wiseman, *The Growth of Public Expenditure in the United Kingdom* (Princeton University Press for the National Bureau of Economic Research, 1961).

finance have not absorbed an increasing share of gross national product. Interest on the public debt has never been a significant factor in the overall picture, and the ratio of interest to gross national product now stands about where it was in 1940. Unanticipated inflation has served as a built-in mechanism of debt repudiation.

But what of the rising ratio for civilian expenditures? While O'Connor recognizes that it is not always possible to assign a particular expenditure item neatly to one or another category, he suggests an interesting formulation of expenditure theory in Marxist terms by distinguishing between the contribution to expenditure growth made by (1) social investment, (2) social consumption, and (3) social expenses. As noted before, the first two are needed for the productivity of private accumulation and add to surplus value, while the third is needed for social harmony. Taking (1) to be reflected in expenditures on economic development, it is seen that the corresponding ratio rose up to 1940 but declined during the forties and by 1977 was still below its 1940 level (see table 1). This pattern hardly supports the hypothesis that monopoly capital has exacted increasing subsidies, based on free inputs by the state. Nor does it seem reasonable to interpret the rise of all development expenditure in these terms. The growth of highway expenditures reflects technological change in transportation, which would have occurred as well under alternative forms of social organization. The fact that such programs benefit the automobile and construction industries is evident, but it does not follow that they should be viewed as subsidies to these groups.[27] Outlays on environmental and energy resource programs and on housing and agriculture ("other" economic development, table 1) have risen over the past decade, but once more they may be viewed as subsidies to the consumers of polluting outputs rather than as subsidies to producers.

In O'Connor's category of social consumption one may include programs in education, social insurance, welfare, and health. It is difficult to hold that the sharp increase in the ratio of education expenditures to gross national product between 1960 and 1970 constitutes increased subsidies to monopoly capital. Even if education serves to socialize the young to conform with the capitalist system (a questionable proposition, given the educational experience of the

27. This is not to deny that industry and consumer pressures have resulted in excessive highway expenditures, thus subsidizing the providers and users of automotive services at the cost of taxpayers.

sixties), most of this increase reflects expanded enrollment in the wake of the postwar baby boom and rising teacher salaries brought on partly by increased union pressure. Indeed, support for rising education budgets has come primarily from the political left rather than the right, with emphasis on democratizing the educational process rather than serving the interests of monopoly capital.

Next, consider the rising ratio of social insurance outlays. As shown in table 1, this trend has been the dominant factor in the postwar rise of public expenditures. Can one plausibly argue that this trend has decreased the reproduction cost of labor, thereby increasing surplus value and permitting capital to reap a larger profit share? Putting it differently, can it be maintained that in the absence of social insurance, wages would have been correspondingly higher and profits lower? This reasoning is difficult to follow under either neoclassical or Marxist theory. Under the former the employee's portion of the payroll tax used to finance social security leaves wages unaffected unless labor supply changes. Under traditional Marxist theory wages are determined by subsistence needs, needs that set a wage floor that cannot be reduced by payroll taxes. As social security benefits reduce the need for private saving, the share of the worker's wage previously needed for that purpose is replaced by his or her payroll tax contribution. Thus social insurance cannot be expected to reduce the necessary wage or to raise profits. On the contrary, the objective of social security is to improve incomes of the aged while possibly raising the labor cost of industry. The social and political pressures for extension of social insurance, like those for education, are to be found on the left rather than on the right of the political center.

Turning finally to O'Connor's "expenses" needed to provide social peace and to legitimize capitalism, it is surprising to find that this category (welfare, table 1) until recently contributed negligibly to total expenditure growth. While part of social security might be included under "consumption" rather than "human capital," the picture hardly supports the notion that mounting bribes have been needed to secure popular acquiescence of capitalism. Notwithstanding decreasing self-employment (rising wage labor), the drastic increase in living standards has provided middle class status rather than proletarianization for the bulk of the labor force. While some severe poverty persists, much of it is now segregated in urban and rural slums, thus (unfortunately) reducing its effectiveness as a social force. As a consequence, increases in legitimization "expenses" have accounted for little of the budget expansion.

In short, table 1 lends little support to the proposition that the capitalist system, by internal logic, necessitates an ever-rising ratio of public expenditure to gross national product. The application of Marxist expenditure categories to the public sector, while an intriguing experiment, proves of little explanatory value.

*Expenditure Growth: An Alternative View*

An alternative explanation, which I consider more useful, is based on a distinction between allocational and distributional causes, with the former economic and technical while the latter are political and social.

Beginning with the allocational causes, the efficient mix of output at a given place and time depends on income, technology, and demography. This holds for both capital and consumer goods. The type of capital goods required in the early stages of development, especially those needed to develop infrastructure, typically yield benefits that, in considerable part, are external and therefore require public investment. Later on, with the rise of manufacturing and the development of urban centers, the requisite form of capital formation is of the private type, and the share of private investment rises. Still later, environmental problems, urban slums, and other contingencies may arise, calling for new forms of public investment. The desired mix of consumer goods similarly changes with rising income. When income is low such necessities as food, clothing, and shelter absorb most of the household budget. As income rises, social goods tend to become increasingly important, being demanded directly or as complementary to the consumption of private goods.

The efficient share of social goods is affected also by changes in technology. The invention of the automobile increased demand for highways and dominated the expansion of state budgets for long periods. Progress with space exploration may come to be a major factor in federal finances of the future, as weapon technology has increased the cost of defense and medical technology the cost of health services in past budgets. Technical change thus affects the appropriate share of gross national product that is provided through the budget.

Finally, demographic changes have important bearing on the size of the public sector. Increased school enrollment was a major factor of rising budgets in the sixties, and the growing aged population will demand growing retirement benefits in the coming decades.

These examples show that expenditure growth may be explained in considerable part by factors largely independent of the social system and that prevail in a socialist as well as a capitalist setting. The future directions of these influences are hard to forecast, but more likely than not they will cause a rising public expenditure share. But although this growth of these public outlays may be determined primarily by technical factors, it nevertheless will have significant implications for the political and social structure. Marxist analysis misses this point, as it pays little attention to the inherent nature of public or social (as distinct from private) goods. By assigning a minor role to consumption patterns, Marxist theory fails to explore the social relations of consumption, notwithstanding the central role that materialistic determinism assigns to the social relations of production.

The social relations of consumption of private goods differs from that for social goods. The former are consumed individually, they may be distributed equally or unequally, and their provision may be related to productive contribution. The terms on which goods become available to individual consumers may be considered a matter of entitlement or they may be used as instruments of social power and discipline. Depending on the nature of the social system, the housing space available to a person may hinge on his or her income, standing in a political party, or political views. In contrast, social goods must be consumed jointly, and their benefits tend to be available more or less freely. Such goods tend to be distributed equally, their provision cannot be used to give economic incentives, and they cannot be withheld for purposes of social discipline. All this has immediate and important bearing on the social system, capitalist or socialist. Increased provision of social goods may be favored or fought as a means of equalization, and the very fact that their provision calls for social cooperation (that is, a political as distinct from a market process) introduces a new form of social relationship.

Different considerations arise from the growth of transfers. Here redistributional considerations are of major importance. Although welfare and relief programs account for only a small proportion of the increase in the ratio of overall expenditures to gross national product, other transfers, such as social security benefits, play a redistributional role. Moreover, a significant share of public services directly benefits lower-income groups. In all, more redistribution is accomplished by expenditures than by taxes.[28] This growth of redistribution is in line with the Marxist hypothesis if interpreted as increased power of the majority to force transfers from a reluctant minority or as increased willingness of the better-off to appease the masses through transfers. However, it may also reflect an increased willingness to reduce inequality based on a changing sense of social justice, and thereby an adaptability of the system to social needs. Clearly all three factors have been present, but there is no evident way to determine their respective weights.

### Limited Revenue Capacity?

I finally turn to the revenue side of the structural change hypothesis. Taxable capacity in the Marxist model is constrained for two reasons. First, taxation of wage income is limited or impossible because wages are at subsistence. Second, there are limits to the taxation of capital income. In Goldscheid's version the state is reluctant to tax capital income because such taxes interfere with private investment and thereby destroy the state's own revenue base. In O'Connor's version monopoly capital benefits from social investment but refuses to return these gains to the state through taxation. Since the monopoly capital sector includes both capital and labor employed in it, a large share of national income is preempted from taxation. Neither limit is realistic. Most wages are not at subsistence and the middle-income group (including most employees of monopoly capital) carries a substantial and perhaps disproportionate share of the tax burden. Capital, notwithstanding its strong voice in the deliberations of congressional tax committees, also falls far short of complete success in escaping taxation.

What then determines the limits of taxable capacity? Economists answer this question in terms of the impact of taxes on the supply of

28. See Richard A. Musgrave, Karl E. Case, and Herman Leonard, "The Distribution of Fiscal Burdens and Benefits," *Public Finance Quarterly*, vol. 2 (July 1974), pp. 259–311. While the transfer structure is clearly more pro-poor than the tax structure is anti-rich, it may be argued that equal provision of general public services bestows a greater benefit in money terms on high-income recipients, since they are willing to pay more. See Henry Aaron and Martin McGuire, "Public Goods and Income Distribution," *Econometrica*, vol. 38 (November 1970), pp. 907–20.

labor, savings, and the willingness to invest.[29] Taxation, and especially the use of high marginal rates, induces the choice of tax-preferred options, thereby imposing an "excess burden." Such burdens may arise especially in a capitalist system, where decisions about saving, investment, and work are made largely in the private sector. They are of more limited importance in a socialist setting, where decisions on investment and saving, and to some extent those on work, are made by the state.

But taxable capacity is not only a matter of economics. Not only may taxpayers respond individually to such taxes as have been imposed on them; they may also act in consort with others to determine what the tax structure should be. This outer limit on taxable capacity is a matter of political power and may be related only indirectly to individual responses and the economics of excess burden. Such is the case especially with regard to the taxation of capital income. Investors can threaten to penalize government by reducing investment and the threat is effective if politicians react. Their reason for reacting, however, is not that revenue will be lost, as Goldscheid thought, but that unemployment will result leading to loss of votes. Unless the state is willing to substitute public for private investment or to reduce the growth of productive capacity, the taxation of capital income has to remain acceptable to the investment community. Continued deductibility of three-martini luncheons may become the price of economic recovery and reelection. Labor does not have so potent a threat. While the individual worker may fight increased taxes by working less, the immediate impact of such responses on the economy is less visible. Nor have unions taken to calling strikes to protest what they consider hostile tax legislation. More generally, tax legislation is not a matter of collective bargaining in the United States, although in line with current tax-rebate proposals such considerations might become imbedded in an incomes policy.

The strategic position of capital is stronger in a setting where much emphasis is laid on economic growth as a policy objective. Tax incentives for growth, by their very nature, provide tax relief for capital income, and direct benefits accrue largely to high-income taxpayers.

29. Economic theory in dealing with tax effects on investment has proven surprisingly fickle. A decade or two ago it was shown that taxation with loss offset need not reduce risk-taking and may increase it. Currently this feature has come to be totally disregarded in the design of investment functions, it being assumed as a matter of course that profit taxation will reduce investment.

While labor will share eventually in the gains from growth, it suffers a short-run loss as revenue is redirected. This lends validity to the Marxist emphasis on capital-labor conflict in the fiscal scene, especially since little has been done to design growth policies with a less-regressive impact.[30]

At the same time, far more voters derive most of their income from labor than from capital, a fact that should be expected to tip the scale in the other direction. Income-tax loopholes exist but so do other taxes. Income from capital is also subject to the corporation profits and property taxes, while labor also pays the payroll tax. In all, it is unclear which source is taxed most heavily. Such is the case especially if actual (as distinct from statutory) incidence is considered and the complexities of tax shifting in an imperfectly competitive economy are allowed for.

Tax distortions are primarily a function of marginal rather than of average tax rates, yet redistribution through the tax system is not possible without permitting marginal rates to rise ahead of the average. Whether or not a crisis of the tax state materializes, therefore, depends more on the pattern than the overall level of taxation. This pattern in turn reflects social attitudes and the level of income. As income rises, society may find redistribution less necessary. Much depends on the depth of concern about poverty, on whether poverty is seen in absolute or relative terms, and on whether the goal is to achieve some given degree of overall distributional equality. As redistributive programs expand, however, the dividing line between those who gain and those who lose from redistribution moves down the income scale. This makes it harder to secure a majority for further redistribution. For this reason, one may expect successful additions to the tax burden to be distributed less and less progressively.

Tables 2 and 3 report on a rather crude attempt to test this hypothesis for the increase in U.S. tax burdens from 1910 to 1975. Based on alternative incidence assumptions, the tables show the estimated distribution, by decade, of the increase in revenue borne by various quintiles. As shown by the more progressive estimates in table 2, trends in federal revenues clearly support my hypothesis. The estimated share of incremental federal revenue collected from the top

30. For an early plea to consider the equity aspects of growth policy see Richard A. Musgrave, "Growth with Equity," *American Economic Review,* vol. 53 (May 1963, *Papers and Proceedings, 1962*), pp. 323–33.

**Table 2. Estimated Distribution of Increase in Tax Burden, by Income Class, under Most Progressive Incidence Assumption, 1910–75[a]**

Percent

| Income class[b] | 1910–20 | 1920–30 | 1930–40 | 1940–50 | 1950–60 | 1960–70 | 1970–75 |
|---|---|---|---|---|---|---|---|
| | | | *Federal taxes* | | | | |
| Lowest fifth | 4 | −30 | 3 | 2 | 2 | 2 | 3 |
| Second fifth | 9 | −60 | 12 | 6 | 8 | 8 | 10 |
| Middle fifth | 12 | −60 | 20 | 9 | 14 | 16 | 17 |
| Fourth fifth | 16 | −40 | 25 | 15 | 26 | 22 | 23 |
| Highest fifth | 59 | 290 | 40 | 68 | 56 | 52 | 46 |
| | | | *Federal taxes, excluding payroll* | | | | |
| Lowest fifth | 4 | −30 | 3 | 2 | 2 | 2 | 3 |
| Second fifth | 9 | −60 | 10 | 6 | 7 | 6 | 9 |
| Middle fifth | 12 | −60 | 13 | 8 | 12 | 13 | 14 |
| Fourth fifth | 16 | −40 | 19 | 13 | 18 | 19 | 20 |
| Highest fifth | 59 | 290 | 53 | 71 | 62 | 60 | 53 |
| | | | *State and local taxes* | | | | |
| Lowest fifth | 4 | 4 | 5 | 5 | 4 | 4 | 4 |
| Second fifth | 8 | 9 | 13 | 10 | 10 | 10 | 10 |
| Middle fifth | 10 | 13 | 20 | 15 | 14 | 15 | 15 |
| Fourth fifth | 14 | 17 | 26 | 20 | 19 | 19 | 20 |
| Highest fifth | 64 | 57 | 37 | 52 | 52 | 52 | 52 |
| | | | *All taxes[c]* | | | | |
| Lowest fifth | 4 | 3 | 4 | 2 | 3 | 3 | 3 |
| Second fifth | 8 | 6 | 12 | 7 | 8 | 9 | 10 |
| Middle fifth | 12 | 10 | 20 | 10 | 15 | 15 | 17 |
| Fourth fifth | 15 | 13 | 26 | 14 | 20 | 23 | 22 |
| Highest fifth | 61 | 68 | 37 | 64 | 55 | 52 | 49 |

Source: Author's calculations based on Joseph A. Pechman and Benjamin A. Okner, *Who Bears the Tax Burden?* (Brookings Institution, 1974). The analysis is based on the assumption that the distribution of the burden for various taxes by quintiles is as shown in the Pechman-Okner results. An exception is made only of pre-1940 income tax, for which 1920 and 1930 patterns were estimated by the author. The procedure was (1) to determine the revenue increments from various taxes decade by decade, (2) to allocate the increment for each tax in line with the noted pattern, (3) to add the incremental burdens from various taxes, and (4) to determine the percentage distribution of the incremental burden among quintiles. This procedure was then followed on a decade-to-decade basis. Since the quintile distribution of income has remained fairly constant, it may not be unreasonable to assume that the distribution of the tax burden resulting from various taxes has also followed a constant pattern.

a. The most progressive incidence assumption is that of Variant 1c, Pechman and Okner, *Who Bears the Tax Burden?* tables 4-9, 4-10.

b. Households ranked by adjusted family income (family income as derived from the national income accounts plus indirect business taxes).

c. Includes payroll taxes.

quintile reached 68 percent in the forties and then declined to 46 percent in 1970–75 as the shares of the third and fourth quintiles rose. A similar pattern prevails if payroll taxes are excluded; the absorption by the top quintile in 1940–50 exceeded 70 percent, with a subsequent drop to 53 percent. The state-local level, on the other hand,

**Table 3. Estimated Distribution of Increase in Tax Burden, by Income Class, under Least Progressive Incidence Assumption, 1910–75[a]**

Percent

| Income class[b] | 1910–20 | 1920–30 | 1930–40 | 1940–50 | 1950–60 | 1960–70 | 1970–75 |
|---|---|---|---|---|---|---|---|
| | | | *Federal taxes* | | | | |
| Lowest fifth | 6 | ... | 4 | 3 | 3 | 3 | 3 |
| Second fifth | 9 | ... | 12 | 8 | 9 | 9 | 10 |
| Middle fifth | 15 | −80 | 19 | 11 | 15 | 16 | 17 |
| Fourth fifth | 18 | −40 | 24 | 17 | 22 | 23 | 23 |
| Highest fifth | 52 | 226 | 41 | 61 | 51 | 49 | 45 |
| | | | *Federal taxes, excluding payroll* | | | | |
| Lowest fifth | 6 | ... | ... | 3 | 2 | 2 | 3 |
| Second fifth | 9 | ... | 11 | 7 | 8 | 7 | 9 |
| Middle fifth | 15 | −80 | 11 | 10 | 14 | 14 | 16 |
| Fourth fifth | 18 | −40 | 25 | 16 | 21 | 21 | 22 |
| Highest fifth | 52 | 220 | 52 | 63 | 55 | 57 | 51 |
| | | | *State and local taxes* | | | | |
| Lowest fifth | 4 | 5 | 4 | 6 | 6 | 5 | 5 |
| Second fifth | 12 | 14 | 13 | 13 | 13 | 12 | 12 |
| Middle fifth | 17 | 18 | 21 | 17 | 18 | 17 | 17 |
| Fourth fifth | 21 | 24 | 25 | 23 | 23 | 23 | 23 |
| Highest fifth | 46 | 40 | 38 | 42 | 41 | 43 | 43 |
| | | | *All taxes[c]* | | | | |
| Lowest fifth | 5 | 5 | 4 | 3 | 4 | 4 | 4 |
| Second fifth | 11 | 14 | 12 | 8 | 11 | 10 | 11 |
| Middle fifth | 16 | 16 | 20 | 11 | 17 | 17 | 18 |
| Fourth fifth | 19 | 21 | 24 | 21 | 18 | 23 | 24 |
| Highest fifth | 49 | 50 | 40 | 54 | 50 | 47 | 45 |

Source: See table 2.

a. The least progressive incidence assumption is that of Variant 3b, Pechman and Okner, *Who Bears the Tax Burden?* tables 4-9, 4-10.

b. Households ranked by adjusted family income.

c. Includes payroll taxes.

does not display this pattern. Under less progressive assumptions regarding incidence the hypothesis is supported less strikingly (see table 3), but the declining share of the top quintile over recent decades remains apparent.

Given the shape of the income pyramid and the level of tax rates already reached, the fraction of voters supporting higher taxes and more redistribution is likely to decline. This trend, joined to the investors' veto over excessive taxation of capital income, suggests that tax increases will become increasingly difficult to enact. As a result, fiscal expansion may well slow and increased fiscal redistribution

may draw to an end. The so-called crisis of the tax state may prove
self-terminating. But it does not follow that a happy equilibrium
must result. The blocking of the fiscal crisis may simply transfer the
crisis into another and less manageable sphere of the socioeconomic
system.

## Conclusion

Four hypotheses regarding possible sources of fiscal crisis may be
distinguished.

First, under the *Marxist* hypothesis the root of the fiscal crisis lies
in the tendency for increasing socialization of costs and rising expenditures to legitimize capitalism, without any corresponding socialization of the resulting gains to monopoly capital. As a result, the
government can no longer pay for needed outlays through taxes. The
result is either rising inflation or reduced outlays, or both, leading
to deepening class conflict and eventual collapse of the system.

History does not support this diagnosis. There is little evidence of
a continuously rising public expenditure share to subsidize private
firms through cost reduction, nor have expenses directed at appeasing
social unrest continuously increased. The rising real income of most
voters, rather than increasing immiserization of the proleteriat, has
been the dominant influence on the social climate. The facts do not
support the hypothesis of fiscal collapse in a redistribution-oriented
class struggle. If anything, the median-voter rebellion indicates the
opposite.

Second, under the *structural change* hypothesis, the root of the
fiscal crisis lies in certain objective forces of change that require more
output to be devoted to social goods to promote economic efficiency.
These changes may be technological, as illustrated by the coming
of the automobile and the resulting need for highways. Or they may
be demographic, such as increased demand for education with rising
population growth or for old age pensions as population growth declines. Finally, there may be structural changes in consumer demand
with rising per capita income. The income elasticity of demand for
public services may exceed unity.

These forces singly and in combination may cause the budget share
and taxes to increase, but higher taxes may distort incentives and
reduce economic efficiency. The conflict may be resolved by limiting

the size of the public sector or by reducing the weight of efficiency costs. Such costs in considerable part are an institutional phenomenon and may be modified also by institutional change. Distortions in investment and savings decisions, and to a smaller degree decisions between work and leisure, can be reduced by adopting other forms of economic organization. Suppose that rising income and changing technology produce an increasing demand for social relative to private goods. An efficiency-oriented economist might then have to conclude that a change in economic organization rather than interference with consumer preferences is the proper answer. A theory of capitalist breakdown might then be derived from neoclassical premises.

The thought is interesting, but the events of recent decades hardly support it. While the structural forces here noted will continue to influence the size of the budget, there are no compelling reasons that the ratio of public expenditure to gross national product need rise. For example, declining needs for education may well offset rising needs for retirement pensions, and emission charges rather than expenditures may be used to deal with environmental issues.

A third source of fiscal crisis might emerge from a growing support for *egalitarianism*. But as voters support egalitarian policies through transfers and public services, rising taxes may once more undercut economic efficiency and may call for changes in economic organization. Under a socialist system investment and savings decisions are transferred to the state.[31] Such a system avoids the unequalizing effects of the distribution of private capital income and is less vulnerable to distorting effects on savings and investment incentives. This, I take it, is the meaning of Schumpeter's prognosis of social change, based on a "widening circle of social sympathy." But again, this does not seem to be where history is pointed. Rather, it appears that redistribution is a self-terminating activity. The egalitarian philosophy hits a median-voter barrier, and future redistribution, for the time being at least, comes to a halt.

Finally, consider the *Santa Claus* hypothesis, which asserts that voters increasingly try to get public services for nothing. This de-

31. It is hardly necessary to add in a paper of this sort that the final choice among economic systems involves more than considerations of economic efficiency and income distribution. Other aspects, such as effects on freedom, must also be allowed for.

terioration of the democratic process could again lead to fiscal and economic crisis. But again, such a trend is improbable. For one thing, a learning process should set in, followed by remedial action. For another, the median taxpayer should call a halt. The budget reform of 1974 illustrates the point as does the sweep of Proposition-13-type measures.[32]

In all, the case for fiscal crisis is unconvincing. The Marxist diagnosis, though interesting, is not supported by economic and social history. The allocative roots of fiscal crisis, though conceivable, do not seem likely to expand in the foreseeable future. Nor does the egalitarian trend in social attitudes seem on the upturn, nor does fiscal irrationality go unchecked. Changes there will be, but as Mark Twain said of rumors that he had died, reports of the demise of the tax state are much exaggerated.

32. Congressional Budget and Impoundment Control Act of 1974, P.L. 93-344. Also see Richard A. Musgrave, "Leviathan Cometh—or Does He?" in Helen Ladd and Nicolaus Tideman, eds., *Tax and Expenditure Limitations,* COUPE Papers on Public Economics, 5 (Urban Institute, forthcoming).

EMIL M. SUNLEY *U.S. Department of the Treasury*

# A Tax Preference Is Born: A Legislative History of the New Jobs Tax Credit

IN 1977 PRESIDENT CARTER proposed a tax credit to encourage the hiring of additional workers. How Congress transformed this fairly simple presidential proposal into an exceedingly complex and probably ineffective piece of legislation—contained, ironically, in the Tax Reduction and Simplification Act of 1977—is the subject of this chapter.

No student of public finance, if left alone, would design a tax incentive as complicated as the jobs credit. Surely the arbitrary distortions inherent in the credit, many of which are discussed below, could have been minimized. As the Tax Reduction and Simplification Act of 1977 moved through Congress, various features of the credit, which can only be understood in the legislative context, were added in response to criticisms of the legislation. What follows, then, is a legislative history of the jobs credit—essentially a case study of the process by which tax proposals are enacted into law—with special emphasis on the specific concerns that ultimately shaped the credit.

## The President's Proposal

Even before President Carter was elected, work had begun on an economic stimulus program for presentation to Congress shortly after

The author would like to acknowledge helpful comments on this paper from Bruce Davie, Larry Dildine, and Jim Wetzler.

391

his inauguration. Following the election, he met in Plains, Georgia, on December 1, 1976, with a panel of economists and businessmen, including two former chairmen of the Council of Economic Advisers, Arthur Okun and Walter Heller; Joseph Pechman of the Brookings Institution; and those he soon was to appoint as secretaries of the Treasury Department and the Department of Commerce, director of the Office of Management and Budget, and chairman of the Council of Economic Advisers.[1]

Economic indicators for 1976 suggested that the recovery from the 1974 recession was petering out. Unemployment had hovered around 7.7 percent through all of 1976 after declining from a high of 9.0 percent in May 1975 to 7.8 percent in January 1976. Many forecasters expected a sluggish economy in 1977 and even in 1978 unless additional fiscal stimulus could be provided. The economists advising the president-elect told him that the achievement of 6 percent growth in real GNP during 1977 and a reduction in the unemployment rate to about 6.5 percent by year-end required $15 billion to $20 billion of additional fiscal stimulus. As a practical matter, only about $5 billion of this additional fiscal stimulus could come from the expansion of nondefense spending.

Thus about $10 billion to $15 billion in tax reductions would be needed for 1977. Despite recognition that temporary tax cuts probably are not as stimulative as permanent tax cuts of the same size, the president's advisers agreed that the largest portion of the tax cut should be temporary or in the form of a partial rebate of the prior year's taxes so as not to mortgage future revenues during the first months of the Carter administration. These revenues would be needed for any expenditure initiatives that the administration might propose or to sweeten the anticipated proposal for comprehensive tax reform.

The advisers also generally agreed that consumers should receive most of the tax cut because consumers spend more of any tax cut they receive and spend it faster than do businesses. The tax program, however, would have to have a business component. The two major contenders for the business portion of the program were an increase in the investment tax credit and an income tax credit for employers for some portion of payroll taxes paid.[2]

It was felt that an increase in the investment tax credit, particularly

---

1. *New York Times,* December 2, 1976.
2. Other contenders included corporate rate cuts and acceleration of tax depreciation.

if only temporary, would have the greatest short-term effect on investment. But it was quite possible that Congress might make permanent any increase in the credit, and there was considerable opposition to temporary business cuts, especially from the businessmen advisers. In addition the credit would tend to favor profitable, capital-intensive businesses and would provide little relief for small business and labor-intensive industries such as retailing and services.

An income tax credit for a portion of payroll taxes had a number of advantages. It would be anti-inflationary and a direct stimulus to employment because it would directly lower labor costs. If refundable, the credit would reach all employers, including tax-exempt ones. It would be an indirect step toward some general revenue financing for social security. Since the removal of an employment credit would be inflationary, that credit, like the increase in the investment tax credit, was apt to become a permanent feature of the law unless it could be removed as part of a program for comprehensive payroll tax reform.

On January 6, 1977, President-elect Carter again met in Plains with his economic advisers and the next day with congressional party leaders. At the end of that meeting Charles Schultze, chairman-designate of the Council of Economic Advisers, announced that accord had been reached on a two-year tax cut costing about $15 billion in fiscal years 1977 and 1978.[3] He indicated that the business portion of the program would probably be an income tax credit for 5 percent of employer's social security taxes paid, but that instead it might include a 2 percentage point increase in the investment tax credit. Because the business portion of the stimulus package was not firmly set, jockeying over it continued during the next two weeks. Large business did not view a cut in the employer payroll tax as a business tax cut since this tax is probably shifted back on labor. Small business, however, strongly supported payroll tax relief.

President Carter announced his program for economic recovery involving tax reductions and expenditure increases on January 31, 1977, just eleven days after his inauguration.[4] The president recom-

3. *New York Times,* January 8, 1977.

4. See "Economic Recovery Program: The President's Message to the Congress Proposing a 2-Year Economic Recovery Package, January 31, 1977," *Weekly Compilation of Presidential Documents,* vol. 13 (February 7, 1977), pp. 120–29. This chapter focuses only on the tax side of that program and touches on tax proposals, other than the employment credit, only to develop the context in which the tax-writing committees made their decisions on the employment credit.

mended $50 income tax rebates or cash payments for almost every American. He also recommended an expansion and simplification of the standard deduction. For businesses he recommended that each firm be permitted to make a binding choice between either a credit against income taxes of 4 percent of social security payroll taxes paid by the employer or an increase in the investment tax credit for machinery and equipment from 10 to 12 percent. The payroll tax credit would have been fully refundable so that all businesses, but not tax-exempt organizations, would benefit whether or not they had current tax liability. The employment and investment tax credit proposals would have reduced business tax liabilities for 1977 by $2.6 billion, of which an estimated $1.1 billion would have been attributed to the payroll tax credit. The business tax reductions and the changes in the standard deduction were intended to be permanent.

## House Action

The House Ways and Means Committee began hearings on February 2 on the tax portions of the president's stimulus program. The committee showed little enthusiasm for increasing the investment tax credit. It had jiggled the credit up and down or on and off just too many times, and members expressed growing skepticism about its effectiveness in stimulating investment. Large, capital-intensive business generally favored the increase in the investment tax credit, while small business favored the employment tax credit.[5]

The proposal to require taxpayers to make a binding choice between an increase in the investment credit or the new employment credit received little support. The economic case for requiring firms to make this choice was also weak. Presumably capital-intensive firms would choose the increase in the investment credit and labor-intensive firms the new employment credit, thus artificially encouraging capital-intensive firms to become more capital intensive and labor-intensive firms to become more labor intensive.

5. Accounts of the committee's opinions and witnesses' testimonies appear in *Panel Discussions on the Tax Aspects of the President's Economic Stimulus Program —Prepared Statements of Panelists,* House Committee on Ways and Means, 95 Cong. 1 sess. (Government Printing Office, 1977); and *Tax Aspects of President Carter's Economic Stimulus Program,* Hearing before the House Committee on Ways and Means, 95 Cong. 1 sess. (GPO, 1977).

In addition, committee members regarded the employment tax credit proposed by the president as too insignificant to be meaningful; it would have had the effect of reducing payroll costs by less than one-quarter of 1 percent (4 percent of the employer's social security rate of 5.85 percent). The committee argued that no firm would expand employment in response to such a small reduction in labor costs, particularly when firms would receive the credit even though they had not increased employment. Similarly, the proposal could not be expected to have a significant anti-inflation effect.

### Ways and Means Committee Action

By mid-February, when the Ways and Means Committee began to mark up the tax portions of the president's stimulus program, a majority of the members wanted to make the employment credit incremental because this approach would deny windfall gains to employers who did not increase employment and would provide greater "bang for the buck."[6] There was major disagreement over whether the credit should be provided only for hiring the disabled, the young, the aged, the long-term unemployed, and employees in distressed areas because such limitations would lead to discrimination in favor of some applicants against others for reasons that are not related to job classifications.

The staff of the Joint Committee on Taxation explored alternative ways to handle an incremental credit that would not require additional record-keeping for firms.[7] It was particularly important that the credit not require firms to develop information for a prior year that was not already readily available. From unemployment or social security tax records firms would know the number of employees for the current and previous year.[8] The firm would not necessarily know how many of these workers had been with it for the entire year or how many had been full-time or part-time workers. An incremental credit based simply on the number of workers, and not on the number of

6. During the campaign for the Democratic nomination for president, Lloyd Bentsen and Sargent Shriver both had proposed incremental employment credits. See *Candidates '76* (Congressional Quarterly, 1976), pp. 25, 71.

7. See *Tax Reduction Program,* prepared for the House Committee on Ways and Means by the staff of the Joint Committee on Taxation, 95 Cong. 1 sess. (GPO, 1977), pt. 4.

8. There are even problems here if during either the base year or the current year there have been mergers or other corporate reorganizations. These problems are inherent in any incremental tax subsidy and must be handled separately.

full-time equivalent workers, would favor the substitution of part-time for full-time workers and would reward firms that have an increase in turnover rates.[9] There are, however, no standard accounting rules for measuring the number of full-time equivalent employees.

The Joint Committee staff suggested that instead of trying to determine the number of full-time equivalent employees an incremental credit could be based on the aggregate unemployment insurance wages under the Federal Unemployment Tax Act. The FUTA base for 1977 consisted of the first $4,200 of wages paid to each employee.[10] Because employers must maintain records needed to file FUTA returns, no additional record-keeping would be needed for such an incremental employment tax credit.

A credit of $x$ dollars per worker or $y$ percent of the first $4,200 of wages would reduce the cost of hiring low-paid workers more than of hiring high-paid workers, thus encouraging employers to hire low-paid workers, a possibly desirable social policy.

On the other hand, such a credit would also encourage the replacement of full-time with part-time workers and would favor firms with high turnover. To restrict such substitutions the joint committee staff suggested that the amount of the credit could also depend on the increase in total wages. Thus a substitution of two part-time workers for a full-time worker would increase unemployment insurance wages, but it might not increase total wages.

The Ways and Means Committee decided to focus the credit on small businesses by placing a cap on the amount of the credit a firm could earn in any one year.[11] It was felt that small businesses are less secure financially and thus are less able to expand employment. There clearly is some potential conflict between the goal of wanting to provide an incentive for firms to hire new workers and of wanting to provide tax relief for small businesses. These trade-offs are discussed below.

9. A credit based on the number of full-time equivalent workers would reward firms that replaced a high-paid, high-productivity worker with two low-paid, low-productivity workers. This might be acceptable as a matter of social policy.

10. The FUTA base was scheduled to increase to the first $6,000 of wages per employee beginning in 1978. For purposes of the employment tax credit enacted by Congress, however, only the first $4,200 of FUTA wages paid in 1978 were to be counted in determining the employment tax credit for that year.

11. An account of the business tax aspects of the Ways and Means Committee's bill appears in *Tax Reduction and Simplification Act of 1977*, H. Rept. 95-27, 95 Cong. 1 sess. (GPO, 1977), pp. 53–60.

Given the considerable sentiment in the committee for providing a tax incentive for hiring handicapped workers, the committee decided to add a supplemental credit for the employment of such workers. It rejected the proposed increase in the investment tax credit but decided that the total cost of the employment credit should be about the same as the business tax reduction proposed by the president. Thus the committee had several variables to play with—the rate of the credit, the FUTA base limitation, the total wage bill limitation, and the cap.[12]

The Ways and Means Committee agreed on a two-year incremental employment tax credit costing about $2.4 billion a year. The credit would have had six features. First, it would have been 40 percent of the excess of each employer's FUTA wage base over 103 percent of the FUTA wage base in the previous year. Second, the credit could not have exceeded 40 percent of the amount by which an employer's total wages paid for the year exceeded 103 percent of total wages paid by the employer in the previous year. Third, the credit would have been limited to $40,000 a year for each employer. Fourth, an additional 10 percent credit would have been allowed for the employment of handicapped workers, but only to the extent that the employer otherwise qualified for the 40 percent credit. The additional credit, however, would not have been subject to the $40,000 cap. Fifth, the deduction for wages paid would not have been reduced by the amount of credit allowed. Finally, the credit was not refundable. The credit could have been carried back three years and forward seven years.

The bill would have required a 3 percent increase in FUTA wages and total wages before the firm was eligible for the credit. This rule was designed so that firms that had not increased employment by the normal growth for the economy as a whole would not have qualified for the credit.[13]

If the Ways and Means bill had been enacted, the maximum credit per worker would have been $1,680 (40 percent of the first $4,200 of wages). Given the $40,000 cap, a firm could have earned the credit with respect to the first twenty-four workers added after a 3 percent increase in its payrolls.

12. The supplemental credit for handicapped workers was not expensive.
13. The Senate Finance Committee improved on this quite imperfect rule. This is discussed later in the text.

On February 24 the Ways and Means Committee reported out the bill containing the tax portions of the stimulus program. Though substituting its own new jobs credit for the president's proposed business tax reductions, the committee generally accepted the president's proposal for $50 rebates and for the expansion and simplification of the standard deduction. The bill was considered and passed by the House on March 8 under a closed rule permitting no amendments.

### Treasury and Administration Positions

The Treasury, in both Republican and Democratic administrations, has generally opposed incremental tax subsidies because of their inherent complexity and general unfairness.[14] Proponents contend, however, that such subsidies can provide substantial incentives at a modest cost.

Incremental credits are complex because the base of the credits is hard to define. Special rules are required to handle corporate acquisitions and dispositions and possibly to handle new businesses. In the case of the incremental employment credit, the House approved and Congress later enacted a special rule denying the credit for self-employed persons who incorporate and become employees. (Under the bill as enacted, the self-employed could not claim the credit with respect to themselves.) Consideration also was given to denying the credit with respect to independent contractors who become employees of firms they used to serve. In the case of partnerships the credit flowed out to the partners, but it could only be used to offset individual income tax attributed to the income from the partnership.

As another example of complexity, the House-passed bill denied the credit if an employee was fired and replaced by another worker in order to earn the new jobs credit. Under this provision, the fired employee was supposed to present evidence to the Internal Revenue Service. The service would then have determined whether the evidence was adequate. This provision had much potential for mischief and was dropped in both the Senate and final versions of the bill to

14. Most of the Treasury criticism of the House-passed bill would apply to the final bill as well. One notable exception to the Treasury's opposition was the incremental investment tax credit proposed by President Kennedy in 1962 but later greatly modified by Congress. In that proposal the usual complexity inherent in incremental credits was held to a minimum by limiting the credit to investment in excess of the current year's allowable depreciation.

the great relief of the Internal Revenue Service, which was not anxious to judge motivations behind firings.

An incremental credit similar to the House-passed bill is procyclical if it becomes a permanent feature of the tax law. The more rapidly an economy is expanding, the greater the tax reductions. As the economy begins to turn down, the credit begins to disappear and taxes go up. This procyclical effect can be muted if the rate of the credit is made to vary over the business cycle, but this would add additional complexity.

According to supporters, incremental tax incentives produce a greater bang for the buck because they reward firms only for doing what they otherwise would not have done. For example, the president's original proposal rewarded firms for all their employment, while the incremental credit rewards firms only for additional employees. The problem is that last year's employment level may be a very poor proxy for what firms otherwise would have done this year. Using last year's employment as the base for an incremental credit provides a nice windfall gain for rapidly growing firms. These firms would have substantially increased their employment in the absence of any tax subsidy. At the other extreme, declining firms may get no benefit at the margin even if they hire more workers in response to the credit, because they cannot clear the hurdle of last year's employment level.

Any additional jobs attributable to a credit such as the one in the House bill or enacted by Congress would be primarily in industries and regions that otherwise would have experienced employment growth; and because of the cap they would be primarily in small and medium-sized businesses. Specifically, trade and construction workers would benefit more than those in manufacturing; rapidly growing regions, such as the South and West, would benefit more than slowly growing, stagnant, or declining regions. The types of jobs that receive the most subsidy are those requiring limited skills and at relatively lower pay. Because the credit would provide a large subsidy for each additional employee during the first year on the job, jobs created because of the incentive are likely to be temporary.

The greater bang for the buck of incremental tax subsidies can be overstated. It is often forgotten that this year's employment goes into the base for determining some future year's tax benefit. Furthermore, the uncertain duration of the credit made planning more difficult for eligible firms.[15] Anyone believing the two-year incremental credit would not be extended beyond 1978 would have had far more incentive to hire in 1978 than in 1977 since additional employment in 1978 would have had no impact on 1979 tax liability.

Though not enthusiastic about incremental credits, the Treasury tried to quantify the effects of the threshold and the cap contained in the House bill.[16] Under the assumption that the percentage distribution of growth rates among employers is similar to the growth rates of detailed industry classes at a corresponding stage of the last two recoveries (1972–73 and 1962–63) and that total employment would grow at 3.5 percent, the Treasury estimated that in 1977, 30 percent of the labor market would have been excluded by the threshold.[17] The $40,000 cap would have effectively excluded at least 36 percent of the labor market from any possible gains from employment in response to the credit. The threshold and cap together excluded nearly two-thirds of the labor market from any benefits under this credit. The Treasury concluded that the House bill would have fought the short-run battle against unemployment with only one-third of the troops available.[18]

The Treasury explored other combinations of the rate of the credit, the threshold or floor, and the cap that cost the same amount in reduced revenues to see if any would be more effective in raising employment. This exercise ignored trade-offs between increased employment and distortions among industries and regions of the country. Maximizing the employment effect may be said to maximize the bang for the buck, but it may cause economic distortions. Nevertheless, the results of this exercise are interesting.

15. This effect applied to incremental credits for exports, investment, or whatever. For a discussion of incremental export incentives, see U.S. Department of the Treasury, *The Operation and Effect of the Domestic International Sales Corporation Legislation: 1975 Annual Report* (GPO, 1977), pp. 15–17.

16. The basic staff work was done by Seymour Fiekowsky and Larry Dildine.

17. The model for estimating the portion of the labor force excluded from the credit was used to make the basic revenue estimates used by the Treasury and the tax-writing committees.

18. The Treasury Department's position is presented in testimony before Senate committees. See Laurence N. Woodworth, Assistant Secretary of the Treasury for Tax Policy, Statement before the Senate Select Committee on Small Business, February 22, 1977; and W. Michael Blumenthal, Secretary of the Treasury, in *Tax Reduction and Simplification Act of 1977,* Hearings before the Senate Committee on Finance, 95 Cong. 1 sess. (GPO, 1977), pp. 93–166.

To get the greatest bang for the buck, the credit had to arbitrarily exclude many employers by means of a floor or a cap. If the floor were lowered from 103 percent to say 95 percent and the rate of the credit correspondingly reduced, the bang for the buck would probably have been reduced. The reduction in the floor ensured that more firms at the margin were eligible for the credit. The windfall was increased, however, for firms that qualified for the credit when the floor was 103 percent. There was a similar trade-off between the cap and the rate of the credit, particularly when the cap was defined in terms of a percentage of the former year's unemployment tax base. An absolute cap reduces the bang for the buck, but it does ensure that the employment credit becomes small business tax relief.

An employment credit that is calculated on the unemployment insurance wage base and limited by the total wage bill is ingenious. It minimizes administrative problems, and firms are not burdened with additional record-keeping. But it encourages the substitution of part-time for full-time workers, discourages the reduction of overtime employment, and provides a tax subsidy for some inflationary wage increases. These distortions arise because for employers not subject to the threshold or the $40,000 cap, the amount of the credit is limited by either the increase in unemployment insurance wages or in total wages, whichever is less.

The unemployment insurance wage base is only a proxy for increased employment. As a consequence, a firm intending to hire one *additional* full-time worker at $10,000 a year can double its credit if it hires two part-time workers at $5,000 each. The total wage bill limitation presumably is aimed at denying the credit to employers who substitute part-time workers for *existing* full-time workers. However, given some growth in money wages—currently on the order of 6 to 7 percent a year—the total wage bill limitation with only a 103 percent floor was largely ineffective against the replacement of current full-time with part-time workers.

For example, take the case of a firm with ten workers, each earning $10,000 last year. This firm decides to replace one full-time worker with two part-time workers each earning $5,350 this year ($5,000 plus 7 percent). In this case the total wage bill limitation is not binding. Assuming a 7 percent increase in wages, total payroll will increase by $7,000, which fully accommodates the $4,200 increase in the unemployment insurance wage base. This result occurs even though there has been no increase at all in total work hours used by the firm. Part-time workers are more likely to be second and third earners in families than are the full-time workers they displaced.

A second distortion arises when firms reduce overtime and hire additional workers. These firms may be excluded from the credit because of the total wage bill limitation. This distortion results because overtime work is paid at higher rates than work during regular hours. Replacing overtime workers with new employees could therefore reduce the total wage bill, thereby bringing the overall wage limitation into play. Thus the credit would have been a disincentive to one kind of spreading of work that may be desirable.

A third distortion arises in those cases where the unemployment insurance wage base has grown more rapidly than total wages. Here employers face an incentive to grant inflationary wage increases so as to relax the total wage limitation and to increase the amount of the credit. These wage increases might be granted only to the officers of the corporation.

The House-passed bill would have introduced one final distortion. Under that bill it would have even been possible for noncorporate employers in tax brackets exceeding 50 percent to make money from the program simply by hiring new workers and telling them to stay at home. For example, for an employer in the 70 percent marginal tax rate bracket, the tax deduction for wages paid would reduce the after-tax labor cost to 30 cents on each dollar. Then the credit would provide an additional tax saving of 40 cents for a net wage cost of minus 10 cents. Thus by paying a dollar of wages qualified for the credit, after-tax income of employers would increase by 10 cents for every dollar of wages paid new employees even if the new employees were totally unproductive.[19]

## Senate Action

Following House passage of the Tax Reduction and Simplification Act of 1977, the administration reviewed its legislative position. Because the Senate Finance Committee seemed inclined to increase the investment credit, there was strong support within the administra-

19. The tax benefit would have been even greater if handicapped persons had been "hired."

tion for pushing this proposal.[20] There also was strong opposition within the administration to the incremental employment credit, particularly to the $40,000 cap and to the very high floor. Though it seemed unlikely that the Finance Committee would eliminate the incremental feature, it was hoped that the committee would greatly modify it. In the end the administration decided to continue to support its original proposal for an option of a 2 percent increase in the investment credit or a credit against income taxes equal to 4 percent of payroll tax payments. Secretary of the Treasury W. Michael Blumenthal outlined the administration's position on March 8, 1977, before the Senate Finance Committee, stressing the arbitrary distortions that would flow from the House-passed employment credit.

### Senate Finance Committee Consideration

The Finance Committee agreed that both labor-intensive and capital-intensive firms should be given an incentive to increase their productive resources.[21] It therefore adopted the administration's approach of requiring firms to choose between a 2 percentage point increase in the investment credit and a new employment tax credit. The committee made a number of important changes in the credit provision of the House bill.

First, it removed the $40,000 cap so that large employers could also benefit from the credit by hiring additional employees.

Second, it increased the total wage bill limitation to 105 percent of last year's wages but retained the 103 percent floor for the unemployment insurance limitation. The 105 percent wage bill limitation reduced the possibilities of employers substituting part-year, part-time jobs for existing full-year, full-time jobs. Because total wages grow more rapidly than the unemployment insurance wage base, it was reasonable to have a higher floor on the wage bill limitation than the unemployment insurance wage limitation.

20. The administration's position following House passage of the bill is outlined in *Tax Reduction and Simplification Act of 1977,* Hearings before the Senate Committee on Finance; and *Tax Reduction Program, Summary of Testimony on H.R. 3477 and the Administration's Economic Stimulus Program,* Committee Print, prepared for the Senate Committee on Finance by the staff of the Joint Committee on Taxation and the Congressional Research Service, 95 Cong. 1 sess. (GPO, 1977), pt. 4.

21. The Finance Committee's version of the bill and reasons for changes are contained in *Tax Reduction and Simplification Act of 1977,* S. Rept. 95-66, 95 Cong. 1 sess. (GPO, 1977). See especially pp. 63–76.

Third, to eliminate the possibility that an employer could make money from the tax credit simply by hiring new workers and telling them to stay at home, the committee provided that the income tax deduction for wages and salaries must be reduced by the amount of the employment tax credit. This adjustment was also justified on conceptual grounds: firms should only be permitted a tax deduction for wages they pay. Wages paid by the federal government through a tax credit should not also be deductible by the firm.[22]

Fourth, under the House bill all employees of a new business, up to twenty-four employees, would have been eligible for the employment tax credit. The Senate Finance Committee believed that this would unduly favor new businesses. To reduce the competitive advantage the new firms would have, the Finance Committee limited the amount of wages eligible for the credit to 50 percent of the current year's unemployment insurance wages. Fifth, the committee eliminated the extra credit for the handicapped.

Finally, the committee reduced the rate of the credit from 40 to 25 percent so that the total revenue loss of the business tax portion of the Finance Committee's bill would be approximately the same as that of the House bill.

Several committee members, most notably Senator Daniel Moynihan of New York, expressed concern that the incremental employment tax credit would favor expanding regions of the country. Consideration was given to lowering the unemployment insurance wage floor for distressed regions or possibly providing increased investment tax credits or additional acceleration of tax depreciation for these regions. In the end the committee decided not to target the tax incentives on distressed regions.

22. Under the legislation enacted by Congress, firms must reduce the deduction for wages by the amount of employment tax credit earned during the year even if the credit currently cannot be used. Self-employed people who employ others and may thus earn an employment tax credit for the year may find that their self-employment taxes have gone up since the deduction for wages has been reduced (and their self-employment income increased) even though they currently may not be able to claim the credit. There is no simple way to adjust the deduction for wages for the amount of the employment tax credit actually used. Any change in the deduction for wages affects taxable income and therefore the amount of tax before the employment tax credit. This in turn affects the allowable employment tax credit which would affect the deduction for wages. One possibility would be to permit firms each year to elect *not* to claim the employment tax credit. The deduction for wages then would not be reduced.

The Senate Finance Committee on March 28, 1977, reported its version of the Tax Reduction and Simplification Act of 1977. It included the president's $50 rebate, the increase and simplification of the standard deduction, and the choice between an increased investment credit or the new incremental employment tax credit.

Before the Finance Committee bill reached the Senate floor, President Carter on April 14 announced that he was abandoning the $50 tax rebate and withdrawing his support for the business tax cuts.[23] (The president continued his support for the standard deduction change and the expenditure increases.) The administration had concluded that its economic stimulus was no longer necessary and that the tax rebate and business tax cuts would increase inflation. After a poor showing in January due to a harsh winter, the economy had had a very strong first quarter with key economic indicators pointing up. Inflation also seemed to be increasing. A week before the president dropped the rebate the Labor Department had announced that the wholesale price increase for March had been 1.1 percent, the highest in seventeen months.[24]

The $50 rebate was in considerable trouble in the Senate, where the opposition rested on the view that the rebate was too gimmicky. This opposition was heightened by the president's insistence on cutting back the funding for a number of politically popular water projects. The Senate Finance Committee quickly agreed to offer a floor amendment dropping the $50 rebate but not the business tax reductions.

### Senate Floor Action

The Senate considered the Tax Reduction and Simplification Act from April 19 to April 29. During that period it adopted four amendments to the new jobs credit. First, the Senate increased the rate of the credit from 25 to 50 percent. Second, the Senate placed a $100,000 cap on the amount of credit a firm could earn in one year. This amendment, strongly supported by small business groups, insured that the final legislation would contain a cap, as both the House and

23. See "Economic Stimulus Package: The President's Remarks and a Question-and-Answer Session on the Withdrawal of the $50 Tax Rebate and Business Tax Credit Proposals from the Package," *Weekly Compilation of Presidential Documents*, vol. 13 (April 18, 1977), pp. 530–32.

24. U.S. Department of Labor, Bureau of Labor Statistics, "Wholesale Price Index, March 1977," *News*, USDL 77-289, April 7, 1977.

Senate versions of the legislation had such a provision. Third, the Senate adopted an additional 10 percent credit for employers who hired certain veterans, handicapped persons, or low-income, long-term unemployed persons. This amendment was broader than the House provision to award the credit for handicapped employees. Fourth, the Senate provided that employers in the twenty-two states that in 1976 had an unemployment rate of 7.5 percent or higher could qualify for the new jobs credit if their unemployment wages exceeded 101 percent of the prior year's wages (compared with 103 percent for employers in other states). The Senate rejected an amendment that would have eliminated the optional increase in the investment tax credit. The Senate amendments increased the cost of the business tax portion of the tax bill to $2.9 billion.

### Conference Committee

It is often said that tax bills are written in the Conference Committee because that committee must reconcile differences between the House and Senate versions of the bill. The Conference Committee did shape the final version of the new jobs credit.[25] At the strong insistence of the House conferees, the Conference Committee agreed to drop the optional 2 percent increase in the investment credit contained in the Senate bill. Otherwise the Conference Committee generally followed the Senate version of the bill except that it reduced the 103 percent unemployment insurance wage limitation to 102 percent, dropped the special rule for high-unemployment states, and narrowed the additional 10 percent credit for handicapped workers.

Specifically, the jobs tax credit enacted by Congress, equaled half the amount by which each employer's unemployment insurance wage base (the first $4,200 of wages paid per employee) exceeded 102 percent of the unemployment insurance wage base in the previous year. But the credit for a tax year was limited to the lesser of (1) half the amount by which an employer's total wages paid for the year exceeded 105 percent of total wages paid by the employer in the previous year (wage bill limitation); (2) 25 percent of the current year's unemployment insurance wage base (new business limitation); (3) $100,000 (small business limitation); and (4) the employer's

25. For the Conference Committee's changes see *Tax Reduction and Simplification Act of 1977*, H. Rept. 95-263, 95 Cong. 1 sess. (GPO, 1977).

income tax liability for the year. Credits that exceeded tax liability for a year could be carried back for three years and forward for seven years. In addition, the income tax deduction for wages and salaries was reduced by the amount of the credit.

Employers received an additional 10 percent credit on the first $4,200 of unemployment insurance wages paid to handicapped people whose first such wages from the employer were paid in 1977 or 1978. The additional credit could not exceed 20 percent of the credit otherwise allowable, disregarding the $100,000 cap.

Special rules were provided for agricultural and railroad employees not covered by unemployment insurance. Moreover, all employees of corporations that were members of the same controlled group of corporations were treated as employees of a single employer, and special adjustments had to be made for corporate acquisitions or dispositions during either the current or previous year.

The incredibly complex credit resulted in a number of arbitrary distortions. Its incremental feature favored rapidly growing firms, industries, and regions of the country. Because of the $100,000 cap the credit primarily benefited small- and medium-sized businesses and negligibly influenced large employers. Because only the first $4,200 of earnings affected the calculation, the credit encouraged the substitution of part-time for full-time workers and discouraged the reduction of overtime employment. It also provided a tax subsidy for some inflationary wage increases, which in some circumstances increased the credit a firm may receive.

The bill reduced revenues by an estimated $2.4 billion, which is just below the cost of the business portion of the president's original proposal for economic stimulus. The 102 percent threshold excluded an estimated 28 percent of the work force from the credit, and the $100,000 cap excluded an additional 27 percent of the work force. Thus firms with 45 percent of employment would, at the margin, be eligible for the credit, compared with 34 percent under the House-passed bill.

The conference compromise did not cure the administration's basic objection to the incremental credit contained in the House-passed bill with its threshold and cap. Nevertheless, the president signed the Tax Reduction and Simplification Act on May 23, just four months after he had sent his original proposals to Congress.

## Summary

The new jobs tax credit was a product of the legislative process, which has often transformed simple proposals into complex laws. The president's original proposal was for an optional income tax credit of 4 percent of social security taxes paid by employers. This credit would have had a small anti-inflationary effect in the short run and would have put general revenues into social security through the back door. Congress wanted instead to provide a greater incentive targeted on *additional* employment, recognizing that the base for any incremental credit must be somewhat arbitrary, as it is not possible to know the number of employees a firm would have had if the credit had not been enacted. The complexity of the jobs credit, which resulted in a number of economic distortions, arose because Congress wanted the credit to be incremental, to do something for the handicapped, and to avoid excessively favorable treatment for new firms that might be competing with old firms. Congress, however, adopted an arbitrary base for its incremental credit. This decision minimized the record-keeping burdens but led to the distortions favoring rapidly growing firms, industries, and regions of the country.

The impact of the credit on jobs was slight. In many firms those who make hiring decisions did not understand the firm's tax status. In addition, some time passes between the employment decision and the determination of eligibility for the credit.

Because the capital stock is fixed in the short run, to increase employment significantly, demand for output must increase. An incremental tax cut tied to employment will not by itself generate that increase in demand. Moreover, a temporary incremental credit is unlikely to affect significantly the long-run substitution of labor for capital.

The short life of the jobs credit ended when President Carter failed to recommend its extension beyond 1978. Instead he recommended as part of his urban program a targeted jobs credit that was not incremental and was limited to the hiring of disadvantaged young people and the handicapped. Congress generally accepted the president's recommendations and enacted a targeted jobs credit as part of the Revenue Act of 1978, allowing the former broader jobs credit to expire at the end of 1978 as scheduled.

# Index